HOW TESTING CAME TO DOMINATE AMERICAN SCHOOLS

PETER LANG
New York • Washington, D.C./Baltimore • Bern
Frankfurt am Main • Berlin • Brussels • Vienna • Oxford

GERARD GIORDANO

HOW TESTING
CAME TO DOMINATE
AMERICAN SCHOOLS

The History of Educational Assessment

PETER LANG
New York • Washington, D.C./Baltimore • Bern
Frankfurt am Main • Berlin • Brussels • Vienna • Oxford

Library of Congress Cataloging-in-Publication Data

Giordano, Gerard.
How testing came to dominate American schools:
the history of educational assessment / Gerard Giordano.
p. cm.
Includes bibliographical references and indexes.
1. Educational tests and measurements—United States—History.
2. National teacher examinations—United States—History.
3. Education—United States—History. I. Title.
LB3051.G516 371.26'2'0973—dc22 2003027185
ISBN 0-8204-7255-7

Bibliographic information published by Die Deutsche Bibliothek.
Die Deutsche Bibliothek lists this publication in the "Deutsche
Nationalbibliografie"; detailed bibliographic data is available
on the Internet at http://dnb.ddb.de/.

Cover design by Joni Holst

The paper in this book meets the guidelines for permanence and durability
of the Committee on Production Guidelines for Book Longevity
of the Council of Library Resources.

© 2005 Peter Lang Publishing, Inc., New York
275 Seventh Avenue, 28th Floor, New York, NY 10001
www.peterlangusa.com

Printed in the United States of America

For My Current and Former Students,
Who Have So Enriched This Book,
and My Life

TABLE OF CONTENTS

ILLUSTRATIONS

PREFACE

*The importance of the [testing] movement lies not only in its past and
present achievements, but in the hope of the future.*
—AYRES, 1918

Sowing Seeds

Early twentieth-century public education was a garden. No one was surprised that
parents wanted to be reassured about the produce from this garden. However,
many observers did not expect industry, the military, and the government to show
intense interest. These groups believed that their own fates and that of the schools
were interconnected. Consequently, they became disconcerted when educational
productivity diminished. They questioned whether the garden's managers had
introduced deleterious elements, held back essential nutrients, or relied on
unproven procedures.

Teachers, textbooks, curricula, and instructional methods were all viewed as
critical elements of a healthy educational garden. Nonetheless, each element was
controversial in its own way. For example, educational consumers argued about
teachers' preparation, responsibilities, rights, accountability, and salaries. In a
similar fashion, they squabbled about the philosophical and practical aspects of
textbooks, curricula, and instructional methods. At one time, religion had been
another essential feature of the educational garden. However, the homogeneous
religious instruction that had been pervasive in the schools proved less relevant as
society became more industrial, secular, and diverse.

As World War I approached, federal, state, and local governments asked the
schools to do a better job of preparing individuals for military service or wartime
employment. Although educators responded, another problem immediately
emerged. A good portion of the students could not meet the higher scholastic
standards. Some of these students were recent immigrants who were unfamiliar
with American customs. Some were unable to speak English. Many of them were
assigned to teachers who were untrained and poorly equipped. If students were
going to be successful, certain conditions had to be met. Schools needed
professional teachers. They also needed effective textbooks, suitable curricula, and
facilities that were safe, clean, and comfortable. Some critics set another
requirement. They demanded that educators monitor the quality of the education
they were providing. In effect, these critics challenged the educators to prove that
they had taken control of their garden.

Gaining Control

At the beginning of the twentieth century, standardized tests were introduced unpretentiously as aids for assigning grades. Scientifically minded teachers were excited about the novel instruments. In addition to helping them evaluate their students, they hoped that tests might elevate the lackluster status of their occupation. Although tradition-minded schoolmasters were upset that their centuries-old grading practices were being challenged, the public was initially uninvolved. This situation changed once it became clear that the new evaluation techniques presented political opportunities. The critics of teachers were one of the first groups to detect these opportunities. Because they were convinced that students' test scores revealed the competence of teachers as well as the talents of learners, they recommended that these scores become a means of identifying unfit instructors. The most adversarial critics wanted the teachers themselves to pass tests as a condition for getting jobs and remaining employed.

Other groups that supported tests had distinct motives, some of which were educational. For example, administrators embraced tests as cost-effective techniques for measuring school achievement. Parents thought tests could pinpoint their children's learning problems and ensure scholastic remediation. The general public hoped tests would make schools answerable to voter-sanctioned directives. Some groups had ulterior reasons for endorsing tests. Political conservatives searched for tests that could be connected to national security or economic health. Employers wanted screening and placement tests that would improve the efficiency of their companies. Military leaders thought that tests were important components of their training and management system. Publishers saw tests as opportunities to expand business with the public schools, colleges, commerce, and industry.

As the number of supporters for academic testing increased, opponents became more strident. Teachers who were employing highly individualized, child-centered activities depicted standardized testing as a strategy that would promote the structured curricula that they dreaded. Some teachers distrusted sampling, statistics, experimental design, and the innovative research concepts on which standardized assessment relied. Immigrants and minority groups feared that their predictably low performance on tests would lead to intellectual, political, economic, and social castes.

Liberals wished to curb standardized testing because of its philosophical assumptions and pedagogical implications. Had they lacked these grounds, they still would have opposed it because of the enormous political power it gave their opponents. Although they were trying to block standardized tests, the liberals recognized that the public was demanding educational accountability. These demands had been extended to educational budgeting, teacher hiring, administrator preparation, curriculum development, career training, selection of learning materials, fostering of student values, control of disruptive student behaviors, synchronization of classroom activities with district-wide objectives, and numerous other school practices. Although standardized tests did not encompass all of these practices, the public had accepted performance on these tests as a convincing way to demonstrate scholastic accountability. Unable to ignore the sustained calls for accountability, the opponents of standardized tests pledged that they would devise alternative measures that were less biased, less costly, less error-prone, less centralized, and less politicized.

This book examines the ongoing disputes about standardized tests. The early dialogues, confrontations, public appeals, marketing efforts, propaganda campaigns, and machinations established a pattern that persisted throughout the century. Although the encounters between the supporters and opponents of standardized tests may have been relatively stable, the public's attitudes were variable. The public responded less to the ways in which these groups couched their scholarly statements and more to the manner in which they addressed the broad social, financial, and military issues that the country was facing. After the disputants became conscious of these subtle dynamics, they used them to their advantages. In fact, some of them became so politically sophisticated that they were able to gauge, predict, and even mold the public's attitudes toward testing.

ACKNOWLEDGMENTS

I cannot express sufficient gratitude to my independent, inventive, and indefatigable research assistant, Becky Packard. Without her collaboration, this book would not have been written. I also depended heavily on Amy Wilberg and Sandranee Bacchus, who showed professionalism and patience while preparing the final copy of the text.

CHAPTER 1

Scientists Nurture Testing

Intelligence [is] what the tests of intelligence test.
—BORING, 1923

To study mental operations, early twentieth-century psychologists developed tests similar to those that were being used in the physical sciences. Some critics disapproved of the tests because they relied on indirect activities, artificial situations, and statistical models. Nonetheless, educators judged that the benefits of intelligence tests outweighed their disadvantages. They wished to administer the intelligence tests to assess the intellectual aptitude of their students. Because they also wished to gauge classroom learning, they devised and administered academic tests. As the number of persons who were taking mental and academic tests increased, so did the amount of criticism that these instruments elicited.

Science Influences Behavioral Studies

At the beginning of the twentieth century, many academicians had been inspired by colleagues in the scientific fields. They particularly were impressed with the manner in which Francis Galton had used statistics to solve technical problems. As impressive as these achievements were, Galton's vision extended beyond the physical sciences. He believed that scholars who studied human behavior could use research methods comparable to those that the chemists, physicists, and biologists employed. Toward the end of the nineteenth century, he had written eloquently that "one of the most important objects of measurement....is to obtain a general knowledge of the capacities of a man by sinking shafts, as it were, at a few critical points" (1890, p. 380).

Psychologists shared Galton's optimism about a new model for behavioral research. Disagreeing with the many persons who thought of them as philosophers, the psychologists tried to convince the public that they truly were scientists. To document how recently this academic and public relations campaign had been made, Whitley (1911) noted that "the history of scientific inquiry into the natures and amount of individual differences dates back only about twenty-five years" (p. 1). During that 25-year period, the many ingenious psychologists who believed in objective measurement had adapted research methods from the physical sciences. One professor wrote explicitly that "the present practices of measuring mental accomplishment are largely modifications of the methods used in the physical sciences" (Weiss, 1911, p. 555). A year later, Kirkpatrick (1912) relied on a simile to underscore the connection between the research paradigms that psychologists and physical scientists were pursuing.

A test of the kind of mental ability a child has is...possible...[and] valuable in determining mental age. The physiologist can judge with considerable accuracy the age of an individual by the texture of his bones and muscles, the proportion of parts and the kind of motions he makes much better than he can by weighing, measuring or testing strength or rate of movement. In a similar way the psychologist may hope by means of [intelligence tests] to determine with considerable accuracy the mental age of children and feeble-minded adults. (p. 337)

In a preface that he wrote in 1926 for a history of mental testing, Freeman (1939) pledged that he would explain some of the "scientific problems which are involved in the design, application, and interpretation of tests" (p. ix). Hoping that he would not be seen as an extremist, Freeman "endeavored to weigh the evidence as impartially as possible." He thought this objective stance was prudent because "due to the recency [*sic*] of the development of mental tests, many of the principles which are involved in them are not very fully agreed upon, and some are not yet very clearly recognized." Thirteen years later, Freeman updated his testing book. Within the introduction to that second edition, Cubberley (1939) confidently assured readers that the preceding 25 years had been "a most fruitful period" for the "experimental study of educational problems." He added that "the new teaching material and techniques which have been evolved have been of many different types, but no aspect of this development has awakened more widespread interest, challenged the thinking of more young workers, or been more fruitful in results than the creation of tests and the application of statistical procedures to the interpretation of the results obtained" (p. v).

Cubberley had pointed with pride to the beneficial union of testing and statistics. However, Cubberley's positive attitudes were far from universal. In fact, Lewis Terman (1922a), an influential psychologist, observed that the "intelligence testers" were being excoriated for their reliance on "statistical formulae, which common people do not understand" (p. 116). With mordant wit, he suggested that "in the interest of freedom of opinion there ought to be a law passed forbidding the encroachment of quantitative methods upon those fields which from time immemorial have been reserved for the play of sentiment and opinion."

Terman had made the preceding comments in response to a set of articles that a popular editorialist had published in a national magazine. He believed that this journalist, like the general public, was confused about statistics. He thought the journalist had misunderstood another feature of testing, namely its critical reliance on scientific objectivity. Terman explained that this reliance had led to several disconcerting but nonetheless "factual" conclusions. Political adversaries had depicted these conclusions as "dangerous doctrines, subversive of American democracy." Terman belittled these critics for adopting the erroneous conviction that "the essential thing about a democracy is not equality of opportunity...but equality of mental endowment" (1922a, p. 117). He then gave examples of some of the "dangerous doctrines" that had stirred up so much controversy.

Intelligence testers...have enunciated, ex cathedra, in the guise of fact, law and eternal verity, such highly revolutionary and absurd doctrines as the following; to wit:

1. That the strictly average representative of the genus homo is not a particularly intellectual animal;
2. that some members of the species are much stupider than others;
3. that school prodigies are usually brighter than school laggards;
4. that college professors are more intelligent than janitors, architects than hod-carriers, railroad presidents than switch-tenders; and (most heinous of all) [*sic*]
5. that the offspring of socially, economically and professionally successful parents have better mental endowments, on the average, than the offspring of said janitors, hod-carriers and switch-tenders. (Terman, 1922a, p. 116)

Terman had the ability to entertain persons with his sarcastic remarks. However, he also could rephrase complicated information in ways that made it accessible to a scientifically unsophisticated audience. This facility was evident when he represented statistical sampling as a process that was similar to the assaying of ore.

> In order to find out how much gold is contained in a given vein of quartz it is not necessary to uncover all the ore and extract and weight ever particle of the precious metal. It is sufficient merely to ascertain by borings the linear extent of the lode and to take a small amount of the ore to the laboratory of an assayer, who will make a test and render a verdict of some many ounces of gold per ton of ore. (Terman, 1919, p. xxiii)

Formats for Intelligence Tests

By extrapolating investigative procedures from the physical sciences, psychologists hoped to transform the examination of mental activity into a science. The development of objective mental tests was essential to their success. However, the psychologists who were intrigued by tests made assumptions that were extremely divisive. In fact, some of the issues they raised remained controversial for decades. An employee of the Psychological Corporation (Wesman, 1968) looked back at these early disputes and identified the parties that were involved as psychologists, educators, sociologists, geneticists, neurophysiologists, and biochemists. He concluded that "despite this attention, however—or perhaps *because* of it—there appears to be no more general agreement as to the nature of intelligence [today] than was the case 50 years ago" (p. 267).

Although he was writing many decades after the initial objections to standardized intelligence tests had been made, Garcia (1981) still censured the early researchers for assuming that intelligence was "a general aptitude to solve any and all problems, to be a fixed quantity determined largely by heredity, and remain constant during growth and development" (p. 1172). He recommended instead that "each social group should be tested and scaled in its own cultural idiom, with test elements and activities from that domain." The specific recommendation that Garcia articulated had been suggested decades earlier. As an indication of this longevity, consider the following remarks from Boring (1923).

If you take one of the ready-made tests of intelligence and try it on a very large number of persons, you will find that they succeed with it in very different degrees. Repeat the test, and you will find that they cannot, with the best will in the world to do well, alter their scores very greatly. Then give the same group another intelligence test, and you will discover that the differences among individuals are approximately, although not exactly, the same. And you can go on. You will find that an adult, after continued exposure to his social and educational environment, does not greatly alter his score on a given test; that children, however, do steadily improve their performances until somewhat between ten and twenty years old; that the average age at which improvement stops is about fourteen years; but that children while improving tend to maintain the same individual differences, so that in a given group every child would keep about the same rank within the group. (p. 35)

Boring explained that a person's performance on any intelligence test depended on the peculiar items that the exam comprised. He emphasized that "there is no such thing as a test for pure intelligence" because "intelligence is not demonstrable except in connection with some special ability." He continued that a certain percent of the performance on menta l tests might be the result of actual intelligence, but that the remainder was from "some special ability that is not intelligence." As a consequence, he suggested that intelligence be defined operationally as "what the tests of intelligence test" (p. 37).

When some disgruntled scholars estimated the portion of test performance that was attributable to an "ability that is not intelligence," they were even more critical than Boring. If these critics were correct, then mental tests might reveal a very restricted type of information, such as the degree to which tested persons could solve the precise problems on that individual test. Other critics conceded that performance on specific mental tests might generalize to other tasks, but only if those tasks were quite similar to those on the mental tests in question. As an illustration, a tested person's performance on a maze puzzle could reveal his or her aptitude for other maze-like puzzles. However, it might not generalize to puzzles that were arranged in distinct formats or that involved discrete abilities such as computation and language. Although early researchers were disconcerted by these objections, they had no alternatives to indirect measures for gauging abstract mental operations. Nonetheless, they did recognize a responsibility to demonstrate that the measures they had selected applied to the widest possible range of mental performances.

Most of the early psychologists who faced these challenges were struck by the solutions that Alfred Binet had proposed. In one of the first h istories of intelligence testing, Pintner (1923) had concluded that this French scholar was important "because of the great stimulus he gave intelligence testing" and because "his concept of intelligence is essentially the one that is held at the present time by psychologists" (p. 24). Binet's ingenuity was revealed in the activities within his 1908 test. For example, he claimed that he needed only five tasks to confirm whether a person employed mental operations that were as sophisticated as those of a three-year-old child.

1. Points to nose, eyes, mouth.
2. Repeats two numbers.
3. Describes pictures.
4. Knows family name.
5. Repeats sentences of six syllables. (Items from Binet's 1908 test, reported by Berry, 1912, p. 444)

Compare the preceding traits with those that characterized a person with the mental age of a seven-year-old child.

1. Shows right hand, left ear.
2. Describes pictures.
3. Executes three commissions.
4. Counts stamps.
5. Names four colors. (Items from Binet's 1908 test, reported by Berry, 1912, p. 445)

Binet suggested equally clever tasks for measuring the intelligence that children, teenagers, and adults displayed. Some of these tasks required tested persons to

Figure 1.1 Pictorial Completion

compare objects from memory (typical of individuals at age eight), identify the 12 months of the year in their order of occurrence (age nine), resist suggestions (age 12), form rhymes (age 15), or explain the difference between a president and a king (adult).

Additional Pretexts for Assessing Intelligence

Squire (1912a, 1912b, 1912c) published a series of early reports in which she gave examples of items from "graded mental tests." For example, she described the "a–test," which had been used in the Chicago Public Schools to assess rate of perception. This test encompassed a single sheet of paper, on which "at the top of the page are printed 100 a's, distributed evenly in rows" and "below there are 100 a's, distributed among one hundred nonsense syllables." The "a–test" was designed to help instructors "abstract the motor time—the time required to mark out the 100 a's—from the finding or perception time—the extra time required to mark out the a's when distributed among the one hundred words" (1912a, p. 370).

Assessing Comprehension

Squire illustrated a variation on the "a–test" in which the task became one of comprehension. When the test was arranged in this format, the students still had to mark the a's that occurred within nonsense syllables. However, they were to do this while listening to a passage that was read aloud. Each student was then "expected to give the substance of the matter read after the completion of his test."

Squire illustrated several other techniques for measuring comprehension, most of which were less circuitous than the tasks in the preceding test. Some of these techniques involved pictorial stimuli. In response to a picture that had been presented to them, students might be required to identify the context, to provide a title, or to form a salient question. Healy (1914) presented a picture-based test to the members of the American Psychological Association at their annual meeting in 1911. He later described this test and the materials it employed.

> The brightly colored picture, 10 X 14 inches, represents an outdoor scene with ten discrete, simple activities going on. When properly mounted...10 one-inch squares are cut out along the dotted lines shown on the picture necessary to complete the meaning of the separate activity [*sic*]. Besides these ten pieces, there are 40 other one-inch squares (produced as part of the original lithograph, but not shown in the illustration), 30 of them bearing other objects, and 10 being blank. Each piece should be so well cut out that it may fit into any one of the ten apertures; there must be no possible rejection of a choice on account of variation in form or size. (Healy, 1914, p. 191)

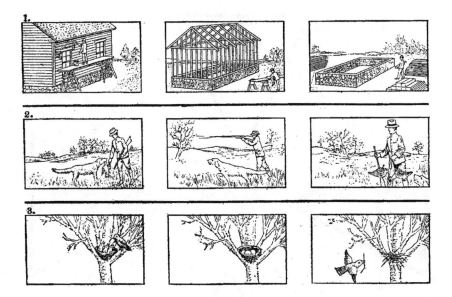

Figure 1.2 Pictorial Sequencing

Figure 1.1 (p. 5) contains this early pictorial test. In this illustration, all of the test pieces have been placed in their appropriate positions. Figure 1.2, which is a portion of another intelligence test, was used by the Army during World War I. It represents a distinct pictorial format for assessing comprehension (Yerkes, 1921).

Assessing Associational Ability

To demonstrate one of the ways that associational ability was being assessed, Squire identified words to which students were to provide antonyms.

> The list is as follows: Series I—day, asleep, absent, brother, best, above, big, backwards, buy, come cheap, broad, dead, land, country, tall, son, here, less, mine. Series II—great, hot, dirty, heavy, late, first, left, morning, much, near, north, open, round, sharp, east, known, something, stay, nowhere, past. Series III—bad, inside, slow, short, little soft, black, dark, sad, true, dislike, poor, well, sorry, thick, full, peace, few, below, enemy. (1912b, p. 430)

To give an idea of a very different format for assessing mental associations, Squire (1912b) described a task that required persons to recreate from memory a Maltese cross. The examinees were to replicate the pattern that they had viewed, arranging the numbered pieces in the same order. Figure 1.3 (p. 8) illustrates the stimulus pattern prior to the shuffling of its pieces.

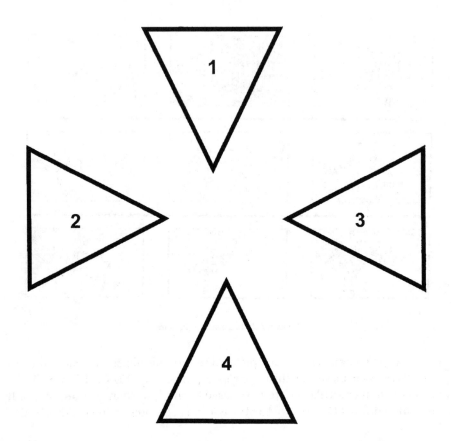

Figure 1.3 Pattern Test

Assessing Creativity

Squire classified some of the tasks on early intelligence tests as "invention and construction problems." Most of these activities required students to assemble cardboard or wooden puzzles. Other activities involved the folding of papers into geometric patterns. One particularly striking task required students "to trace [a] figure without crossing a line, lifting a pencil or tracing any part twice" (Squire, 1912b, p. 436). Figure 1.4 contains a reproduction of the pattern to which the preceding instructions referred.

Bronner, Healey, Lowe, and Shimberg (1932) later reviewed a singular test of creativity that employed a mechanical puzzle box. The mechanical device that this test required is illustrated in Figure 1.5. The examinees had five minutes to solve the puzzle, the goal of which was described in the instructions.

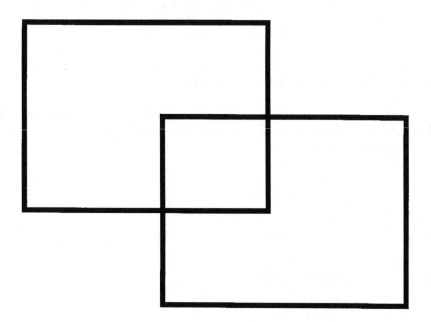

Figure 1.4 This Figure Was to Be Copied Without Lifting a Pencil, Crossing a Line, or Retracing

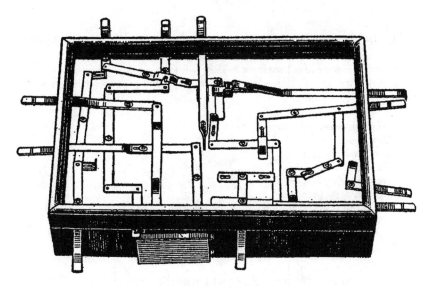

Figure 1.5 Mechanical Puzzle Test ("Puzzle Box Text." *Stoeling Company. Reprinted by permission of the publisher. All rights reserved.*)

Tell S that if he moves the levers the little door in front will spring open. He is told to study the box carefully so that he may move the levers in the right order. He is warned not to use force. (Bronner, Healey, Lowe, & Shimberg, 1932, p. 102)

Assessing the Ability to Make Judgments

Squire illustrated several formats for those test items that were intended to elicit judgments, conclusions, or summaries. The following items focused on the ability to make judgments.

```
              longer
   1.   Days are            in summer than in winter.
              shorter
                   more
   2.   Glass breaks      easily than tin.
                   less
                   up
   3.   Water always flows        hill.
                   down
              softer
   4.   Iron is        than wood.
              harder
                   before
   5.   Christmas comes      Thanksgiving. (Squire, 1912c, p. 493)
                   after
```

Unlike the previous tasks, some items on tests assessed "selective judgments."

The following reasons have been given to show why grass grows in summer and not in winter. Write "yes" after those reasons you consider good and "no" after the reasons you think poor.

1.   Summer is warm and winter is cold.
2.   Grass is green.
3.   Grass needs warmth.
4.   Grass needs sunshine.
5.   Cows and horses eat grass.
6.   Grass needs moisture.
7.   The ground is frozen in winter.
8.   Children skate in winter.
9.   Grass is sometimes cut for hay.
10.   Grass could not grow in the frozen earth. (Squire, 1912c, p. 495)

Squire contrasted the preceding tasks with the straightforward format of "problem questions." She listed five examples of questions that were arranged in this format.

1. A boy said: "I know ten good men who are doctors and ten bad men who are policemen." Did he prove it? Why? Or Why not? [*sic*]
2. If all the boys who are good in arithmetic are good in spelling, will all the boys who are good in spelling be good in arithmetic? Why? Or Why not? [*sic*]
3. If there were no bread or flour, would everyone starve?
4. Is this true, "The more we eat the more we grow?"
5. If there were no schools, would children learn anything? (Squire, 1912c, p. 497)

Assessing the Ability to Define

The "definition test" provided still another opportunity to assess intelligence. Squire gave examples of pairs of words that could occur within this type of test.

1. *key* and *chain*
2. *sweet* and *hot*
3. *kindness* and *pleasure*
4. *to read* and *to write*
5. *time* and *number* (Squire, 1912c, p. 498)

Assessing Decoding Proficiency

Clarence Gray (1913) reported about popular tests that relied on military encoding or decoding practices. In fact, one of the strategies that Gray suggested required persons to use an actual Civil War cipher to write the phrase "caught a spy." Providing another example to demonstrate the way this technique was being applied to mental assessment, he wrote that "a number is to be substituted for each letter in the alphabet as 25 for 'a,' 7 for 'b,' etc." He added that "the key is placed at the top of the page, the material to be written is printed in short lines down the left hand side of the page, and the substitutions are to be made in blank squares to the right of each printed line" (p. 293).

Pintner and Paterson (1917) also became fascinated with decoding tests. Working with deaf children, they tried to "assemble a group of tests which did not involve any kind of language response" (p. I). The Digit Symbol Test was one of these instruments. The instructions that were given to students, even though these could have been written more clearly, revealed the simplicity of this test.

In the circles at the top of the sheet before you are written in the blank squares below for the digits to which they correspond [*sic*]. Work as fast as you can and try to fill as many of the squares as possible without making mistakes. (Pintner & Paterson, 1917, p. 591)

Figure 1.6 (p. 12) and Figure 1.7 (p. 13), which have been taken from the Army's World War I intelligence tests (Yerkes, 1921), demonstrate two additional formats for assessing decoding skills.

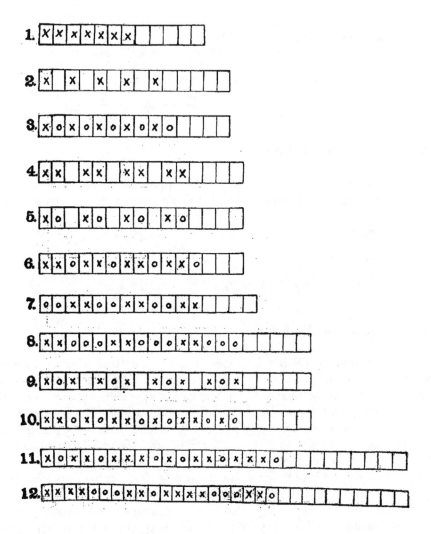

Figure 1.6 Pattern Replication Test

Weaknesses of Mental Tests

As the popularity of mental tests increased, so did the frequency with which testing was denigrated. Although these attacks became glaringly evident after World War I, they were discernible earlier. Squire (1912a) reported that Binet's initial tests had "received their full share of criticism." Most of this criticism had focused on technical issues. This tendency was reflected in the five categories that Squire (1912a) used to summarize the criticism.

(1) Certain tests are too easy and others too difficult for the grades to which they are assigned... (2) The tests are not entirely independent of school training. (3) The number of tests for different ages vary....(4) The tests are not standardized....(5) The tests for the different ages are not comparable; at one age certain specific mental capacities and at another stage entirely different capacities are tested. (p. 366)

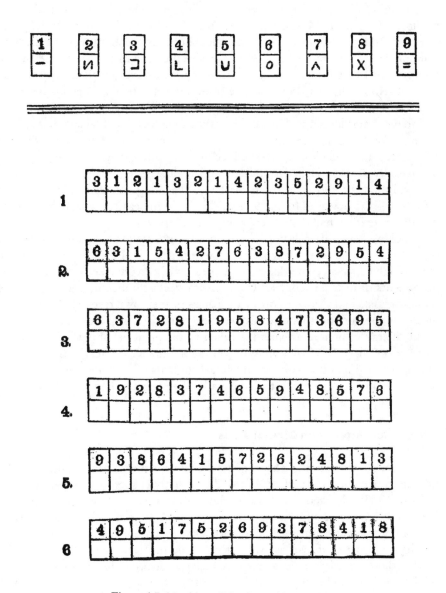

Figure 1.7 Matching of Numbers with Symbols

A year later, Doll (1913) agreed that Binet's mental tests had been "severely criticized." However, he thought that critics had complicated matters by misdirecting their attention to philosophical issues rather than the problems' true sources, which were the many incompetent examiners who were "mechanically" administering the tests. Doll and several colleagues (Bell, Berry, Cornell, Doll, Wallin, & Whipple, 1914) subsequently pointed to additional technical faults of the standardized tests. For example, it often had been unclear to practitioners which editions of tests were to be used under specific circumstances. Some of the creators of tests had failed to define normal performance on their instruments. Many developers had used variably sized samples to standardize their instruments, eccentric measures to designate chronological age, different ranges for chronological intervals, and incompatible techniques for calculating mental age. In all, Doll and his colleagues made 18 suggestions for improving mental tests. Although most of their recommendations concerned technical features, they did note that some of the test creators had failed to address fundamental issues. For example, they had not explained the rationale for those tests "that hinge on the child's stock of information (as opposed to his capacity)" or, in some cases, "what is it, after all, that the scale [they had developed] aims to test" (p. 98).

Looking back through the literature on mental testing, an Indiana principal (Orr, 1925) chastised the advocates of testing for not being evenhanded. He observed that "teachers' marks and estimates have been criticized severely" by the proponents of tests. He contrasted this critical zeal with the indifference that the same scientists had shown to the inadequacies of their own research. Speaking of himself in the third person, he explained that "the writer fails to find any reference in the 'literature' where attention is called to the great variability in scores and ranks given to individual pupils by different intelligence tests" (p. 50). The principal added that the scores of individual students on various intelligence tests were correlated less positively than the grades their teachers had assigned to them.

Accelerated Attacks on Mental Tests

Although testing was challenged from its incipience, the confrontations became more aggressive after World War I. This change was apparent when Ballard (1923) admitted that British schoolmasters were altering their opinions about the advocates of standardized assessment. Whereas they had formerly thought of them as "amusing" or "dry-as dust," they were increasingly inclined to see the proponents of tests as "sinister." Writing that same year, Whipple (1923) lamented the merciless attacks that were being made upon the "mental testers" in the United States. He noted that "the favorite indoor sport of journalists, feature writers, and some even of the 'purer' variety of psychologists appears of late to be that of attacking, in tones that range from thinly veiled sneers to patronizing admonitions, the intelligence testing program of the educational and applied psychologists" (p. 561). Whipple reported about one writer who, mixing metaphors, had characterized mental testing as a "fetich [*sic*]" that was "exploding" in the schools. This same author also advised the public to be aware of a "rebellion against misuse of mental test figures by educators" (W. Allen, 1922, as quoted by Whipple, 1923, p. 561). Whipple cited another critic who had referred contemptuously to the "riddles of our busy little sphinxlets [*sic*], the intelligence testers" (A. Johnson, 1922, as quoted by Whipple, 1923, p. 561).

Whipple identified Walter Lippmann as the author of some of the most widely read and influential attacks on mental testing. Even though he disagreed with Lippmann, Whipple had to admit that this critic's caustic and witty prose made "interesting reading." Paraphrasing and quoting, he summarized Lippmann's allegations that "'the intelligence tester starts with no clear ideal of what intelligence means,' then proceeds 'to guess at the more abstract mental principles which come into play' in what looks like intelligence, and then makes up his tests by inventing puzzles which can be employed quickly" (W. Lippmann, 1922, as restated by Whipple, 1923, p. 561).

Even as they were highlighting the practical inadequacies of mental testing, critics showed their displeasure with some of its broad implications. For example, they worried about the unprecedented rapidity with which tests were taking hold of society. Convinced that the testing movement had "swept everything else before it," Young (1923) elaborated on the reasons that this had happened.

> The present tendency for statistical and quantitative classification is part and parcel of the general trend toward mechanization and standardization of life, consequent upon the application of science to human endeavor, in industry, in education, in the military. It is an inevitable effect of a materialistic civilization. In this mad rush for mass production, be it in the classroom product or in business enterprise, the trend is ever and anon toward those values which are expressible in quantitative units. We are rapidly losing our older notions of quality, of calm and divergently integrated personalities....[and] the present statistical treatment of [man] in terms of I.Q. and score, buttressed by averages of correlation quotients, tends to make man a psychological robot with no emotion, no quality, no personality. (p. 48)

Dixon (1929) paraphrased some of the philosophical arguments about tests that school board members, parents and teachers had been expressing.

> Those who object to the tests and the classifications made upon this basis, state that these tests result in labeling the several groups as the very bright, the average, and the slow; that the pupils so grouped are aware of the nature and significance of this grouping, and that the grouping tends strongly to foster caste feeling and intellectual snobbery. They further say that such a classification tends not only to produce an undue egotism on the part of many of the upper groups, but that it brings about an "inferiority complex" in members of the lower group, and that the sense of inferiority so engendered tends to persist as a permanent character trait. (p. 33)

In the preceding remarks, Dixon identified the reactions of anti-testing factions to the disconcerting statements that Lewis Terman and his supporters had made. In the popular magazine, *World's Work*, Terman (1922b) had written an article with the piquant title "Were We Born That Way?" His answer to this question was apparent when he lectured the readers that "intelligence is chiefly a matter of native endowment" that "depends upon physical and chemical properties of the cerebral cortex" (p. 659). He added that "like other physical traits," intelligence was "subject to the laws of heredity." Based on these convictions, Terman was sure that scores on tests revealed the operation of genetic laws within the student population.

In the revision of his classic 1919 textbook on public education, Cubberley (1934) conceded that intelligence tests had "provoked an enormous controversy." He explained that "for a time the battle of nature *vs.* nurture raged rather fiercely" because "the conception of the biological inequality of human beings, though clearly recognized as to size and strength and endurance and ability to perform, seemed particularly difficult for some educators to accept when applied to mental capacity" (p. 700). As to those educators who had found it "particularly difficult" to accept a biological theory of intelligence, Cubberley concluded that they eventually did change their minds. He believed they had made this adjustment after recognizing "that nurture and environment, while very important in the education of the individual, cannot to any material extent overcome the handicap of poor heredity." Needless to say, Cubberley made a grave miscalculation when he reported that this dispute had been resolved.

Response to Criticism

Some of the anti-testing critics had addressed their concerns to the relatively small audiences that were reading professional journals. However, they eventually were joined by reporters who discussed the anti-testing arguments in popular newspapers and magazines. As the assaults upon them broadened, some of the psychologists presented counterarguments. However, a group of psychologists made concessions that they hoped would appease their adversaries. For example, they modified the ways they were administering and developing tests. When Edmund Huey (1910) wrote an early article advising American readers about Binet's work on mental testing, he explained that "we have here an immediately available means of measuring retardation which can be of immediate and extensive use in the schools and institutions of America" (p. 436). Despite his enthusiasm, he still cautioned his readers that Binet's scales had not been validated with American subjects. In view of this limitation, he recommended that the tests be "tried out" and then "revised wherever revision is certainly indicated." He added that "these Binet tests must be used with judgment and trained intelligence, or they will certainly bring themselves and their authors into undeserved disrepute" (p. 444). Huey's pragmatism was again evident when he urged his readers to view the tests as "the right 'idea' for the construction of a still better scale."

Other researchers shared Huey's attitudes about the limitations of the current tests. Kirkpatrick (1911) suggested restrictions on the implementation and interpretation of any mental imagery tests that would be used with elementary-school children. Davies (1912) recommended alternative techniques for reporting testing data to the general public. Fernald (1912) described ways in which statistical standardization could increase the utility of tests for delinquents. Also addressing delinquency, Jennings and Hallock (1913) recommended that practitioners employ comprehensive batteries to measure both physical and psychological traits. Scott (1913) endorsed "a combination of tests designed to measure different sides or kinds of intellectual performance" (p. 509). Carpenter (1913) urged teachers to validate intelligence tests with school records and personal observations. He thought that a comprehensive approach of this sort would reveal inappropriate items on exams. It would also ensure that any unsuitable exams were identified and then supplemented with sound ones.

Dougherty (1913) reminded any teachers who were going to employ tests that they needed to be aware of children's attitudes. He explained that "when a child fails continually on test after test if he is conscious of his own failure, as he must sometimes be in spite of the examiner's efforts to encourage him, it is not wise to proceed until he merely fails from habit" (p. 339). Agreeing that a child's attitudes and ability to remain attentive had to be taken into account, Kuhlmann (1913) added that even technical aspects of tests, such as the order in which tasks were arranged, could influence a student's performance.

After he had recapitulated objections about the use of standardized mental tests in schools, Dixon (1929) conceded that "there can be no question but that there is some truth" to the opposition. Nonetheless, he pleaded with critics to be fair and consider "whether this system of testing and classification involves a sufficient number of these negative characteristics to make the system undesirable" (p. 33). He pedantically pointed to six benefits of mental testing that more than compensated for its weaknesses.

> [Testing is desirable] because its aim is democratic, because it places each pupil in the working niche where his opportunities will be greatest, because it is the nearest approximation to the truth…because it is essentially the method of the open door to bigger things, because it refuses to emphasize unduly merely book learning ability, and because in actual practice it works out by keeping pupils in school and interested and happy. (p. 34)

Sympathetic to the arguments that Dixon had articulated, Tiegs (1931b) believed that the anti-testing factions had inappropriately dramatized the dangers of tests. He thought they were "seeing elephants where only mice exist" (p. 1931b). To buttress this metaphor, he listed several of the positive features of mental tests.

The use of intelligence tests makes it possible to provide for children a more adequate quality of education....Through their use, the slow pupil is saved from discouragement and disappointment....[and] the intelligence test...has vindicated them of the charge of laziness....In other words, the intelligence test is one instrumentality through which the ideal of equality of opportunity is being realized. (p. 45)

Transition to Education

Attempting to characterize the educational impact of Binet's intelligence tests, Bell (1912) wrote that "perhaps no device pertaining to education has ever risen to such sudden prominence in public interest throughout the world" (p. 102). Equally aware of the excitement about mental testing, Pyle (1912) predicted that it "means much for the future of education" (p. 95). A year later, he judged that everyone recognized the value of tests, including their suitability for grading and classifying "pupils, methods of teaching and, to a considerable extent, the nature of the curriculum" (Pyle, 1913, p. 61). Courtis (1915b) applauded testing because it had provided a new point of view from which educators were able to recognize "that both the materials and the techniques of teaching must be varied according to the results to be secured" (p. 44).

After World War I, John Dewey (1922) simultaneously acknowledged and bemoaned the remarkable progress of the testing movement. He judged that contemporary educators were fascinated by the achievements of psychologists in the same way that earlier psychologists had been impressed by the accomplishments of scientists. As a result, misguided educators had attempted to extrapolate research procedures that originated in science and engineering. To make sure his audience understood this point, he added that these educators were "excessively concerned with trying to evolve a body of definite, usable, educational directions out of the new body of science" (p. 91). Although he characterized their efforts as "pathetic," he recognized that some educators felt the need for "assurance that the best methods of modern science are employed and sanction what is done" (Dewey, 1922, p. 91).

That Dewey had depicted his psychological and educational opponents accurately was clear from their own remarks. Cattell (1905), whom many historians considered the father of modern psychological testing, had written that "the extraordinary growth of the material sciences with their applications during the nineteenth century requires as its complement a corresponding development of psychology" (p. 367). Fifteen years earlier, he had warned that "psychology cannot attain the certainty and exactness of the physical sciences, unless it rests on a foundation of experiment and measurement" (Cattell, 1890, p. 373). As a "step in this direction," he had recommended the application of "a series of mental tests and measurements to a large number of individuals." Cattell added parenthetically that "the science and practical value of such tests would be much increased should a uniform system be adopted, so that determinations made at different times and places could be compared and combined."

Wallin (1914) compared psychological tests to medical examinations. Although medical examinations had been implemented in the schools in order to restrict the spread of contagious diseases, Wallin pointed out that "there is another function of school medical inspection which is even more important for the proper development of the individual child" (p. 1). This additional function was the detection of any physical problems that would prevent children from achieving their full potential in the schools. Some of the physical problems were "defective vision, defective hearing, defective nasal breathing, adenoids, hypertrophied tonsils, cardiac diseases, defective teeth and palate, malnutrition, orthopedic defects, tubercular lymph nodes, lateral curvature of the spine, stoop shoulders, nervous exhaustion and pulmonary disease" (Wallin, 1914, p. 1). He advised teachers that psychological tests were necessary because the mental problems that they were able to detect could be as devastating as physical ailments.

Reminiscing about the early period of testing, Stark (1925) recounted that he personally "had a fairly scientific training in preparation for engineering." Consequently, he had adopted the dictum, "Don't rely upon mere opinion, collect the facts" (p. 79). After he had turned to a career in education, he understandably became a member of the educational group that was attracted to the testing movement. Thorndike (1920a) was another scholar who forthrightly admitted his fascination with science.

> In the last hundred years the civilized world has learned to trust science to teach it how to make the powers of wind and water, the energy of chemicals, and the vibrations of the ether do man's will and serve his comfort. Physical forces are being conquered by science for man. We may hope that man's own powers of intellect, character, and skill are not less amenable to understanding, control, and direction; and that in the next hundred years the world may improve its use of man-power as it has improved its use of earth-power. (Thorndike, 1920a, p. 227)

Orleans and Sealy (1928) also alluded to the physical sciences to justify the use of objective educational testing. They observed that, just as "the strength of a beam is 'tested' to see whether it will stand a given weight or strain...[and] a chemical solution is 'tested' to determine whether it is strong enough for a given purpose...in the same way pupils are tested to determine whether their achievement is 'strong' enough" (p. 1). Tiegs (1931a) later compared educational testers to those engineers who had "suspended wonderful bridges and reared great temples" by relying on "tests for strengths of materials and measures of stress and strain" (p. 10). Tiegs was equally impressed that "the medical profession, with its physical, chemical, and other tests and measurements" had "so improved preventative and reparative procedures that fifteen years, on the average, have been added to the span of life" (1931a, p. 10).

Like many of his positivist colleagues, Kandel (1936) believed that education was transforming itself from a provincial practice into a substantive science.

> The demands imposed upon educators by the conditions which from the beginning of the century were peculiarly American and the criticisms of the traditional practice of examinations coincided with, if they did not actually stimulate, the development of what has been called the scientific movement in education, that is, methods analogous to those employed in the physical sciences. (p. 73)

Psychologists and educators had adapted mental tests so that they would be better suited for school applications. They had modified them for students who were developing normally, students who were gifted, students with learning problems, students with disabilities, and juvenile delinquents. They had made these changes in order to lance a bacteria-like strain of criticism that had festered within education for decades. In the middle of the nineteenth century, Chadwick (1864) already had identified this criticism. He wrote that "much of the scepticism [sic] prevalent as to the power and value of popular education arises from the inability of the educationist, or of the school teacher, to adduce satisfactory statistical evidence of the moral or the intellectual results from any special courses of instruction or training" (p. 479).

Almost fifty years after Chadwick had made the preceding observations, De Sanctis (1911) wished to eliminate any lingering skepticism about the disciplinary integrity of education. He attempted to demonstrate that educational problems could be resolved through test-based investigations. Using the demeaning terminology of his era, he explained that he had devised mental tests that could be applied within "a special school for abnormal children" or "an institution for idiots." He continued that "this is important from the medico-psychological standpoint, since the morons should be sent to special schools, or as day pupils to asylum schools, while the idiots and imbeciles should be entrusted to institutions" (p. 505).

A principal (Adler, 1914) in the New York City public schools wrote that tests were invaluable because they could help administrators and teachers differentiate students with genuine learning problems from those who had been placed in this category erroneously. With regard to those students who had been misdiagnosed, she reasoned that "there must be numbers of children whose native ability is never discovered, who probably always pass as dull, and who consequently live up to their reputations." Convinced that this was the case, she declared that "it is of utmost importance that some form of mental test other than the regular school examination be used by those upon whom falls the task of classifying pupils" (p. 23).

Many educators recognized the need for a carefully developed and standardized educational test. Such a test would set a high standard to which other objective tests could then be compared. Whipple (1921) recounted that several preeminent psychologists had wished to develop precisely this type of test. Prior to World War I, they had made a request to the National Association of Directors of Educational Research, asking for the financial support to commence "the measurement of the intelligence of a good-sized group of pupils." Consideration of their request was postponed until the war had ended. During the intervening period, the members of this association had been impressed by the success of military intelligence testing. As a result, the National Research Council, which was a unit within the National Association of Directors of Educational Research, eventually did provide the funding to tailor a group intelligence test specifically for the schools.

The National Research Council designated five psychologists to develop and standardize the assessment device that it would fund. The researchers included Edward Thorndike, Lewis Terman, and Robert Yerkes, three of the most influential psychologists of their generation. The experimental prototypes for their tests involved 22 different kinds of tasks: printed directions, disarranged sentences, arithmetical problems, information, opposites, practical judgment, number series, analogies, series completion, symbol-digit, comparison, picture completion, geometrical construction, copying designs, vocabulary, picture sequence, pictorial analogies, recognitive pictorial memory, sentence completion, pictorial similarities, computation, and logical selection. From the preceding items, the psychologists finally selected 10 tasks. The tasks were organized into a booklet "that could be applied to any child in the elementary school who could read well enough to participate in a group examination" (Whipple, 1921, p. 17). Their final product, which was marketed as the National Intelligence Tests, was so popular that it sold 200,000 copies during the first year that it was available. Whipple, who was one of the committee members who had developed the National Intelligence Tests, could not conceal his delight with this project. After admitting that he might have been influenced by "unconscious bias," he still wrote that "I feel that the committee has a right to feel a tinge of pride in what it has accomplished" (p. 31).

The intelligence test that the National Research Council had funded was not the first group measure of intelligence. In fact, Pintner (1919) had observed that "the usefulness of group tests for the measurement of intelligence is resulting in the appearance of a great number of such tests" (p. 199). Nonetheless, the test that the National Research Council sponsored was unlike its precursors. The fact that it was distributed in several different but comparably difficult forms was one indication of this test's distinctiveness. The precaution of developing multiple forms had been insisted upon by Thorndike, who was worried about "the dangers of coaching." Although Whipple believed that Thorndike's fears were unrealistic, he dutifully summarized his colleague's thoughts on the matter.

> [Thorndike] felt that not only would intelligence testing become a common feature of public school administration, but that it would become also a common feature of business

administration, e.g., that business men would use mental tests in selecting young boys and girls for beginners in their establishments. He argued also that within some five years practically every city of over 25,000 population would establish special classes for gifted pupils and that many parents would seek to coach their children to pass intelligence examinations given for the selection of pupils for these classes. On this account, he urged that any intelligence examination that came into general usage ought to be capable of almost unlimited expansion, that it was desirable to include in our examinations only tests the materials of which could be so extensive that it would be possible to produce even as many as thirty or forty different forms of the test just by drawing material by chance from the general reservoir of items prearranged for each test. (Whipple, 1921, pp. 18–19)

Within a history of mental testing, Goodenough (1949) acknowledged that the public had showed "rapid" and "widespread" interest in the novel assessment instruments. In fact, she thought the excitement had been so extraordinary that it had led to "the promulgation of erroneous as well as sound theories." She also cautioned that "the use of the new methods by many enthusiastic but poorly trained persons has not always worked out to the advantage of the tested individual or society" (p. vii). Despite the problems and limitations of mental testing, Goodenough believed that "few if any other fields of psychology have aroused so widespread an interest." Within the range of professionals who had become interested in testing, she included psychiatrists, anthropologists, sociologists, lawyers, and educators. Although Goodenough's observations may have been accurate, not all of these groups were invested to the same degree in testing. Furthermore, they did not have comparable opportunities to influence the ways in which testing was being used. Unlike the psychiatrists, anthropologists, sociologists, and lawyers, the educators controlled the primary market for tests. Consequently, they were in the pivotal position to shape the testing movement.

Summary

Although nineteenth-century psychologists initially resisted the research methods that scientists and engineers had been using, their attitudes changed as standardized intelligence tests emerged. Anti-testing critics disparaged these new instruments as crude, impractical, technically flawed, and socially biased. However, the psychologists were determined to experiment with and refine the measurement techniques. They also were determined to develop the popular base that they needed to expand the use of the techniques. The political strength of the psychologists grew noticeably after military leaders and school administrators endorsed their efforts. In addition to administering intelligence tests, these groups devised exams that were peculiarly suited to their needs. The extensive media coverage that resulted attracted the attention of the general public, which learned about the benefits and the liabilities of standardized testing.

CHAPTER 2

Educators Adapt to Standardized Tests

[Because each teacher] has, consciously or unconsciously, set himself up as a designer of educational yard sticks...the general outcome has been that we have had in the same system of schools, the same institution, school building or department as many standards of marking as there have been teachers.
—H. O. RUGG, 1915

Nineteenth-century teachers had evaluated their students subjectively. However, some of them became dissatisfied with this unreliable technique. Using shared examination items, common curricula, and universal thresholds of mastery, they devised standardized measures of academic achievement. They developed these measures for core subjects such as reading, writing, mathematics, social studies, and the sciences. They also developed them for specialized academic subjects and even for noncurricular traits.

Subjectively Graded Exams

Although testing may have been as old as schooling itself, nineteenth-century schoolmasters limited themselves to a single form of assessment. Typically conducted in a group setting, the type of testing that they employed was known as recitation. It was a procedure in which students orally recapitulated key information. Teachers would then judge the degree to which the students had mastered the material. Although it was once universal, recitation was eventually denigrated. Looking back on this assessment practice, Cubberley (1934) dismissed it as little more than "personal opinion." He reported that "the test and measurement movement arose, something like a quarter of a century ago, largely as an attempt, on the part of a few students of education, to find a means for transforming guess work as to school progress into procedures having scientific accuracy" (p. viii).

In a classic study about academic achievement in the Philadelphia public schools, Phillips (1912) had attempted to explain the differences between those students who were progressing adequately and those who were retarded, by which he meant "those who are one year or more behind the 'normal' grade for their age." After observing that the number of retarded students varied dramatically in the different schools throughout the school district, he speculated about possible causes, such as class size, poverty, medical care, and the number of African American or immigrant families within neighborhoods. However, the feature of this study that would later stand out the most was his failure to consider the possibility that the teachers at the different schools were making assessments unevenly. As a matter of fact, Phillips made no mention about the basis for assigning grades.

A year later, Strong (1913) assumed a more sophisticated perspective when she studied children in South Carolina. She explained that she had decided to make "practical use" of a standardized intelligence test, even though this test had some weaknesses. To emphasize the value of standardized testing, she referred to New Jersey, where "legal enactments require the segregation and special training of backward and defective children" and where "some standard is necessary to determine which children are sub-normal" (p. 485). Strong added that "although the primary object in devising the [standardized intelligence] tests was the determination of defective children," the identification of students who "are backward, or normal, or endowed with more than average mental ability…cannot fail to result in increased efficiency of teaching."

Like Strong, most of the early twentieth-century proponents of standardized tests recognized the significant practical problems that they faced. However, they were equally aware of the problems inherent in subjective judgments. Summarizing the drawbacks of subjective grading, Squire (1912a) had written that the schoolmasters, who were attempting to measure "the amount assimilated of the knowledge in the school curriculum," could never complete this task because "there are…as many measuring rods as there are courses of study" (p. 364). Whipple (1913) argued tautologically that subjective evaluation was "an absolutely uncalibrated instrument." Finkelstein (1913) lamented that subjective evaluations often were based upon students' zeal and enthusiasm rather than their academic performance. He added that "the variability in the marks given for the same subject and to the same pupils by different instructors is so great as frequently to work real injustice to the students" (p. 6). A year later, Doll (1914) agreed that "different schools are of as varied efficiencies as are the different teachers in these schools, so that we are at present unable to say what is a standard performance in scholastic ability for a child" (p. 347).

The educators who questioned subjective grading were impressed with the ways that their fellow researchers in psychology had been addressing somewhat comparable problems. Buckingham (1914) complimented these educators because they had not merely carped at the prevalent system of assessment but actually searched for a way to improve it. He judged that "for a number of years there has been a growing disposition among educational thinkers to seek to base their conclusions upon data quantitatively determined rather than upon the dictum of an authority" (p. 199). He chided those teachers who had set themselves up as "dogmatists" to adopt "the scientist's precise statement of fact." Buckingham urged the substitution of "numerical expression" for fine words, especially because "one of the fields to which this [new] method has been applied with attractive prospects of success is the measurement and standardization of school products." He continued that "what we really need is a series of several tests in fundamentals and another series in reasoning, each test more difficult than the preceding one by a known amount" (p. 203).

Judd (1916) agreed that students should be systematically and objectively assessed. He was especially distressed by the situation in Cleveland, Ohio, where "in June, 1914, 10,000 pupils in the elementary schools failed to be promoted" (p. 17). He added that nearly 1,400 of these pupils, who already had been left back at least once, were failing the same course work for a second or even third time. After noticing a discrepancy between the scores that students had earned on objective academic achievement tests and the grades that they had received from their teachers, Judd placed his confidence in the tests. He wrote sarcastically that the grades from teachers were a better indication of "special policies in the individual schools" than they were of students' scholastic abilities. In fact, Judd singled out arbitrary grading practices as the primary reasons for the many students who already had been held back and who subsequently continued to fail. Using turgid vocabulary, he portrayed the Cleveland schools' grading system as one that lacked "symmetrical and wholesome development" (p. 234). More than 30 years later, Thorndike (1948) used equally stodgy and censorious prose when he looked back on this period. He postulated that "all competent students of measurement" eventually came to recognize that scholastic assessment had to be "characterized by very small personal equations and close agreement in the scores given to the same examinee by different examiners" (p. 21).

Some of the teachers who relied on oral assessment did supplement by evaluating their students' written work. However, the subjective manner in which they graded writing had the same weaknesses as the subjective way in which they evaluated oral remarks. Cattell (1905) reported about one researcher who had discovered that high grades in university Latin courses correlated with high grades in Greek. In the event that this seemed reasonable, he added that the students who were excelling in Greek were "almost as likely to receive a high grade in mathematics or gymnastics" (p. 367). The witty Cattell concluded that, "grades assigned to college students have some meaning, though just what this is remains to be determined."

Kelly (1914) specifically addressed some of the problems associated with subjectively graded writing. He surmised that the "disposition to depend more and more upon the individual teacher's notion of what is proper to expect in the way of student achievement" had resulted "in wide differences in demands because the standards of teachers are far from uniform" (p. 2). Hillegas (1912) had argued that a uniform scale for testing English composition was essential if educators wished to measure "the efficiency of instruction in a school system or to evaluate different methods of education procedure." Furthermore, such a scale "would make it more difficult for mere opinion to control so much of our school-room practice" (p. 1).

Starch and Elliott (1912) conducted a study in which they discovered that different teachers, who had all been given copies of the same English paper, assigned it radically different grades. Because the grading of English presented obvious opportunities for subjective assessment, Starch and Elliott conceded that some educators might have anticipated these results. The two researchers therefore replicated their experiment with a mathematics exam. To the embarrassment of those teachers who were endorsing the prevalent approach to grading, "the marks of this particular paper [varied] even more widely than those of the English papers" (Starch & Elliott, 1913b, p. 258). Although they reviewed potentially ameliorating circumstances, Starch and Elliott concluded that it was "fully evident that there is no inherent reason why a mathematical paper should be capable of more precise evaluation than any other kind of paper."

Hillegas (1912) wished to "make it more difficult for mere opinion to control so much of our school-room practice" (p. 1). He therefore published a "scale for the measurement of quality in English composition by young people." He believed that this scale could "compare with certainty the work done in one school or system with that done elsewhere." Prefiguring the politically conservative rhetoric that would be popular 80 years later, he extolled objective testing because "every attempt to measure the efficiency of instruction in a school system...serves to emphasize the importance of standards."

Monroe, DeVoss, and Kelly (1917) identified several subtle but substantive problems with subjective grading. They pointed out that those teachers who asked the same questions about the identical content still faced challenges because they would assign different weightings to those questions. These investigators were even more troubled when they discovered that individual teachers, if given the chance to do so, would change the grades that they previously had assigned. This situation seemed patently unacceptable. Canning (1916) expressed the convictions of many educators who believed that "fairness in the award of honors, justice in determining failures and dismissals, and incitement of the student to better work can be attained only to the extent to which a common standard for the awarding of marks is understood, accepted, and acted upon" (p. 196). Standardized testing was proposed as the remedy for this unfair situation.

Standardized testing was recommended as the solution to another early twentieth-century problem. This problem had resulted from individual teachers who were defining their own idiosyncratic curricula. Pressey and Pressey (1922) made this point when they wrote about weak tests that "consisted of a number of questions selected by the teacher, and covering what she thought to be the important points" (p. 7). Thorndike and Gates (1931) pointed out that individual teachers inevitably defined the scope and content of the curriculum differently. As a result, teachers were likely to have judged students distinctly even if they had assigned the same grades for the class work that had been done in courses with comparable titles. Thorndike and Gates provided evidence to confirm that "even in determining the most obvious achievements of pupils in their own class, expert teachers with the results of weeks of work, of special examinations, and other data before them, are strikingly inaccurate and variable" (p. 283).

The educational damage caused by teachers who defined their own curricula was compounded when those teachers were poorly trained. To protect children from incompetent instructors, parents and school administrators insisted that the teachers use textbooks as de facto curricula (Giordano, 2003). Cast (1919) encapsulated this sentiment when he reported that many persons were viewing the textbook as "a substitute for the teacher." As a result of this expectation, textbook authors began to assume a role that had formerly been assigned exclusively to teachers.

Despite the uniform curricula that they created, textbooks could not eliminate all of the problems of subjective grading. To demonstrate the degree to which educators were disturbed by the practice of subjective grading, Rugg (1915) referred to 38 articles, all of which had been published during the preceding 10-year period and all of which had been critical of subjective grading. For example, Johnson (1910) demonstrated that the grades assigned to students in elementary school did not predict their high-school grades. He believed that poor assessment was responsible for this breakdown in the educational system. The editors of the journal in which this study appeared praised Johnson's research as "a full, concrete illustration of the application of impersonal scientific methods to elementary-school problems" (p. 63).

Lowell (1919) also saw the educational damage inflicted by unsophisticated or sentimental teachers. He wrote that "teachers frequently persuade themselves that since a child is sweet, docile and attractive, he must necessarily be bright; or, because he is doing good work in his grade, he is undoubtedly normal, regardless of the fact that he is two or three years older than his classmates." He used an anecdote to illustrate this point.

> In one rural school, the teacher, on being asked about the work of twin girls in the third grade, said with great assurance, "Oh, those girls are very bright. They do good third grade work, and they are such nice children." The twins in question had a chronological age of twelve years, a fact entirely overlooked by the teacher in her estimation of their ability. Mentally, they were found to be 7 5/8 and 8 3/8 years. (pp. 215–216)

Figure 2.1 is an illustration from the April 1922 cover of the *American School Board Journal*. The personification of the "new method of education" is using "intelligence tests" to carefully examine a single pupil. On her desk are books about mental forces, scientific methods of mental investigation, and the psychology of individuality. An accompanying insert depicts the "old method of education." The personification of the old method is using a huge scoop to haphazardly assign students to educational categories.

Another reason that objective testing was alluring to so many persons was that it complemented the standards movement, which was germinating at the same time. McConn (1935) observed that the pressure to establish high academic standards had "come to the fore in American education in the late nineties" (p. 44). He reported that he had "learned that gospel in my first job, from men who were leaders in their generation, and that for twenty years I never doubted that it contained practically everything needful for educational salvation." He continued

Figure 2.1 1920s Depiction of Changing Examination Practices
(*Reprinted from American School Board Journal, April 1922.*)

that "to set standards, and enforce standards, and raise standards, and raise them
evermore, was nearly the whole duty of teachers and principals and superintendent and state departments and college presidents." Like the testing movement,
the standards movement was a reaction to the public's demand for scholastic
accountability. Schudson (1972) concluded that the educators who had adopted the
standards philosophy needed credible testing programs to confirm that their
standards were being met. As such, the movement to set standards and the
movement to standardize assessment became politically as well as philosophically
entwined.

In the event that scholarly arguments did not convince teachers, McCall (1920) advanced a practical rationale for adopting objective tests. He estimated that the 600,000 teachers in the United States annually spent 36,000,000 hours constructing, administering, and scoring their personal examinations. In view of this daunting commitment, he thought it was self-evident that tests "are and will be for some time and may possibly always be the most important form of educational measurement" (p. 33). He adjured the proponents of traditional examinations to cease fretting, recognize that standardized tests were "nothing but improved examinations," and embrace them enthusiastically.

Focusing on administrative, scholarly, or theoretical issues, most of the opponents and proponents of testing restricted their arguments to pedagogy, curriculum, and educational administration. However, not all of the disputants followed this course. For example, a Michigan superintendent noted that "the oral method of testing is undoubtedly the oldest of all forms" because "the Old Testament records that an oral examination was given the Ephraimites by the Gileadites at the passage of the Jordan in regard to the former's ability to pronounce the word "*shibboleth*" (Giddings, 1936, p. 21). Although he also had consulted the Bible, McCall (1923) believed that this sacred text contained the rationale for a more scientific type of educational testing. He explained to his colleagues that Jesus had "tacitly accepted and practiced mental measurement when He estimated the quantity of faith on a mustard-seed scale" (p. 4).

Pioneers of Objective Educational Tests

Within the second edition of a book about assessment, Webb and Shotwell (1939) included a chapter on the history of educational testing. They wrote that this movement was part of a broader initiative to "apply scientific procedures to the solution of educational problems." Nonetheless, they thought that the testing advocates stood out from other modern educators because they "went one step further and stressed the objectivity of the measuring instruments" (p. 14). Webb and Shotwell called particular attention to a physician, J. M. Rice, whom they lionized as "the first [American] to make a radical departure from the usual methods of measuring achievement in the schools" (1939, p. 18). Most scholars who contemplated the early history of educational measurement agreed about Rice's prominence among the brilliant and foresighted scholars who had been responsible for the success of educational testing. Scates (1947) wrote that two of Rice's 1897 articles about spelling were "usually taken as the beginning of the modern movement for the objective study of education" (p. 241). Two-and-a-half decades before Scates had made these remarks, Trabue (1924) had characterized Rice as the "'inventor' of comparative educational tests in America." Even though he added his personal opinion that this reputation was undeserved, Trabue did concede that Rice's research "received a great deal of public notice and criticism." In a still earlier history of educational testing, Ayres (1918) had not qualified his admiration for Rice, whom he acknowledged as the individual who had instigated the current educational revolution.

Within his seminal, two-part report, which he entitled *The Futility of the Spelling Grind*, Rice (1897a, 1897b) had argued oxymoronically that teachers who increased the amount of classroom time devoted to spelling could not be assured that their students' scores on spelling tests would improve correspondingly. He wrote that he had "endeavored to prove that the first step toward placing elementary education on a scientific basis must necessarily lie in determining what results may reasonably be expected at the end of a given period" (1897a, p. 163). As such, he systematically gathered and analyzed data about spelling instruction before he formed his final conclusions.

Even though he was personally sympathetic to Rice, Ayres (1918) admitted that this controversial scholar "did not meet with the approval of the educators of the day." He explained that contemporaries objected to Rice's research because they thought "that the object of [classroom spelling] work was not to teach children to spell, but to develop their minds" (p. 11). Anticipating this objection at the time that he had published his research, Rice had written sardonically that "as some of our most scholarly people are deficient in spelling, and as, in this subject, some of the brightest pupils cannot keep pace with the dullest, our high-pitched sensibilities on the spelling question may be regarded as one of the mysteries of civilization" (1897a, p. 163).

Cubberley (1917) noted that subjective evaluation, which had been challenged initially by comparative testing, recently had been replaced by "a still better method for the evaluation." The new approach involved "the setting up, through the medium of a series of carefully devised 'Standardized Tests,' of standard measurements and units of accomplishments for the determination of the kind and the amount of work which a school or a school system is doing" (p. vi). Cubberley had made the preceding remarks in the introduction to a book by Monroe, DeVoss, and Kelly (1917). These authors identified Edward Thorndike as the scholar who had pioneered and popularized standardized educational tests. Other educational historians agreed about Thorndike's professional stature. Ayres wrote that "if Dr. Rice is to be called the inventor of educational measurement, Professor E. L. Thorndike should be called the father of the movement" (1918, p. 12). Pintner (1923) wrote effusively that "no one man has had more to do with stimulating the measurement movement in this country than Professor Thorndike" (p. iv). Even Trabue (1924), who had been skeptical about Rice's research, did not question the value of Thorndike's work. Trabue wrote that Thorndike had made an epic contribution through "a scale for the measurement of merit in children's handwritings...[which] was the first of the scientifically constructed instruments for measuring the quality of children's educational products" (1924, p. 73).

The handwriting scale to which Trabue had referred consisted of a "graphometer." This instrument rank ordered samples of students' handwriting. Each exemplar in the graphometer was accompanied by a numerical value. In a subsequent review of his own study, Thorndike (1923) explained that the values on this assessment instrument comprised "a scale for merit in handwriting in the same way the $5, $7, $9, etc., are a scale for purchasing power, and in almost the same way that a series of lines 5, 7, 9, etc., inches long would be a scale for length" (p. 213).

The graphometer, like Thorndike's other educational scales, reflected his strong positivist dispositions. These dispositions had been discernible in 1904 when he had declared that "the facts of human nature can be made the materials for quantitative science" (Thorndike, 1904, as reproduced in Thorndike, 1913, p. v). Thorndike's positivist attitudes were just as strong nine years later when he recommended that "a student of education should first know many facts of biology, psychology, sociology, ethics and the other sciences of man" (1913, p. 1). Describing his philosophy as the same one that had characterized "those who, in the last decade, have been busy trying to extend and improve measurements of educational products," he recapitulated its major assumptions in succinct, encyclopedia-like prose.

> Whatever exists at all exists in some amount. To know it thoroughly involves knowing its quantity as well as its quality. Education is concerned with changes in human beings; a change is a difference between two conditions; each of these conditions is known to us only by the products produced by it—things made, words spoken, acts performed and the like. To measure any of these products means to define its amount in some way so that competent persons will know how large it is, better than they would without measurement. To measure a product well means so to define its amount that competent persons will know how large it is, with some precision, and that this knowledge may be conveniently recorded and used. (Thorndike, 1918, p. 16)

Academic Tests Proliferate

Proponents of objective assessment were able to accommodate the content in some academic subjects more easily than that in others. As contemporaries might have expected, the learning of mathematics was an area that seemed especially suited to testing. Monroe (1918a) reported that 24 standardized mathematical tests were available at the end of World War I. Eleven of these assessed fundamental operations, six assessed arithmetic reasoning, and seven involved algebra. However, nonstandardized mathematical tests were available as well. A year later, Monroe (1919) simply noted that "a large number of tests have been devised to measure the results of teaching arithmetic" (p. 91). He described several of these, such as the *Cleveland Survey Tests*, which consisted "of fifteen tests, including four in addition, two in subtraction, three in multiplication, four in division, and two in addition and subtraction of common fractions" (Monroe, 1919, p. 93). *Starch's Arithmetic Scale* contained "a series of arithmetical problems which are arranged in order of increasing difficulty." Monroe's own *Standardized Reasoning Tests* comprised problems that had been "carefully selected so as to be representative of the one-step and two-step problems in the arithmetic tests now in use." The *Courtis Standard Research Tests* measured "the rate and accuracy with which the pupil can perform these operations with one type of example." Courtis (1911) had written earlier that his own mathematics tests were especially attractive because of "the elaborate provision for uniform conditions through instructions, record sheets, answer cards, [and] special methods of computation" (p. 274).

Toops (1925) recounted that he had received numerous requests for copies of a general science test that he had constructed six years earlier. Although he was willing to share this test, he urged teachers to create their own science exams. He advised them to follow a three-stage process in which they were to "select the facts or principles which are to appear as questions," "select some objective or technical word or numerical fact for an answer," and then "try out the questions thus formulated upon some critical person whose business it is to attempt to evade giving the intended answer by answering some other 'correct' answer" (p. 817).

Other scholars had given advice about ways in which teachers could devise their own exams. Many of these persons had focused on science tests. For example, Herring (1919) advised teachers about the construction of tests to measure "scientific thinking." Chapman (1919) gave examples of items that he had used on physics tests and the procedures by which they had been developed. He encouraged teachers to follow his procedures and create additional items. Although Cooprider (1925) recommended a similar set of procedures, he applied them to biology tests.

Reading Tests

Looking back at the early research about learning to read, William Gray (1946) documented that it "was begun in the eighties and nineties by surgeons and neurologists" who "influenced to a large extent the thinking of teachers and specialists in reading during the next two decades" (p. v). Other reading educators repeatedly acknowledged the impact that medical researchers had made on them. For example, consider Thorndike's momentous adjuration.

> Educational science and educational practice alike need more objective, more accurate and more convenient measures....Any progress toward measuring how well a child can read with something of the objectivity, precision, commensurability, and convenience which characterize our measurement of how tall he is, how much he can lift with his back or squeeze with his hand, or how acute his vision is, would be of great help in grading,

promoting, testing the value of methods of teaching and in every other case where we need to know ourselves and to inform others how well an individual or a class or a school population can read. (Thorndike, 1924, pp. 1–2)

In the rep ort from which the preceding remarks were taken, Thorndike provided actual reading tests that teachers could employ. One of his tests required students to follow eight directions as they parsed a list of words. The list began with the words "camel, samuel [*sic*], kind, lily, cruel, cowardly, dominoes, kangaroo, pansy, tennis" and ended with "opossum, poltroon, begonia, equitable, pretentious, renegade, reprobate, armadillo, iguana, philanthropic" (pp. 3–4). Their first task was to "look at each word and write the letter F under every word that means a *flower*" (Thorndike, 1914, p. 3). Subsequent tasks required the students to differentiate words that identified animals, names of males, games, books, and "something to do with time." He also asked students to isolate words that meant "something *good to be* or *do*" as well as those that meant "something *bad to be* or *do*" (p. 3). Two years later, Thorndike (1916a, 1916b) increased this list and organized the words into graded categories. Haggerty (1917) expanded Thorndike's list again "in order to extend this scale and to provide duplicate scales for further testing" (p. 39).

Gray (1916a, 1916b) developed an early test of reading that required students to answer questions about the passages that they had read. The following passage was intended for students who could read at either the seventh-grade or eighth-grade levels.

There is no more interesting study to marine architects than that of the growth of modern ships from their earliest form. Ancient ships of war and of commerce equally interest them; but as they study the sculptures and writings of the ancients, they find records of warships far out-numbering ships of commerce. (1916b, p. 285)

Gray formulated ten questions about this passage. The first was, "To whom is the study of the growth of modern ships interesting?" Another question was, "How do the records of warships compare with the records of the ships of commerce?"

Thorndike's and Gray's tests were not the only reading assessment devices available. Gray (1915) published a *Selected Bibliography upon Practical Tests of Reading Ability* in which he listed eight instruments. Courtis had developed one of these measures. Sharing Gray's enthusiasm for reading tests, Courtis (1915b) extolled the "yardstick men" who were responding to the "widespread interest in the movement for measurement in education" (p. 44). In an article about reading assessment, Starch (1915) agreed that "material progress has been made during the last five years in the endeavor to devise accurate methods for measuring the actual efficiency of pupils in school studies" (p. 1). Starch concluded that testing had become "one of the three or four most important fields of investigation in the scientific study of educational problems."

Monroe (1918b) believed that the "widespread use" of the *Kansas Silent Reading Tests* was evidence "that school men generally feel the need for a simple instrument for measuring the ability of pupils to read" (p. 303). The following passage occurred on this instrument.

> They rested and talked. Their talk was all about their flocks, a dull theme to the world, yet a theme which was all the word to them.
>
> What do you suppose was the occupation of these men?
> carpenter   doctor   merchant   shepherd   blacksmith (p. 309)

Although scientifically minded educators recognized the need to measure reading achievement, they disagreed about the features of reading that should be examined during this measurement. Mead (1915) assumed the constrained view that "the getting of the thought which the writer wishes to impress is the main purpose for our reading" (p. 345). Although he concurred with Mead about the importance of comprehension, Brown (1916b) added an additional element to the equation. He wrote that "the two things, then, which must be accurately weighed in order to have a complete measure of reading ability are: (1) rate of reading, and (2) comprehension" (p. 590).

Other experts had their own ideas about the essential characteristics of the reading process. Wells (1916) judged that "a test of reading ability which is concerned alone with the facility in gaining thought from the printed page naturally raises various doubts and questions in the minds of teachers accustomed to look upon the oral element in reading as the essential factor" (p. 585). Although Wells clearly believed that an evaluator should be attentive to the "oral element" in reading, he did not elaborate. In contrast, Starch (1917) was not at all reluctant to explain his own thoughts on this matter. He believed it was "obvious" that reading comprised not only comprehension but speed and "the correctness of pronunciation, or elocution" (p. 20). McLeod (1918) evaluated oral reading achievement by analyzing speed, comprehension, and the errors that students made. Gray (1921) recounted that teachers at the University of Chicago's laboratory school analyzed the mechanics of reading, speed of oral reading, accuracy of oral reading, speed while silently reading simple materials, comprehension while silently reading simple passages, and comprehension while silently reading a set of passages that became increasingly more complex. Thorndike (1917) had assumed a truly eclectic viewpoint when he identified reading as "a very elaborate procedure" that included "all the features characteristic of typical reasonings."

Greene and Jorgensen (1929) reported about tests that measured the versatility and speed of readers. For example, the Chapman-Cook Speed of Reading Test required students to quickly read passages and locate the single word that "spoiled the meaning" in each paragraph. The following paragraphs illustrate the types of tasks that the students faced on this test.

Tom got badly hurt the other day, when fighting with his older brother. As soon as this happened, he ran home to his mother, laughing as hard as he can.

Mary said she mailed a letter to me at the post office the day before yesterday, but the milkman did not leave anything for me when he came this morning. (Passages from the Chapman-Cook Speed of Reading Test, as cited by Greene & Jorgensen, 1929, pp. 27–28)

Because they were impressed with the usefulness of the research that their medical colleagues had conducted, reading educators explored practical applications for their own research. Some of these applications were intended to establish school accountability. Brown (1916a) noted that "one of the leading educational problems of the present day is that of measuring in a competent manner the efficiency of the work of the public school" (p. 3). He added that "it is true, also, that a large part of the educational practice of the past has had no scientific foundation and that the results of much of the teaching have been meager....[and] that this, too, may be accounted for in part by the lack of adequate means of measuring the efficiency of instruction" (p. 3).

Medical scientists had demonstrated the value of their research by applying it to patients with physical problems. In a similar manner, reading educators applied their own research to students with learning problems. Uhl (1916) advised teachers "to use the results of the tests in reading as bases upon which to plan remedial work for defects in reading" (p. 266). Two years later, Gray (1918) assured skeptics that "the technique of improving instruction through the use of tests has been worked out more or less successfully" (p. 121).

One of the primary ways to ensure that tests would improve classroom learning was to make certain that the tasks on the exams were similar to those on instructional materials. Figure 2.2 and Figure 2.3 contain sections from a reading test (passages from the *Sangren-Woody Reading Test*, 1925, as reproduced in Sangren, 1932, pp. 99–102). They illustrate tasks for measuring comprehension. Compare the congruity between these test items and the workbook tasks depicted in Figure 2.4 (activity from Buswell, n.d., as reproduced in Sangren, 1932, p. 129), Figure 2.5 (activity from *Thought Test Readers*, 2nd ed., 1925, as reproduced in Sangren, 1932, p. 113) and Figure 2.6 (activity from *Tests and Practice Exercises*, Merton, 1925, as reproduced in Sangren, 1932, p. 131).

Just as medical personnel had been drawn to diagnostic tests, so were reading educators. Within a study about the difficulties of learning to read, Freeman (1920a) lectured that "when the question of failure in learning...arises in the case of an individual, it is necessary not only to know that a condition may arise...but it is necessary to know what condition or conditions actually produce the failure" (p. 141). To demonstrate one of the ways that this type of information might be gathered, Freeman analyzed photographic records of readers' eye movements. Five years later, Zirbes (1925) judged that diagnostic reading procedures were plentiful, varied, and effective. Making this same point, Tinker (1932, 1933) offered "a rather complete bibliography on the subject of diagnostic and remedial reading." His bibliography contained 180 citations. Characterizing the 1930s as the "golden era" of diagnostic and remedial reading instruction, Giordano (2000) documented the multiple educational initiatives that were explicitly modeled after medical practices.

Figure 2.2 Following Directions (*"Sangren-Woody Reading Test."* *Copyright 1926 by The Psychological Corporation, a Harcourt Assessment Company. Reproduced by permission. All rights reserved.*)

DIRECTIONS: Do what each paragraph tells you to do.

1. Mary was sent to the store by her mother to buy a dozen oranges. On her way home she became hungry and ate two of the oranges. Then she had only ten. On the line at the right write the number that tells how many oranges Mary ate on her way home from the store.

2. When Helen came home from school the other day, she hurried into the house and began hunting for something to eat. There were three apples lying in a row on the table. Helen took the apple in the middle because it was the largest. The apples are shown at the right. Mark with a cross the apple that Helen took.

3. The clock struck nine times, and it was time for the boys to go to bed. One of the boys tried to draw a short line for each time the clock struck. The lines are shown at the right, but there are only seven. Draw enough more lines to the right of those drawn to show how many the boy should have drawn.

4. Jack and Harry were playing ball late one after-noon. Finally, when Jack threw the ball, it slipped from his hand in some way and crashed through the window of the schoolhouse. The window is shown at the right. Draw a small circle in the upper right-hand corner of the window to show where the ball went through.

5. This noon Helen's mother told her to be very careful not to spill anything on the clean tablecloth. Helen tried to be very careful, but she soon forgot and laid her spoon, all covered with strawberry juice, down on the cloth. When she picked up the spoon, a bad spot was left. Place a black dot on one corner of the tablecloth at the right to show where the spot is.

6. At the right you see a circle and a cross. The circle stands for a pig pen, and the cross stands for a pig. We want to have another pig in the pen; so make another cross to show a pig in the pen. We want to have a pen around the pig that is out of the pen; so draw another circle to make a pen around that pig. You will then have two pigs in their pens.

7. James had three nickels that he earned carrying in wood and water for his mother. When he went down to the store, he bought candy with one nickel and a package of gum with another nickel. He then had one nickel left. At the right are the three nickels. Draw a line around the ones he spent, to show that he has but one left.

8. Tonight, after school, Harold is going after nuts. In the figure at the right H is where Harold lives, and N is where the trees are from which he will gather nuts. Harold does not want to go all the way around the road, but wants to go across the field because it is nearer. Draw a line to show how Harold will go across the field after the nuts.

Figure 2.3 Applying Information (*"Sangren-Woody Reading Test."*
Copyright 1926 by The Psychological Corporation, a Harcourt Assessment Company.
Reproduced by permission. All rights reserved.)

Mary is Dick's sister. She has two dolls. One is named Jean and the other is named Joan. Mary is pulling Jean in Dick's little wagon. Dick is sitting on Mary's chair. He is looking at Jean. Mary's dress is red and Dick's suit is blue The wagon and chair are red.

———————

1. Make the wagon and chair the color they are in the story.
2. Color green what Dick is looking at.
3. Make Mary's dress and Dick's suit the colors they are in the story.
4. Write your name above Jean.

Figure 2.4 Testing Comprehension

GRANDMA'S VISIT

Grandma came to see Betty and John.
She brought them pretty toys.
Betty said, "I know the book and doll are mine."
John said, "You may have them but the top and ball are mine."

GRANDMA'S VISIT

Here are some pretty toys.
They belong to Betty and John.

1. Write "Betty" under what Grandma brought Betty.

2. Write "John" under what Grandma brought John.

Figure 2.5 Workbook Resembling a Reading Test

PICTURE ONE

Place the house at the right of the picture.
Place the tree at the left.
Hang the swing from the tree.
Put the little girl in the swing.
Place the bird house between the house and tree.
The bird is flying to the bird house.
The dog is watching the little girl.

Figure 2.6 Workbook Requiring Manipulation

History Tests

Although many social studies teachers may have found it hard to accept objective tests, they had an even harder time defending subjective grading. Researchers such as Starch and Elliott compounded those difficulties. Having already demonstrated the weaknesses of subjectively evaluated English and mathematics exams, Starch and Elliott (1913a) revealed the unreliability of subjectively graded history exams. A year later, Gathany (1914) joined in the attack on subjectively graded history exams. Like so many other critics, he heartily endorsed objective tests as alternatives to teacher-graded exams. However, he stood out from other critics when he recommended that objective tests be shared with students before they were administered to them. He thought this change in procedure would increase the validity of the assessment, motivate students, and encourage the students to view the exams as meaningful learning experiences. Gathany then identified the "greatest advantage" for the novel assessment procedure that he was recommending.

> It gives the teacher an excellent opportunity to help develop in his pupils the sense of historical proportion. Many distorted judgments, much real harm, and considerable injustice have been results of a lack of this sense. Of course a great deal here depends upon the skill of the teacher in framing questions. Well-phrased questions compel careful thinking and furnish one of the best ways in the world for developing in the pupil sane, safe, skillful, and analytical judgment of men, institutions and movements. (p. 521)

Despite opposition from progressive educators and tradition-bound schoolmasters, objective history tests became more popular. As World War I was ending, Monroe (1918a) was aware of six standardized history tests. Not limiting his inventory to standardized tests, Earl Rugg (1919) counted 11 tests "that aim to measure some phase of history." Rugg concluded that the pressure to create these objective history tests had come from "the quantitative movement in such school subjects as spelling, arithmetic, algebra, and handwriting." However, he warned that the history tests had not been "well standardized." Rugg still believed that objective history exams, even with their limitations, were valuable because they "test the aims and outcomes of this subject, and because they will aid in improving classroom instruction" (p. 771).

Buckingham (1917) described statistical procedures to help teachers standardize the items on the history tests that they created. To illustrate these procedures, he applied them to "information" and "thought" questions. His information questions required simple recapitulation of the facts that students could extract from lectures or printed materials. In contrast, thought questions required the students to make judgments, reorganize facts, or place themselves in the context of historical situations. Below are three of his thought questions:

> "For many years after the coming of Columbus, explorers wandered about in the forests of the New World and paddled their canoes up and down its great rivers without thinking very seriously of colonization." What were they thinking about and trying to do?

> Under what topic would you place the following events: Missouri Compromise, Dred Scott Decision, "Uncle Tom's Cabin," and the Thirteenth Amendment to the Constitution?

> In 1790 ninety per cent. of the people of the United States lived on farms. At the present time only thirty per cent. of the people live in the country. How can you account for the change suggested by these facts? (p. 447)

Van Wagenen (1919) agreed with Buckingham that objective history tests should not be restricted to factual information. Like Buckingham, he devised a test that measured knowledge of facts as well as the ability to draw inferences from historical data. However, Van Wagenen was especially proud that his own test assessed a student's "ability to judge character and motives from facts about persons, especially about their public life" (p. 1). To make this measurement, he had placed passages about historical events next to sentences about motives. He instructed students to "put a check mark in front of those three of the ten motives which you think most likely prompted the people to do what they did in each story" (p. 20). For example, a passage about an Indian massacre of white persons was followed by ten statements about the possible motives of the attackers. Within this list were the three statements that Van Wagenen identified as the correct responses.

> They may have wanted to take revenge on the white men for having injured some of their kin.
>
> They may have been in a rage over some act which they thought the white people had done to injure them.
>
> They may have been at war with the white people and this action may have seemed perfectly right to them. (p. 64)

Following the lead that many of his professional colleagues had taken, Harlan (1920) developed still another objective history test. Like those colleagues, he paired it with advice so that teachers could model their own tests after his instrument. He advised the teachers to create exams that would "cover a wide range of facts," "demand the use of a variety of mental functions," "be independent of attainment in other subjects," "require unequivocal answers," and "be easily given and scored" (p. 852).

Harlan could not conceal the positive and self-serving opinion he had formed about his own test. Not all of his contemporaries shared that opinion. Griffith (1920) pointed to one of the key features of reputable testing that Harlan had ignored.

> In history there are many items of information, some important, others unimportant. Since authorities agree on the importance of some facts and disagree on others, the selection of questions for texts is very difficult. Moreover, the questions must be carefully evaluated in order that the amount of credit to be given for each question may be scientifically determined. (p. 700)

Griffith thought that Harlan's test also failed to assess "the most important objective of history," which was the use of information from the past to solve current problems.

Three years later, Kepner (1923), who was looking back on the testing movement, detected 22 tests that had been designed exclusively for secondary history students. Of these, "2 are for use in the field of ancient history, 15 for American history, and 5 for the testing of general ability in history" (p. 309). He added that 16 different "agencies" had developed these tests. Furthermore, 13 of the tests were available on "prepared forms." A year later, Brinkley (1924) looked through educational journals and concluded that "many high school [*sic*] teachers are using the new type of examinations in an unstandardized form to supplement or supplant the ordinary examination" (p. 1). As to the value of the changes that were transpiring, Brinkley reported that "the experimental evidence based on the results got when the tests are administered to students indicates with only one exception that the new type examination is a better measure of pupil achievement than the old type examination" (p. 9).

Other Specialized Academic Tests

Horn (1919) judged that "there is perhaps no subject in the course of study to which general experimentation in psychology and special experimentation in the subject itself have contributed more than in the case of spelling" (p. 52). Since this subject was being studied so exhaustively, contemporary educators should have anticipated that researchers would create spelling tests. A year before Horn had made his observation about the extensive interest in spelling, Monroe (1918a) had identified 11 standardized spelling tests. Other academic subjects in which 10 or more standardized tests were available included mathematics, handwriting, language development, reading, and foreign language.

Although educators probably expected that standardized tests would be developed for the core subjects in the curriculum, they may not have anticipated them for art appreciation. Karwoski and Christensen (1926) began a report with the unqualified exclamation that "there is need for objective tests in art" (p. 187). To adapt art appreciation to the constraints of objective testing, these researchers forced "the subject to give an opinion of why one art example is preferred rather than another." Tiegs (1931a) reported about other art tests such as the *Thorndike Drawing Scale*, the *Kline-Carey Drawing Scale*, the *Lowering Tests of Fundamental Abilities of Visual Art*, the *Williams Scale for Judging Kindergarten Drawing*, and the *Detroit Freehand Lettering Scale*.

Carlson (1925) was interested in bookkeeping exams. He began a report with the statement that "in recent years educational measurements, scientific testing, standardized tests, and test programs have been receiving especial emphasis in all educational circles." He thought that the ambitious testing programs that had been developed in most academic disciplines augured the future of assessment for bookkeeping courses. To help instructors devise objective exams of their own, he provided advice about optimal formats for business-education questions. For example, he endorsed questions that could be "answered by yes or no, the true-false, the completion type, multiple-choice, matching, arranging in series, and one word answers" (p. 12). Carlson added that these types of questions would produce business-education exams that were objective, reliable, valid, easy to administer, simple to score, and an adequate basis from which to make comparisons between students.

Not content with the application of objective tests to required subjects and elective courses, educators developed them for areas outside of the curriculum. For example, Briggs (1923) developed a dictionary test. Laycock (1925) suggested one for biblical information. Chassell and Chassell (1924) produced an objective test for citizenship. Because government was a standard course within high-school curricula, other teachers already had developed objective tests for factual recall and analytical reasoning within political science. Wishing to set a higher standard, Chassell and Chassell designed their test to measure the "ability to weigh foreseen consequences."

Several years later, two researchers (Hartshorne & May, 1928, May & Hartshorne, 1928) at Columbia University's Teachers College developed a battery of exams to measure "the nature of character." Their work was funded by the Religious Education Association, the members of which were concerned because "hundreds of millions of dollars are probably spent annually by churches, Sunday schools, and other organizations for children and youth with almost no check on the product" (Hartshorne & May, 1928, p. 5). The executive secretary of this association acknowledged that the organization's directors had been worrying about this issue for years. Nonetheless, they had not acted more quickly because of the difficulty of designing "a careful and scientific investigation of the question." Recognizing that wholesome character was an amorphous trait that was difficult to observe, document, and analyze, Hartshorne and May proposed to assess it indirectly. They suggested that they could record the deceitful behavior that correlated with poor character and then use the results to draw inferences about wholesome character. As an example of the way in which they proceeded, the researchers allowed students to mark and score their own responses to tests. However, they subsequently determined whether the students had inflated the grades they had assigned to themselves. The actual character test consisted of the students' behaviors while they were resisting or succumbing to the opportunities for cheating.

Tiegs (1931a) reviewed several measures of character, including *Olson's Problem Tendencies in Children*, the *Cornell-Coxe-Orleans Rating Scale for School Habits*, and the *Raubenheimer Test of Potential Delinquency*. The *Raubenheimer Test of Potential Delinquency* contained seven sections, two of which were "overstatement on books read" and "overstatement on knowledge claimed." Tiegs explained the types of tasks within these sections.

In the knowledge overstatement test appear such questions as the following:

1. Do you know who discovered America?
2. Do you know who wrote Huckleberry Finn?

The pupil scores his own test and adds up his score. A second part of the test which he takes immediately afterward contains items of this type:

1. America was discovered by Drake, Columbus, Balboa, Cook.
2. Huckleberry Finn was written by Alger, Dickens, Henty, Mark Twain.

To these the students must respond. (Tiegs, 1931a, p. 429)

Specialized University Exams

During the first part of the twentieth century, public-school educators used science-based approaches to investigate and resolve scholastic problems. Their confidence in this educational movement was reflected in the many specialized academic tests that they adopted. Standardized testing, which was a critical element within science-based approaches, enabled the educators to address curricular problems that previously had seemed insurmountable. Standardized testing also enabled them to prepare their students for colleges with restrictive admission policies. Well before the twentieth century, White (1888) had expressed the frustration that high-school teachers were experiencing as they prepared their students for elite colleges. He wrote that "the work of preparing students for the three or four leading colleges of America…has become so complicated that it can be thoroughly done only by the expert teacher who keeps himself thoroughly informed as to the methods used in the various colleges and the peculiarities of the individual examination papers presented" (p. iii).

Test performance provided an obvious basis upon which to make decisions about university admissions. However, a widely implemented, and preferably universal, system of testing was needed. Otherwise, comparable assessments could not be made by the staffs at the different educational institutions. McConn (1931) recounted that the American Council on Education had organized the Co-operative Test Service to commence precisely this type of assessment program. He indicated that its efforts were the response to "general interest in personnel methods, which for a number of years has been growing apace in college and schools" (p. 225).

University administrators and professors agreed with high-school educators that standardized testing benefitted college aspirants and the colleges to which they applied. However, some of them pointed to additional benefits. Miller (1927a, 1927b) described a meeting of the faculty senators at the University of Michigan in which they had decided to implement special programs that would "further benefit our superior students." The faculty had commenced experiments to demonstrate that "superior pupils in at least technical subjects and probably in all subjects can derive an additional profit…when segregated" (p. 120). As far as the inferior students were concerned, Miller judged that "no apparent harm" had resulted from the placements with their "mental equals." Many professors, university administrators, parents, and college students shared the philosophy that had inspired Miller and his colleagues. It seemed reasonable to them that academic competence should determine which students were admitted to certain classes and programs within the universities.

Some persons went further and suggested that students' academic competence should limit the type of careers that they could pursue. In his review of pre-World War II professional testing programs, Kandel (1940) endorsed the exams that were being used to screen candidates for medicine, law, and engineering. Even though he gave his professional approval to this practice, Kandel urged persons to use the test scores cautiously and balance them against other types of information. After the war, Eysenck (1947) judged that "the national need for trained personnel in practically all the professions is such that laissez-faire methods of selection will have to give way to a more scientific approach which can, up to a point, be provided by the use of psychological tests" (p. 32).

Criticism of Educational Testing

Even though educational tests became more popular, their opponents remained implacable. They doggedly censured tests for a broad range of inadequacies, many of which concerned practical issues. Alexander (1921) paraphrased these allegations and gave multiple examples of practical problems. For example, some of the technical aspects of tests had been presented in ways that were not accessible to teachers and the public. Alexander added that the "measurement work is too costly for the results secured," that "too little constructive help is given after tests," and that "some measurement workers do not seem to use enough commons [*sic*] sense" (pp. 348–354). With regard to this last accusation, he explained that "commons sense [*sic*] is indicated by frankly recognizing that there are still many phases of school work where measurements cannot be profitably used" and that "in some cases they probably never can be" (pp. 350–351). He continued that "some school children are being assigned to grades or promoted largely on the basis of one brief intelligence test—'in twenty minutes branded for life.'" A year later, Pressey and Pressey (1922) reported about teachers who shared these sentiments.

Many teachers and administrators are still skeptical of the value of the new 'tests' advocated by educationalists and psychologists. These practical schoolmen are skeptical not only of the practical value of the results obtained by use of these tests, but of the essential soundness of the present test movement. There is a feeling that testing is a time-consuming, artificial, and one-sided way of obtaining information which the teacher may acquire much better by her own observation of her pupils and their work. (p. 7)

Some of the criticism about the impracticality of testing was directed at the ways in which instructions were phrased, the formats into which the questions were arranged, and even the style in which examination forms were organized. Brinkley (1924) noted that persons had attacked multiple-choice and true-false exams because they enabled students to improve their scores through guessing. Other critics judged that objective tests encouraged memorization, over-emphasized factual information, and limited the types of knowledge that could be assessed. Figure 2.7, which is the initial page from a 1915 reading exam, demonstrates efforts by this test's developers to minimize some of the predictable difficulties that students would encounter. Notice how the test developers related the novel activities on the exam to tasks with which the students were familiar and toward which they were positively disposed.

Stenquist (1933) wrote about the excessive strain that was placed upon teachers who were required to administer, score, summarize, and then interpret objective tests.

Another critical issue is the need for mechanization of test procedures to the time and labor cost. To make full use of even the tests already available requires more time and energy than is generally available under present-day school conditions. Since a large part of the work, particularly that of scoring and gross tabulating is essentially mechanical in nature, there is great need for mechanical means for carrying out this work so as to relieve teachers and test technicians for more interpretive work. (p. 60)

Some critics resisted objective tests because of the unnatural restrictions of statistical models and experimental procedures. Woody and Sangren (1933) acknowledged that "uninformed" teachers had initially opposed educational testing because they saw it as "an educational innovation perfected by specialists utilizing materials and methods foreign to their experience and understanding" (p. 1). Two years earlier, Tiegs (1931a) had observed that some evaluators assumed that "the logical approach to the problem is through a study of statistics; that as pure arithmetic precedes problem solving, so pure statistics should precede its application in educational measurement." Tiegs noted that "this approach has served as an obstacle to the development of measurement in education because of the teacher's fear of mathematics" (xi).

Weld (1917) had studied educational assessment during that early period about which Woody, Sangren, and Tiegs had made observations. He had detected "a great deal" of criticism that seemed to corroborate his colleagues' observations. Weld had noted that this criticism was being directed at those World War I teachers who aspired to be scientific but who actually were "constrained to

---

Test II.

State Normal School,
EMPORIA, KAN.
Bureau of Educational Measurements
and Standards.

Put
Pupil's
Score
Here.

THE KANSAS SILENT READING TEST.

Devised by F. J. Kelly

FOR

Grades 6, 7 and 8.

City.................................... State................ .... Date.... ... ...

Pupil's Name.. .. Age............ Grade............ .

School .... Teacher............ ....

Directions for Giving the Tests.

After telling the children not to open the papers ask those on the front seats to distribute the papers, placing one upon the desk of each pupil in the class. Have each child fill in the blank spaces at the top of this page. Then make clear the following:

Instructions to be Read by Teacher and Pupils Together.

This little five-minute game is given to see how quickly and accurately pupils can read silently. To show what sort of game it is, let us read this:

> Below are given the names of four animals. Draw a line around the name of each animal that is useful on the farm:
>
> cow   tiger   rat   wolf

This exercise tells us to draw a line around the word cow. No other answer is right. Even if a line is drawn *under* the word cow, the exercise is wrong, and counts nothing. The game consists of a lot of just such exercises, so it is wise to study each exercise carefully enough to be sure that you know exactly what you are asked to do. The number of exercises which you can finish thus in five minutes will make your score, so do them as fast as you can, being sure to do them right. Stop at once when time is called. Do not open the papers until told, so that all may begin at the same time.

The teacher should then be sure that each pupil has a good pencil or pen. Note the minute and second by the watch, and say, BEGIN.

Allow exactly five minutes.

Answer no questions of the pupils which arise from not understanding what to do with any given exercise.

When time is up say STOP and then collect the papers at once.

Figure 2.7 Reading Test from 1915 (F. J. Kelly, *"Kansas Silent Reading Test."*
Kansas State Normal School, Bureau of Educational Measurements and Standards,
copyright 1915. Reprinted by permission of the publisher. All rights reserved.)

exercise arbitrary rules of judgment in order to make the results of their grading fulfill certain theoretical conditions" (p. 412). Sympathetic to this criticism, Kohs (1920) wrote that "at this time when mass tests are rapidly multiplying, and when their range of application is becoming more and more widely extended, it is necessary that we frequently reexamine [*sic*] the mathematical and statistical trellis work upon which such tests necessarily depend for sanction of reliability" (p. 1). Even though he was calling for the reappraisal of the theoretical and statistical substructure for testing, Kohs confided somewhat pessimistically that only time could compensate for the "fallacies of method and logic" that were inevitably associated with "mushrooming development in any branch of science."

Almost two decades after Kohs had made his rueful remarks, Courtis (1938a) adopted a more philosophical attitude toward the ongoing criticism of standardized educational assessment. He advised those who were "much distressed" by the negative allegations to realize that "some criticism is an aid to healthy growth" (p. 546). He took exception to the "extremists who characterize the prevailing uncritical but practical use of measurement by schools as the grossest pseudo-science." In fact, he judged that tests, even if they turned out to be "totally invalid," still had value; for "it cannot be denied that many a teacher has been stimulated by their use to new effort, new enjoyment of his work, and new interests in his children." Courtis concluded that "to some extent we are all pragmatists; if we believe we can get benefit from an activity, we are likely to continue the activity."

Other groups had distinct reasons for challenging objective tests. For example, some of them were concerned about the fundamental validity of the tests. Looking back at the early years of the testing movement, Mort and Gates (1932) detected "a strong tendency on the part of teachers to criticize the tests as covering work not taught, or as measuring factual material only, or as omitting much that was thought essential and stressed by the teachers" (p. 109). Remarks that were made during these early years validated the observation by Mort and Gates. For example, Breed (1918) had warned that the "basic assumptions" underlying many tests had not been adequately investigated let alone confirmed. Sharing Breed's skepticism, Starch (1918) wrote that "with the development of methods for measuring achievement in school subjects, it is becoming an increasingly important problem to determine the accuracy and reliability with which the various tests and scales actually measure the particular capacities which they are designed to measure" (p. 86). Anticipating that the criticism of tests would persist and grow stronger, Myers (1922) demanded that testing advocates demonstrate the predictive validity of their instruments. He wrote poetically that the "test which proves a good prophet of school progress is counted good; that one which proves a poor prophet, poor" (p. 300).

Broom (1931) recognized that some opponents of the assessment movement earnestly believed that testing was "just another educational fad, one that has almost run its course" (p. 175). Although he was convinced that this conviction was misplaced, he recapitulated several of the philosophical problems to which these critics had alluded. The most "potent" accusation was that tests would "mechanize education and educators, leading to the production of a product as alike as the buttons which are turned out by a machine" (p. 176). Two other conceptual challenges were that "testing places the emphasis of teaching on wrong aspects of the teacher's job" and that "the child's mind is too complicated to be measured adequately by tests" (pp. 177–178). Aware of the "antagonism to measurement…[that was] evident on many sides," Broom tried to bolster support for standardized testing by a demonstration that it was more practical, economical, and accurate than any of the alternatives to it.

Responding to Criticism

Hawkes (1933) made a succinct, ingenuous, and undeniably pragmatic defense of educational tests. He wrote that all the problems with educational tests "would have been settled ages ago" if it had not been for "the imperfect [instructional] techniques that we have" (p. 136). In other words, how could one censure educational tests for their imperfections when the instructional processes that they were designed to complement were so imprecise?

Hardly an advocate of standardized testing, Myers (1926) did not intend to defend it. In fact, he sternly lectured teachers to "put more emphasis upon teaching and less on testing." In spite of his personal attitudes toward this issue, Myers provided a rejoinder to those traditional teachers who wished to eliminate testing and go back to recitation as the principal activity in their classrooms.

> Most of the so-called recitations consist in giving the child oral or written examinations. So-called drills are practically all examinations upon what had been imperfectly learned or not learned at all. Even schoolroom games in the elementary grades are for the most part kinds of examinations. (p. 47)

Myers had highlighted the similarities between objective tests and the recitation techniques that they had replaced. A return to those recitation techniques would not be advantageous if recitation and informal grading turned out to be variations on the standardized testing that many traditional teachers so detested.

Lathrop (1927) provided another pragmatic defense of objective testing. He explained that the adoption of new forms of testing was inevitable because "a considerable proportion of the teaching profession" had been aroused against the "great evils" associated with subjectively graded exams. He certainly did not console traditional teachers when he assured them that the advocates of the new testing methods were committed to finding "a remedy for past evils and defects."

He enthusiastically quoted one educator who viewed standardized testing as a dispassionate procedure in which a student would be fairly "measured when he has been correctly spaced along a scale of merit in such a way that his relative achievement with respect to other members of the group has been reliably portrayed" (G. M. Ruch, 1924, as quoted by Lathrop, 1927, p. 362). Lathrop counseled his opponents to accept objective testing, which, even with imperfections, was vastly superior to the error-filled system it was replacing.

Lathrop had cited passages from a book entitled *The Improvement of the Written Examination*. Within that textbook, Ruch (1924) had made arguments in support of objective tests. He depicted them as alternatives to the oral "examination methods [that] have persisted throughout the centuries with modifications that are almost microscopic" (p. 1). He judged that modern objective tests made numerous other invaluable contributions to the success of the schools. In the preface to Ruch's book, Horn (1924) listed reasons why the use of objective educational testing, which was already sizeable, should be expanded.

1. To show the pupil the efficiency with which he has worked.
2. To show the teacher the efficiency with which she has taught.
3. To measure the value of a given textbook.
4. To measure the value of a given method of teaching.
5. To compare the efficiency of teaching in one school with that in another school.
6. To guarantee a thorough and rigorous attack, not only in study but also in teaching.
7. To get a general but useful index of the status of teaching in any given school system. (p. iii)

Ruch and Rice (1930) collated some of the "objective or new-type examinations" that had been developed during 1927 and 1928. They indicated that "the examinations presented in this volume represent a collection adjudged the best of more than four hundred entries in a contest of a national character" (p. iii). They organized the prizewinning tests into topical categories such as English, social studies, natural sciences, mathematics, foreign languages, and home arts. They also included tests for the commercial subjects, under which they placed bookkeeping and shorthand, and for the manual arts, under which they listed mechanical drawing, cabinetmaking, and machine shop. Ruch and Rice explained that they had arranged this competition in order to display "the present state of the objective testing movement," to create a textbook for university courses in assessment, and to compile "examinations worthy of study and imitation by teachers initiating or perfecting their study of objective testing" (p. iii).

In an earlier book, Ruch and another colleague (Ruch & Stoddard, 1927) identified scores of published tests that were appropriate for high-school use. Moreover, they conceded that "a great many [additional] tests have not been mentioned chiefly because of the lack of adequate data for their evaluation" (p. iii). One of the reasons they adjured teachers to use these tests was that many had diagnostic value. To underscore this point, they identified 17 diagnostic tests for students who were taking high-school courses in English, foreign languages, physics, grammar, American history, mathematics, and music.

Although Ruch and Stoddard extolled the diagnostic application of tests in their 1927 book, Ruch had not even commented on this attribute in a previous book (Ruch, 1924). One of the reasons that some educators initially hesitated to endorse diagnostic testing was the controversy about the genetic determinants of intelligence. This tension had been evident during the 1920s when Lewis Terman was editing a series of books on tests and measurement for the World Book Company. Each volume contained a paragraph-long statement about the common philosophy that united all of the books in the set. Within that paragraph, which almost certainly was written by Terman himself, was a statement that "scientific method in education...involves adjustment of organization, subject matter, and methods of instruction to the varying needs and abilities of pupils" (passage from the paragraph on the copyright page, Dickson, 1924). Although these remarks might seem to support the diagnostic use of tests, Terman's precise intentions were occluded by his strong convictions about the degree to which inherited intelligence limited educational attainment.

Approvingly citing Terman's research about the constancy of IQ scores, Loree (1925) made guarded observations about the diagnostic value of educational testing.

> There is a feeling among many educators and patrons that [the administration of an IQ test] creates a feeling of despondency for a dull pupil to be definitely referred to as having limited capacity to learn. The fact is that the pupil already knows this, and his parents have known it for a long time. By use of intelligence tests and other tests we try to help him *in his limited capacity.* (p. 54)

Not all educators shared these stern views about the unalterable limits on learning. Those who disagreed thought that tests were necessary so that teachers could decipher the causes of their students' learning problems. For example, Woody (1917) had expostulated that "unless measurements aid in the diagnosis of school conditions they are useless" (p. 63). He wrote metaphorically that "if you go to a physician and he takes your temperature, counts your pulse, looks at your tongue and asks a few questions concerning your diet, and then does no more, you are no better off than if you had not gone to the physician." Despite the personal tone of the metaphor, Woody was referring to broad diagnostic procedures that would produce system-wide educational analyses.

During the 1920s, some educators did refer clearly to the benefits of individual diagnosis. In the introduction to a book about educational measurement, Strayer (1924) noted that educational testing not only had enabled teachers "to determine more accurately the achievements of pupils, but also to diagnose their particular difficulties" (p. 3). A Connecticut superintendent (Mills, 1925) advised teachers that intelligence testing, which "leads us from the study of the group to the study of the individual," could be used to for "diagnosis of cause of failure" (p. 141). Although he did not identify the date on which it had first appeared, Malin (1930b) referred to diagnostic testing as a critical milestone in the "second phase" of the measurement movement. He explained that, during this latter phase, "data collected from the diagnostic tests were put to use" and "the teachers now began to apply remedial measures in the teaching process as a result of these tests" (p. 155).

Within an essay about his 50-year professional career, Buros (1977) chronicled his involvement with the educational testing movement. He did not conceal the fact that he had made many critical remarks about testing. In fact, he still believed that standardized tests were "poorly constructed, of questionable or unknown validity, pretentious in their claims, and likely to be misused more often than not" (p. 9). Despite this adversarial stance, Buros fondly reminisced that "in many ways, the year 1927 was a banner year in testing." He wrote that he could not "recall a year which produced so many scholarly books in testing." Buros concluded that the books and tests available that year were of such luster that one "might be surprised that so little progress has been made in the past fifty years—in fact, in some areas we are not doing as well." To underscore this last point, he emphasized that the early consumers of tests had "more tests to choose from than they have today" (Buros, 1977, p. 9).

Buros provided another reason that 1927 was so remarkable. During this year, two groups of educational extremists had substantively changed their attitudes toward assessment. One of these groups comprised the testing advocates, who began to recognize that some of their initial expectations had been set "unreasonably high." The other group, which included the anti-testing factions, learned to appreciate some of the positive values of tests. Making an observation just after that transitional era to which Buros had referred, Mort and Gates (1932) conceded that "in the first years of educational testing, a great many abuses developed which retarded the progress of the movement." However, these researchers judged that modern educators eventually were "able more and more to view the objective test with the perspective necessary to a realization of its shortcomings." As a result, objective tests had come to be "generally looked upon as useful devices the limitations of which are so well known that they need not be feared" (p. iii).

Summary

To evaluate learning, nineteenth-century schoolmasters required that their students orally recapitulate information from classroom lessons. Even when evaluating written work, the individual teachers defined the content for which students were responsible and the criteria for passing. Dissatisfied with this subjective approach, scientifically disposed educators searched for valid, reliable, and objective forms of assessment. They developed discipline-specific tasks, geared them to common curricula, incorporated them within standardized tests, and agreed upon thresholds of mastery. Although contemporaries might have anticipated objective tests in core subjects such as reading, writing, and mathematics, they were surprised to see them emerge in specialized courses, elective subjects, and even noncurricular activities. Because the different scholastic disciplines entailed diverse types of learning, educators had to c reate specific tasks for assessing each type of academic achievement. Despite the strain that this placed on them, they prized the results, which had direct instructional implications.

CHAPTER 3

Military Backing for Tests

On every kind of test that was employed, even the most non-verbal, the average score earned by [World War I] draftees was less than that earned by average fourteen-year-old school children.
—*TERMAN, 1922a*

Prior to World War I, mental testing had not attracted much attention. The attitudes of the public changed after the Army tested soldiers to see if they qualified for active duty or specialized types of training. The Army's testing generated interest because of its large scale, novelty, and practicality. However, the greatest publicity was created by the low scores that many of the servicemen earned. Political conservatives depicted these scores as indicators of serious problems in the schools. Some of them went further and characterized the low scores as symptoms of profound problems that threatened the nation's future security. In contrast, anti-assessment critics simply dismissed the scores as inappropriate, inefficient, and invalid.

Tests Reveal a National Crisis

Hersey (1959) wrote about the distress that he and other liberals felt after World War II. They were upset because a good many citizens were viewing "human beings as statistics," "children as weapons," and their "talents as materials capable of being mined, assayed, and fabricated for profit and defense." Hersey chastised a public that seemed to "think that we can order up units of talent for the national defense." He rejoined that "the only sure defense of democracy will be…something far less grandiose…than a National Defense Education Act" (p. 28).

Hersey discerned that the 1950s public had linked education with national defense. Giordano (2004) documented that this perception, although it was common during the 1950s, had emerged during World War I. The conservatives of that earlier era had supported an approach to education that emphasized discipline, basic academic skills, physical fitness, patriotism, science, mathematics, and vocational training. They saw these as the qualities that prepared students for military service and industrial employment. Robert Yerkes, who was one of the persons most responsible for the Army's testing program, expressed these sentiments when he wrote that "relatively early in this supreme struggle, it became clear to certain individuals that the proper utilization of man power, and more particularly of mind or brain power, would assure ultimate victory" (Yerkes, 1920, p. vii).

Both contemporary and later scholars agreed about the immense impact of the Army's testing program. Immediately after the war, Doll (1919) also had noted the effects of the publicity that military testing had generated. He observed that the military tests "seemed to indicate that 16 years was the upper life age limit in the growth of intelligence of average individuals" (p. 524). As if these statistics were not sufficiently disconcerting, he added that "new data seem to indicate that this age should be reduced to 13 years." Summarizing the results of military testing in an equally disquieting manner, Myers and Myers (1919) wrote that "approximately 25 per cent. [*sic*] of the recruits of the American Army could not read an English newspaper, write an English letter, or had not reached the fifth grade of school" (p. 355). Myers and Myers censured the Surgeon General for failing to broadcast these data. In the second edition of a book that he had published originally in 1929, Boring (1950) remarked that "the Armistice of 1918 came too soon to get much use out of the results [of the Army testing program], but the advertising that this testing gave psychology in America reached into the remotest corner of the laboratory and swelled college classes" (p. 575). Gould (1981) later made a comparable observation. He acknowledged that the tests administered to World War I soldiers had convinced the public that education was a vital component of national security. However, he concluded that "the primary impact of the tests arose not from the army's lackadaisical use of scores for individuals, but from general propaganda that accompanied Yerkes's report" (p. 195).

In the popular *Atlantic Monthly*, Link (1923) had written that the most controversial conclusion drawn from the military testing program concerned the relatively few persons who had scored in the *superior* or *very superior* ranges. Link himself had anticipated these results. He wrote in a matter of fact style that "it is surprising that these claims should even be questioned; for, regardless of the validity of intelligence tests, it must be obvious to any person that a certain proportion of the people in any group are superior in intelligence to the rest" (p. 374). He proceeded to give examples of normally distributed data that would be expected of "any test whatsoever, whether of height, weight, spelling, or speed in copying a letter."

Even though Link disagreed with the factions that opposed military testing, he did not dispute the fact that their "widely advertised" challenges had stirred up a gigantic controversy. Long (1923) also attested that "the report of the army examining presented numerous data which have provoked many discussions" (p. 22). Long added that "so popular are mental tests today that even the man in the street knows of them and has his prejudices." Robert Yerkes (1923b), one of the designers of the military's testing program, wrote calmly that he was "not at all concerned, much less alarmed," by the results of the assessment program. In fact, the results struck him as quite reasonable, especially when one considered the high number of examinees who spoke only limited English. Despite these understated remarks, Yerkes was quite aware of the severe disagreements about testing. He demonstrated this awareness when he selected a "popular magazine" passage that was "typical of much that has been written about 'army mental tests.'"

> The army mental tests have shown that there are, roughly, forty-five million people in this country who have no sense. Their mental powers will never be greater than those of twelve-year-old children. The vast majority of these will never attain even this meager

intelligence. Besides the forty-five millions [*sic*] who have no sense, but a majority of votes, there are twenty-five millions [*sic*] who have a little sense. Their capacity for mental and spiritual growth is only that of thirteen- or fourteen-year-old children, and your education can add nothing to their intelligence. Next, there are twenty-five millions [*sic*] with fair-to-middling sense. They haven't much, but what there is, is good. Then, lastly, there are a few over four millions [*sic*] who have a great deal of sense. They have the thing we call "brains." (Passage from an unidentified popular magazine, quoted by Yerkes, 1923b, p. 358)

History of Military Tests

Looking back on the First World War, Malin (1930a) recounted how psychologists had been commissioned to create tests. He thought that they had been given this responsibility by the War Department because "necessity is still the mother of invention." To clarify his selection of this adage, he explained that "group intelligence tests were sorely needed to classify the men [in the Army] according to mental abilities" (p. 75). A decade later, Paterson (1940) also connected the rise of mental assessment to the war. His own perception about the significance of that connection was revealed when he wrote that the "birth-labor of applied psychology began in April, 1917, and was completed on the day of the Armistice in 1918" (p. 1). Thompson (1943) was another analyst who agreed that World War I "gave great impetus to the entire field of educational measurement" (p. 565).

During the period to which these scholars referred, wartime psychologists had developed, administered, and applied the results of several famous tests. Long (1923) recounted that "in 1917, when the country was amassing an army under pressure, a group of eminent psychologists were invited to assist in an economical allocation of the army personnel so as to prevent mistakes and loss of time" (p. 22). Chapman (1921) gave several reasons why military leaders hoped to get help from psychologists, particularly those with industrial experiences.

While the ordinary commercial industry, under normal conditions, is able to make up for mistakes in the selection of its personnel by hiring more personnel, the army at the outbreak of the war, and more particularly later, was not in a position to apply this easy but highly wasteful remedy. Man power [*sic*] for the army was by no means inexhaustible, for industry was at the same time sorely pressed to maintain its production. It was incumbent upon the army to use the knowledge and skill of each member to the best advantage, for the industrial situation was such that the number of skilled men the army could call upon was strictly limited. It was under this urgent necessity that the army in 1917 turned to industry to see if any methods in use at that time for determining the skill of workmen would help it to meet its placement problems. (p. 5)

Yerkes (1918), who was the president of the American Psychological Association, described some of the early steps that the Army had taken to establish an assessment program. The Army initially had allocated $2,500 for Yerkes and 14 associates to measure the intelligence of 4000 soldiers. Half of this money was intended to cover the staff's traveling and living expenses. The remainder was used to print tests, purchase special assessment materials, and furnish examination rooms. Yerkes observed that the prototypical program was quickly expanded once the military's leaders realized that "the demand for psychologists and psychological service promises, or threatens, to be overwhelmingly great" (p. 113). To ensure that the supply of persons needed for this program was adequate, the Army established a special school for training its psychologists.

Yoakum and Yerkes (1920), both of whom were principal investigators in the military's measurement program, recollected that they originally were asked to devise a test to identify three groups of soldiers: "drafted men who were too low-grade mentally to make satisfactory privates in the Army," "exceptional types of men who could be used for special tasks that demanded a high degree of intelligence" and "those who were mentally unstable or who might prove incorrigible so far as army discipline was concerned" (p. xii). The two psychologists admitted that they had not been able to devise methods for detecting the last group, wh ich comprised the mentally unstable and incorrigible servicemen. However, they had been able to designate persons with extremely low or exceptionally high intelligence. They also had been able to achieve several special goals, such as the establishment of "development battalions of men who are so inferior intellectually as to be unsuited for regular military training," "[the creation of] organizations [in which all of the men had] uniform mental strength," "the selection of men for...military training schools, colleges, or technical schools," and "the formation of special training groups...in order that each man may receive instruction suited to his ability to learn" (pp. xii–xiii).

The Alpha Test

The Army's Committee on Classification of Personnel rated 3,000,000 soldiers, most of whom took either the Alpha test or the Beta test (Chauncey & Dobbin, 1963, Kevles, 1968). Lewis Terman (1918) contributed significantly to these two exams. He based them on a group-administered intelligence test that he and one of his doctoral students had crafted. As for the Alpha test, it was so "arranged that its 212 questions are answered by checking or underlining, thus permitting the answers to be scored by the use of stencils" (Terman, 1918, p. 180). Terman described the skills that these questions measured.

> *Alpha* [is] a group test for men who read and write English. The Alpha test measures a man's ability to comprehend, to remember and follow instructions, to discriminate between relevant and irrelevant answers to common sense questions, to combine related ideas into a logical whole, to discover by logical reasoning the plan present in a group of abstract terms, to keep the mind directed toward a goal without yielding to suggestions, and finally, to grasp and retain miscellaneous items of information. (p. 180)

Writing several years after the war, Yoakum and Yerkes (1920) indicated that the Alpha test could be administered to a group of 200 soldiers in less than an hour. Figure 3.1, Figure 3.2, and Figure 3.3, which are actual sections of the Alpha test, reveal the types of tasks to which the servicemen responded (Yerkes, 1921). The portion of the test contained in Figure 3.1 measured "practical judgment." That in Figure 3.2 comprised verbal analogies. The section in Figure 3.3 assessed soldiers' knowledge of general information.

TEST 3

This is a test of common sense. Below are sixteen questions. Three answers are given to each question. You are to look at the answers carefully; then make a cross in the square before the best answer to each question, as in the sample:

SAMPLE
- Why do we use stoves? Because
- ☐ they look well
- ☒ they keep us warm
- ☐ they are black

Here the second answer is the best one and is marked with a cross. Begin with No. 1 and keep on until time is called.

1 Cats are useful animals, because
- ☒ they catch mice
- ☐ they are gentle
- ☐ they are afraid of dogs

2 Why are pencils more commonly carried than fountain pens? Because
- ☐ they are brightly colored
- ☒ they are cheaper
- ☐ they are not so heavy

3 Why is leather used for shoes? Because
- ☐ it is produced in all countries
- ☒ it wears well
- ☐ it is an animal product

4 Why judge a man by what he does rather than by what he says? Because
- ☒ what a man does shows what he really is
- ☐ it is wrong to tell a lie
- ☐ a deaf man cannot hear what is said

5 If you were asked what you thought of a person whom you didn't know, what should you say?
- ☐ I will go and get acquainted
- ☐ I think he is all right
- ☒ I don't know him and can't say

6 Streets are sprinkled in summer
- ☐ to make the air cooler
- ☐ to keep automobiles from skidding
- ☒ to keep down dust

7 Why is wheat better for food than corn? Because
- ☒ it is more nutritious
- ☐ it is more expensive
- ☐ it can be ground finer

8 If a man made a million dollars, he ought to
- ☐ pay off the national debt
- ☒ contribute to various worthy charities
- ☐ give it all to some poor man

☞ Go to No. 9 above

9 Why do many persons prefer automobiles to street cars? Because
- ☐ an auto is made of higher grade materials
- ☒ an automobile is more convenient
- ☐ street cars are not as safe

10 The feathers on a bird's wings help him to fly because they
- ☒ make a wide, light surface
- ☐ keep the air off his body
- ☐ keep the wings from cooling off too fast

11 All traffic going one way keeps to the same side of the street because
- ☐ most people are right handed
- ☐ the traffic policeman insists on it
- ☒ it avoids confusion and collisions

12 Why do inventors patent their inventions? Because
- ☒ it gives them control of their inventions
- ☐ it creates a greater demand
- ☐ it is the custom to get patents

13 Freezing water bursts pipes because
- ☐ cold makes the pipes weaker
- ☒ water expands when it freezes
- ☐ the ice stops the flow of water

14 Why are high mountains covered with snow? Because
- ☐ they are near the clouds
- ☐ the sun seldom shines on them
- ☒ the air is cold there

15 If the earth were nearer the sun
- ☐ the stars would disappear
- ☐ our months would be longer
- ☒ the earth would be warmer

16 Why is it colder nearer the poles than near the equator? Because
- ☐ the poles are always farther from the sun
- ☒ the sunshine falls obliquely at the poles
- ☐ there is more ice at the poles

Figure 3.1   Military Test of Practical Judgment

TEST 7

SAMPLES
{
sky—blue :: grass— table green warm big
fish—swims :: man— paper time walks girl
day—night :: white— red black clear pure
}

In each of the lines below, the first two words are related to each other in some way. What you are to do in each line is to see what the relation is between the first two words, and underline the word in heavy type that is related in the same way to the third word. Begin with No. 1 and mark as many sets as you can before time is called.

1　gun—shoots :: knife— run cuts hat bird.................. 1
2　ear—hear :: eye— table hand see play..................... 2
3　dress—woman :: feathers— bird neck feet bill............. 3
4　handle—hammer :: knob— key room shut door.............. 4
5　shoe—foot :: hat— coat nose head collar.................. 5

6　water—drink :: bread— cake coffee eat pie.............. 6
7　food—man :: gasoline— gas oil automobile spark........... 7
8　eat—fat :: starve— thin food bread thirsty............... 8
9　man—home :: bird— fly insect worm nest................. 9
10　go—come :: sell— leave buy money papers.............. 10

11　peninsula—land :: bay— boats pay ocean Massachusetts...... 11
12　hour—minute :: minute— man week second short........... 12
13　abide—depart :: stay— over home play leave............. 13
14　January—February :: June— July May month year 14
15　bold—timid :: advance— proceed retreat campaign soldier.... 15

16　above—below :: top— spin bottom surface side.......... 16
17　lion—animal :: rose— smell leaf plant thorn............. 17
18　tiger—carnivorous :: horse— cow pony buggy herbivorous..... 18
19　sailor—navy :: soldier— gun cap hill army............... 19
20　picture—see :: sound— noise music hear bark............ 20

21　success—joy :: failure— sadness success fail work......... 21
22　hope—despair :: happiness— frolic fun joy sadness........ 22
23　pretty—ugly :: attract— fine repel nice draw............. 23
24　pupil—teacher :: child— parent doll youngster obey....... 24
25　city—mayor :: army— navy soldier general private....... 25

26　establish—begin :: abolish— slavery wrong abolition end..... 26
27　December—January :: last— least worst month first......... 27
28　giant—dwarf :: large— big monster queer small.......... 28
29　engine—caboose :: beginning— commence cabin end train..... 29
30　dismal—cheerful :: dark— sad stars night bright.......... 30

31　quarrel—enemy :: agree— friend disagree agreeable foe...... 31
32　razor—sharp :: hoe— bury dull cuts tree............... 32
33　winter—summer :: cold— freeze warm wet January........ 33
34　rudder—ship :: tail— sail bird dog cat............... 34
35　granary—wheat :: library— desk books paper librarian........ 35

36　tolerate—pain :: welcome— pleasure unwelcome friends give.. 36
37　sand—glass :: clay— stone hay bricks dirt.............. 37
38　moon—earth :: earth— ground Mars sun sky............ 38
39　tears—sorrow :: laughter— joy smile girls grin........... 39
40　cold—ice :: heat— lightning warm steam coat............ 40

Figure 3.2　Military Test Using Analogies

TEST 8

Notice the sample sentence:

People hear with the   eyes   ears   nose   mouth

The correct word is ears, because it makes the truest sentence.

In each of the sentences below you have four choices for the last word. Only one of them is correct. In each sentence draw a line under the one of these four words which makes the truest sentence. If you can not be sure, guess. The two samples are already marked as they should be.

SAMPLES { People hear with the   eyes   ears   nose   mouth

France is in   Europe   Asia   Africa   Australia

1 America was discovered by Drake Hudson Columbus Cabot..................... 1
2 Pinochle is played with rackets cards pins dice............................... 2
3 The most prominent industry of Detroit is automobiles brewing flour packing...... 3
4 The Wyandotte is a kind of horse fowl cattle granite........................... 4
5 The U. S. School for Army Officers is at Annapolis West Point New Haven Ithaca.. 5

6 Food products are made by Smith & Wesson Swift & Co. W. L. Douglas B. T. Babbitt 6
7 Bud Fisher is famous as an actor author baseball player comic artist............ 7
8 The Guernsey is a kind of horse goat sheep cow............................... 8
9 Marguerite Clark is known as a suffragist singer movie actress writer........... 9
10 "Hasn't scratched yet" is used in advertising a duster flour brush cleanser....... 10

11 Salsify is a kind of snake fish lizard vegetable............................... 11
12 Coral is obtained from mines elephants oysters reefs........................... 12
13 Rosa Bonheur is famous as a poet painter composer sculptor.................... 13
14 The tuna is a kind of fish bird reptile insect................................. 14
15 Emeralds are usually red blue green yellow................................. 15

16 Maize is a kind of corn hay oats rice...................................... 16
17 Nabisco is a patent medicine disinfectant food product tooth paste............... 17
18 Velvet Joe appears in advertisements of tooth powder dry goods tobacco soap...... 18
19 Cypress is a kind of machine food tree fabric............................... 19
20 Bombay is a city in China Egypt India Japan................................ 20

21 The dictaphone is a kind of typewriter multigraph phonograph adding machine...... 21
22 The pancreas is in the abdomen head shoulder neck........................... 22
23 Cheviot is the name of a fabric drink dance food............................. 23
24 Larceny is a term used in medicine theology law pedagogy...................... 24
25 The Battle of Gettysburg was fought in 1863 1813 1778 1812.................... 25

26 The bassoon is used in music stenography book-binding lithography............. 26
27 Turpentine comes from petroleum ore hides trees............................. 27
28 The number of a Zulu's legs is two four six eight............................ 28
29 The scimitar is a kind of musket cannon pistol sword......................... 29
30 The Knight engine is used in the Packard Lozier Stearns Pierce Arrow........... 30

31 The author of "The Raven" is Stevenson Kipling Hawthorne Poe............... 31
32 Spare is a term used in bowling football tennis hockey........................ 32
33 A six-sided figure is called a scholium parallelogram hexagon trapezium......... 33
34 Isaac Pitman was most famous in physics shorthand railroading electricity......... 34
35 The ampere is used in measuring wind power electricity water power rainfall...... 35

36 The Overland car is made in Buffalo Detroit Flint Toledo...................... 36
37 Mauve is the name of a drink color fabric food.............................. 37
38 The stanchion is used in fishing hunting farming motoring..................... 38
39 Mica is a vegetable mineral gas liquid..................................... 39
40 Scrooge appears in Vanity Fair The Christmas Carol Romola Henry IV........... 40

Figure 3.3 Military Test of General Information

The Beta Test

Terman (1918) noted that "of whites, ordinarily about 75 per cent. [*sic*] receive their ratings on Alpha, about 20 per cent. [*sic*] on Beta." He indicated that the Beta test, which was "given to all men who cannot understand or read English well enough to take the Alpha test," was presented in a distinctive fashion. For example, the instructions were provided through pantomime and demonstration. Terman clarified the type of audience for which the Beta test was intended and the nature of the tasks on it.

> *Beta* [is] a group test for foreigners and illiterates....Like Alpha, Beta measures general intelligence, but it does so through the use of concrete materials instead of by the use of written language. It measures particularly the ability to understand instructions given in pantomime, degree of foresight and ingenuity, the ability to discover a plan in given materials, the power to form arbitrary associations quickly, the ability to find likenesses and differences among printed symbols, to detect absurdities, to remember, and to combine related items into a logical whole. (p. 180)

Yoakum and Yerkes (1920) indicated that the Beta test, which required 50 to 60 minutes to complete, was designed for groups of 60 soldiers or less. Disagreeing on this point, Terman (1918) thought the test could "be given equally well to any number of men up to four or five hundred, according to available space" (p. 180). Figure 3.4 contains some of the illustrations that were used to train the administrators of the Beta test (Yerkes, 1921). The administrators could use these chalkboard drawings to demonstrate the types of performance required for some of the tasks on the exam. Figure 3.5 and Figure 3.6 are items from the test itself (Yerkes, 1921). Figure 3.5 contains diagrams that soldiers were to match. Figure 3.6 contains pictures for which soldiers were to identify the missing features.

Other Military Tests

The military mandated testing for all enlisted men and lower ranking officers. In addition to the Alpha test and the Beta test, some soldiers completed "individual mental tests" such as the Stanford-Binet. Terman (1918) estimated that only five percent of the servicemen took an individual test. He indicated that those persons who had failed the Alpha test or the Beta test would not be discharged, rejected, or assigned to a "development battalion" until they had been screened with an individual test. He was convinced that the imposition of an individual test was "a necessary precaution to prevent malingering." Without providing an explanation, he declared that the proclivity for malingering would not invalidate an individual test because "attempts to cheat [on an individual test] are not common" (pp. 180–181).

Although the Alpha test had been designed as a general screening device, it did have explicit vocational implications. This was clear in the explanations for the letter grades that soldiers received. As an example, consider Terman's remarks about the military careers that were appropriate for those persons who had been assigned the highest or lowest possible test scores.

A. *Very Superior Intelligence.*—This grade is earned by only four or five soldiers out of a hundred. The "A" group is composed of men of marked intellectuality. "A" men are of high officer type when they are also endowed with leadership and other necessary qualities....

D– and E. *Very Inferior Intelligence.*—This group is divided into two classes (1) "D–" men, who are very inferior in intelligence but are considered fit for regular service; and (2) "E" men, those whose mental inferiority justifies their recommendation for Development Battalion, special service organization, rejection, or discharge. (Terman, 1918, pp. 181–182)

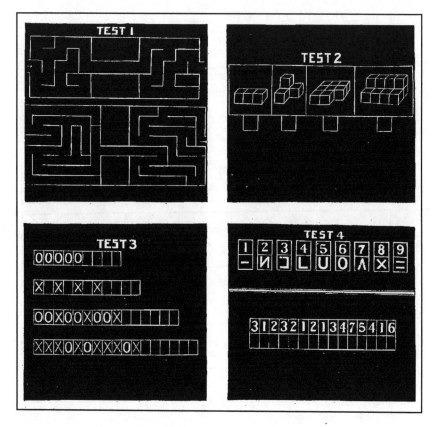

Figure 3.4 Chalkboard Illustrations for Explaining Tests

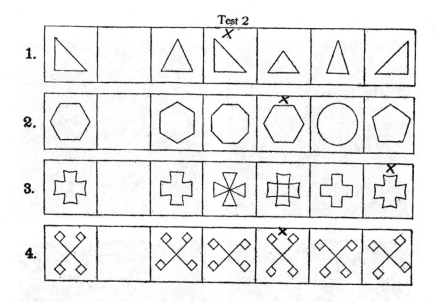

Figure 3.5 Nonverbal Matching Test

Figure 3.6 Nonverbal Pictorial Test

Paterson (1940) reported that military psychologists had collaborated with human resource directors from industry to develop new types of tests during World War I. The novel tests were to replace the seniority-based promotion system that historically had dominated the armed forces. Writing during World War I, Hard (1918) illustrated one of these new evaluation procedures.

First, you make a "rating-scale." You make a "rating scale" for each of the five considerations on which you are going to "rate" your subordinates. These considerations are: Physical Qualities, Intelligence, Leadership, Personal Qualities, and General Value to the Service. The greatest number of "points" which you can give to any subordinate for General Value to the Service is 40. The greatest number you can give him for any one of the other four considerations is 15. The greatest possible total of "points," therefore, for the perfect officer, is 100....Among the Majors in your acquaintance, which one would you pick out as ranking highest, in your estimation, for Leadership....You mark him down at

the top....Now, among all of the Majors you know, which one is worst for Leadership....You mark down the worst major, at the bottom....You now have a scale for
Leadership, and it is made not of theories but of Majors. It is made of flesh and blood. (p.
284)

One observer claimed that this scale's inter-rater reliability was so high during a
particular trial that "the average of several hundred candidates differed by less than
two points" ("Rating Scale," 1918, p. 206).

Ruml (1919) endorsed the collaboration between military and industrial
psychologists and the new evaluation procedures that they devised. He wrote that
the Army's psychologists were responsible for investigating each recruit's
"physical, mental, educational and technical qualifications and [making] the record
of these qualifications instantly available." This responsibility was very much like
that which the industrial psychologists had been discharging for years.

An army itself is in a very real sense an industrial unit,—industrial in that like industry it
must meet and solve problems of fabrication, maintenance, transportation and distribution.
Like industry, the army found the solution of these problems to be dependent to an
important degree on the effective utilization of available skilled personnel, and in order that
jobs requiring men with special qualifications might be acceptably filled, the army created
within itself a body with functions like that of the employment manager of industry, that
is, functions of bringing man and job together with due regard to the qualifications of the
former and the demands of the latter. (p. 38)

Kohs and Irle (1920) recounted that the leaders in the armed forces had turned
to psychologists to analyze individual servicemen and to synthesize "more or less
fragmentary mental evidence for the purpose of more clearly indicating or
prognosticating what one might expect in the future" (p. 73). The military had
made this move after discovering that the high-school achievements of students
and the subjective evaluations from their teachers were less accurate predictors of
military success than the psychologists' "prognosticating machinery."

Military leaders did not limit their interest to mental achievement instruments.
Yerkes (1921) reported that their success with intelligence tests persuaded the
military leaders to make greater use of career aptitude exams and vocational
assessment instruments. In his cumbersome writing style, Yerkes explained that
"the relationship between intelligence as measured by the Army psychological
examinations and various occupations groups was a by-product of the development of the Army psychological work" (p. 819). Figure 3.7 contains a vocational
scale that was derived from the research to which Yerkes had referred. It indicated
the average scores that persons from various occupations had earned on the Alpha
test.

Yerkes (1923b) suggested that scales such as that in Figure 3.7 could be used
to match soldiers with their appropriate military occupations. Because similar tests
could identify the ideal civilian careers for public-school students, he predicted that

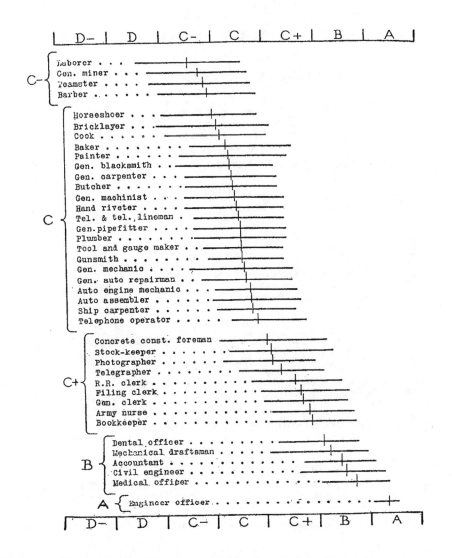

Figure 3.7 Mental Test Scores That Have Been Scaled to Occupations

"vocational and avocational choices, instead of being left to the wish or whim of parent, guardian, or self, to necessity, to ease and openness of road, will come more and more to rest on adequate knowledge of the traits and capacities of the self, and the demands, requirements, and opportunities of different classes of occupation" (p. 370).

TRADE TEST

BUTCHER. — Butcher

ORAL

COMMITTEE ON CLASSIFICATION OF PERSONNEL
IN THE ARMY

Trade Test Division

Reproduced by permission of the Adjutant General

QUESTION 1

Q. From what part are pork chops usually cut?
A. Loin.   Score 4

QUESTION 2

Q. How many ribs are cut to a rib of beef?
A. (1) 7.   Score 4
    (2) 8.   Score 4
    (3) 9.   Score 4

QUESTION 3

Q. What are two knives which a butcher uses?
A. (1) a. Steak (cutting).   Score 4
      b. Boning (trimming).

QUESTION 4

Q. From what part of the hog do you get picnic or California hams?
A. Shoulder.   Score 4

QUESTION 5

Q. What is located between the first rib and the hip?
A. Loin (porterhouse).   Score 4

QUESTION 6

Q. What is the average weight of sweet-breads?
A. ½ to 1 pound.   Score 4

QUESTION 7

Q. From what is tripe made?
A. (1) Stomach (belly).   Score 4
    (2) Paunch.   Score 4

QUESTION 8

Q. From what part of a hog is salt pork made?
A. Belly.   Score 4

QUESTION 9

Q. How many ribs are left on a chuck of beef?
A. (1) 4.   Score 4
    (2) 5.   Score 4

QUESTION 10

Q. What is the average weight of a plate from a 500 pound dressed
   steer?
A. 20 to 40.   Score 4

Figure 3.8 Military Exam for Butchers

Persons who were accountants in their civilian careers generally made fine accountants in the military. The same was true of persons who had learned about accounting through educational programs. Nonetheless, the Army needed to assure a prerequisite level of occupational competence before it assigned recruits to the numerous military jobs that had to be filled. It relied on trade tests for these evaluations. Figure 3.8 represents the first 10 questions from an individually administered oral exam that was posed to prospective military butchers (Chapman, 1921, pp. 144–145).

Figure 3.9 contains an illustration that was part of an orally administered trade test for lathe operators (Chapman, 1921, p. 226). The tested person would view illustrations of machinists' tools and then name them. Figure 3.10, which displays types of flames, was used to question potential welders (Chapman, 1921, pp. 249–250). Figure 3.11 contains a portion of the pictorial test administered to aspiring cobblers (Chapman, 1921, p. 247).

Trade tests could demonstrate that recruits and draftees were ready to assume some types of vocational assignments. However, readiness for combat duty was more difficult to verify. The difficulty resulted from the fact that general intelligence tests, school curricula, and previous civilian experiences failed to indicate the ways in which persons would behave under hostile fire. Although the prediction of vocational success during combat was important to many military jobs, Henmon (1919) thought that "no where has this been more true than in the Air Service." Incidentally, the Army did not require a minimal level of educational experience for pilots until 1920, when it insisted that all applicants possess a high-school diploma. This requirement remained in place until 1927, when the excessive number of pilot applicants enabled the educational requirements to be raised to two years of college (Rogers, Roach, & Short, 1986). With educational standards set so low during World War I, the Army had searched for ways to identify those persons who would succeed in flight school. Henmon (1919) reported that "when war was declared the need for selecting thousands of men for training as pilots, observers and balloonists was met by the creation of Examining Boards and Physical Examining Units" (p. 103). Despite the special screening performed by these units, more than six percent of the candidates who commenced flight training "were discharged or transferred because of inaptitude for flying." Although a candidate completion rate 94 percent might seem impressive, it was not acceptable to the Army leaders of that era.

In their attempt to ascertain which candidates would successfully complete combat flight training, the Army's psychologists developed a special set of tests. The tests in this battery measured emotional stability, perception of tilt, reaction to swaying, visual acuity, auditory acuity, equilibrium, perception of depth, mental alertness, athletic achievement, and athletic interest. The military examiners fully appreciated the complexity of the problem they were confronting after they unexpectedly discovered that emotional stability was the best predictor of flying

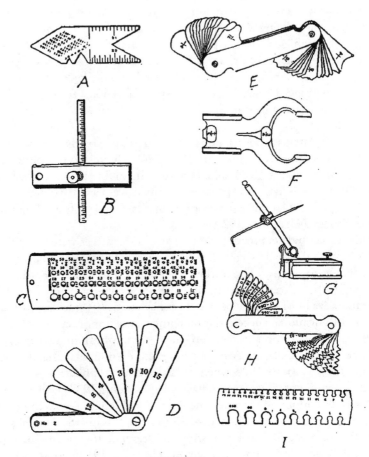

PICTURE 16

19. Q. Name the gages in that picture.
    A. (a) Center Gage.
        (b) Depth Gage.
        (c) Drill Gage (Wire Gage).
        (d) Feeler (Thickness) Gage.
        (e) Radius (Curve) Gage.
        (f) Snap Gage.
        (g) Surface Gage.
        (h) Thread Gage.
        (i) Wire Gage.   (All nine required)

Figure 3.9   Military Exam for Lathe Operators

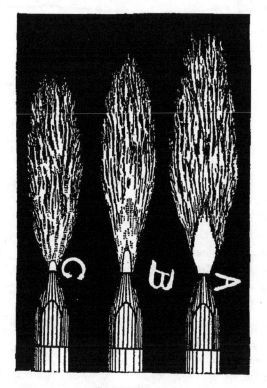

PICTURE 1

1. Q. What kind of flame is shown at A?
   A. (1) Carbonizing.
      (2) Excessive acetylene.
      (3) Crystallizing.   (One sufficient)

2. Q. What kind of flame is shown at B?
   A. (1) Neutral.
      (2) Welding.   (One sufficient)

3. Q. What kind of flame is shown at C?
   A. Oxidizing (oxygen).

Figure 3.10 Military Exam for Welders

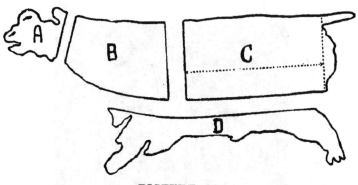

PICTURE 14

17. Q. This is a side of leather,
     (a) From what part do you get heel stock?
     (b) From what part do you get light soles?
     (c) From what part do you get insoles?
     (d) From what part do you get prime soles?
    A. (a) A. and D.   (b) B.   (c) A. and D.   (d) C.   (Any 3)

PICTURE 15

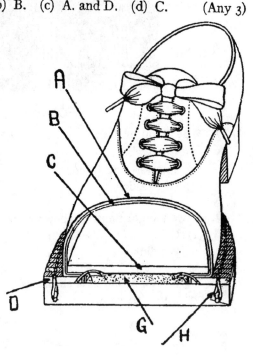

18. Q. This picture shows shoe cut across.
       What part of the shoe do you call part at " A "?
    A. Upper (vamp).
19. Q. What is the name of the part of the shoe at " B "?
    A. Lining.
20. Q. What do you call " C "?
    A. Insole.
21. Q. What is " D " called?
    A. Welt.

Figure 3.11 Military Exam for Cobblers

ability. Henmon (1919) described the situation that they used to elicit this trait and the manner in which they measured it.

> [The emotional stability test] measures the liability of the subject to incoördinate [*sic*] purposeless reaction upon a receipt of a sudden shock, the discharge of a pistol. Measurements were made of amplitude of hand tremor, time of recovery from tremor, changes of frequency of pulse, changes in frequency and amplitude of respiration, and the effect of the shock on rate of solving examples in addition. Of these measurements amplitude of hand response and changes in frequency in respiration were found to be especially significant. (p. 105)

Parsons and Segar (1918) also studied the likelihood that persons would succeed in combat flight training. They focused on the validity of a widely used equilibrium test. Their research was particularly important because military leaders had, on the basis of their intuitions, established high performance on this test as the indispensable condition for commencing flight instruction. In their understated style of writing, Parson and Segar reported that "the evidence…seems to point to an absence of correlation between equilibrium tests…and actual flying ability" (p. 1065).

Figure 3.12 illustrates equipment that was used to test the "psychomotor coordination" of prospective pilots. This photograph, which was taken during World War II, demonstrated an examination on which cadets engaged in tasks that resembled the physical act of piloting an airplane. In the depicted testing center, the examiner could observe four cadets simultaneously.

Thurstone (1919b) investigated whether general intelligence tests and previous academic accomplishments predicted the degree of skill that telegraph operators would display. After determining that previous academic experience was not a useful predictor, he administered exams for spelling, arithmetic, forming analogies, designating opposites, and following directions. He even administered a rhythm test. He was unable to establish meaningful correlations between any of these measures and the soldiers' subsequent proficiency as telegraph operators. Thurstone eventually concluded that "ability in telegraphy is probably a special ability" (p. 117).

Curtailing Military Testing

The Army authorized its testing program during the last week of 1917. The March 7, 1919, issue of *Science* contained an evaluation of this massive assessment initiative ("Measurement and Utilization," 1919). The reporter who had written this piece acknowledged that the Army was "at first naturally and wisely skeptical concerning the practical values of psychological services." However, the reporter continued that "skeptics, of course, still exist and there are inevitable misunder-

Figure 3.12 Testing the "Psychomotor Coordination" of Pilots

standings and prejudices, but the data at hand indicate that at least seventy-five per cent. [*sic*] of the officers of the United States Army have been won by actual demonstration of values and first hand acquaintance with psychological service to its hearty support" (p. 222). This author indicated that Major Robert Yerkes, the Chief of the Army's Section of Psychology, had read and approved the final version of his report. Despite the writer's confident tone and optimism, the Army discontinued most types of testing. It had made this decision only weeks before this report was published and less than 13 months after the assessment program had been initiated.

Yerkes (1921) opined that the wartime research by the Army's psychologists would have continued "had not the military situation changed so radically" (p. 819). Because Yerkes was involved directly in this research, his explanation could have been biased. Almost 20 years later, Paterson (1940) also examined the end of military assessment. However, he did not proffer the reason for this cessation. He simply concluded that "with the signing of the Armistice, the majority of our military psychologists returned to civilian life with a deep-seated ambition to put psychology to work in everyday life....[and] this will account, in large part, for the healthy and vigorous growth which characterized the post–war [*sic*] history of applied psychology" (p. 3). Writing several decades later, Kevles (1968) viewed these events from a different perspective. Struck by correspondence in which senior officers had referred to the psychologists as pests, Kevles judged that the officers' discomfort with testing had led them to place limits on it. In fact, the only postwar assessment responsibility that they left to the psychologists was the identification of the persons who were unfit for service.

Irrespective of the prevailing attitudes of senior officers, the military's tests did produce widespread publicity. Their tests were illustrated, paraphrased, editorialized, and debated in newspapers and magazines. Although testimonials abounded about the inaccuracy of the tests, even opponents had to acknowledge that the once arcane psychological instruments had captured the nation's imagination. The practicality of tests had been demonstrated by the fact that more than 1,000,000 persons had completed them. Even more momentous, the tests had revealed sensational information about widespread educational deficiencies. Some persons thought that these deficiencies might be undermining the long-term interests of America's armed forces. This lesson was not lost on political conservatives. They demanded academic reforms to ensure that scientific, mathematical, and technical training would meet higher standards. They believed that these standards were appropriate during an era of increasingly sophisticated warfare. Because academic accountability was critical to their reforms, testing was the indispensable tool for confirming that they were achieving their objectives.

Objections to Military Tests

The popular journalist Walter Lippmann did not conceal his skepticism about the Army's mental testing program. Although he was not the only critic, he stood out because of his acumen, wit, and extremely persuasive rhetoric. All of these assets were evident in a highly publicized set of articles, most of which he published in the *New Republic* (Lippmann 1922a, 1922b, 1922c, 1922d, 1922e, 1922f, 1923a, 1923b, 1923c, 1923d, 1923e).

Lippmann used rapier-like language to dispute allegations that a significant number of Americans were mentally incompetent. He began one of his articles by analyzing a controversial book by Lothrop Stoddard (1923).

> A startling bit of news has recently been unearthed and is now being retailed by the credulous to the gullible. "The *average* mental age of Americans," says Mr. Lothrop Stoddard in *The Revolt Against Civilization*, "is only about fourteen." Mr. Stoddard did not invent this astonishing conclusion. He found it ready-made in the writings of a number of other writers. They in their turn got the conclusion by misreading the data collected in the army intelligence tests....The average adult intelligence cannot be less than the average adult intelligence, and to anyone who knows what the words "mental age" mean, Mr. Stoddard's remark is precisely as silly as if he had written that the average mile was three-quarters of a mile long. (Lippmann, 1922d, p. 213)

Lippmann deflated the "pretensions" of psychological tests by insisting that "these are not 'intelligence tests' at all nor 'measurements of intelligence,' but simply a somewhat more abstract kind of examination" (1922a, p. 11). He added that "as examinations they can be adapted to the purposes in view, whether it be to indicate the feeble-minded for segregation, or to classify children in school, or to select recruits from the army for officers' training camps, or to pick bank clerks."

When Stanford psychologist Lewis Terman decided to challenge Lippmann, the journalist relished the opportunity to debate the issues with him. Block and Dworkin (1976) later collated the articles and letters that these two intellectuals exchanged. Lippmann and Terman's highly publicized allegations, responses, and counterresponses were read by a large audience. Making observations about the debate while it was transpiring, Dickson (1923) indicated that it was stirring up "so much controversy...about mental tests or intelligence tests that many teachers are in doubt as to what to believe, whom to believe, what to do or what not to do in the field of tests and measurement" (p. 176).

Lippmann used the debate with Terman as a forum for demonstrating some of the methodological shortcomings of the military's testing program. He also pointed to some of the questionable decisions that military psychologists had made when they had reported their data. For example, they had decided that they would not sort test scores by states or regions. Had they done so, they might have detected the degree to which scores were influenced by the variable economic, social, and educational opportunities that correlated with the distinct geographical areas. Lippmann wrote skeptically that "for some reason the army editors...left that comparison alone" (1923a, p. 99).

Within each of his articles about military testing, Lippmann predictably used the lead paragraph to display his stylized sarcasm. This tactic was evident in a piece that he published in the popular *Century Magazine* (Lippmann, 1923a).

When a man of science announces that seventy millions [*sic*] of Americans have "little or no brains" and that "education can add nothing to their intelligence," it is perhaps time to see whether it is possible to say a word in defense of education. For if seventy millions [*sic*] are predestined and irretrievable fools, this democracy is probably a predestined and irretrievable failure. Even eugenics, the one hope held out, is not promising, for you can hardly expect in any visible future to breed a more intelligent race out of people who have little or no brains to transmit to their children. (p. 95)

Although Lippmann had used a particularly biased article as the pretext for his remarks, he wished to discredit that entire crowd of psychologists, politicians, and educators who had proclaimed that intelligence was genetically constrained, impervious to education, and measurable through tests. Lippmann cleverly stated that "I do not see why anybody should either deny this hypothesis [that all people may be born with a certain fixed intellectual capacity] or insist upon it, unless he can prove that he has found a way of separating inborn capacity from all of the effects of environment, schooling, occupation, disease, health and opportunity." Lippmann then used his opponents' own data in an attempt to demonstrate that they had failed to "find a way of unscrambling the egg by the use of the army tests" (1923a, p. 95).

In one of his articles, Lippmann (1923a) had made derogatory comments about Lothrop Stoddard and this writer's commitment to "eugenics." Echoing the language of those Germans who had been extolling the superiority of the Aryan race, Stoddard had written a book entitled *The Revolt against Civilization: The Menace of the Under Man*. After beginning the preface with a dire warning about the danger to the nation, Stoddard suggested an appropriate response.

The revolutionary unrest which to-day [*sic*] afflicts the entire world goes far deeper than is generally supposed. Its root-cause is not Russian Bolshevik propaganda, nor the late war, nor the French Revolution, but a process of racial impoverishment, which destroyed the great civilizations of the past and which threatens to destroy our own... In the light of these biological discoveries, confirmed and amplified by investigators in other fields of science, especially psychology, all political and social problems need to be re-examined. (Stoddard, 1923, p. I)

In a history of the American eugenics movement, Haller (1963) referred to Stoddard's popular book as "the low point of pessimism" within the debate about race and intelligence. Stoddard (1923) had focused attention on the opportunities to improve humanity through "race cleansing," a crusade that he thought was manifest in "the segregation of the insane and feeble-minded in public institutions." He warned that institutionalized individuals were "merely the most afflicted sufferers from taints which extend through the general population" (p. 245). To expand the campaign, he suggested "the prevention of all obvious degenerates from having children" by "segregating most of them in institutions" (p. 247). Stoddard employed a tautology to dismiss Lippmann and his other critics.

The environmentalist argues that social unrest is due to bad social conditions, but when we go into the matter more deeply we find that bad conditions are due largely to bad people. The mere presence of hordes of low-grade men and women condemned by their very natures to incompetency [*sic*] and failure automatically engender [*sic*] poverty, invite [*sic*] exploitation, and drag [*sic*] down others just above them in the social scale. (p. 246)

The racist Stoddard hardly represented the many reputable psychologists who believed that genetic traits significantly influenced the scores that persons were receiving on intelligence tests. To help the public understand the details of the debate in which highly regarded psychologists were engaged, Freeman (1923) developed a "survey of opinion on mental tests." This questionnaire was designed to reveal the psychologists' views toward the popular practice of administering military intellige nce tests to adults and then expressing their scores as the equivalents of those that children might have earned. The questionnaire also attempted to discern the attitudes of the respondents toward the educational implications of these test scores. Freeman published the results in *Century Magazine*. Although only 12 persons were offered the survey, they included Cattell, Yerkes, Terman, Thorndike, and other preeminent psychologists. Freeman had solicited their expert remarks to offset those of the "journalists, educational theorists, and other non-technical writers [who had written so much] on the subject of intelligence tests and their broader implications" (p. 237).

After examining the psychologists' responses, Freeman concluded that the practice of taking adult scores on the Army tests and characterizing them "in terms of the mental age of children must be scrutinized with the greatest caution" (1923, p. 237). He explained that adults and children who performed comparably on intelligence tests were not equal in their overall maturity and experiential knowledge. He assured his readers that "the scare-head announcement that nearly half of us are stupid must be taken strictly for what it is worth" (p. 245).

Freeman also summarized the psychologists' thoughts about the educational limitations of the persons who had scored poorly on the Army's mental tests.

[The psychologists assume]: first, that human nature is not indefinitely modifiable by education...second, that the capacity of different persons to profit by education differs...and third, that mental tests enable us, with a degree of accuracy that makes them practically serviceable, to pick out the persons who can profit largely by education and distinguish them from those who can profit slightly. (1923, p. 245)

Implications for Education

In the introduction to an exhaustive report about the Army's testing program, Yerkes (1921) tried to impress his audience with "the novelty, practical success, and military value" of these tests as well as their "educational, industrial, and scientific significance" (p. 5). The psychologists released from the armed services after the war were in an ideal position to reinforce this message. Many of these discharged psychologists applied for employment in the schools. Claxton (1919), the Director of the United States Bureau of Education, provided postwar school administrators with several reasons why they should hire the psychologists.

> The fact that two or three hundred young men who have for several months been working in the psychology division of the Army are now about to be discharged offers an unusual opportunity for city schools to obtain the services of competent men as directors of departments of psychology and efficiency, for such purposes as measuring the results of teaching and establishing standards to be attained in the several school studies, applying mental tests and discovering defective children and children of superior intelligence, and investigating various other vital questions necessary to establish an intelligent basis for promotion, class organization and special schools. (pp. 203–204)

Claxton thought that the services of these highly skilled professionals were needed in every city with 30,000 or more residents. He adjured school administrators to make employment offers before businesspersons had a chance to do so. Once the businesspersons had entered the competition, Claxton reckoned that "it will hardly be possible to obtain their services without offering them salaries sufficiently large to tempt them from work in which they will then be engaged" (p. 204).

This prediction about the emerging influence of psychologists in the schools turned out to be accurate. A year after Claxton had made his plea for hiring testing and measurement personnel, Freeman (1920b) judged that the military "tests, the publicity which has been given them and the large number of men who gained experience in giving tests by using them as psychological examiners in the army, are doing very much to popularize intelligence tests" (p. 353). Several years later, Cardozo (1924) reported that "public school authorities have felt it necessary to organize departments of research or of standards and measurements" (p. 797). Cardozo estimated that most cities were paying about $16,000 a year to staff these departments. New York City, which had the largest assessment budget, was paying more than $100,000 annually for a director, an assistant director, 2 assistant supervisors, an examiner, scorers, and clinicians. Cardozo concluded that school systems were hiring measurement personnel because of "the revelations that have come out of the World War as to the lack of intelligence in humankind." The responsibilities of the assessment specialists included the selection and administration of tests, as well as the interpretation and reporting of the scores that resulted from them.

Madsen and Sylvester (1919) made observations about the use of the Alpha test in three Midwestern cities. They hoped that their data would help "others who have applied Alpha to high schools." Madsen published additional articles that were based on the same data but from which he drew more ambitious conclusions. For example, he argued that the data demonstrated "the possibilities of using the Army Intelligence test or similar group tests as means of prognosis in high school"

(1920b, p. 625). In yet another article, Madsen showed that younger students scored higher on the military test than older students who were in the same grade. Madsen speculated that "this is what should be expected if the Army Test really measures native intelligence....[because] a twelve-year-old who has reached the freshmen class [should] be mentally superior to the older students in the same class" (1920a, p. 299).

Universities Use Military Tests

Within a review of recently published psychological research, Freeman (1920b) wrote that "the widespread experimentation with the army tests, particularly Scale Alpha, and their influence on the development of other tests, makes it appropriate to give [military testing] the place of emphasis in this year's review" (p. 353). The authors of many other articles provided evidence that substantiated the appropriateness of Freeman's selection. At Ohio State University, Noble and Arps (1920) did not conceal their pride when they enticed 6,350 of the school's 6,750 students to take the Alpha test. Hunter (1919) compared the scores of students who took the Alpha test at the University of Illinois, Southern Methodist University, and Dickinson College. Other institutions in which professors reported about postwar students taking this exam included the University of Minnesota (Van Wagenen, 1920), Oberlin College (Jones, 1920), Purdue University (Roberts & Brandenburg, 1919), and the University of Arkansas (Jordan, 1920). After reviewing the scores that university students had been earning on military tests, Freeman (1920b) observed that freshmen at Yale had led the pack while those at the University of Oklahoma had finished in last place.

Bregman (1926) reported about "the general and wide-spread use of the Army Alpha Examination as an intelligence examination for adults" (p. 695). To make the exam even more practical, he developed a scale for "converting scores on the Alpha test into percentiles for use with the total population." Wells (1932) alluded to five forms of the Alpha test and then proposed still another version from which obsolete or military items would be removed. A year later, Wells and a colleague (Atwell & Wells, 1933) actually did alter the original examination materials. As a result of these changes, they thought that they had made the tests "shorter, yet still reliable." Like its counterpart, the Beta test was revised. As an example of these changes, Kellogg and Morton (1934) developed printed activities that were to precede each portion of this test and substitute for those earlier instructions that had been pantomimed or blackboard-based.

Toward the end of the 1930s, Bingham (1937) noted that "there are newer, better group tests than the Army Alpha for measuring scholastic aptitude and general intelligence." Despite these developments, Bingham conceded that the newer tests were based on relatively small samples. Additionally, the scores on recent exams had not been correlated with occupational requirements. Bingham concluded that "for these reasons [the Army's] epoch-making battery has been kept in use, both in certain of its original forms and in several revisions" (p. 330).

Military tests appealed to those persons who believed that students' native intelligence restricted the degree to which they could benefit from schooling. Both psychologists and educators who were dealing with high-school students exhibited this attitude. However, these attitudes were discernable even among some of the persons who were working with students in the early elementary grades. As an example, Dickson (1920) had judged that the intelligence test scores of "first-grade children have shown that mental age and I.Q. are important factors in revealing a child's chances for success in his school work" (p. 480). Terman had concluded that not all elementary and high-school student dropout "is traceable to inferior mental ability, but that a large part is due to this cause there is no longer room for doubt" (Terman, as quoted by Stenquist, 1921, p. 242).

Terman (1924) advised educators that they should sort children on the basis of their test scores. He explained that this procedure was "absolutely essential if the public school is to be made a real instrument of democracy" because a "true democracy does not rest upon equality of endowment, but upon equality of opportunity" (p. xiv). He added that it was as "unjustifiable and dangerous for the educator to prescribe the same educational treatment for all as it would be for a physician to prescribe the same medical treatment for all." Terman made the preceding remarks within the introduction to a text by Dickson (1924). Aware that his own ideologically biased views had produced a severe public backlash, Terman referred antagonistic members of his audience to Dickson's book. He specifically recommended the book for members of "women's clubs, parent-teacher associations, and other groups interested in education."

The philosophy that Terman and his colleagues had articulated became known as "educational determinism." Buckingham (1921) stated one of the explicit assumptions of this philosophy.

> The notion that the school produces its results through training alone is too naïve to be entertained. It is true that we sometimes hear teachers and other school officers speak as if the success of their pupils in after life were wholly attributable to instruction. Those who have sought to measure the results of teaching have often been told to look for them ten, twenty, or thirty years later. The fact is that our students have certain endowments long before they come under our influence. We may help them to realize their possibilities, or we may hinder them in their development; but we cannot create capacity. (pp. 138–139)

Anticipating that these remarks would be seen as "fatalistic and depressing," Buckingham added that "the real question is not a question of fatalism but of truth."

Buckingham correctly anticipated a hostile response to his statements. Some critics, such as Cobb (1922), were struck by the fact that Buckingham had not supported his contentions with data. She counseled readers that "there is here a fertile field for pioneer work in originating a curriculum which will fit their needs, for discovering what these children can and should be taught and what methods of presentation best reach them" (p. 554). The scholars who were most alarmed depicted educational determinism as a threat to democratic government. Even though he recognized that educational determinism had "received a sanc-tion…from the unquestionable success of the tests in the Army," Bagley (1922) labeled it "a specious sanction" that was "fraught with educational and social dangers of so serious and far-reaching a character as to cause the gravest concern" (p. 373). Reigner (1924) thought that the sponsors of the measurement movement were scheming "to segregate children of 'low native intelligence' into special classes." He added derisively that "on the other hand, society—and a democratic republic in particular—will be vastly benefitted if it is possible to segregate its supernormally [*sic*] 'intelligent' children and give them training which will enable them to translate their superior 'intelligence' into terms of leadership" (p. 573).

As one would expect, the advocates of educational testing were upset by these accusations. They blamed the press for sensationalizing problems that actually were no greater than those that had accompanied other new educational developments. They were particularly disturbed by the disproportionate publicity that the press had given to the theory of educational determinism. Kelley (1923) judged that the journalists had taken scientific and scholarly remarks out of their original context and misrepresented educational determinism as the foundation for standardized testing. As far as the more serious charge that the leadership of the measurement movement was "undermining democracy," Kelley remonstrated that it was "as innocent as a new born babe" (p. 19).

The genuine educational determinists paired their narrow view of the students who would benefit from elementary and high-school education with a comparably contorted view of those who would profit from college education. The president of the Carnegie Foundation for the Advancement of Teaching detected an emerging attitude that "too many young men and women are to-day [*sic*] enrolled in our universities, and that the country would be better off if that attendance were, by some process or other, cut down" (Pritchett, 1923, p. 556). Many of the persons who shared this disposition saw tests as the ideal "process" for reducing university enrollments.

Almack, Bursch, and DeVoss (1923) were worried that students were relying on their own opinions about whether they should attend universities. They thought this was problematic because "some of us do question college classes [of students] concerning their estimates of their own intelligence" (p. 293). The only alternatives to self-evaluations were subjective estimates made by teachers or the results of objective tests. Both of these alternatives were controversial. A robust professional literature documented the multiple problems with subjective evaluations. As far as test-based admissions to universities were concerned, these had been denounced as dangerously elitist. Almack, Bursch and DeVoss (1923) struggled to address this last objection logically.

> If this is true, then instead of devising means for making classification accurate, we should exert our energies to remove from our course of study in English, civics, history, literature, etc., every item which would tend to make them think in terms of social levels or castes, or else we should build a hierarchy of social levels and castes and tell them all that they may climb ever upward on this ladder. Just where in this view of affairs should we place the man who must handle large groups of people and sort them for the purpose of his organization, such as the manager of a factory, the head of the police department, the general in the army and others? It would appear that we must have esoteric and exoteric views of ourselves if we make this assumption. (p. 294)

Opponents of exam-based university admissions alleged that performance on tests was an indication of students' social and economic backgrounds. Critics such as Lippmann (1923a) had highlighted the predictable correlations between students' test scores and their environments. He and sympathetic colleagues argued that test-based university admissions created a gate beyond which racial minorities, immigrants, and poor persons could not pass. Scott (1922) had expressed these sentiments when he wrote that the debate over university admissions tests had become focused on "the ethical laws and the philosophy that should...prevent their use as an instrument merely for closing the doors of institutions of higher learning to the ambitious youth of mediocre intelligence but possessing sufficient brain and grit to graduate from high school" (p. 384).

Gauss (1927), a dean at Princeton University, reinforced Scott's argument. Even though he was associated with a university that few minority, immigrant, or economically lower-class students attended, he pointed out that some of the socially upper-class students at elite universities lacked the intelligence or temperament to profit from the opportunities they had been given. He lamented that the wealthy parents of these students had failed to dispassionately appraise their children's limitations. He probably struck very few persons as sincere when he exclaimed that "blessed...are the poor" because "poorer parents of high-school boys know their children better than parents who have sent their sons away to preparatory schools and summer camps after they reached the age of ten or twelve" (p. 412). Five years earlier, the president of Dartmouth College, who had made this same point, probably appeared equally disingenuous. This administrator had decried "the use of the college to define an aristocracy of birth or wealth" and suggested an alternative.

> [I am calling for] an aristocracy of brains made up of men intellectually alert and intellectually eager, to whom, increasingly, the opportunities of higher education ought to be restricted, if democracy is to become a quality product rather than simply a quantity one, and if excellence and effectiveness are to displace the mediocrity towards which democracy has such a tendency to skid. (M. Hopkins, 1922, quoted in "Who Should Go," 1922, p. 12)

Summary

Most of the public was unaware of mental testing at the beginning of the twentieth century. This situation changed after the military adopted standardized assessment. One exam required soldiers to answer written questions. A separate test used pictures and symbols to assess the intelligence of illiterates and non-English speakers. Additional military instruments measured career dispositions, vocational achievements, and special aptitudes. Many citizens were struck by the efficiency and value of this massive testing program. They were also impressed by the low scores that many of the examinees earned. Political conservatives publicized these problems, linked them to the schools, insisted on reforms, and demanded ongoing assessment.

CHAPTER 4

Entrepreneurs Create an Industry

To devise and apply the best methods of determining fitness is the business of the psychological expert, who will probably represent at the close of this century as important a profession as medicine, law or the church.
—CATTELL, 1905

Assessment enthusiasts insisted that the early intelligence tests were fair, practical, and accurate. This issue became critical to the public, which wanted to know why so many World War I servicemen had scored poorly on tests. The pro-assessment factions claimed that the military testing had been valid and that a comparable type of assessment was needed in the public schools. Businesspersons responded to this suggestion with numerous educational tests. They also devised assessment instruments for higher education, the government, the military, commerce, and industry.

Expanding Markets

Many beginning-of-the-century educators remarked on the extraordinary expansion of the testing market. Ayres (1918) admitted that the initial use of educational testing had been sparse in England, Germany, France, and several other European countries. However, this situation changed to such an extent that tests became popular "around the world." Ayres called special attention to the impressive growth of standardized assessment in Australia, New Zealand, India, and Hawaii. As far as the United States and Canada were concerned, he reported that tests were being used throughout their "length and breadth."

Monroe (1918a) agreed that "during the past decade and especially during the past five years, the number of tests available for measuring the abilities of children in school subjects has grown very rapidly" (p. 71). To substantiate this point, he identified 109 standardized educational tests. Three years later, Alexander (1921) used a simile to characterize the situation. He wrote that "this growth has been so phenomenal that mere figures are too weak to express it...[and] we need to employ forceful images such as likening it to the gigantic business expansions of the war period" (p. 345). Long (1923) reported that, "in a short period of years," testing had turned into "a robust type of psychological development" (p. 22). Unable to conceal his personal envy of those professors who had benefitted from this development, he added that the movement "had brought into prominence and fame persons who otherwise could hardly be ranked as eminent in the field of psychology" (p. 22).

During the 1920s, many writers continued to offer testimonials about the growth of testing. Bliss (1922) observed that the "air is filled with tests and talk of tests" (p. 33). McCall (1923) indicated that testing had "developed at such a phenomenal rate in the last few years as to make this movement for the mental measurement of children the most dramatic tendency in modern education" (p. v).

Wishing to help his readers conceptualize the "immense proportions" of the testing movement, Dickson (1924) advised them that "hundreds of thousands, if not millions, of school children are being tested annually" (p. iii). Gilliland and Jordan (1924) were aware of so many publications about testing that they felt obliged to offer "some definite justification" for writing still another book on the subject. Burtt (1926) reported about the Psychological Corporation, a testing company that had been founded five years earlier. He indicated that the organization had been so successful that it already had opened branches in Massachusetts, Pennsylvania, Maryland, Ohio, Michigan, Illinois, Iowa, Kansas, Missouri, California, and the District of Columbia. Referring to the increasing numbers of test and measurement courses into which teacher candidates were enrolling, Alexander (1921), Terman (1928), and Cubberley (1939) all pointed to this trend as an indirect indication of the growth in testing.

Symonds (1928) noted that standardized high-school and college tests had not become popular until the postwar era. Nonetheless, he discerned "a sizable body of material and of techniques" that had been assembled after World War I. He concluded that additional growth was assured because so many new uses for tests had been devised. He gave examples of 15 of these applications.

1. To inform pupils of their achievement.
2. As incentives to study.
3. To promote competition....
4. To determine promotion.
5. To diagnose weak spots in the pupils' achievement.
6. To determine the quality of instruction.
7. To determine admission to high school.
8. To place a pupil in the school.
9. To determine admission to college.
10. To provide reports to parents.
11. To determine credits, honors, etc.
12. Educational and vocational guidance.
13. To rate teachers.
14. To predict a pupil's success.
15. To study the efficiency of the school. (pp. 1–2)

Advertisements constituted another indirect indication of the popularity of testing. Many of these advertisements, which were designed to sell products other than exams, used terminology from the assessment movement. For example, one of the advertisements from the I-Q Teachers Association, which was an employment agency for teachers, noted that "we enroll only candidates who pass our standard mental test, which is carefully administered" ("Mental Test," 1930). An advertisement for instructional materials from the Winston Company emphasized that these were "not just another series of work books in arithmetic....these are exact instruments of pupil diagnosis and they provide preventive treatment against arithmetic disorders" ("New! Diagnostic Tests," 1929). The

Kalamazoo Vegetable Parchment Company announced that its products "must go through severe tests and close examination—before they can 'pass with honors'" ("Every 'Examination' Passed," 1931). The Natural Slate Blackboard Company urged school administrators to purchase its product, which "passes every test in school service" ("Passes Every Test," 1937). An inkwell manufacturer attracted attention by exclaiming, "Speaking of tests—Why not take advantage of our free trial offer" ("Speaking of Tests," 1936). Figure 4.1 contains a portion of an advertisement identifying schoolroom windows that "will pass your examination" ("This Window," 1931). These companies and their advertising firms would not have linked their products to the testing movement unless they had viewed that movement positively.

Figure 4.1 Use of Testing Jargon to Market Schoolroom Windows

Bibliographies of Tests

Personal estimates, testimonials, observations about new courses in teacher education programs, and advertisements all provided indirect measures of the degree to which assessment was expanding. One of the reasons that contemporary scholars sometimes referred to indirect measures may have been the difficulty they had identifying and cataloging tests. Webb and Shotwell (1932) had specifically addressed this issue. They wrote that "the number of standard tests has become so large that any adequate treatment of them must be of parts rather than of the whole" (p. v).

Instead of listing the many tests that were available, Hawkes, Lindquist, and Mann (1936) wrote a manual in which they advised high-school teachers about techniques for constructing their own tests. They illustrated ways in which these techniques could be applied to social studies, natural sciences, foreign languages, mathematics, and English. They also included a bibliography with the names and addresses of individuals who could provide information about several statewide testing programs. These programs had been implemented in Alabama, Colorado, Georgia, Indiana, Iowa, Kentucky, Minnesota, New Mexico, North Carolina, Ohio, Texas, South Carolina, and Wisconsin.

Echoing the remarks that other scholars had made, Hildreth (1933) acknowledged that "the rapid increase in recent years in the number of available tests and rating scales" had created an inadvertent problem in which "locating a specific test is often...baffling" (p. 7). Like her colleagues, she recognized the "indispensable" need for "a comprehensive list of tests and rating scales." Unlike her colleagues, she did not shrink from this task. The final version of her bibliography, which was 175 pages long, catalogued and described over 3,500 tests. Six years later, she revised this book (Hildreth, 1939). To justify the updated bibliography, she noted that numerous new tests had been published. This was especially the case for tests of personality, speech, and vocational aptitude, as well as tests aimed at high-school and college students. Her second bibliography contained an astounding 4,279 entries.

Buros (1937) assembled a list of educational, psychological, and personality tests to supplement Hildreth's 1933 bibliography. Within a roster of those instruments that had appeared between 1933 and 1935, he catalogued 503 tests (Buros, 1936). A later list, which included only those items that had been published during 1936, catalogued and reviewed 868 tests (Buros, 1937).

Buros (1937) had entitled his second volume, *Educational, Psychological and Personality Tests of 1936: Including a Bibliography and Book Review Digest of Measurement Books and Monographs of 1933–36.* As indicated by the subtitle, he had incorporated some critical remarks about tests. He included these reviews so that his book would stand out from that of Hildreth. With regard to Hildreth's book, the managing editor of her publishing house had recounted that "the purpose of

[Hildreth's] book is not to serve as a critique of tests or the testing movement, but to meet the need for a handy first reference as to what measurements of this kind have been attempted and the devices that have been tried" (Achilles, 1933, p. v). Buros pursued a different tact within his bibliography. In the preface to the 1938 edition, he explained that "because of the warm reception given this book-review-excerpt section, the decision was made to expand the scope of the series so as to include in this issue original reviews" (Buros, 1938, p. xiii). In the foreword to the same volume, Partch (1938) commented that "for the first time, a large number of frankly evaluative reviews by able test technicians, subject-matter specialists, and psychologists are available to assist test users in making more discriminating selections from among the hundreds of tests on the market" (xi).

Ross (1941) wrote that an earlier generation of educators had been frustrated because they did not have the types of references that Hildreth and Buros later assembled. Prior to these landmark bibliographical publications, educators hoped that textbook authors would list tests. However, "the rapid increase in the number of tests and scales published had made it impossible to keep the [textbooks] up to date" (p. vii). Ross continued that "fortunately, in recent years the appearance of rather complete and frequently revised bibliographies of published tests, together with critical evaluations, has made detailed lists and descriptions of available measuring instruments in textbooks no longer necessary."

The number of tests continued to increase after World War II. To help his readers understand the rapidity of this growth, Sundberg (1954) remarked that the newly published *Fourth Mental Measurements Yearbook* contained 4,417 references. Intelligence tests accounted for less than 25 percent of the listed items. The remaining instruments assessed a full range of specialized aptitudes and achievements. Contrasting the recent bibliography with one that had been compiled during World War I, Sundberg observed that "the testing world has changed radically since 1917 not only in quantity of tests but also in kinds of tests." In that early bibliography to which Sundberg referred, Boardman (1917) had arranged seven to eight items on each sheet of a 110-page volume. However, she included not only tests but also articles and reports about them. The vast majority of her references pertained to informative articles rather than tests. A full 52-page section contained articles that exclusively referenced the Binet-Simon intelligence tests. As a result, the number of tests that Boardman listed in her bibliography was relatively modest. Sundberg was understandably amazed at the thousands of tests that became available in the succeeding 35 years.

Expense and Income

Early educational analysts had a hard time calculating the cost of large-scale assessment. The difficulty that they faced was brought into relief when later analysts admitted that they still had not solved this problem. Adopting a commonsense attitude, Phelps (2000) remarked that "it is generally agreed that, as tests go, ordinary standardized student tests are inexpensive" (p. 343). To win support for this opinion, he pointed out that "it would take relatively enormous resources…for an individual school to develop tests from scratch that contain the reliability and comparative properties of the standardized tests produced by commercial vendors and state education agencies." In an earlier study, Phelps (1996b) had analyzed the average expenses for the tests that were administered during the 1990–1991 school year. He acknowledged that the fee for each exam, which had averaged $5.00 per student, was not a realistic estimate of a test's true cost. He suggested that the actual cost had to incorporate another $10.00 in personnel expenses for each examinee.

Not all persons agreed with Phelps about the reasonableness of testing. More than a decade earlier, Alkin and Stecher (1982) had referred derisively to those individuals who maintained "a 'common sense' notion that equates program costs with dollars appearing on a ledger sheet" (p. 3). Providing examples of the types of information for which financial records did not account, they noted that "the time teachers contribute while administering a test and the time students spend taking a test are parts of the total cost of the evaluation." Other items that might not be included on a ledger sheet but which had costs associated with them were the salaries and benefits of the professionals who administered the tests. This point also applied to the salaries and benefits of clerical persons and external consultants. Still more expenses might be the result of facilities, equipment, supplies, and data processing. In a subsequent publication, these authors (Alkin & Stecher, 1983) identified the professional staff as the most expensive aspect of a testing program. They estimated that this budgetary item by itself accounted for 70 percent of assessments' expenses.

A decade after Alkin and Stecher had argued that the costs of tests should be estimated broadly and inclusively, Bauer (1992) used a comparable financial model to calculate the average expenses associated with the testing programs in 38 large school districts. He concluded that 25 percent of the districts had spent less than $2.30 for testing each student while another 25 percent had spent more than $6.14. The average expenditure per test had been $4.79. Gifford (1992) also addressed the cost of tests. Although he did not calculate the average cost for administering an individual test, he did suggest that the annual national expense for all state-mandated or federally mandated tests was a figure between $70,000,000 and $107,000,000. Gifford explained that this figure represented only the direct costs. He estimated that the typical indirect costs, which included teacher and administrator time, were four times greater than the direct costs. Two years earlier, the members of an anti-testing organization had reckoned that "mandatory testing consumes…the equivalent of $700 to $900 million in direct and indirect expenditures annually" (National Commission on Testing and Public Policy, 1990, p. x).

Monk (1995) thought it was important that the cost of testing be ascertained during "the advent of authentic pupil performance assessment on a large scale as a means of transforming entire educational systems" (p. 363). Despite its importance, this complex estimate was difficult to compute. To help his audience understand this point, he differentiated costs from expenditures.

> Costs are measures of what must be foregone to realize some benefit, and for this reason they cannot be divorced from benefits. Expenditures, in contrast, are measures of resource flows regardless of their consequence. A cost analysis requires a comparison of benefits; an expenditure analysis does not....We hire armies of accountants to keep track of expenditures; there is no comparable corps of cost analysts. (p. 365)

Monk added that the prospects for accurate cost analyses in education were "impeded by the multiplicity of possible benefits coupled with a rudimentary knowledge of how resources are translated into educational outcomes" (p. 365). Unable to conceal his frustration, he concluded that the fiscal analysts who examined testing programs would be unable to distinguish expenditures "that are required...[from] those that are due to inefficiency and waste."

Monk specifically challenged a study from the U.S. General Accounting Office in which researchers had attempted to demonstrate the relatively modest expenses associated with large-scale, test-based educational reforms. Defending the way the General Accounting Office had acted, one of those researchers (Phelps, 1996b) dismissed Monk for "mis-coneptualizing" the cost of assessment. Using the polite rhetoric of scholars in educational finance, Monk (1996) retorted that "I believe policymakers are well served by surveys of perceptions of current costs" and that "I do not believe that anyone is well served when those engaged in this work begin to overstate the virtues of their chosen methodologies" (p. 591). Addressing this same issue from a different perspective, Monk and another colleague had argued that "isolated numerical estimates of costs...are perhaps the least valuable and most problematic of the contributions cost analysis can make to ongoing reform efforts" and that these should be replaced by analyses that could "provide the reformer with insight into the origins and implications of costs" (Monk & King, 1993, p. 132).

Calculating the expense of testing and its profits turned out to be a divisive practice. The total expenses for testing certainly included more items and services than the prices of the tests themselves. Even so, the assessment companies had to carefully calculate the prices of their tests. Prices had to be set with care so that their clients and the public would judge that the expense of testing was fair and reasonable. Prices also had to be set so that the assessment companies would generate profits. Although the profits could be considerable, the financial risks that the testing companies assumed also were significant. In fact, progressively fewer companies competed in the assessment business precisely because the development and marketing of the products was so expensive.

Writing in the early 1970s, Holmen and Docter (1972) had calculated that six large organizations were responsible for 75 percent of the tests that were being sold in the United States. These organizations were the California Test Bureau, the Educational Testing Service, Harcourt Brace Jovanovich, Houghton Mifflin, the Psychological Corporation, and Science Research Associates. Even though it had the least seniority, the Educational Testing Service was the largest and most successful competitor. Unlike the other five companies, which were publicly owned and profit-making, the Educational Testing Service was a private, nonprofit organization. Although they did not estimate the average prices for the tests, assessment forms, and ancillary materials that were purchased during the early 1970s, Holmen and Docter did judge that the number of these items sold annually to educators exceeded $150,000,000.

Profits From Early Tests

At the end of the twentieth century, analysts wrote about the difficulty of estimating the direct and indirect costs of recent testing. Early twentieth-century analysts had encountered even greater problems when they had tried to make this calculation. Attempting to estimate New York City's early assessment budget, one newspaper editorialist wrote with dismay that the city "last year spent nearly $35,000,000 for education, and hardly a dollar of it went for measuring results" (unidentified editorialist for the *Springfield Republican*, quoted by Taylor, 1912, p. 348). This writer noted that "lately we had a striking demonstration of what experimental science could do by reducing motions in laying bricks and the fatigue in handling pig-iron." With unconcealed frustration, the editorialist added that "it will hardly be pretended that scientific efficiency is of less consequence in the schools."

The amount of testing conducted in New York's schools and the budget required to support it would change quickly. Just a dozen years after the editorialist had made the remarks that were quoted in the preceding paragraph, New York City was spending more than $100,000 annually just for the salaries of its assessment staff (Cardozo, 1924). After adding to these expenses the costs of tests and the time diverted from the normal responsibilities of teachers and clerical staff, one could hardly question that the school administrators of New York had altered their commitment to testing. Cardozo concluded that this commitment had increased because postwar constituents were demanding a higher level of school accountability.

Most educational administrators recognized the relationship between soldiers' poor performance on World War I military tests and the public's increased skepticism about the schools. Wishing to demonstrate accountability, many administrators implemented educational testing. However, not everyone was pleased with this turn of events. After lamenting that "of giving tests there is no end," a professor at the Cleveland School of Education judged that many of the "supervisors and administrators think they must be doing it just to be in style" and that "a few of their teachers try also to keep up with the fashion" (Myers, 1926, p. 47). One New York superintendent (Rhoads, 1926) observed that "every village school, as well as the most progressive city systems, are [*sic*] using the tests" (p. 67). Despite the phenomenal rate at which educational testing was spreading, this administrator detected "an under-current of thought among many of our best teachers that the testing movement is being carried too far and that the results obtained do not justify the large amount of time and money spent" (Rhoads, 1926, p. 67). After surveying the superintendents in California's rural school districts, Russell (1925) noted that their annual assessment budgets had ranged from $35 to $2,000. Twenty-four of these superintendents had confidence in intelligence tests, 13 questioned their value, and three "do not think they are worth while" (p. 68).

The strongest support for standardized testing came from the school administrators in urban school districts. This clearly had been the case in New York City. It was also true in Baltimore, where administrators established a Bureau of Research that was to conduct large-scale educational assessment. Although Stenquist (1929a, 1929b) did not identify the precise size of the Baltimore Bureau of Research, he wrote articles in which he included photos of eight of the individuals on his staff. Aware that some critics were questioning the expense of the services that he and his staff were providing, Stenquist confided that "the first problem" he had confronted in Baltimore had been posed by colleagues who required "general education and propaganda" about the advantages of a large testing unit. He advised those persons who were planning to establish assessment offices of their own to be sure that the benefits of their services had been "*well sold* to principals, teachers and all others involved" (1929a, p. 41).

Stenquist (1933) acknowledged that many persons opposed testing because they thought it was too expensive. One way that publishers could reduce these expenses was to hold down prices. Even with low prices for their tests, they could still make significant profits if they were able to sell the tests to large markets. However, this strategy did not solve another financial problem, which was the high cost of scoring the exams. This cost of scoring had been apparent to Scates (1937) when he had administered the Stanford Achievement Tests in the Cincinnati schools. In fact, Scates had taken steps to reduce these costs.

> The tests were scored by a group of college students trained for the purpose. They worked 4½-hour shifts per day, receiving therefor [*sic*] $2.25. Each person scored only a single test in each battery, thus gaining familiarity with it. Celluloid scoring stencils were used, and 10 per cent of each scorer's work was checked each day for accuracy. (p. 56)

To place these expenses in perspective, Scates pointed out that the price of each test had been only 8.8 cents. In contrast, the cost of scoring it had been 18.1 cents.

Many persons were concerned about the difficulty as well as the expense of scoring exams. To simplify this process, the IBM Corporation developed a mechanical "test scoring machine" during the 1940s. The machine is illustrated in Figure 4.2. However, the price of these machines placed them beyond the budgets of many small and poorly funded school districts. Fortunately, inexpensive devices to reduce the time and complexity of scoring were available. For example, Scates (1937) had indicated that his staff had used special stencils to score exams. Just as the World War I military had supplied scoring templates to facilitate the grading of intelligence tests, testing companies provided similar devices to their clients. The "scoring key" depicted in Figure 4.3 accompanied a 1940s version of the Iowa Every-Pupil Tests of Basic Skills.

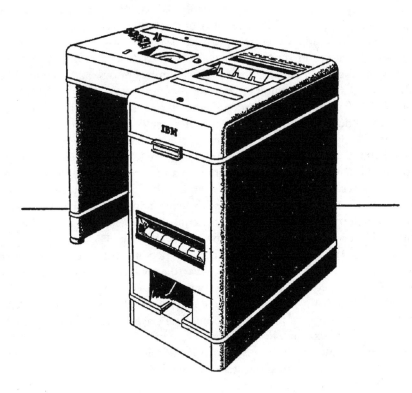

Figure 4.2 Machine for Scoring Tests (*"International Test Scoring Machine."* Copyright *1954 by International Business Machines Corporation. Reprinted by permission.*)

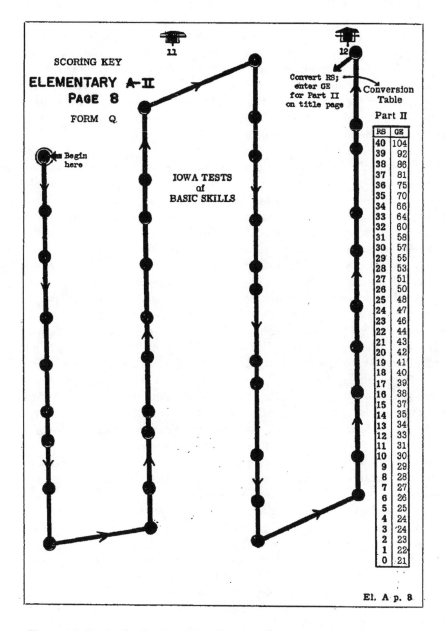

Figure 4.3 Key for Grading Tests (*"Iowa Every-pupil Tests of Basic Skills." Copyright 1947. This work is granted by permission of the Houghton Mifflin Company.*)

The public's uneasiness about the quality of learning in large school districts had prodded test-based accountability. This same uneasiness accounted for the public's enthusiasm about a national achievement test. Whipple (1921) chronicled the development and marketing of the National Intelligence Tests. Two hundred thousand copies of this exam were purchased during the first year that it was available. Attempting to deflect any charges about conflicting interests, Whipple emphasized that he and the other authors had not profited from this venture, for "the authors' royalties...are turned over to the National Research Council for use in further studies of tests" (p. 16).

At the same time that the National Intelligence Tests appeared on the market, James Cattell, the distinguished psychologist, organized the Psychology Corporation. Sokal (1981) later described this company as "one of applied psychology's great successes" (p. 54). Among the organization's founders were the most prominent psychologists of that period—Edward Thorndike, John Watson, Robert Yerkes, and Walter Dill Scott. Although persons who published their exams through the Psychology Corporation could make personal profits, a portion of the revenue was sequestered to cover the cost of future research. Cattell explained that "the psychologists of this country...have taken the lead in forming a Psychological Corporation whose objects are to conserve for research part of the profits from the applications of our science and to conduct new research on an economic basis....[so that] scientific men should take the place that is theirs as masters of the modern world" (Cattell, 1926, quoted by Sokal, 1981, p. 58). Holmen and Docter (1972) reported that the Psychological Corporation took other extraordinary measures during the late 1920s. To discourage charges of profiteering, it appointed the American Psychological Association as its ethical reviewer. It also gave this association the "perpetual right" to buy all of the company's stock. Twenty years later, the American Psychological Association waived this prerogative and returned unqualified ownership to the authors of the corporation's tests. After another 20 years, Harcourt Brace Jovanovich, a major scholastic textbook publisher, purchased the Psychological Corporation and reorganized it as a profit-accountable subsidiary.

One of the reasons that the directors of the Psychological Corporation went to great lengths to represent their organization as science-centered rather than profit-focused was their desire to reassure the public about the costs of tests. Alexander (1921) had reported that one of "the chief objections to measurement work" was the concern that it was "too costly for the results secured" (p. 348). He added that "it is certain that in the present flush of enthusiasm some measurement workers have forgotten that the public will judge their activities by the same economy standards which they [*sic*] employ in evaluating school work." Using an approach to cost analysis that was remarkably similar to that which would be advocated 70 years later, he explained the complex accountability that had been connected to testing.

[Any school system's] measurement bureau should…be prepared to show that its own expenditures are justified. It spends some money and it consumes time and energy of both teachers and pupils. This time and energy represent the same cash value when expended upon measurements as when devoted to arithmetic or the keeping of school records. The measurement bureau must be ready to show better results for such cash equivalent than would have been secured by the regular school work [*sic*] that would otherwise have gone on. If approximately the same results can be secured with a twenty-minute test as with a forty-minute one, or if a five-cent test will do instead of a ten-cent one, or if the clerical labor involved in one is only a fraction of that needed for a similar test, or if a rough oral test will suffice for an elaborate written one, the bureau should do the economical thing and advertise the fact. (p. 349)

Although some skeptics certainly shared Alexander's sentiments toward testing, the use of standardized assessment increased. In a retrospective analysis, Weitzman and McNamara (1949) observed that "during recent decades, an increasingly large share of all educational achievement testing in elementary and secondary school has been accomplished through formal standardized tests constructed by specialists in measurement" (p. v). As the use of tests increased, so did the profits that were derived from them. At the beginning of the era to which Weitzman and McNamara had referred, Peterson (1925) reported that "a considerable amount of money" was being spent on educational tests. However, Peterson judged that the most lucrative market comprised college admission tests, which determined "in advance of their training, by means of tests, the abilities of students who enter these institutions" (p. iii). Assuming an even broader perspective on the expanding market, McConn (1931) reported a "general interest in personnel methods…[that] for a number of years has been growing apace both in colleges and schools and also in industry and among commercial organizations" (p. 225). Kelley and Krey (1934) observed that the publishers of textbooks who were turning to tests were entering a market that was already profitable. They added that this market would become even more lucrative. They explained that "enterprising publishers of textbooks, recognizing in the new-type test a coming vogue of the educational world, had begun to develop tests to accompany their textbooks" (p. 3).

In 1947, the year that the American Psychological Association severed its relationship with the Psychological Corporation, another major assessment unit commenced operation. The directors of three educational organizations—the American Council on Education, the Carnegie Foundation for the Advancement of Teaching, and the College Entrance Examination Board— jointly founded the new unit, which they called the Educational Testing Service. Like the executives at the Psychological Corporation, the directors of the Educational Testing Service worried about the way in which they would be perceived by the public. To protect themselves from accusations of conflicting interests, they established their unit as a private, nonprofit organization. The size of the market that this new unit addressed was revealed by first-year sales of nearly $1,000,000. This robust market grew even stronger. For the next 30 years, the Educational Testing Service's sales revenues consistently doubled every six or seven years ("Pleasures of Nonprofitability," 1976).

Vocational Tests

Publishers designed educational achievement tests to measure the academic success of students in the elementary schools and high schools. They developed other tests to assess those high-school graduates who were vying for admission to selective institutions of higher education. For obvious reasons, parents held high-school administrators and teachers responsible for their children's performance on these critical examinations. The parents also had high expectations for the vocational educators who were preparing students to take the tests that determined admission to competitive apprenticeships and training schools.

In an early book on industrial and vocational psychology, Münsterberg (1913) had chided his fellow psychologists for "slowly and reluctantly" approaching "the apparently n atural task of rendering useful service to practical life" (p. 4). Münsterberg identified vocational analysis and guidance as two ideal and preeminently useful applications for the new science of psychology. Despite Münsterberg's criticism, vocational and industrial psychologists had been influential during the early decades of the twentieth century. Quite predictably, the emergence of their profession had paralleled that of vocational education, which had grown so dramatically during World War I (Giordano, 2004). The wartime contributions of industrial and vocational psychologists were recognized widely after they devised tests for assigning soldiers to military vocations.

Once the war had ended, some vocational educators predicted that the civilian market for vocational tests would expand. As just one example, Bingham (1919) observed that "of the improvements in personnel technique, which has emerged from Army experience, perhaps no phase has greater promise of worth for industry than the development of standardized trade tests" (p. 2). Publishers agreed with this forecast. Patterning vocational tests after those that the Army had used, they assembled massive inventories of products. Once employers, parents, and the public had expressed their confidence in vocational tests, the publishers anticipated that this market would remain healthy.

Even during the period prior to World War I, some psychologists and educators had seen opportunities for employers to use tests. Cattell (1905) had written that the role of the psychologist was "to devise and apply the best methods of determining fitness." He predicted that this expansive approach to psychology "will probably represent at the close of this century as important a profession as medicine, law or the church" (p. 369). Although he was not concerned about psychological testing, Frederick Winslow Taylor may have done more than any other professional to predispose employers toward vocational tests. In his classic 1911 book, *The Principles of Scientific Management*, Taylor (1998) had articulated a philosophy of "maximum prosperity" characterized by "large dividends for the company" and "development of the business to its highest state of excellence" (p. 1). A key corollary of Taylor's approach was "the development of each man to his state of maximum efficiency, so that he may be able to do, generally speaking, the highest grade of work for which his natural abilities fit him, and it further means giving him, when possible, this class of work to do."

As Taylor's philosophy became more popular, persons began to demand that schools implement it. Irrespective of the applicability of the entire "maximum prosperity" paradigm to educational programs, vocational testing had an obvious role to play. This connection was evident to Walter Dill Scott, the psychologist who had supervised much of the military's research on vocational testing during World War I. Before the United States had entered that war, Scott (1916) described the dysfunctional models of recruitment and promotion that industry and commerce were using.

> Historically it has been the practice of many commercial and industrial organizations to recuperate their forces of employees by the employment of young boys and girls as helpers for menial service. The wages paid these employees were small and no careful selection was deemed essential....Promotion from the ranks was insisted upon in many instances even though no attention was given to preparation for such promotions. The children who accepted such positions were frequently those who had already failed in school....The ranks were, therefore, filled by many who had already proved themselves to be incompetents. No attempt was made to make the most of this defective native ability and yet the executive assumed that the higher positions must be filled by recruits from this untrained group of intellectual weaklings. (p. 182)

As an alternative to the prevalent but "absurd method" that he had described, Scott suggested that employers select their workers through "quantitative determinations." Hiring decisions would involve data about an applicant's previous employment, personality, physical condition, intelligence, and vocational skills. He described a role-playing activity that illustrated how this procedure could be implemented when evaluating persons for sales positions.

> In a Room A is a merchant who is to be regarded as a "buyer." You are to enter Room A, introduce yourself to Merchant A, and try to sell him some kind of merchandise. You will spend five minutes with Mr. A, then pass on to Room B and repeat your selling talk to Merchant B. You will keep this up till you have called on all the "buyers." You may sell any line of merchandise....Present your merchandise for five minutes in such a way that the "buyer" will actually want to purchase your line. Sell as you would if the "buyer" were a real prospective. (pp. 191–192)

Thorndike (1920b) used Taylor's philosophy to establish a rationale for vocational testing. He wrote that "both the employer and the employee gain in proportion as men work at a job for which they are more fit than any other men are, as each man is given the job for which he is better fitted than for any other job" (p. ix). He continued that "if sufficient ability and effort are expended it is possible to measure the comparative fitness of any number of men for any one given job, or the comparative fitness of any one man for any number of different jobs." Six years later, Burtt (1926) concurred that "we should consider the capacities and the interests of the man and attempt to adapt him to his work and adapt the work to him so that that unit will be of maximum effectiveness" (p. 508). Although Burtt conceded that efficiency "should not be achieved at the expense of happiness," he soberly added that "nor should happiness be obtained at the expense of efficiency."

Looking back on the vocational assessments that were conducted during World War I, Scott and Clothier (1949) described the screening of more than 1,000,000 men, who then "could use their special abilities in a degree that would have been impossible otherwise" (p. ix). They highlighted this accomplishment so that their readers would "acknowledge the contributions of the men," recognize that "while the work in the Army was far from perfect...it was done better than ever before under such emergency conditions," realize that this work "did much to formulate certain of the basic principles underlying personnel work in industry," and appreciate the fact that this effort "provided an unprecedented stimulus to American employers to study the adaptation of these principles to the personnel problems of industry" (p. ix).

Employers were not the only group that was impressed with the military's vocational assessment programs during World War I. Educators also were impressed. They quickly recognized that the vocational tests being administered to soldiers could be just as appropriate for students in high school. In the introduction to a book about educational assessment, Cubberley (1918) judged that intelligence testing, which already was being used to assign students to appropriate scholastic levels, was "also certain to play an important part in educational and vocational guidance" (p. vii). Cutten (1922) made an even more ambitious prediction. He wrote that "when the tests for vocational guidance are completed and developed, each boy and girl in school will be assigned to the vocation for which he is fitted, and, presuming that the tests are really efficient, he will in the future not attempt any work too advanced for this ability and hence make a failure of it" (p. 480). He added that "neither will he be found in any occupation too elementary for his ability and hence be dissatisfied."

Fryer (1922) agreed with Cutten. He wrote that intelligence could limit a person from achieving appropriate employment goals under two different circumstances. For example, this could happen when the person was "attempting to succeed in an occupation demanding greater intellectual capacity than is his." Intelligence also could restrict productivity when the person "is in an occupation which fails to make sufficient demands upon his intellectual capacity to keep him interested and at work" (p. 273). Relying on the research that had been conducted by military psychologists, Fryer hoped that intelligence tests would identify the careers at which persons would succeed. These careers could be sorted into levels such as "professional work with very high educational…standards," "professional work with slightly lower educational…standards," "technical work," "skilled mechanical work of [a] concrete nature," "skilled mechanical work demanding some occupational skill," and "manual work demanding no skill" (p. 274).

The demonstrated industrial value of Frederick Winslow Taylor's philosophy and the evidence of the Army's success with its World War I testing program had convinced many persons that vocational assessment was viable. Some popular authors attempted to articulate additional supportive arguments. In the most original presentation, Wiggam (1922) developed a new set of commandments to replace the original 10 recorded in the Bible. One of his commandments recognized a responsibility to support vocational education. He discursively elaborated that "civilization has always failed, because it has never succeeded in fitting each and every man to its new form of evolution" (p. 649). He continued that "for this reason vocational education must discover every human worth and fit the individual possessing it to an ever-widening and more complex environment, which the increasingly intelligent descendants of such a scientific social order are certain, from their inborn excellence, to build." Haller (1963) later looked back on Wiggam's referral to "inborn excellence" as an indication of the extreme racism that Wiggam had propagated in his other writings.

In contrast to the bizarre arguments that Wiggam made to support vocational assessment, Yerkes (1923b) devised one that was extremely pragmatic. He pointed out that choices about careers, if they were not guided by "adequate knowledge of the traits and capacities of the self, and on the demands, requirements, and the opportunities of different classes of occupation," would be "left to the wish or whim of parent, guardian or self, to necessity, or to ease and openness of road" (p. 370). Using the same logical strategy, other critics of traditional educational practices endorsed those scholastic reforms that purported to help students acquire useful skills. The writers of a report from the Carnegie Foundation for the Advancement of Teaching expressed this position when they pointed out that "in no country in the world does so large a proportion of the energy of the teaching profession devote itself to the tedious task of lifting ill-prepared children and youth through courses of study from which they gain little or no good" (passage from a Report of the Carnegie Foundation for the Advancement of Teaching, 1923, quoted in "Fundamentals in Education," 1923, p. 57). The editorialist who had cited the Carnegie Report noted that recently "the growth of the high school [*sic*] population has increased a thousand-fold" because of the retention of students who previously had been dropping out of school to work in farming or industry. Moreover, many of the new students were immigrants who did not or could not aspire to a college education. If vocational education were not available, what other portions of the curriculum would be left for this segment of the burgeoning high-school population?

Testing for General Vocational Aptitude

Hollingworth (1915) saluted those employers who had abandoned "primitive magic, medieval clairvoyance, phrenology and physiognomics" and turned to specialized vocational tests to hire workers. Nonetheless, Hollingworth reminded employers that these instruments, even though they might eventually become highly scientific, were "still in process of trial." Because the early vocational assessment products were tenuous, many of the test developers designed these instruments so that they would apply to the largest possible market. As an example, Kemble (1917) proposed a set of examinations that he redundantly entitled "standard tests for testing employees." One of his exams, a measure of "thought speed," required examinees to answer as many "easy questions" as they could during a 30-minute trial. Kemble thought this test could be used to screen persons for any job that required "constant and quick decisions." The first 10 questions on the test are listed.

> Give the name of any vegetable.
> Give the name of any metal.
> Give the name of any insect.
> Give the name of any reptile.
> Give the name of any fish.
> Give the name of any man.
> Give the name of any woman.
> Give the name of any ocean.
> Give the name of any lake.
> Give the name of any town. (p. 22)

Kemble also referred to the ergograph, a mechanical device illustrated in Figure 4.4. This piece of equipment provided an additional measure of general vocational aptitude.

> The ergograph is used for fatigue tests. The arm and fingers are strapped in a certain position and the fingers pull a weight up by repeated operations, the action being recorded by waving lines on the cylinder shown. As fatigue increases, the waves become larger. This test is theoretically useful where continuous pulling operations are liable to fatigue the hand. (p. 214)

The Stoelting Company had devised the ergograph. Kemble referred to another assessment device that this company had manufactured. Depicted in Figure 4.5, this second instrument comprised tools and devices with which students interacted. The students' facility at the respective tasks revealed their

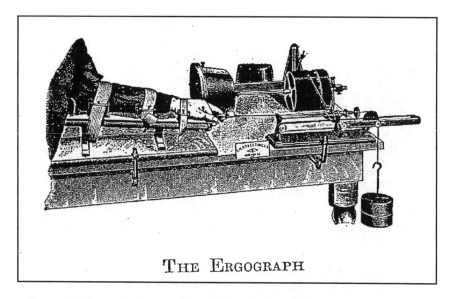

THE ERGOGRAPH

Figure 4.4 Device for Measuring General Vocational Aptitude. (*"The Ergograph." Stoelting Company. Reprinted by permission of the publisher. All rights reserved.*)

aptitude for mechanical, technical, and applied types of work. Figure 4.6 indicates a comparable test that the Stoelting Company developed for females. This alternative test assessed aptitude for the types of applied tasks that female workers were likely to encounter.

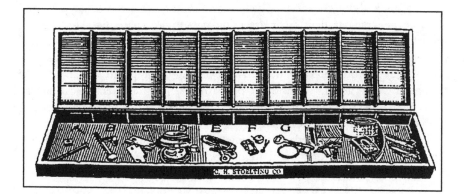

Figure 4.5 Instruments for Assessing Specialized Vocational Skills. (*"Stenquist assembling test of general mechanical ability." Copyright 1923, the Stoelting Co., 620 Wheat Lane, Wood Dale, Illinois 60191. All rights reserved. Reproduction by permission.*)

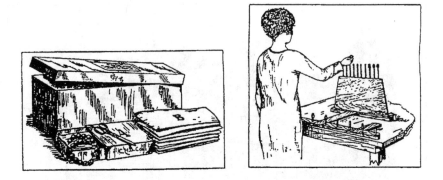

Figure 4.6 Devices for Assessing Skills of Female Workers (*Copyright 1923, the Stoelting Co., 620 Wheat Lane, Wood Dale, Illinois 60191. All rights reserved. Reproduced by permission.*)

Robinson (1919) referred to devices such as the preceding ones as instruments that could analyze trade ability. He explained that trade ability did not "refer to occupations mainly concerned with the exchange of goods, but rather to occupations, emphasizing an acquired facility in the use of certain tools, instruments and machines for the achievement of certain classes of physical results" (p. 353). He referred to the skills of carpenters or interior wirers as trade skills that characterized "all men skilled in a given trade and marking them off as a single group." He differentiated trade skills from the "very simple and oft repeated" actions and the "ordinations typical of the operation of much standardized factory machinery."

In a book about vocational psychology, Hollingworth (1919) gave examples of three general paradigms for assessing persons' preparedness to engage in specialized forms of work. One of these paradigms was the "method of the vocational miniature" in which "the entire work, or some selected and important part of it, is reproduced on a small scale by using toy apparatus or in some way duplicating the actual situation" (pp. 109–110). The mechanical aptitude assessment kits depicted in Figure 4.5 and Figure 4.6 clearly represent this approach to vocational assessment.

Viteles (1925) described another ingenious assessment device that illustrated the "method of the vocational miniature." The apparatus consisted of two motorized conveyor belts. A marker indicating a pedestrian was attached to one of these belts. A marker representing a streetcar was attached to the other belt. The belt with the pedestrian moved at speeds that were variable and that the examinee could not control. The belt with the car moved at speeds that the tested individual could control. A person who aspired to be a streetcar motorman was to demonstrate an ability to judge the effects of distance and time. Viteles explained that "the subject controls the movement of the marker representing the street car (which is activated by a motor) and is required to speed it up as fast as possible and at the same time prevent the two markers from colliding" (p. 108).

Hollingworth's second paradigm for vocational testing was "taking an actual piece of the work to be performed and sampling the candidate's ability by his success in this trial" (Hollingworth, 1919, p. 110). Burtt (1926) described two civil service examinations that had this feature. He wrote of an agency that had "developed various tests…for mail distributor, in which they classify names of cities according to various boxes or have to discriminate specimens of rather illegible handwriting" (p. 495). He continued that "tests for policemen have likewise been developed embodying such things as ability to evaluate evidence, the significance attached to different acts, and judgments as to the action an officer should take in a particular situation."

Hollingworth's third assessment paradigm embodied a task in which "the attitude and endeavor of the worker seem to be much the same" as in the vocational work for which the tested person was being assessed. He gave several examples of general tests that demonstrated this approach and that were "slowly being correlated with various types of occupational activity." One of these instruments was the *Following Instruc tions Test*, the first portion of which is illustrated.

> With your pencil make a dot over any one of these letters, F G H I J, and a comma after the longest of these three words: BOY MOTHER GIRL. Then, if Christmas comes in March, make a cross right here _____, but if not, pass along to the next question, and tell where the sun rises _____. If you believe that Edison discovered America, cross out what you just wrote, but if it was someone else, put in a number to complete this sentence: "A horse has _____ feet." Write "yes," no matter whether China is in Africa or not _____; and then give a wrong answer to this question: "How many days are there in the week?" _____. Write any letter except G just after this comma, and then write "No" if two times five are ten _____. (Hollingworth, 1919, pp. 296–297)

Snow (1926) developed tests to reveal prospective chauffeurs' reactions to automobile accidents. Some of these tests, such as that which measured emotional stability, made it "necessary to devise some artificial test." In other words, this particular test relied on Hollingworth's third assessment paradigm. Snow conceded that "persons may ask how we know that the emotional stability test really tests emotional stability….[and] the answer is, of course, that we do not know." However, he immediately added that "we do know that these tests show a high degree of correlation…[and] do *accomplish the purpose for which they were intended*, and after all, that is what is important" (p. 37).

Anderson (1921) recounted still another method for indirectly assessing vocational aptitude. He reported that some employers were using photographs of job seekers as aids in determining the applicants' intelligence. To confirm the validity of this approach, he conducted an experiment in which he gave employers photos of individuals who were either executives or menial workers within an actual company. Without revealing the official positions of the photographed individuals, he asked the employers to discern the jobs for which these persons were suited. After the employers failed at this task, Anderson concluded that "selecting employees by a study of photographs would be a very haphazard way of selection" (p. 155).

Chapman (1921) also reviewed a vocational test that involved photographs. However, in this test, the applicants for jobs were given the photographs. These applicants were handed ten portraits, each with a name beneath it. Figure 4.7 contains the initial set of pictures with which they were provided. It also contains the altered display that they were given after a two-minute study period. The instructions that accompanied the initial set of photographs described the performance that was required with the second set.

> When you look at the next page you will see ten photographs with names attached. You will be given two minutes to memorize the names as connected with the faces. At the end of two minutes you are to turn to the following page where you will find the same faces but in different rotation. Write as many names as you remember on the margins above and below the faces. (p. 28)

Chapman explained that "this test has proved of little significance for ordinary clerks or executives; but it is of importance for hotel clerks, waiters, and salesmen" (p. 31).

Hull (1928) judged that general tests rather than those specific to certain careers had become the chief means for estimating vocational aptitude. He summarized the different types of tests on which employers and school personnel were relying.

> These tests range through tests of the higher mental processes, such as reasoning and ability to learn; tests of character and temperamental traits; tests of sensory acuity; tests of motor speed, coördination [sic], and strength; tests of physiological traits, such as basal metabolism; chemical tests of the bodily secretions, such as of the blood and the saliva; etc. Though not tests, properly speaking, there may be included in the list of the aptitude psychologist's resources the determination of the various anatomical dimensions and proportions, past environmental conditions of the subject, and even the behavior and achievements of his ancestors. (p. 2)

Testing for Specialized Vocational Aptitude

Hull (1928) believed that vocational aptitude testing was similar to medicine and engineering in that it was "ceasing to be a job for amateurs and is becoming the work of technically trained professionals." After noting the tremendous growth

Figure 4.7 Testing Recall of Names and Faces

in the number of general tests for vocational aptitude, he observed that the number of assessment instruments that had been paired with specific jobs was "already very extensive" and "rapidly increasing." He identified a "partial list" that included 31 different occupations in which specialized tests were being used. This list included prison guards, retail salesmen, department-store cashiers, restaurant waitresses, telephone operators, business executives, office boys, messenger boys, general clerks, and musicians.

While listing the many specialized tests that were available, Hull highlighted those for evaluating office workers. Kornhauser and Kingsbury (1924) had made a similar observation four years earlier. They also gave advice about a simple procedure with which to validate any business test. The procedure required that a test be administered to workers "whose ability in the job is already known." The administrators would then determine "if the test scores agree sufficiently closely with the known ability of the persons tested" (p. 45). They identified the *National Business Ability Tests* as a set of instruments that had met this standard. Stressing that only those parts of these tests that were appropriate for a specific job were to be administered by employers, they listed the multiple parts from which they might choose.

> The applicant must tabulate items according to certain somewhat complicated conditions....memorize and later reproduce some detailed instructions concerning the use of sales slips....fill in some sales slips in accordance with instructions and facts given....[be] tested in the fundamental arithmetical operations....[employ] business arithmetic....[complete] tests in English....and letter writing....[complete] stenographic tests....[complete a] test on copying for the mimeograph....[and complete a] test on addressing envelopes with a pen, and on filing. (p. 85)

As an indication of the degree to which employers were relying on standardized tests when hiring office workers, Thurstone (1919a) estimated that one of the early clerical tests had been administered to over 5,000 job applicants.

Book (1924) provided another indication of the popularity of clerical tests. Within his study of typists, he gave an historical overview of the many "tests previously devised for selecting typists and learners of typewriting" (p. 283). As a part of this study, he wished to identify the most accurate measures of typing success. He therefore attended the 1923 International Typewriting Contest, where he persuaded elite typists to participate in several experiments. Incidentally, he discovered that "the world's champion typists possess an exceptionally high degree of voluntary motor control" and that "this same superiority…is found…in almost direct proportion to the skill in typing which each displayed" (p. 305).

Martin (1923) described an aptitude test for policemen that relied heavily on the examinees' corollary experiences. He noted that those applicants who had served in the armed forces had a "tremendous advantage" because of the automatic examination points they were awarded on civil service exams. Objecting that "this provision has not demonstrated relation to the candidate's fitness for police work," Martin proposed "a method to show the relationship between previous occupation and success in police work" (p. 392). He suggested that all applicants receive scores that ranged from one to seven points, depending on the suitability of their previous employment. Without providing any rationale, he suggested that a guard receive a single point, a roofer two points, and a corset cutter three points. A chauffeur was to be granted four points while a bartender would be given five. Salespersons received six points and journalists received the maximum credit of seven points.

Many of the specialized vocational tests were designed for oral administration to a single person. Chapman and Toops (1919) wrote that the "Army Trade Test Division was, on *a priori* grounds, extremely skeptical of written trade examinations" and that, as a consequence, oral tests had been employed. Figure 4.8 is a portion of the World War I military test that was given to soldiers who aspired to be electricians. Figure 4.9 and Figure 4.10 are sections of other highly specialized oral tests. They were respectively intended to help the military identify typewriter repairpersons and lathe operators.

Chapman and Toops (1919) preferred written tests. They thought that written tests reduced examination time, eliminated subjective judgments, decreased the scoring effort, and rapidly eliminated the "bluffers" who otherwise would consume a disproportionate amount of attention. They gave an example of a written test for bricklayers. Five of the 62 multiple-choice items from this test are listed.

1. The top course of stone on a wall is called: coping, bond-stone, clip-course, capstone.
2. A brick set on end is called: upright, soldier, rowlock, stud.
3. Before plumbing up a corner, one should lay: 3-courses, 6-courses, 9-courses, 12 courses.
4. A brick that is set on the narrow edge is called: stretcher, oarlock, rowlock, header.
5. In coming to a height, if there is a course of brick difference in the level, you would call it a: haunch, filler, line-level, hog. (p. 359)

Both the oral and written specialized trade tests were popular. This popularity was revealed by the advertisements in educational and vocational journals. Figure 4.11, which is an advertisement for vocational tests and the materials associated with them, was printed in the back of a World War I era textbook about vocational assessment (Kemble, 1917).

Bibliographies of tests provided another indication of the popularity of specialized trade tests. For example, these bibliographies showed the number of specialized vocational instruments that were developed during the 1920s and 1930s. Ruch (1929) identified 41 vocational tests that had been devised and published by the Bureau of Public Personnel Administration. These tests included exams for prison guards, hospital attendants, janitors, road inspectors, probation officers, steam firemen, food inspectors, and blacksmiths. Hildreth (1933) developed an extensive bibliography of tests in which she included an 18-page

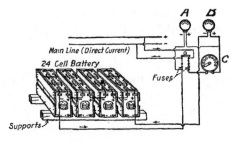

1. Q. What is being done in that picture?
   A. Charging.

2. Q. What is at " A "?
   A. Voltmeter. (Note: "Voltmeter or ammeter" is wrong.)

3. Q. What is at " B "?
   A. Ammeter. (Note: "Voltmeter or ammeter" is wrong.)

4. Q. What is at " C "?
   A. (1) Rheostat.
      (2) Resistance.

(One sufficient)

(Note: "Starting box" or "Controller" is wrong.)

PICTURE 2

5. Q. What is that apparatus used for?

   A. Burning.

6. Q. What is supplied at " A "?

   A. (1) Gas.
      (2) Hydrogen.

(One sufficient)

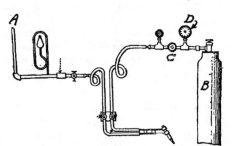

7. Q. What is in the tank at " B "?

   A. (1) Oxygen.
      (2) Air.

(One sufficient)

8. Q. What is at " D "?

   A. (1) Pressure gauge.
      (2) Pressure meter.
      (3) Pressure indicator.

(One sufficient)

(Note: "Pressure regulator" is wrong.)

Figure 4.8 World War I Exam for Electricians

QUESTION 1

Q. How are the feed rolls cleaned?
A. Alcohol.   Score 4

QUESTION 2

Q. How many feed rolls are there on a Remington No. 10?
A. 6.   Score 4

QUESTION 3

Q. How many column selector keys are there on a Remington No. 10?
A. 5.   Score 4

QUESTION 4

Q. What do you use to bend a type bar?
A. A nine-prongs.   Score 4

QUESTION 5

Q. What would be the result if the teeth on the rack would not mesh
   with pinion wheel?
A Skipping (jumping) (wrong spacing).   Score 4

QUESTION 6

Q. How are bell cranks fastened to the segment?
A. Screws.   Score 4

QUESTION 7

Q. How is type fastened to type bars on a Remington No. 10?
A. (1) Pressed in (forced in).   Score 4
   (2) Squeezed in.   Score 4

QUESTION 8

Q. Name the different standard lengths of carriages on a Remington
   No. 10.
A. (1) a. A ($7\frac{1}{2}$) (76 pica).   Score 4
       b. B ($9\frac{1}{2}$) (95 pica).
       c. C (12) (120 pica).
       d. D (16) (160 pica).

QUESTION 9

Q. What are <u>metal</u> platens made of?
A. Brass.   Score 4

QUESTION 10

Q. What mechanism is inside of the governor cup?
A. (1) a. Fan (propeller) (paddle).   Score 4
       b. Graphite.
       c. Shot.

Figure 4.9 World War I Exam for Typewriter Repairpersons

TEST EQUIPMENT

Equipment:

1 Cast iron surface plate $7 \times 7\frac{1}{2}$ inches, weight approximately 10 lbs.

1 Cadillac steering spindle.[2]

Tools:

1 6 inch Outside spring caliper, Brown & Sharpe No. 806.

1 6 inch Inside spring caliper, Brown & Sharpe No. 807.

1 9 inch Combination square.

1 o to 1 inch micrometer caliper with ratchet stop.

1 1 to 2 inch micrometer caliper with ratchet stop.

1 Pencil.

INSTRUCTIONS TO THE EXAMINER

1. Make certain that the TEST EQUIPMENT is complete and ready for the test.

2. Hand the candidate blue-print 6-L, No. 1.

INSTRUCTIONS TO THE CANDIDATE

1. Say to the candidate: "Look at the instructions on this blue-print while I read them." Read distinctly and slowly all legends and measurements. Point to each thing as you read it.

2. Say to the candidate: "Are there any questions?"

3. Repeat, if necessary, all or any part of the instructions on the blue-print. Do not change them in any way.

4. Answer any questions the candidate may ask during the test by repeating the instructions on the blue-print.

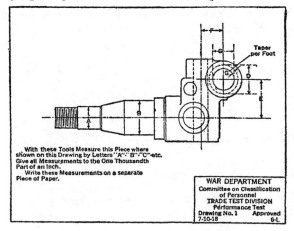

Figure 4.10 World War I Exam for Lathe Operators

No. 1.   TESTS FOR CLERKS AND EXECUTIVES
          (Pamphlet containing twenty-two tests outlined
          in Chapter II.)   One dozen, $1.50; 100, $10.00;
          1,000, $80.00.
No. 2.   TESTS FOR CLERKS AND EXECUTIVES
          (To replace No. 1.   Gives another set of questions
          of the same character.)   One dozen, $1.50; 100,
          $10.00; 1,000, $80.00.
No. 10.   STANDARD INDEX CARD (page 52).
          On Paper: 100, $2.00; 1,000, $17.50.   On Card:
          100, $3.00; 1,000, $25.00.
No. 11.   SELLING TALK AND SELLING METHOD TEST (pp. 332,
          333)
          One Dozen, 50 cents; 100, $2.50; 1,000, $10.00.
No. 12.   EXPERT MACHINIST TEST (p. 324)
          One Dozen, 50 cents; 100, $2.50; 1,000, $10.00.
No. 13.   HUMAN INTEREST TEST (p. 327)
          One Dozen, 50 cents; 100, $2.50; 1,000, $10.00.

                INDUSTRIAL MANAGEMENT
                 140-142 NASSAU STREET
                       NEW YORK

Figure 4.11 Advertisement for Vocational Tests and Materials

section on vocational assessment. Just six years later, she published a second
edition and added over 100 new vocational tests (Hildreth, 1939). She included
entire sections for tests of general business, clerical work, stenography, typing,
mechanical trades, motorized streetcar operation, truck driving, and manufactur-
ing. Within a five-page section on miscellaneous vocations, she identified 77
additional tests, including those for screening railway switch operators, typesetters
of Russian text, makers of paper bags, goldsmiths, opticians, blueprint readers,
shoemakers, and Bavarian police officers.

The growth in employment-centered tests was synchronized to the expansion
of vocational education. Although they did not list all of the vocational tests that
were available, Newkirk and Greene (1935) did identify those publishers who had
produced "test material likely to be of interest to industrial education students,
teachers, and supervisors" (p. 243). Even after they had eliminated "many of the
important distributors and publishers of tests of more general interest," they still
were able to identify 15 different publishing houses that had assembled significant
inventories of vocational tests.

In the preface to the second edition of his textbook about mental tests, Freeman (1939) candidly acknowledged that he had deleted the chapter on vocational assessment that had been part of the 1926 edition. He explained that the topic had not been omitted because its importance had diminished. To the contrary, vocational testing had "become so elaborate that it warrants a more detailed discussion than can be given in a general text" (p. viii). A 1940 survey (Scott, Clothier, and Spriegel, 1949) of 325 companies provided another indication of vocational assessments' growth. This survey revealed that 66 percent of the companies were using vocational tests to select workers.

Objections to Vocational Tests

After chronicling the success of military testing during World War I, Hull (1928) noted that "the moment that the war was over, there was a mad rush to transfer the testing methods found so useful in the army directly into industry, particularly in employment and personnel work" (p. 18). He described some of the negative reactions to this initiative.

> The attempt was made, often with little or no modification, to use the army tests to forecast aptitudes of the most diverse kinds. The endeavor to use tests designed for this one aptitude, to detect aptitudes of a very different sort, could have but one outcome. The result of this hasty and often ill-advised exploitation of an instrument really useful in its own field was temporary failure and disillusionment. There followed in industry a distinct reaction against aptitude testing. (p. 18)

Ten years after the war, Hull was able to identify an impressive number of vocational tests. Nonetheless, he counseled his audience that "the most accurate method of determining the aptitude of an individual for a vocation or other activity is the test of life itself" (1928, p. 1). A decade later, Taylor and Russell (1939) complimented Hull's prescience. Even though they conceded that employment assessment had continued to expand, they questioned its value. Their skepticism was evident when they challenged test publishers to prove that individuals who were scoring high on vocational tests would not score equally high "with a selective device of no validity" whatsoever.

Many critics had underscored the limitations of vocational testing in the hope of slowing its growth. Link (1920) reported about critics who had dismissed the entire field of vocational psychology because it treated "human nature in a manner altogether too mechanical and the human being too much as if it were a mere automaton to be adjusted and shifted accordingly" (p. 377). He could not resist observing that "now, strange as it may seem, even the manufacturer sometimes adopts a hostile attitude and resents the method of employment psychology on the ground that it is too scientific and too formal for application to human beings."

He pointed to an ironical incident in which an employer had applied "scientific methods to the inspection, classification, and treatment of his material equipment" but then was "satisfied with the application of crude clerical methods to the treatment of his human equipment" (p. 377). Link added that some other employers, who fully understood the value of vocational psychology, still had not implemented it because they thought it was too costly. Still other employers had hesitated because they were intimidated by some of the hermetic features of the new practice.

Some persons rejected vocational tests because they were too detached from real-world job markets. Stenquist (1935) thought this fault was especially apparent during the Great Depress ion. He wrote that "techniques of diagnosis and prediction in the vocational field involve the same basic principles as those in the academic fields...[and] what is worse, they demand also analysis and measurement, not only of the mental and manual traits of the individual but of *vocational opportunities in the world as well*" (p. 435). He added that "in this financial depression it should be unnecessary to emphasize that it is the latter that presents by far the greater difficulty." Two years later, Bingham (1937) offered similar cautions. He urged persons who completed vocational aptitude tests to deliberate carefully before making any decisions on the basis of those tests. He specifically suggested that they consult current data about any career that they might be contemplating. These data could reveal average earnings, job security, opportunities for advancement, career prestige, the ratio of employment opportunities to qualified applicants, and other variables that might influence their vocational decisions.

Summary

Objective academic assessment started out as a minor movement in the schools. Its stature changed during World War I, when the public learned about soldiers' low scores on military tests. C ritics claimed that these failure s, which had originated in the schools, imperiled the security of the nation. They demanded new educational programs that were to be valid ated through systematic testing. Detecting a promising market, publishers developed innovative instruments for a full range of applications.

CHAPTER 5

Early Twentieth-Century Politicians Embrace Testing

[Because] survey after survey has revealed unsuspected inadequacy or inefficiency in American education...both teachers and teaching...have been exposed to severe public censure.
—CALDWELL & COURTIS, 1925

At the beginning of the twentieth century, many politically liberal teachers joined the progressive education movement. Emphasizing individualized, spontaneous, and activity-based approaches to instruction, they opposed those teachers who relied on textbooks and skills-based lessons. Standardized testing became a critical point of dispute between these factions. While the progressive educators depicted standardized testing as elitist and racist, the pro-assessment educational faction saw it as a preeminently useful scientific innovation. Both groups took advantage of this scholastic altercation to advance their ulterior political interests.

Politicizing Assessment of Students

Most early twentieth-century educators did not think of themselves as excessively political. This was certainly the case when Thorndike (1908) tried to determine the cause of student dropout. He purposely avoided divisive rhetoric and confined his observations to the data before him.

> At least 25 of 100 children of the white population of our country who enter school stay only long enough to learn to use, and perform the four operations for integers without serious errors....Only about half have any teaching of consequence concerning the history of their own country or any other or concerning the world's literature, science, or art....The superiority of one city over another in the retention of pupils is apparently caused far more by the nature of the population than by any peculiarities in the curricula or schemes of administration of the schools....One main cause of [student dropout] is incapacity for and lack of interest in the sort of intellectual work demanded by present courses of study. (pp. 9–10)

These remarks did not elicit an emotional retort from the public. One of the reasons that Thorndike's observations did not stir up a greater response may have been the ingenuous manner in which he admitted his own preconceptions. Although the situation about which he reported was far from acceptable, Thorndike was sure that teachers, the methods they employed, their textbooks, the facilities in which they taught, and their system for organizing classroom content were not the exclusive causes of failure. He did not blame teachers, methods, or materials because of his strong conviction that students' own aptitudes and attitudes significantly influenced whether they would learn and the degree to which they would learn.

Another reason that some contemporaries refrained from indicting the schools was their skepticism about the evidence on which these accusations had been made. After all, the primary indications of academic failure were teacher-assigned grades, which had been demonstrated to be notoriously erratic. Johnson (1911) made an observation about grading that was restated with increasing frequency. He remarked that "the amount of time and labor expended by high-school teachers in grading their pupils…is enormous" but that "the value of the results is in no way commensurate with the effort involved" (p. 13). He added that "in general, very little use has been made of these records."

Even though many early twentieth-century educators prioritized pedagogy before politics, the issues that they addressed inevitably had political nuances. Colvin (1912) agreed with other critics that grades were being assigned in an inconsistent and unpredictable fashion. In fact, he thought the "incentive to study" was compromised once students realized that their grades were more or less arbitrary. He warned that "the plain man, the man who has no [educational] theory, but who is responsible for the public schools as a tax-payer and a patron, is demanding…[that] the school system be efficient" (p. 561). Certain that objective tests would become the basis for assigning grades, Colvin wrote with mock eloquence about those teachers who were resisting the new system of assessment.

> [They] consider themselves the true bearers of the torch of learning; they are the inspired ones to whom it is given to see the promised land from the mountain tops; they need not the letter for they have the spirit and this cannot be reduced to a definite form; it can be felt and in a sense comprehended, but never stated in exact terms, nor expressed in measurable ways. (p. 560)

That same year, a New York superintendent (Bliss, 1912) expressed sentiments that were similar to those of Colvin. He warned the readers of the *American School Board Journal* that "unless all signs fail education is entering upon a period during which present ideals will be radically modified or wholly changed" (p. 12). As a specific example of this imminent change, he pointed to the "rightful demand of the public for something in the nature of a balance sheet." He believed that objective tests were a convincing response to this demand. He thought that the tests, which he characterized as "standards of efficiency," could eliminate those problems in which "the estimate of various [exam] papers may be unduly influenced by the personal bias of the examiner" (Bliss, 1912, p. 12).

Courtis (1915a) was the director of educational research for the Detroit public schools. As one would expect, he was a strong proponent of standardized tests. Unlike some other advocates of testing, he recognized the great power of the new instruments. He warned that schoolwide testing could have consequences that went much deeper than school board members and district administrators might envisage. One of these results could be the arousal of "public attention to the fact that there are still many unsolved problems in education" (p. 89). He then made remarks that would resonate well with political conservatives. Using italics to underscore his key points, he noted that "because education *is* so vitally important in the life of the nation, schoolmen everywhere should not be content with simply drawing *attention* to existing defects." Instead, they should "make constructive use of the knowledge gained." Conservatives accepted this challenge as an opportunity to restructure education.

Instead of speculating about the philosophical relationship of tests to school accountability, Clarence Gray (1917) decided to provide an actual demonstration of accountability. He first administered tests so that he could document the extent to which students were learning. After discovering that "certain high-school pupils cannot read with success selections which many fifth-grade pupils read fluently and with understanding," he demanded that the "causes be discovered" (p. 1). Like Thorndike, he thought that a portion of the failures could be attributed to the limited abilities of the students themselves. However, some of the problems had resulted from instructors who had selected inefficient pedagogical approaches. He pointed out that a simple change from an inappropriate to an appropriate instructional approach could sometimes produce a "large change" in learning.

Pressey and Teter (1919) gave multiple examples of situational variables that could influence students' academic learning or their performance on tests. Referring specifically to African American students, they pointed to several environmental factors that might have some bearing on this group's examination scores.

> The unsatisfactory school work of colored [*sic*] children may be, in part at least, merely an indication of lack of adaptation of the schools to their special needs. It may surely be questioned whether tests given by white examiners to colored pupils can give reliable data for a comparison of the races. There may even be some doubt as to whether, with examiners of their own race, the reaction of the colored children to the test situation would be quite the reaction of white children. In any case, the fact must not be forgotten that the colored children come from a social and psychological environment which is subtly but powerfully different from the environment which molds the mentalities of the white children; standards of living, moral and religious ideas, sentiments and interests and ideals, are all pervasively different. (p. 278)

The superintendent of the New York City schools ("Newark System," 1930) made similar observations when he identified factors that were "beyond the control" of instructors but that still influenced educational achievement. As an example, he noted that all children do not mature according to the same chronological schedule and "in the cases of many thousands of children it is a well known fact that their presence in a sixth grade does not prove that they are not possessed of either fourth-grade or eighth-grade ability in a given subject." Some of the other extraneous determinants of learning were "poor racial stock, low mentality, alien tongues, holy days and holidays, ill health, frequent transfers,...lack of balance in the teaching strength of grades,...lack of special classes, lack of shop instruction in the upper grades, cumulative effect of maternity leaves...and failure to provide financial resources to fill normal positions speedily" (Superintendent William Grady, quoted in "Newark System," 1930, p. 409).

Conflict Between Political Conservatives and Liberals

At the end of the nineteenth century, Rice (1896) had written that "in former years I entertained the belief...that the cause of the obstacles to educational progress might be attributed to...politics in school boards, incompetent supervision, [and] insufficient preparation on the part of teachers" (p. 385). However, he had recently changed his mind and come "to the conclusion that these elements are not the ultimate cause of the evil, but constitute only the symptoms." He confided that the true "evil" that was hindering educational reform was the pervasive condition in which "educators themselves cannot come to an agreement in regard to what changes, if any, are desirable or feasible" (p. 386).

Rice had not concealed his scorn for the divisive feuds in which nineteenth-century educators had engaged. Giordano (2000) documented that the bitterness among these early educators anticipated that which their twentieth-century successors would display. When partisan conflicts later surfaced during the twentieth century, they polarized around two groups of educators, those who saw themselves as conservatives and those who professed politically liberal principles. These factions differed on a full range of issues. They supported distinct approaches to classroom instruction, curriculum, and behavior management. They disagreed about the responsibilities of teachers and administrators. They had distinct ideas about selecting learning materials and furnishing classrooms. Even the names that respectively described these two parties conveyed the impression that they viewed society differently. The term *conservative* implied an attempt to maintain the political, social, and economic establishment. Conversely, the term *liberal* connoted a willingness to consider a full range of alternatives to the status quo. Although these depictions of the two groups were generally correct, they did not accurately characterize their respective attitudes toward assessment in the schools. Because objective testing was one of the most intrusive reforms within early twentieth-century schools, contemporaries might have anticipated that the liberals would have been predisposed to it. To the contrary, they opposed it. Meanwhile, the conservatives supported it wholeheartedly.

Political conservatives supported objective testing for several reasons. One of these was that testing had the potential to reassure citizens about the quality of their educational system, which the conservatives viewed as a critical component of the nation's internal security. Ayres (1909) had paraphrased comments by early twentieth-century political conservatives in the opening sentence to his classic book, *Laggards in Our Schools*. He wrote that "during the past decade it has been increasingly realized that the education of children who are defective in body, mind, or morals is a matter of great importance to the future of the state" (p. xiii). Giordano (2000) provided citations from the numerous other critics who had made comparable warnings. Although such forebodings initially seemed speculative, they became credible after war emerged in Europe. Once the United States had joined the combat, the public recognized that a new era of warfare required home-front as well as battlefront contributions. Politicians demanded that the schools assume a critical role in the home-front campaign.

Giordano (2004) described the skill with which political conservatives lobbied for wartime educational reforms. These reforms, which included a renewed emphasis on basic academic skills, seemed especially urgent in view of servicemen's dismal performance on military intelligence tests. Other World War I scholastic issues that the conservatives addressed were foreign-language instruction, pre-induction training, nationalistic textbooks, vocational education, patriotic school activities, the inclusion of international cooperation as a topic in the curriculum, and the acceleration of graduation schedules.

The conservatives cleverly depicted themselves as the champions of educational changes that were current, efficient, and scientific. The rationale for these changes seemed especially persuasive after the conservatives linked them to the nation's war interests. Camp (1917) exclaimed that the conservative educational agenda had given a "jolt" to those school administrators and teachers who dwelled in "the land of steady habits." Political liberals such as John Dewey and his disciples, who had opposed science-based reforms because they conflicted with their own developmental philosophy, suddenly realized that they were being portrayed as de facto academic conservatives. As irritating as they found this turn in the debate, they could not extract themselves from their predicament without sacrificing some of their fundamental principles.

The conservatives would not have advanced their educational agenda so rapidly without the impetus of World War I. Hull (1928) explained that wartime testing attracted unprecedented attention because it was executed on a massive scale and "carried out...during intense public interest in everything pertaining to military affairs" (p. 18). He concluded that these conditions, as well as the public's impression that testing was useful and successful, gave testing "enormous publicity and prestige." Irrespective of their wartime agenda, the conservatives were predisposed toward objective testing. Two of their perennial educational goals had been the detection and elimination of scholastic inefficiency. Stone (1908) had hoped that a new generation of researchers would carefully examine "the relation between distinctive educational procedures and the resulting products" (p. 7). Looking back at the period during which Stone was writing, Caldwell and Courtis (1925) reported that "survey after survey has revealed unsuspected inadequacy or inefficiency in American education" and that "both teachers and teaching accordingly have been exposed to severe public censure" (p. v).

Politicizing Assessment of Teachers

The modern era of instructor assessment began when states decided to regulate teaching. Vold (1985) recounted some of the events that transpired after the Ohio legislature of 1825 required that teachers be examined and certified by county-appointed boards. Because of the way in which this regulation was crafted and the manner in which the responsibilities for enforcing it were assigned, it is likely that political factors were introduced each time the members of examination boards were appointed or aspiring teachers summoned before those boards. Unable to eliminate the bi ases demonstrated by county-regulated teacher credentialing boards, state governments eventually assumed their responsibilities. This shift had been evident in an 1899 Alabama law.

> A state board of examiners has been constituted which prepared all questions for the examination of teachers throughout the state. Two regular examinations are to be held each year, and on the same days throughout the state. Special examinations may be given in Montgomery and at the normal schools only. All teachers, not teaching in cities of two thousand or more inhabitants, are required to take this examination, even graduates of the Alabama normal schools not being exempt. A fee of from one to three dollars must be paid by every applicant, varying with the grade of certificate desired. The members of the state board of examiners are each to be paid "five dollars per day, including Sundays, for the time they are engaged in conducting the examinations." Certificates are issued by the secretary of the state examinations. Certificates are issued by the secretary of the state board of examiners to those who pass, and these certificates "entitle the holder to teach in the public schools of any county in this state for the following period of time: a third-grade certificate, two years; a second-grade certificate, four years; and a first-grade certificate, six years." No teacher shall be granted a second-grade certificate more than twice, and when a teacher has taught ten years on a first-grade certificate, it may become a life certificate. (Cubberley, 1906, p. 48)

Two years before this Alabama law had been enacted, Rice (1897a) had examined the issue of instructional competence from a distinct perspective. Wishing to determine "what results may reasonably be expected at the end of a given period of instruction," Rice had focused his attention on teachers and the "results the more successful ones had been able to obtain" (p. 163). Because of his strong conviction that "nothing can take the place of that personal power which distinguishes the successful from the unsuccessful teacher," he recommended that academic reform "efforts should be primarily directed toward supplying our schools with competent teachers" (1897b, p. 419).

Although Rice resisted the opportunity to politicize teacher evaluation, some of his early twentieth-century colleagues showed less restraint. Strayer (1911), a professor of educational administration at Teachers College, enunciated a simple dictum with which few of his peers were likely to disagree. He wrote that "efficiency in any line of human endeavor depends upon our ability to evaluate the results which are secured" (p. 3). He was sure that an assessment of the educational system would demonstrate its overall efficiency. Even though he was confident about the general result of an evaluation, he was not sure that recent educational progress would turn out to be in proportion to the money that had been spent on it. He added that he also worried about "the effort and devotion of those who have engaged in teaching." Two years later, he published another article (Strayer, 1913) in which he instructed readers that it had become possible to evaluate teachers with "scientific accuracy." Expropriating some of the contemporary arguments about teachers who were grading students subjectively, he reasoned that superintendents might be replicating the errors of these teachers. This would be the case if superintendents were evaluating their teachers subjectively. Strayer lectured educational administrators that subjective teacher evaluations were "based upon some prejudice or special interest which has little or no relation to the results actually achieved" (p. 256). He then pointed to an alternative, which was objective teacher evaluation.

Four years later, Bradford (1917) advised her fellow administrators about objective teacher evaluation, which she referred to as the merit system. After dispassionately observing that this new system "is coming to be established," she used anecdotal information to convince readers that this change was as desirable as it was inevitable.

> A man with two daughters about to graduate from the high school of a certain city got himself elected to the school board with the purpose of securing places for these daughters in the school force. This was accomplished, and the man retired to private life. Later when the successor of the preceding superintendent reported against the competency of one of these girls and she was denied a place, the father immediately became again a candidate for the board, this time with the avowed purposed of getting rid of the obnoxious superintendent. (p. 19)

Cubberley (1918) noted that "within recent years a number of personal-estimate scales have been devised by students and superintendents for charting, in visual form, the important characteristics of teachers" and that "practically within the past five years an entirely new series of instruments for estimating teaching efficiency has been made available in the form of the new Standardized Tests" (p. v). He added that "to a superintendent of the drill and memorization and martinet type, a creative and stimulative [*sic*] and original teacher probably would be classed as poor; whereas such a teacher would be highly prized by a superintendent in close sympathy with the creative and expressive tendencies in modern education." Cubberley believed that objective tests of teaching were advantageous to teachers because, otherwise, "against such personal opinion [as that expressed by a biased superintendent] the teacher has had almost no means of defense" (p. v).

Product-Based Assessment

Those persons who supported the objective approach to teacher evaluation had different opinions about how this assessment should be conducted. Haggerty (1916) referred to one superintendent who believed that students' scores on reading tests indicated not only the academic achievement of the students but also the instructional skills of the teachers. Haggerty explained that this superintendent would make "the amount of error of a child missing a particular word relative to the number of times that word has occurred in his reading" and then conclude that any "teacher is less efficient if her pupils miss the more frequently occurring words" (p. 114). Even administrators who did not make this type of assumption were likely to associate students' performance on tests with the competence of teachers. For example, questions about the professional fitness of the teachers in Cleveland must have been difficult to repress after a researcher reported that "in rate of silent reading Cleveland is ahead of thirteen other cities, but behind these cities in ability to interpret what is read" (W. S. Gray, 1917, p. 141). Less than a decade later, Deffenbaugh (1925) sent a survey to administrators of "elementary, junior high, and high schools in cities having a population of 10,000 or more." He discovered that 57 percent of the 215 respondents were using the scores from student achievement tests to make a "comparison with other school systems." Furthermore, 38 percent were using these scores as the basis for "determining comparative efficiency of teachers."

Brooks and Buckingham (1922) endorsed standardized tests to measure "the progress of pupils and to tell when they were ready for promotion." However, they added that "at the same time, we were measuring the ability of the teachers to get results" (p. 69). To illustrate the logic that guided them, they referred to product-based procedures for assessing the efficiency of workers.

> Is it not customary to measure the efficiency of the workman, professional or otherwise, by the amount and quality of the work he turns out? The efficiency of the wood-chopper is gauged by the number of cords of wood he can chop in a definite length of time; of a bricklayer, by the number of bricks he can lay in a day; of a farmer, by the per-acre yield and profit of his crops; of the lawyer, by the percent of cases he wins for his clients; of the doctor, by the proportion of cases he cures. (p. 70)

To make sure that their audience did not miss the political undertones of their message, Brooks and Buckingham emphasized that "experience has set certain standards of achievement in every kind of work" and if a worker "does only three fourths as much as the standard, he is only seventy-five per cent efficient" (1922, p. 70). McAndrew (1920) had relied on popular literature from business to advance the same message. He concluded that, if a principal "doesn't follow up the work of those he is put to supervise he is not doing his duty as a financial manager" and "if he doesn't keep an account of his appraisal of work he is likely...to be a poor business man [*sic*]" (p. 243).

When Brooks and Buckingham (1922) suggested that administrators use teacher productivity to rate their employees, they noted that teachers "of the time-serving variety" displayed a "marked lack of interest" (p. 72). The authors indicated that they initially decided to ignore this group. A year earlier, Brooks (1921), who was a New Hampshire superintendent, had persuaded his school board to pay bonuses of two dollars per week to those teachers whose students were earning high scores on standardized tests. Somewhat unsophisticated about conflict of interest, he concluded that all of the teachers in his district endorsed this plan because none "who failed to get such a raise made any complaint of favoritism" (p. 264). Brooks later did concede that some teachers had made substantive objections to his evaluation scheme.

> Their chief objections were: (1) that knowing they would be judged by the results of the tests, some teachers would be tempted to cheat in giving these tests, thereby perhaps gaining a higher rating than would better and more conscientious teachers who gave the test honestly; (2) that since there are in most schools a sprinkling of mentally deficient or even feeble-minded children who under the most efficient teacher cannot be expected to make normal progress, the records of such pupils, when averaged with those of normal children, would seriously and unjustly lower the rating of the teachers; and (3) that of two teachers of equal ability one might have a school whose pupils averaged so much higher in intelligence than those of the other than she would undeservedly obtain a much higher rating. (Brooks & Buckingham, 1922, p. 72)

Reminiscing about his 1920s appointment as a Texas superintendent, Deck (1932) recalled the skepticism that he had displayed toward the teachers in the Crockett School District. Even though he had been advised "from various sources that the Crockett schools were superior in achievement to most schools of the state," he decided to confirm this claim through standardized testing. He thought this assessment was necessary after some members of the school board had confided "that a few teachers were giving grades to please the pupils or to hold the good will of certain parents" (p. 25). Additionally, "several elderly married women [who] had been teaching for years in the local schools, and [who] resented supervision and changes," had formed high impressions of their pedagogical skills, even though the superintendent's "observation of their teaching did not seem to warrant their good opinion of themselves." Deck hoped that the results of academic tests would "shake the exalted opinion of the high achievements of the schools." At the same time, he hoped that the testing would shield him from "some of the faculty, probably a few school-board members, and a part of the public." He indicated that he had wanted to use the test scores to substantiate his conviction that "the whole school system needed a thorough overhauling" (Deck, 1932, p. 25).

Aware of the many misgivings about teacher productivity ratings, Russell (1926) tried to win teachers over through a philosophical dialogue. He agreed with those educators who believed that "we cannot say that a teacher has any definite percentage of teaching efficiency, as we can measure the development of horse power in a gasoline engine" (p. 4). Russell insisted that "we can, however, through the analysis of a series of tests, say that a teacher is doing better with his pupils than teachers of similar children elsewhere, or as well, or more poorly." Framing his conclusion to show that instructors could benefit from teacher productivity ratings, he wrote that "it becomes possible in this way to increase efficiency by preventing unnecessary repetition of teaching or by providing more clearly for teaching-needs" (Russell, 1926, p. 4).

Many teachers were unimpressed by these arguments. Even those who recognized the strengths of standardized tests worried about concomitant liabilities. These drawbacks were especially disconcerting to teachers who felt that their jobs might be placed in jeopardy by faulty tests. A 1930s article about a convention of the National Educa tion Association ("In Classroom and on Campus," 1932) was subtitled *The Test Dethroned.* The byline for this *New York Times* article explained that "standardized measures of achievement [are] said to have bad effect." The author of the article observed that "standardized tests, those present-day gods of the educational machine, came in for a good many unkind words at the annual convention of the National Education Association" (p. 8).

Content-Based Assessment

Some of the methods for evaluating teachers were modeled after business practices in which an employee's productivity determined whether that individual would receive a positive or negative rating. However, teachers could also be evaluated through an objective test of the content for which they were account-able. In order to determine which methods currently were being used to judge teachers, Boyce (1915) surveyed superintendents in school districts with a general population of at least 10,000 persons. Two hundred and forty-two of the superintendents responded. Of these, only 14 were using "promotional examina-tions." Boyce explained that promotional exams, which were used to "determine the advance of teachers from one salary group to another," consisted "of the earning of credits in college ex tension courses or summer schools, or the presentation of theses on professional problems, or papers reviewing certain professional reading, or they may be regular examinations set on professional or academic subjects" (p. 12). Boyce added that "in most instances the taking of the examinations is optional, but the fact that further increase of salary depends on it is compelling enough" (1915, p. 12).

Eight years after Boyce had reported about the limited use of promotional examinations, Abbott (1923) published a standardized test "of some of the essentials in the preparation of an English teacher." Abbott had made a request to the readers of the *English Journal* to assist him in the identification of the content that should appear on this test. One thousand teachers responded. They helped Abbott develop an exam about vocabulary, the interpretation of poetry, and Shakespearean quotations. They also helped him designate appropriate test content that was related to "child literature, biblical and mythical allusions, books commonly read in school, established classics less common in school, and leading works of contemporary authors" (p. 664). Even though he initially had referred to his test as one that measured "some of the essentials" of the material for which English teachers were responsible, Abbott later waffled on this claim. He indicated that the alleged essentials on his test were actually just the "minimum equipment" for teachers. Effective instructors had to supplement the minimal equipment with the "prime essentials," which he evasively identified as "the kindling imagination, the power of leadership, the personal tact, the idealism, without which all these things that can be measured and standardized are but as ashes in the mouth" (p. 671).

Many of the objective tests for evaluating teachers were developed during the late 1920s and early 1930s. Within her bibliography of tests and scales, Hildreth (1933) listed 23 items within the category of *Achievement Tests to Assess Teachers*. Some of the instruments to which she referred were the *Comprehensive Objective Examination for Graduate Students in Education*, the *Odell Standard Achievement Test on Principles of Teaching in Secondary Schools*, the *Weber Standard Achievement Test on Aims, Purposes, Objectives, Attributes, and Functions in Secondary Education*, the *Aptitude Tests for Elementary and High School Teachers*, the *Teachers' Professional Judgment Test*, and the *Classroom Procedure Test for Rating Teachers of History and the Social Studies*.

Adopting a sophisticated diagnostic perspective, Brueckner (1935) challenged those tests that purported to evaluate teachers but that only measured their knowledge of content information. Convinced that these tests had to be balanced with information about a teacher's knowledge of content-specific pedagogy, he gave detailed examples from mathematics education.

> The teacher may have a very narrow view of the functions of arithmetic instruction and emphasize the computational function to the neglect of the other important objectives; the teacher may lack the technical information required by the arithmetic curriculum that emphasizes an enriched conception of the subject; the teacher may be unskilled in developing number concepts; the teacher may stress speed too much; the teacher may fail to adapt instruction to the varying needs of pupils; when pupils show a low performance on a test, the teacher may assign further practice without attempting to determine the nature of the difficulty that caused the poor work, and thus fix bad habits of work; the teacher may fail to recognize the need of an adequate program for maintaining the skills in arithmetic, which then rapidly deteriorate; the teacher may fail to use legitimate types of motivation of drill work, such as progress charts, rewards, and similar incentives, which experiments have demonstrated contribute significantly to growth in arithmetic; the teacher may fail to teach the pupils efficient, economical methods of work; the practice provided may be poorly distributed and insufficient in amount. (p. 278)

Rating Scales

Instead of requiring teachers to take achievement tests, some superintendents and principals chose to assess instructors with rating scales. Hildreth (1933) identified 50 of these instruments. Some of them were general, such as the *Practical Teacher Rating Card*, the *Teachers' Efficiency Record*, and the *Standards for Judging Teachers*. She also reviewed specialized checklists, such as the *Rating Scale for Shop Teachers*, the *Conduct Scale for the Measurement of Teaching*, the *Score Card for Rural Teachers*, the *Supervisor's Rating Card for Home Economics Teachers*, the *Personality Rating of Prospective Physical Training Teachers*, and the *Scale for Judging Manual Arts Teachers*.

The Committee of Southern Educators (1921) reported that "the first definite attempt to reach a scientific estimate of the relative values of the various qualities of merit in teachers was made by E. C. Elliott, of the University of Wisconsin, in 1910" (p. 44). The committee members noted that Elliott had assigned numerical values to the traits on which "rating officials" were to evaluate teachers. His traits included "the results of teaching" as well as "physical, moral, executive, professional, projective, and social qualities." The committee members then contrasted the features on Elliott's rating scale with those on a scale that Ruediger and Strayer had developed later that year. The latter researchers had recommended that supervisors pay attention to "educational qualifications, number of years of teaching experience, general teaching merit, health, initiative, personality, teaching skill, ability to carry out suggestions, accord between teacher and pupil, progressive scholarship, and social factors outside the classroom" (Ruediger & Strayer, 1910, as paraphrased by the Committee of Southern Educators,1921, p. 44).

Witham (1914) conducted a survey of "fifty prominent school men including superintendents, college presidents, college professors of education, teachers and normal and high school principals, from Maine to California" (p. 268). He asked them to identify the percentage of school success attributable to teachers. Because the average estimate was 60 percent, he took this as a confirmation of the teacher's central role in the educational process. Witham then proposed to measure teachers with a 46-trait scale. Lacking the facility to coin succinct titles, he called his instrument the "Measuring Scale for Teacher Measurement." The first five traits Witham listed were morals, leadership, personality, personal appearance, and ideals. Next to each trait he placed three descriptive phrases to denote superior, average, and deficient teachers. For example, superior personal appearance was indicated by attire that was "commanding but without pomp." The teacher with average personal appearance was "clean but inclined to neglect the charm of good dress." The inferior teacher was "untidy" and "undignified." Witham boasted that this rating scale would help "the reduction of guess work in the important function of rating teachers" (p. 267).

Writing just three years later, Landsittel (1917) was more business-like when he developed his "Inspector's Score Card." He gave supervisors an opportunity to distribute up to 1000 points on his card. The points were to be divided within five areas: personality, scholarship, teaching methods, pupil reactions, and room conditions. Twiss (1919) also gave supervisors the chance to assign 1000 points on a performance score card. Although he retained Landsittel's five categories, he added *cooperation*, which included teachers' interrelationships with their supervisors, colleagues, community leaders, pupils, and the members of educational associations. Two years later, Cook (1921) pointed out the limited extent to which score cards had been adapted. He claimed that the "score card for teachers is not yet in general use." To substantiate this contention, he had sent requests for current teacher rating scales to 100 superintendents. The superintendents were employed by cities with populations of 25,000 to 75,000 persons. Thirty-two of the administrators responded. Cook wrote that "only about 50% of those replying had score cards to furnish, 35% reported none in use, and 15% reported their rating system in a state of formation or revision" (p. 2).

Administrators who relied on their personal intuitions were unsure about the new rating instruments. Those teachers who feared that the instruments could be abused by their political opponents were even less trusting. Despite the many objections to standardized tests, the public insisted that school administrators methodically account for the performance of their instructors. Acknowledging this mandate, Wrinkle (1927) declared that "the fundamental objective of supervision must necessarily be that of raising the levels of teaching efficiency through the improvement of the work of the teacher" (p. 425). He thought that the public's insistence on this matter was quite understandable. He was personally sympathetic to the criticism because of his impression that the "vast majority" of teachers exhibited an "astonishing lack of professional preparation" (p. 425). Believing that these situations provided "overwhelming evidence of the inability of the school to furnish the high quality of teaching which the situation justly warrants," he concluded that educational supervisors had to systematically evaluate their employees.

Wrinkle had specified that the evaluations of instructors were to be conducted by supervisors. His insistence on this point was a reaction to those progressive educators who wanted the teachers to write up their own evaluations. Six years before Wrinkle had made his remarks, Woolley (1921) had rejected the proposal that teachers complete their own rating scales. In fact, he judged that resistance from progressive educators was the chief reason that rating scales had not been implemented more widely. He assumed an avuncular tone as he counseled the recalcitrant teachers to accept an approach to evaluation that was as reasonable as it was scientific.

> We are exhibiting the reverse side of our human nature when we do not accept a rating from above by an administrative office. Yet some of us believe that it is the bitterest medicine that does us the most good, and since we must be judged anyway, why not have it done in a scientific way? (p. 5)

Progressive Educators Defy Objective Tests

While addressing a group of New York schoolmasters, Mitchill (1913) articulated a principle of instruction that must have infuriated any progressive educators who were in the audience. He declared that "the peculiar function of the schoolmaster—the task to be performed that distinguishes him from all others—is to teach, to conduct recitations." Mitchill added that instructors achieved this goal through "force of personality, aided to a greater or less extent by the general tone of school discipline" (pp. 8–9).

Progressive educators disagreed completely with Mitchill. They depicted the child, not the teacher, as the focal point of the classroom. They viewed learning as a student-initiated and developmentally constrained process of discovery for which the instructor was only a facilitator. They opposed the identification of precise learning skills, the organization of information into sequential academic units, the synchronization of instruction to textbooks, the linking of chronological schedules with the mastery of skills, and classroom environments that encouraged deference to the subject matter or the instructor (Giordano, 2000). Because progressive educators opposed the pedagogical approach to which objective tests had been connected, they opposed the tests as well.

Even though they personally resisted objective tests, progressive educators recognized that the public's attitudes on this matter had changed. The public was demanding evidence that students, academic programs, and teachers were meeting explicit expectations. Performance on objective tests had become the most widely accepted evidence of this achievement. The public's shifting attitudes made progressive educators nervous. Their anxiety was evident in some of the remarks that Rugg and Shumaker (1928) made in their book about progressive education. In that book, these authors placed two photographs opposite the title page. One photo showed children scurrying freely about a classroom as they worked on various projects. The other illustration showed students with folded arms as they sat in precisely aligned seats. The first picture was described with the following statements: "Freedom! Pupil initiative! A life of happy intimacy—this is the drawing-out environment of the new school." Rugg and Shumaker described the second photo in quite a different manner: "Eyes front! Arms folded! Sit still! Pay attention! Question-and-answer situations—this was the listening régime." On the basis of these remarks, as well as the fact that one of the authors was a teacher in a famous progressive school, readers should have had no doubt about the philosophical allegiance of Rugg and Shumaker. Nonetheless, the readers probably were surprised when these authors conceded that "the extreme individualism of the [progressive] teachers" had contributed to situations in which "the staff as a team does not plan the whole school curriculum" (p. 315).

Three years later, Shumaker again acknowledged the criticism that was being directed at progressive scholars. She wrote that progressive educators had been "frequently criticized for their failure to test scientifically the propositions on the basis of which they are operating" (Shumaker, 1931, p. 100). This time, she added a retort.

> While it is true that progressive schools have been more interested in formulating these propositions than in testing them, it must also be acknowledged that the kind of testing most research scientists have in mind would fail to measure the outcomes toward which the progressive schools are working....The new schools are establishing larger values than can be indicated by the scientific educational techniques now available. This does not absolve them, however, from the necessity of devising research techniques in terms of new and broad values. (p. 100)

Other progressive educators restated Shumaker's remarks. Ganders (1932) acknowledged allegations that progressive education was "unscientific" and that it had failed to place "emphasis upon measurement of results." However, he shared Shumaker's suspicion that the use of objective measures could lead to the "eviction of the sympathetic and observing eye, the recording hand, and the creative mind" (p. 379). Ganders awaited the "evolution of a new Thorndike or Cattell" who would figure out how to measure the educational traits that progressive educators valued. These traits included "freedom, initiative, intensity of willing, self-mastery, social co-operation, planning, organization and judgment, and the quality of dependent thought" (p. 379). Three years later, Caldwell (1935) still could not identify the visionary scholar who would figure out how to make evaluations that would appeal to progressive educators and simultaneously appease the public. He concluded that "for such appraisal, there have not been available necessary tests or measures." Like Ganders, Caldwell was a progressive educator. Both of these scholars had acknowledged the pressure to devise a system of assessment that could compete with objective testing. Caldwell wrote that "for some years, it has seemed desirable to appraise the results [of progressive educational initiatives] by more accurate and reliable measurements than have appeared in articles and addresses by earnest advocates" (1935, p. iii). He anticipated that these assessment devices would focus on personality, responsiveness, cooperativeness, dependability, and other traits to which the creators of the popular objective tests had been inattentive.

Wrightstone (1935) also wrote of the assessment expectations that had been set for progressive educators. He characterized the failure to demonstrate the "relative value" of progressive educational programs as "one of the controversial problems of education" (p. 3). Although he alleged that "the comparative measurement of certain intellectual factors, dynamic factors, and social performance factors" comprised a "tentative proof of the validity" of progressive education, he conceded the need to develop "tests of an objective nature." These tests eventually would assess "the ability to interpret and generalize from social and scientific data, ability to integrate data from several fields, [and] ability to create original works of art" (p. 116).

Near the end of the decade, some progressive educators still had not relinquished the hope that they could devise convincing educational achievement tests. Brownell (1937) noted that the popular tests on the market were being judged "on the basis of such technical criteria as their validity, reliability, objectivity, adequacy, and the like" (p. 485). He promised readers that he would reveal conceptual criteria that were "fully as important but much less commonly recognized" (p. 485). These conceptual criteria would discredit objective tests and validate the type of assessment to which progressive educators were predisposed. For example, Brownell praised tests that would "enable the teacher to observe and analyze the thought processes which lie back of the pupils' answers." In the unlikely event that the preceding criterion failed to discount any objective tests, Brownell introduced other restrictions that were sure to do the job. He suggested that teachers reject exams that did not "encourage the development of desirable study habits," "lead to improved instructional practise [sic]," and "foster wholesome relationships between teacher and pupils."

Progressive Educators Propose Alternatives

At the very end of the nineteenth century, Todd and Powell (1899) published their classic textbook about an alternative, literature-based approach for teaching reading. In it, they described the amorphous and almost spiritual philosophy that had guided them.

> [Children's literature] is first used as environment, an enriching source from which, or a force by which, interest is stimulated. It lifts the subject in hand into the realm of safe emotional delights. Yet it is at no time intangible; its effects are legitimate and rational, safe yet satisfying. It is next used as a source of knowledge. New knowledge of the subject is secured by use of the very power the subject has itself induced, and becomes a means of refinement, and also a field for drill in fixing forms and correlating memories for further interpreting uses in future school or life work. (p. 128)

The teachers who adopted this philosophy had to fall back on their personal intuitions to assess whether their students were succeeding. Anticipating this difficulty, Todd and Powell had presented their instructional activities with extraordinary specificity. They hoped that this attention to detail would provide the teachers with a common viewpoint from which to make observations. Their thoroughness was evident in a lesson about India rubber, which is reproduced in Figure 5.1.

During the 1920s and 1930s, progressive teachers still were relying on the approach to assessment that Todd and Powell had recommended in 1899. They were confused about how they could maintain their philosophical principles and

India Rubber.

Material: Rubber and many articles made of rubber. Turtle shell and palm nuts.

Lead children to describe the picture.

Have them write after the oral description is given.

Have them read their descriptions.

Lead them to tell the story which the picture suggests.

Reproduce the story on paper.

Have the children read their stories.

Tell them of the country in which rubber trees grow.

Have them read the book lesson silently before reading it orally.

Have pupils reproduce the lesson without reference to the book.

Making Paper.

Material: Different kinds of paper.

Collecting rags.

Where taken ? Paper mill.

Sorting, removing buttons, pins, hooks and eyes, etc.

Cleansing. Soaking and boiling in soda water.

Cutting by a machine furnished with sharp knives.

Put into a vat called a "draining chest," where the water is drained from the rags.

Pasty mixture bleached with chloride of lime, after which it is again put into the machine, where it is boiled, washed and chopped until it looks like thick cream.

Put into a vat, where it is beaten and churned until it is just the right thickness.

Figure 5.1 Observation-Based Assessment From a Nineteenth-Century Textbook

still adopt some form of evaluation that would compete with objective tests. Lingenfelter (1930) suggested that progressive teachers enrich their conception of individual differences by gathering information about students' home lives and social activities. This information would help the teachers explain academic progress to the students and their parents. Hughes (1934) was sympathetic to the suggestions that Lingenfelter had made. He distinguished progressive education, which stressed "the intangible traits of personality," from traditional education, which emphasized "the measurable outcomes of scholastic learning" (p. 25). He predicted that "scientific measurement will not be discarded" by progressive educators but that it would be "practically developed in the field of personality" (p. 28). He anticipated tests that would look beyond the "narrow scholastic abilities of children" and express "standards of accomplishment...in terms of interests, appreciations and ideals of the learner" (p. 28).

Washburne (1932) agreed that progressive teachers could benefit from tests. However, he suggested a different approach for resolving their objections. He thought that the progressive teachers would get the greatest benefit from assessment if they individualized the content of tests and the schedules for administering them. Furthermore, they had to accept tests as diagnostic tools rather than measures of achievement. Although an individual student's progress still could be determined, this would have to be accomplished by regularly administering different but comparable versions of the same test. Washburne acknowledged that "this is easier to do in skill subjects like arithmetic, formal language, and grammar than it is in content subject like history and geography" (p. 5). In spite of the difficulty, he reassured teachers of content subjects that "it can be done." Three years later, Whipple (1935) reported that "the discussion of diagnosis in such familiar fields as arithmetic, English, and science traverses ground familiar to many readers" while "that of diagnosis in the social studies will probably enter terrain that is unexplored to most of us" (p. ix). He continued that "more novel still, perhaps, is the discussion of diagnosis as applied to such fields as health education, mental health, art, education for leisure, and the creative aspects of education." Within the book that Whipple had edited, his fellow educators proposed assessment instruments for each of the atypical areas he had listed.

Wishing to help progressive educators who were searching for alternative tests, Wrightstone (1933, 1934b) pointed to case-study procedures, questionnaires, and variations on "the observational method." He thought they might especially be attracted to the observational method because it was unobtrusive, applicable to classroom situations, and a potential source for statistically analyzable data. To help teachers make and record observations, Wrightstone provided a taxonomy of classroom behaviors. For example, he directed the teachers to focus on incidents in which students voluntarily prepared reports, made extemporaneous contributions to discussions, asked questions, praised contributions from classmates, challenged contributions from classmates, or suggested solutions to problems. Even though he encouraged the teachers to make these observations systematically, Wrightstone did acknowledge several weaknesses in the procedure. Some of these were the inability to normalize data, the difficulty of identifying other groups of students to which the observations generalized, the high costs, and the excessive amount of time that the procedure required. Wrightstone failed to confront the procedure's most obvious weakness, which was its similarity to the discredited practice of recitation.

Wrightstone (1934a) provided a questionnaire with which progressive teachers might assess their students. On this questionnaire, which he referred to as a "social background data sheet," he included items that would be scored differentially, based on the students' personal circumstances. For example, one of these items queried each student about his or her father's occupation. If the father worked in a professional field, such as architecture, medicine, law, or engineering, that student would receive 40 points. Accountants, agents, and teachers merited 30 points toward their children's exams. Foremen and the owners of small businesses produced only 20 points. Barbers and clerks earned 10 points; domestic workers and "common laborers" earned no points. In the case of children's homes, teachers were to divide the total number of rooms in each domicile by the number of family members. Quotients of at least 2.2 produced a score of 40 points. A figure of .4 or less did not earn any points. The numerical value for a child's social status would increase by 4 points if his or her home contained any of the following items: a radio, piano, library of 400 books, telephone, or automobile.

Looking back six years to the time that he had joined the group of progressive educational faculty members at Teachers College, Wrightstone (1938) recounted that he had committed himself to "the construction of new instruments of evaluation" and their applications. His professional efforts produced a book in which he identified the "cardinal objectives" of education. These objectives were social relationships, individual aptitudes, critical thinking, appreciation of worthwhile activities, the integration of knowledge with skills, physical health, and mental health. Within each category, he listed specific sub-skills and the "instruments of appraisal" that were suited to them. For example, under the category of appreciation of worthwhile activities, he identified "participation for enjoyment in such activities as art, music, reading, games, experimentation, and travel" (p. 164). To assess this participation, he proposed a "specially constructed questionnaire on participation in voluntary extra-school leisure activities." To evaluate mental health he offered a "specially constructed *Personality Trait Indicator.*" For the assessment of "aptitudes such as telling and writing stories, writing poetry, drawing and painting, construction, music, and dancing" he suggested a special questionnaire, an observational rating scale, and a test of artistic judgment.

Scates (1938) identified Wrightstone as one of the progressive educators who had been "attacking the problem" of assessment and who was not "limited by preconceptions of what form the instrument should have." He added that Wrightstone and likeminded colleagues had "taken recourse to various means, such as anecdotal records, checklists, ratings, observer-diary records, questionnaires, informal reports, and interviews" (p. 534). Scates did caution that these instruments, even though some of them were being used in schools, were only in their preliminary stages of development.

Progressive Educators Assess Teachers

Just as they were pressured to prove that their students were competent, progressive educators were pressured to demonstrate their own competence as instructors. The superintendent in Berkeley, California, (Smith, 1933) made this point. He acknowledged that "sch ools and the public have been markedly influenced by the enthusiastic proponents" of progressive educational practices. However, he worried that "education in this respect is undoubtedly going through the same process of overemphasis which has occurred many times before in our history, and 'the activity' has been magnified into a cult" (p. 669). He reminded his fellow administrators as well as the public that any school system would be "lacking in the discharge of its duty if it does not make a check of the actual service rendered" by progressive educators. He added that "certain essential educational procedures are likely to be neglected unless sanity governs the policy of the schools in this respect as in all other matters."

The educational system's constituents were demanding information about the academic progress of students. They also wanted evidence about teachers' effectiveness. Many of those constituents had already decided that the scores from standardized tests comprised the scholastic information they needed to evaluate both the students and their teachers. The teachers disagreed. They did not believe that students' scores fairly measured the effectiveness of instructors. They opposed these measures because some of the factors that influenced students' test scores were elements over which the teachers had no control. In addition to opposing the use of students' test scores for instructor evaluation, the teachers also resisted those standardized tests that had been designed to assess the instructors' knowledge of course content. They opposed the content tests because they believed these were invalid. McConn (1936) suggested a compromise plan in which the teachers would have to accept the results of students' test scores. However, they would use these results "for self-appraisal, including the discovery of their own shortcomings." McConn thought this was appropriate because teachers "can be trusted to give themselves the benefit of the grave technical uncertainties involved, whereas administrators, even department heads, dealing with others than themselves, might often be tempted away from the necessary caution and come to treat as definite evidence results which would have at most some uncertain probability" (pp. 464–465).

Because they questioned the fundamental validity of objective achievement tests, progressive educators were not enthusiastic about the compromise that McConn had offered. At the same time, they knew that they had failed to keep their promise to advance distinctive but objective measures of student achievement. Under duress, they decided to devise techniques that would assess their students' growth in creativity, social cooperation, appreciation of the arts, independence, and the other curricular goals to which they assigned high priority. The progressive teachers hoped that these alternative measures of student growth would be accepted as substitutes for standardized tests. They also hoped that the measures would be viewed as an indirect indication of their own instructional competence. Most of all, they hoped that the proposed measures would protect them from the fusillade of hostile criticism to which they were being subjected.

Numerous progressive educators had responded to the call to develop alternative measures of assessment. For example, Collings (1926) designed an assessment scale to evaluate students and teachers simultaneously. In her "conduct scale for the measurement of teaching," she stipulated that the primary purpose of the instrument was "to enable the teacher to grow continuously in stimulating and directing the purposeful activities of boys and girls" (p. 98). Her approach was based on six assumptions. The first was that "life is interpreted as purposeful activity" (p. 97). The second supposition was that "purposeful activity is considered in its analytical aspect as the response of boys and girls along their drive in the initiation of goals, initiation of means, evaluation of means, choice of means, organization of means, execution of means, initiation of improvement, evaluation of improvement, choice of improvement, consummation of improvement, and leading to further goals" (p. 97). She arranged the traits that she had specified in this second assumption into a checklist so that the behaviors of students could be recorded. These records became an indication of teaching efficiency, which she believed was "revealed through measuring the extent of functioning of children's response." Needless to say, this amorphous assessment scale did not appease the critics who were demanding that progressive educators demonstrate greater accountability.

Tiegs (1928) developed an approach to teacher evaluation that was philosophically similar to that of Collins. He summarized his recommendations in one of the longest sentences ever penned on this topic.

> It appears, therefore, that the most promising way of progress in the evaluation of teaching service, and the prediction of teaching success, must contemplate procedures which given [*sic*] an increasing emphasis to the minutiae of teacher and pupil activity; that such evaluations as are made should be based on a number of individual samplings, made over a period of time and in each instance, on a definite piece of work; and that the criterion of teaching success should become more and more a combination of definitely defined goals and methods of achieving them toward which teachers may consciously strive, rather than

the often indefinite, intangible, and personal concepts of success, on the basis of which we are at present striving to make adequate professional judgments. (p. 79)

Because this approach was as nebulous as the other ones that his progressive colleagues had proposed, it was susceptible to the same criticism.

As more time transpired, progressive educators desperately wished to retort to the criticism about their failures in assessment. Wrightstone (1934c) judged that observational techniques, which were being used by many progressive educators to evaluate their students, could become an expedient tool for assessing teachers as well. To expedite this shift, he identified an observational taxonomy that encouraged administrators to report whether progressive teachers exhibited model classroom behaviors. For example, did they allow their students to make voluntary contributions to discussions, encourage them to participate in classroom activities, refer them to appropriate supplementary materials, pose questions, suggest explanations, relate classroom discussions to textbooks, and maintain discipline with words, looks, and gestures? As should have been expected, critics were not satisfied with Wrightstone's proposal for evaluating teachers. The critics preferred to draw conclusions about teachers by administering competency tests to the instructors or achievement tests to their students.

Rating scales had been another instrument that educators had used to demonstrate the effectiveness of teachers. However, rating scales gave a great deal of discretion to the administrators who were completing the evaluations. Giordano (2000) recounted that progressive educational programs, despite the significant publicity that they generated within educational journals, were not implemented extensively in the public schools. For this reason, progressive teachers did not relish the ratings that the many traditionally minded supervisors might make. They undoubtedly felt additional uneasiness because most of the teacher rating scales did not emphasize the instructional goals to which progressive educators assigned high priority. Harold Rugg (1920), who would eventually establish himself as one of the most influential progressive educators, proposed two adaptations that would solve these problems. One change would be the development of a rating scale that was sensitive to progressive educational goals. The scale he suggested had the following parts: skill in teaching, skill in the mechanics of managing a class, teamwork qualities, qualities of growth, qualities of keeping up-to-date, personal qualities, and social qualities. He proposed a second change in which teachers would become the subjects and administrators for the ratings. Although this situation would create an obvious conflict of interest, Rugg's philosophy of self-improvement persuaded him that his idea still had merit.

Rating schemes are not aimed primarily at self-improvement. It is the viewpoint of the present writer that for a rating scale to be truly helpful, its chief element must be *self-improvement through self-rating*. Improvement of teachers in service rests directly upon the initial step of *self-criticism*. It is conceivable that this could be stipulated by the personal exhortation of the principal. It rarely is, however. It can be stimulated from within more helpfully and continuously, provided objective, impersonal schemes can be developed by which teachers can be made critically conscious of their strengths and weaknesses. Thus, rating schemes to the present time have revealed an important defect in that they were nearly always an administrative scheme superimposed from above. (pp. 675–676)

Flory (1930) argued for a "personality rating of prospective teachers." He explained that "the idea that teachers need a given personality seems to be an assumption generally accepted" (p. 143). He believed that the individual teacher should make these ratings because he or she "can determine his strength or weakness in personality about as well as his friends are able to when a rating scale with traits defined in terms of trait actions is used." Among the positive traits for which Flory encouraged teachers to search were impartiality, sympathy, appearance, patience, and interest in extracurricular activities. The first three items on his rating scale demonstrated the format that was used throughout this instrument.

1. Adaptable   1 2 3 4 5
   a. I can easily fit into a new situation.
   b. I can change rapidly from one task to another.
   c. I talk as easily to prince as to pauper.
2. Alert   1 2 3 4 5
   a. I see what is happening.
   b. I am quick of thought.
   c. I sense trouble quickly.
3. Cheerful   1 2 3 4 5
   a. I wear a sunny disposition.
   b. I am not irritated by little things.
   c. I enliven the group by my presence. (Flory, 1930, p. 140)

Some progressive educators assumed that teachers could use "impersonal" rating scales to objectively measure their own professional behaviors. Not all of their colleagues shared this optimism. Even though he did acknowledge that rating scales "will necessitate definite concrete thinking on the problem, and will aid in analysis and the avoidance of snap judgments," Freyd (1923) judged that they had a character that was discrete from that of the objective tests. In fact, one of the primary reasons for devising rating scales had been to judge "applicants for positions on traits which are at present impossible of objective measurement" (p. 101). As such, he believed that rating scales could not replace objective measurement. Most progressive educators eventually agreed with him.

Summary

Political conservatives maintained strong, partisan opinions about education. For example, they viewed schools as the source of the skilled laborers that industry and the military needed. They were able to generate enormous publicity during World War I, when they portrayed scholastic problems as obstacles to national defense. In addition to raising doubts about academic progress, they questioned whether wartime schools were instilling discipline, patriotism, and important social values. Performance on tests became a key piece of information about potential problems. To redress weaknesses among the students, the conservatives demanded higher expectations and curricula focused on reading, writing, mathematics, science, physical education, and vocational education. To remedy problems among teachers, they insisted that school administrators hire qualified instructors and then strictly evaluate them.

In contrast, the liberals advanced educational initiatives to enhance critical thinking, appreciation of the arts, and cooperative problem solving. Although they resisted objective tests, they were pressured to provide evidence of educational accountability. They eventually proposed distinctive assessment techniques with which individual teachers could make judgments about their own students. As for the assessment of instructors, they proposed that teachers evaluate themselves. These subjective assessment techniques were not implemented widely.

CHAPTER 6

Charges of Racism

I.Q. tests sometimes systematically underpredict for lower-income children [and] this is largely because it is middle- and upper-income Ph.D.s who make up tests.
—GREEN, 1975

Some early twentieth-century psychologists, politicians, and educators believed that the predictably low scores of certain racial and ethnic groups were indications of inferior mental aptitude. Anti-assessment factions retorted that the genuine abilities of these minorities had been misrepresented by the extensive cultural and linguistic biases within the tests. The most radical members of these factions attracted wide publicity by accusing the assessment companies of deliberately designing faulty tests. A diversified coalition of educational stakeholders eventually concluded that biases did not invalidate standardized exams.

Early Allegations of Test-Based Racism

While using tests to analyze the academic performance of African Americans, Stetson (1897) had been open to the possibility that environmental factors accounted for their different scores. Providing an explanation that would be restated throughout the following century, he argued that African Americans might not be less intelligent than other racial groups but only less proficient in their use of Standard English. He observed that "the fundamental, discouraging, and almost insurmountable difficulty in the education of the Negro is his ignorance of our language" (p. 289). He added that "the great mass of the Negro population of the country very rarely hears the English language spoken in its purity, and the children fortunate enough to be taught by one of their race who has acquired it, only hear it in the school room or in the houses of their white masters." When he noted that African Americans "exhibit a decadence of the observing faculties from earlier conditions," Stetson was referring to years of slavery as an additional situational factor that had limited their intellectual achievement.

Although Stetson had not explicitly referred to racial and ethnic discrimination, he anticipated that these issues would be linked to intelligence testing. In fact, allegations that tests promoted racial and ethnic discrimination were endemic to the testing movement. In the final pages of his book, *The Mental Capacity of the American Negro*, Mayo (1913) not only drew conclusions about race and intelligence but also estimated the degree of similarity between his perceptions and those of his contemporaries.

From all the observations and measurements that have come under consideration we arrive at the conclusion that as regards the mental heredity of the negro [*sic*] and white races...the average mental ability of the white race, so far as this ability is exercised in school studies, is higher, but not a great deal higher, than that of the colored race; and that as regards the matter of mental variability, the white race is more variable, but not a great deal more

> variable, than is the negro race….The foregoing conclusion seems clearly deductible from the data compiled and presented. They are also in accord, except in their moderation, with the teaching of history and anthropology, and with the views commonly accepted among those who have made extensive observations upon the races. (pp. 69–70)

Mayo detected "no statistical grounds for holding to the view of substantial racial mental equality." Nonetheless, he disagreed with those who had detected major differences in intelligence among the races. By insisting that the intelligence of white Americans was not "a great deal" higher than that of African Americans, Mayo portrayed himself as an individual with moderate views about this politically explosive issue.

Morse (1914), a professor at the University of South Carolina, decided to administer standardized intelligence tests to white and African American children. He thought that the results of the exams would help him decipher some of those problems that had not been resolved by mere "discussions of race problems, even when the opinions have been held by scientists eminent in their own special domains" (p. 75). To emphasize this point, he described two scientists with antipodal views about race and intelligence. Whereas one of these scientists could "see no essential difference between the negro [*sic*] and white races," the other was "equally certain that a 'mental abyss' forever separates the two peoples." To settle the matter, Morse decided to initiate investigations that employed psychological tests. He wrote that this course of action seemed appropriate because "important human problems need the spirit, methods and instruments of science applied to them" (p. 79).

At the beginning of the twentieth century, the poor test performance of African Americans, as well as Italians and Slavs, had been amply documented (Knox, 1914). This performance confirmed the racist impressions that many scholars already had formed. For example, Phillips (1914), who was the principal at the Harriet Beecher Stowe School in Philadelphia, focused on African Americans. After administering intelligence tests to both the African American and white children at his school, he noted certain "facts of interest [that] were fortunately thrust upon" his attention.

> In the first place the colored [*sic*] pupils as a class were good in the memory tests and poor in those requiring judgment. They were generally slower in response. The testing of the colored children took much longer time than the white. Their reaction time was greater, they were less animated. It is significant to note that the younger white children were more advanced than the colored children of the same age. This is in contradiction to the generally accepted fact that colored children are quicker when young. (p. 196)

That same year, Lind (1914) pointed to some of the "diagnostic pitfalls" that could "beset the uninitiated in the mental examination of negroes [*sic*]." Despite his adjuration to avoid those pitfalls, Lind himself fell into one when he warned that "the negro [*sic*], especially the negro with little or no white admixture, [is] a somewhat primitive psychological type whose cultural levels overlook but slightly those of the savage" (p. 1286).

The *Eugenical News* regularly published highly editorialized articles about the practical implications of ethnicity and race. One of these reports ("Negro Efficiency," 1916) concluded with the denigrating types of statements that were so predictable in that journal.

> In view of all the evidence it does not seem possible to raise the scholastic attainments of the negro [*sic*] to an equality with those of the white. It is probable that no expenditure of time or of money would accomplish this end, since education cannot create mental power, but can only develop that which is innate. (p. 79)

Some of the early twentieth-century scholars did assume sophisticated perspectives when they were discussing racial differences in test scores. For example, W. E. B. DuBois (1914) disputed an experiment in which one researcher had attempted to prove that the inferior test performance of African American high-school students in New York had been the result of "causes that are fundamental and ineradicable."

> As a matter of fact the colored children in the high schools of New York suffer:
> 1. From poor training in southern schools, whence the majority of them come;
> 2. From the necessity of working their way through school, thus having little time for study or recreation;
> 3. From home surroundings, which do not encourage study and do not afford the kind of help which high-school home study calls for;
> 4. From a lack of that general social contact out of which the ordinary white boy in the big city gets so much of his education. (DuBois, 1914, p. 558)

Pyle (1915) also contemplated situational explanations for the depressed test scores of African American children. He noted that "what these differences would have been had the negroes [*sic*] been subject to the same environmental influences as had the whites, it is difficult to say." Even though he lacked evidence, he speculated about the questions that would remain unresolved if data were to be collected about the intelligence of white children and African American children who had been raised in comparable environments.

> The result obtained by separating the negroes [*sic*] into two social groups would lead one to think that the conditions of life under which the negroes [*sic*] live might account for the lower mentality of the negro [*sic*]. On the other hand, it may be that the negroes [*sic*] living under the better social conditions are of better stock. They may have more white blood in them. (p. 360)

By predicting some of the conflicting interpretations that might be imposed on the results of a carefully designed research investigation, Pyle had revealed several of the prevalent theories about race-based abilities. Many scholars commented on the tension created by these competing but incompatible theories. Weintrob and Weintrob (1912) wrote in exasperation that "the relative power of nature and nurture to affect mental ability is one of those mooted points of psychology which have been interminably discussed" (p. 577). Two years later, Bruner (1914) specifically recounted race-based explanations for the relationship of learning to test performance. Within another discussion of these explanations, Schwegler and Winn (1920) highlighted two theories that stood out from the others because they had been "consistently and plausibly stated." These two explanations were that "the social status and traditions of the negro [*sic*] encourage meager intellectual standards" and "that the mentality of the negro [*sic*] child is essentially different from that of the white child" (p. 838). Although they did not directly address the possible impact of differentially funded and racially segregated schools, Schwegler and Winn did comment on it indirectly. They noted that southern "state agencies have been awakened by patriotic, religious, and philanthropic forces to a new and productive interest in education for the colored race." With regard to the bearing of their own research on the question of differential test performance by African American and white children, the authors drew a somewhat oblique conclusion. They judged that fundamental differences were "indicated by the very fact that the colored children approached the test cheerfully and without concern as to the outcome, while the white children were obviously concerned lest they 'fail the test'" (p. 847).

Robert Yerkes (1923a), one of the designers of the influential World War I military testing program, wrote the foreword to the postwar book *The Study of American Intelligence.* He began with an adjuration that two "extraordinarily important tasks" confronted the nation. One of these tasks was improvement of the industrial system; the other was the "protraction and improvement of the moral, mental and physical quality of its people" (1923a, p. v). As to the book for which Yerkes had written the foreword, he indicated that he had the "satisfaction of recommending" it. Brigham (1923), who was the author of that book and a professor of psychology at Princeton University, did not conceal his extremist thoughts about race.

> In general, the Mediterranean has crossed with primitive race types more completely and promiscuously than either the Alpine or the Nordic, and with most unfortunate results. We must now frankly admit the undesirable results which would ensure from a cross between the Nordic in this country with the Alpine Slav, with the degenerated hybrid Mediterranean, or with the Negro, or from the promiscuous intermingling of all four types... The 1920 census shows we have 7,000,000 native born whites of mixed parentage, a fact which indicates clearly the number of crosses between native born stock and the European importations... According to all evidence available, then, American intelligence is declining, and will proceed with an accelerating rate as the racial admixture becomes more and more extensive... The deterioration of American intelligence is not inevitable...[and] there is no reason why legal steps should not be taken which would insure a continuously progressive upward evolution. (pp. 208–210)

Not all observers agreed with Brigham's warnings about the intellectual degradation of the nation and the need for the federal government to slow down, halt, or reverse racial integration. Bond (1924b) pointed out that "the boasted superiority of the white over the Negro stock does not seem so impressive when the Negroes of Illinois make a score of 47.35 [on the Army's alpha test] while the whites of a least four Southern States [*sic*] were making a score of 41" (p. 202). He added that testing was "a valuable instrument of classification" but not "the shibboleth which would determine the right of a race to higher avenues of expression and advancement." In a separate article in which he specifically denounced Brigham's book, Bond (1924a) concluded that racism posed a greater threat to the nation than integration. Bond highlighted the irony of the situation in which African American soldiers had fought to maintain a government that allowed racist professors to speak and publish freely.

> It is in the post-war period…that [the Army's Alpha tests] have received greatest publicity; and far from their original purpose, they now serve as reservoirs of information, accurate or not, for the use of showing the intellectual inferiority of some of the races who gave without stint of their lives for the maintenance of their country! (p. 62)

Many of the participants in the debate about intelligence and race did try to maintain their objectivity. However, even the more dispassionate observers did not always present a very flattering picture of minority learners. For example, Sheldon (1924) had reviewed research reports about immigrant children and then constructed a table that used race to "tentatively" predict their intelligence. He determined that the average I.Q. of American and English children was 100. The average I.Q. score of Hebrew children was 98 and that of Chinese was 90. However, the respective scores for Mexican Americans, American Indians, Slavs, Italians, and African Americans were 85, 83, 83, 77, and 75. Needless to say, racist groups referred to data of this sort to justify their radical political initiatives.

Walter Lippmann, an influential journalist, was an articulate critic of intelligence testing during this period. He effectively highlighted the inconsistency and inconclusiveness of the data from which racist ideologues had been drawing their conclusions. Although many of his articles targeted the prominent Lewis Terman, Lippmann clearly intended to rhetorically impale that entire cohort of psychologists who believed that intelligence tests validated racial superiority.

> How does it happen that men of science can presume to dogmatize about the mental qualities of the germplasm when their own observations begin at four years of age? Yet this is what the chief intelligence testers, led by Professor Terman, are doing. Without offering any data on all that occurs between conception and the age of kindergarten, they announce on the basis of what they have got out of a few thousand questionnaires that they are measuring the hereditary mental endowment of human beings. Obviously this is not a conclusion obtained by research. It is a conclusion planted by the will to believe. (Lippmann, 1922a, p. 9)

In another article, Lippmann (1922c) observed that "the most prominent testers...believe that they are measuring the capacity of a human being for all time and that this capacity is fatally fixed by the child's heredity" (pp. 297–298). He warned that "intelligence testing in the hands of men who hold this dogma could not but lead to an intellectual caste system in which the task of education had given way to the doctrine of predestination and infant damnation."

Opposition From Civil Rights Advocates

Throughout the early part of the twentieth century, critics had condemned the views that racial supremacists maintained toward test scores. However, these protestations had not always attracted the broad sympathy that the anti-testing opponents would have liked. With the shift of political priorities during the civil rights era, the opportunities for recruiting political supporters multiplied. Keppel (1966) expressed the spirit of the times when he wrote that "in the last decade, the American majority has come to recognize that schools segregated by local law or custom, or by real estate covenants, are insupportable in modern society" (p. 31). Although a national majority denigrated segregated schools, a much smaller group had extended that criticism to tests. A member of New York City's Board of Education represented that smaller group when he wrote that "the validity of the group intelligence test, used extensively all over the nation, is being widely criticized." He added with pride that "New York City, with the largest public school system in the country, has recently discontinued its use" (Loretan, 1965, p. 10).

Tyler and White (1979) characterized the 1960s as a period when criticism of educational testing was no longer "confined to academic debate" and became the "center of public controversy" (p. v). Some of those who attacked tests believed that the instruments were not only the basis for biased assessments but also the foundation for unfair social practices. This attitude was apparent when members of the American Psychological Association (APA) provided educators with *Guidelines for Testing Minority Group Children* (Fishman, Deutsch, Kogan, North, & Whiteman, 1963).

> American educators have long recognized that they can best guide [those who] can assist minority children in overcoming their early disadvantages, fully or at least in part, and can enable them to live more constructively and to contribute more fully to American society. Educational and psychological tests may help or hinder the attainment of this desired state of affairs, depending on how carefully and intelligently the tests are employed. Persons who have a genuine commitment to democratic processes and to the deep respect for the individual, without which no democracy can function, will certainly seek to use educational and psychological tests with minority group children in ways that will enable these children to attain the full promise that America holds out to all of its children. (p. 1)

To underscore the racial bias in tests, the authors of these APA guidelines noted that "a Negro child [who] has had little contact with white adults other than as distant and punitive authority figures" would probably "have difficulty in gaining rapport with a white examiner or reacting without emotional upset to his close presence" (p. 6). The authors continued that "the examiner, reacting in terms of his own stereotypes, might add to the unreliability of the test results by assuming that the child's performance will naturally be inferior." One of their suggestions for correcting this problem was "making more use of everyday behavior as evidence of the coping abilities and competence of children who do not come from the cultural mainstream" (pp. 21–22).

The authors of the APA guidelines had pointed to the negative repercussions that testing had on children who were excluded from "the cultural mainstream." Clements, Duncan, and Taylor (1969) explained that minority children scored poorly on tests because they were part of an impoverished class that was being referred to as *socioeconomically deprived, socially and culturally disadvantaged, chronically poor,* or *poverty-stricken.* Members of this class were penalized because of their own idiosyncratic value systems, their failure to comprehend the purpose of testing, the unsympathetic attitudes of the persons who evaluated them, the imposition of unreliable measures, and the imposition of invalid tests.

Some zealots argued that even methodologically valid research studies should be suppressed if they had incorporated tests that were not aligned with their specific political values. Addressing the question of whether social scientists "have an obligation to consider the social consequences of the work they do and the discoveries they make," Hyman (1969) concluded that each scientist should "consider carefully the social impact of his pronouncements in the light both of the assurance with which they can be offered and of their impact upon the social scene" (p. 30). Wolff (1971) took this argument a step further. He questioned whether the performance of examinees on valid tests, even if this performance enabled the examinees to occupy the social positions in which they could make their greatest contributions, was worth the price of the caste system that resulted. Wolff speculated that "perhaps we would be willing to sacrifice added excellence in the management of our corporations, but not in our hospitals" (p. 106). In any event, he resented those researchers who had presumptuously used "the logic of genetics or statistics" to address problems that should have been resolved through "collective social choices."

The editor (Houts, 1976) of a leading elementary-education journal later reframed the argument that Hyman had used.

No one should interpret the current controversy over standardized tests as an effort to abandon assessment. Rather, it is an effort to develop assessment procedures that are more in keeping with a new set of educational and social assumptions that we as a society are working on: that the purpose of education is not to sort people but to educate them... Assessment of students must begin to reflect that philosophy, and that is the true reason for the current call for test reform and an end to IQ testing. (p. 673)

Houts was the editor of *National Elementary Principal*, which was a publication of the National Association of Elementary School Principals. Under his editorial direction, that journal published a fusillade of anti-testing articles. This barrage was especially evident during 1975. In one of the reports from that year, Olson (1975) railed against the National Assessment of Educational Progress, which he explained was "an assessment that, at best, asks powerless communities to assess themselves in terms provided by the powerful" (p. 46). In another article, Cottle (1975) demanded that the "multimillion dollar [*sic*] testing business" accept responsibility for "the hundreds of thousands of children who, on the basis of some test, will stop going to school and lead a life in which this early sense of incompetence, failure, and lack of grace will never be erased from their self-concept" (p. 62).

Also writing for *National Elementary Principal*, Walden (1975) advised readers about several court cases in which the judges had declared that standardized tests were invalid. He explained that one basis for the legal disqualification of tests had been "using tests standardized to middle class [*sic*] children for youngsters from low socioeconomic backgrounds" (p. 81). The two other principal conditions that had prompted courts to invalidate tests were the use of "vocabulary items that reflect the white middle class [*sic*] culture" and the circumstance where "the test is not administered in the person's primary language."

Writing in *National Elementary Principal*, Taylor and Schwartz (1975) were equally concerned about the legality of standardized testing. They recommended that the provision of "due process" permission slips become a precondition for standardized testing. This document, which was intended for parents, would require a description of the test, designation of the group of children who would be taking it, a rationale about how those children were expected to benefit from the test, specification of the ways in which they would benefit, designation of all persons who would use the results, indication of whether a participant's name would be revealed to those who were analyzing the results, information as to whether the test's results would become part of the child's permanent school records, specification of the consequence for any child who chose not to participate in the testing, specification of the consequences for any teacher or school administrator who chose not to participate, and a description of the type of report that would be presented to the parents, who "must be accompanied by the child" in a meeting that would take place after the test results were available.

The confrontational attitudes of other authors who published test-related pieces in *National Elementary Principal* during 1975 were apparent even in the titles of their articles. These included *How to Avoid the Dangers of Testing* (Patterson, Czajkowski, Hubbard, Johnson, Slater, & Kaufman, 1975), *The Numbers Game: How the Testing Industry Operates* (Kohn, 1975), *The Politics of IQ* (Kamin, 1975), the *Score against IQ: A look at Some Test Items* (1975), *The Bell Shaped* [*sic*] *Pitfall* (Morrison, 1975), *The Hidden Agendas of IQ* (Purvin, 1975), *The Virtues of Not Knowing* (Duckworth, 1975), and *On the Misuse of Test Data: A Second Look at Jencks's "Inequality"* (Lazarus, 1975).

The March 1976 issue of *Citizen Action in Education* was co-sponsored by the National Association of Elementary School Principals and the Institute for Responsive Education. It contained eight challenging articles. The following remarks indicated the politicized views of the authors and their sponsoring organizations.

> The purpose of this issue of Citizen Action in Education [*sic*] is to encourage our readers to ask questions, become informed, and take appropriate action in their own communities to control testing... Many have argued for abolishing tests entirely, or for drastic cutbacks in their use. Testing may or may not be a monster to be destroyed. But as with any of society's technological tools, testing must be harnessed by the citizenry to serve goals which are clearly understood, equitable, and humane. (Davies, 1976, p. 14)

Many of the assaults that were made during this era focused on the linguistic as well as the cultural features of standardized tests. Although they initially did not address the issue of testing, one group of scholars had highlighted the similarity between teaching persons who spoke a language other than English and those who spoke a dialect other than Standard English. The U.S. Office of Education judged that the topic of "social dialects and language learning" was of sufficient importance to merit a national conference (Shuy, 1964). In agreement about the significance of the topic, the National Council of Teachers of English (Shuy, 1964) published the papers from these proceedings.

Goodman (1965) employed a syllogism of sorts to define the peculiar linguistic problems of the students who were learning to read in "big city" classrooms.

> Since it is true that learning to read a foreign language is a more difficult task than learning to read a native language, it must follow that it is harder for a child to learn to read a dialect which is not his own than to learn to read his own dialect. This leads to an important hypothesis: *The more divergence there is between the dialect of the learner and the dialect of learning, the more difficult will be the task of learning to read.* [original emphasis] (p. 853)

Dillard (1967) was sympathetic to the points Goodman had made. He observed that "what was basically a rural language problem, of the plantation and of the sharecropper's farm, has recently become a full-fledged urban language problem" (p. 115). However, Dillard parenthetically noted that some liberal educational theorists had suggested that African Americans be segregated for certain types of instruction. Aware that these suggestions were politically volatile, he predicted that "many a liberal teacher will be dismayed...that the newly unified classroom should be broken up even for a few moments by the use of differing teaching techniques for some groups of students." He reassured the many liberals who were dismayed by these proposals that "special drills for such studies need not be lengthy to be effective" and "a drill unit of five to ten minutes, using pattern practice procedures from English as a Foreign Language methods [*sic*], has proved to be most effective" (p. 120).

Baratz (1969) warned that "the disadvantaged Negro must not only decode the written words, he must translate them into his own language." This posed "an almost insurmountable obstacle since the words often do not go together in any pattern that is familiar or meaningful to him" (p. 201). To demonstrate ways that "disadvantaged" African Americans were "baffled by the confrontation with...a new language with its new syntax," Baratz gave examples of "Negro non-standard" expressions that were grammatically equivalent to Standard English expressions. "He going," "John he live in New York," and "I don't have none" were identified as the non-standard translations of the following phrases: "He is going," "John lives in New York," and "I don't have any" (p. 200).

Extending Baratz's logic to assessment, Green (1971) reasoned that "a biased test...contains a substantial proportion of items that would not have been selected had some other particular group been the tryout sample" (p. 21). As a result of this sampling bias, "the scores of some groups are unfairly low because the test does not adequately measure all the relevant abilities of knowledge, and in particular, does not measure well those relevant attributes on which the group in question happens to score well." After examining standardized assessment from this viewpoint, he concluded that "probably most tests are biased against most groups."

Some critics suspected that the test developers had deliberately contrived items in ways that would frustrate learners, especially those from minority groups. To illustrate this practice, Meier (1973) gave examples of sentences that she thought were similar to those in the California Reading Achievement Test.

> I have read *(those, them)* books before.
> Beth *(come, came)* home and cried.
> We *(was, were)* told to sit down.
> I didn't hear *(no, any)* noise.
> A man *(came, come)* to the door.
> Is *(this, this here)* your pencil. [*sic*]
> She *(doesn't, don't)* read well.
> When *(may, can)* I come again. [*sic*] (p. 8)

Meier faulted test items of this sort because "in no case would the 'wrong' answers lead to a failure of communication" and "in most cases they correspond to one or more of the rather common dialects in America (which may well be why they were chosen)" (p. 8).

In a booklet that they published during the 1970s, Cook and Meier (n.d.) advised that "the people who make standardized tests design them so that half the children must 'fail' (score below 'grade level')" (statement on the inside of the front cover of the booklet). They contrasted these faulty assessment practices with the behaviors of teachers, who gave tests in the "hope that all children will pass" and in order to confirm that "the children have learned what has been taught to them."

Cook and Meier cautioned their readers about the profound effects that normalized tests had on schooling. They explained that "standardized tests...often determine children's future class placement...put pressure on teachers to spend large portions of time coaching children for tests...affect the skills, and the values of the school...[are linked to the] large sums of money [that] are given to schools to improve their reading programs...[cause] children [to] judge themselves by how they did on the tests...[and persuade parents to] judge their children by their test scores" (passage on the inside of the back cover of a 1970s booklet, Cook & Meier, n.d.). To demonstrate a way in which tests inflicted damage, Cook and Meier gave examples of ambiguous questions. They disapproved of test questions that instructed students to designate answers that "best completed" sentences but that actually required them to select synonyms. They highlighted one test item that was needlessly restrictive because it penalized students who designated *old* rather than *wise* as the best description of a *sage individual*. They were equally annoyed at the test authors who had required students to specify whether a *giant* was always *huge, fierce, mean*, or *scary*. Cook and Meier reasoned that "if children pick *scary*, does that mean they are 'wrong' or that they can't read *huge, fierce*, or *mean* [original emphasis]?" They skeptically asked, "Are the 'correct' answers always the best ones?" Although they did not reveal the sources of these examples, they assured readers that they were "from actual standardized tests used in the past few years" (statement on the front cover of a 1970s booklet, Cook & Meier, n.d.).

Cook and Meier expressed additional indignation about a test passage that had portrayed police officers as trustworthy professionals who cared about children. Even though the information that students needed to answer the questions about police officers had been explicitly stated in an accompanying passage, the authors predicted that minority children would be frustrated.

> While some children might agree that policemen are their friends or the policemen "scold people, but only when the people do something wrong", [*sic*] there are other groups of children who do not share this view based on their life experience. Their response to this paragraph does not determine whether or how well they read. Is it fair to penalize them for their different beliefs? (p. 8)

Cook and Meier gave another example of a passage with which they were particularly displeased. The passage in question had occurred on a test that had been administered to children in New York City. Even though the relevant passage described a young girl who lived in a crowded tenement house where "many families live...people often run into each other in the halls, and children play tag,"

Cook and Meier asked whether the passage "was included in order to be 'fair' to inner city children?" They also objected to this item because it employed Standard English. They explained that the wording might not be "familiar to innercity [*sic*] children or any others" (p. 9).

Many of the anti-testing sallies were stridently political. Beard (1986) reminisced that those who had practiced this provocative style of criticism had characterized testing "as a racist means of denying educational credentials such as high school [*sic*] diplomas to minority, and particularly Black, students" (p. 2). The writing of Karier (1972) exemplified this sort of writing. In an essay that he entitled *Testing for Order and Control in the Corporate Liberal State*, Karier inserted a footnote expressing gratitude to a colleague "for calling my attention to the material used in this article which reflects the racial bias of the currently used Stanford-Binet test." He listed several of the features of this test that had made him concur with his colleague's advice.

> The test discriminated against members of the lower class—Southern Europeans and Blacks—indirectly by what they [*sic*] seemed to leave out, but more directly by what they [*sic*] included; for example: On a Stanford-Binet (1960 revision), a six year old child is asked the question, "Which is prettier?" and must select the Nordic Anglo Saxon type to be correct. If, however, the child is perhaps a Mexican American or of Southern European descent, has looked at himself in a mirror and has a reasonably healthy respect for himself, he will pick the wrong answer. Worse yet, is the child who recognizes what a "repressive society" calls the "right" answer and has been socialized enough to sacrifice himself for a higher score... Neither Blacks nor Southern Europeans were beautiful according to the authors of the Stanford-Binet, but then, there was no beauty in these people when Goddard, Laughlin, Terman, Thorndike and Garrett called for the sterilization of the "socially ina dequate," the d iscriminatory closing of immigration, [and] the tracking organization of the American school. (p. 166)

The editors of *Psychology Today* devoted a 1972 issue of their magazine to the topic of "I.Q. abuse." In the introduction to that issue, Harris (1972) noted that "Black groups had fought tests because they saw them as a weapon of the white liberal establishment" (p. 39). Although some of his readers must have been confused when he associated testing with the "white liberal establishment," Harris did not offer any explanation. He simply applauded the editors of *Psychology Today* for challenging this oppressive tradition. Harris thought that the editors had shown their courage by selecting articles from "competent researchers [who] took the I.Q. myth seriously" and who pursued "the long careful studies that should have been done long ago" (p. 39). These articles confirmed his own belief that "the day will soon come when it will be the applicant, not the college or company, who decides which tests to take, which results to submit." Harris added that "the only authority on me is me [*sic*]."

Writing in the same issue of *Psychology Today*, Garcia (1972) entitled his essay *I.Q.: The Conspiracy*. He began this piece with remarks about the demeaning techniques that racehorse breeders used. Losing a grasp on what could have been a salient metaphor, he referred to the I.Q. test as "a sort of social contract between educators and mental testers" that had degenerated into "a social conspiracy to label particular groups inferior and to propagate the status quo" (p. 40). Also writing in *Psychology Today*, Mercer (1972) entitled his essay *I.Q.: The Lethal Label.* He claimed that "a large number of minority persons who can cope very well with the requirements of their daily lives are being labeled mentally retarded" (p. 44). This misrepresentation was occurring because "what the I.Q. test measures, to a significant extent, is the child's exposure to Anglo culture" and "the more Anglicized a non-Anglo child is, the better he does on the I.Q. test."

Rivers, Mitchell, and Williams (1975) reviewed a 1969 declaration from the Association of Black Psychologists. The statement in question indicated that the members of this association fully supported "those parents who have chosen to defend their rights by refusing to allow their children and themselves to be subjected to achievement, intelligence, aptitude and performance tests" (statement from the Association of Black Psychologists, 1969, quoted by Rivers, Mitchell, & Williams, 1975, p. 63). The authors then explained that "in 1972 the National Association of Black Psychologists adopted a much stronger position on testing." One of the nine recommendations within the strengthened position paper encouraged current and future examinees to demand fair testing policies. In fact, this group wanted the new policies to apply retroactively to examinations that had already been completed.

> [The members of the National Association of Black Psychologists will] work and encourage efforts to have removed from the cumulative records of all Black students attending public schools, the personnel records of all Black employees in industrial organizations, the personnel files of all Black employees in local, state and national agencies all quantitative and qualitative data obtained from performance on past and presently used standard psychometric, educational achievement, employment, general aptitude and mental ability tests. (Statement from the National Association of Black Psychologists, 1972, quoted by Rivers, Mitchell, & Williams, 1975, p. 64)

Another group of researchers (Cleary, Humphreys, Kendrick, & Wesman, 1975) indicated that the 1969 testing ban that African American psychologists had proposed was a response to injustices that were ongoing but that had originated in the early years of the assessment movement. They alleged that racially analyzed test scores had "been used without justification as data supporting genetic causation...and in turn as justification for discrimination" (p. 15). As an indication of the extent to which some anti-testing adjurations were followed, De Avila (1976) referred to a 1971 memorandum from the Director of the U.S. Office of Civil Rights. This official had "put virtually every school district in the United States on notice that the use of student assessment and assignment procedures which were based on 'criteria which essentially measure or evaluate English language skills' would be seen as a violation of the Civil Rights Act of 1964" (De Avila, 1976, p. 93).

In an article that he published in *Psychology Today*, Williams (1974) depicted the testing companies as the coconspirators in a racist plot that was designed to discredit minority students.

> The American testing industry goes hand-in-hand with the university in fostering the misuse of tests, and it is no mom-and-pop corner store. It is a multimillion-dollar-a-year supermarket of oppression. If the captains of this industry would admit the truth about testing, they would face bankruptcy. But the economic survival of the testing industry depends upon is symbiotic relationship with educational institutions; and both have constructed elaborate defenses against outside criticism. (p. 34)

To dramatize his point, Williams suggested that white Americans take a test that was based on experiences peculiar to African Americans. He believed that this test would be "as fair to the majority of blacks as the Wechsler Intelligence Scale for Children was to the majority of whites" (p. 101). He gave examples of five items from his prototypical exam.

1. *the bump*
   a. condition caused by a forceful blow
   b. a suit
   c. a car
   d. a dance

2. *running a game*
   a. writing a bad check
   b. looking at something
   c. directing a contest
   d. getting what one wants from another person or thing

3. *to get down*
   a. to dominate
   b. to travel
   c. to lower a position
   d. to have sexual intercourse

4. *cop an attitude*
   a. leave
   b. become angry
   c. sit downs
   d. protect a neighborhood

5. *leg*
   a. a sexual meaning
   b. a lower limb
   c. a white
   d. food (p. 101)

Using the colloquial parlance of the late 1970s as a reference, the correct answers were respectively items *d, d, d, b,* and *a.* Williams warned that practitioners of racist assessment were using "intelligence tests as their hired guns." To make sure that his readers fully appreciated this imagery, he entitled his report *The Silent Mugging of the Black Community.*

The authors ("Now Have a Taste," 1977) of an article in the *American School Board Journal* asked their readers to "imagine that your entire education, career and lifetime prosperity were to be determined significantly by standardized tests" with culturally inappropriate questions. As Williams (1974) had done several years earlier, these authors gave sample questions that were designed to help that journal's readers understand the academic plight of African American students.

If a man is called a "blood," he is a
    (A) Fighter
    (B) Mexican American
    (C) Negro
    (D) Hungry hemophile
    (E) Redman or Indian

Cheap chitlins (not the kind you purchase at a frozen food counter) will taste rubbery unless they are cooked long enough. How soon can you quit cooking them to eat and enjoy them?
    (A) 45 minutes
    (B) 2 hours
    (C) 24 hours
    (D) 1 week (on a low flame)
    (E) 1 hour

A "hype" is a person who
    (A) Always says he feels sickly
    (B) Has water on the brain
    (C) Uses heroin
    (D) Is always ripping and running
    (E) Is always sick

Hattie Mae Johnson is on the county. She has four children and her husband is now in jail for nonsupport as he was unemployed and was not able to give her money. Her welfare check is now $286 per month. Last night she went out with the biggest player in town. If she got pregnant, then nine months from now, how much more will her welfare check be?
    (A) $80
    (B) $2
    (C) $35
    (D) $150
    (E) $100 ("Now Have a Taste," 1977, p. 31)

The authors noted that item *C* was the correct answer for each problem. Incidentally, Walter Dill Scott (1915), who had influenced the Army's testing program during World War I, may have been the first psychologist to have based a test on information from African cultures. In his presentation of "a series of tests made by big corporations representing the most important development in sales management in the past dozen years," Scott illustrated one instrument on which persons had to match English and African proverbs. His list of African proverbs included "one tree does not make a forest," "distant firewood is good firewood," and "ashes fly in the face of him who throws them" (p. 96).

Concerned about the many 1970s allegations of cultural and racial biases in standardized testing, the National School Boards Association (1977a) conducted a survey to ascertain the attitudes of its members. This survey revealed that half of the respondents "accept that 'many current standardized tests discriminate against minorities,' while more than a third accept that standardized testing programs are 'not worth their required investment of time and money,' and that 'schools rely heavily on standardized tests out of ignorance about the tests' limitation'" (p. 25). More than 50 percent of the school board members thought that tests discriminated against persons from minority groups and that teacher judgments were more valuable indicators of students' academic achievement. Eighty-eight percent of them agreed with the statement that "most citizens do not understand standardized test results and misinterpret them." As to their own sophistication about educational assessment, 51 percent of the responding school board members believed that neither they nor their colleagues understood the results of standardized testing.

In an article that he entitled *The Politics of I.Q., Racism & Power*, Williams (1975) had written that "standardized testing and the entire educational system are highly correlated" because both were "Anglo-centric, ethno-centric, academo-centric [*sic*] and collegio-centric [*sic*]" (p. 1). Diatribes of this type specifically depicted tests as the oppressive devices of a racist society. However, even some of the reports that were not focused on testing embodied similarly confrontational rhetoric. This proclivity was apparent in titles such as *How Racists Use "Science" to Degrade Black People* (Rowan, 1970), *Sterilization: Newest Threat to the Poor* (Slater, 1973), and *The Black Six-Hour Retarded Child* (Simpkins, Gunnings, & Kearney, 1973).

At the beginning of the 1980s, Cole (1981) looked back and concluded that "the most prominent issues associated with testing in recent years have involved questions of test bias" (p. 1067). She added that "test critics, the courts, test developers, and scholars of testing" had addressed these issues. Over and above the problems created by accusations of test bias, she identified six significant "social policy" problems to which testing had been connected.

1. In selecting for employment, what is the best policy to combine concerns for compensating for past wrongs with current employer needs and current individual rights?
2. What role should selective admissions play in higher education and how should it be balanced with the desire to broaden opportunities?

3. What form should the education of children with handicaps, such as mental retardation, take?
4. How should we deal educationally with people who are behind desired levels of learning?
5. How should we deal socially and educationally with people for whom English is not a first language?
6. What should a high school [sic] diploma mean and who should have control of certifying its meaning? (p. 1074)

Owen (1983) agreed that the complex social issues associated with standardized testing had a scope that went beyond test bias.

> Leaving aside the technical debate over bias, the simple fact is that from the beginning—the Army Alpha exams—standardized testing has been associated with racial and cultural prejudice and has served to reinforce the established hierarchy rather than to shake it up. And even apart from who in particular is helped or hurt, the question remains as to why, in a democracy, it should be considered desirable to rank people from 200 to 800 every time they turn around. (p. 37)

Because he was convinced that a majority of the public would soon share his views, Owen predicted that the Educational Testing Service, which he characterized as the "nerve center of American meritocracy," was experiencing the "last days" of its societal dominance.

Haney (1981) acknowledged that many liberal educators had not only excoriated standardized testing but also forecast its imminent end. However, this prediction was based on ideological zeal rather than verifiable data. In behavior that was equally self-serving, some of the conservative educators who venerated testing had pretended that none of the opposition to it was significant. Their view did not accurately consider the immense publicity that the anti-testing factions had summoned. Haney, who was a political realist, was not sympathetic to either faction in this feud. Aware that testing had strengths and weaknesses, he observed dispassionately that "standardized testing is on the upswing at the same time that tests are subject to widespread criticism" (p. 1021). As for persons who genuinely wished to understand this paradox, he curtly counseled them to look to the past and examine "the history of public concerns over standardized testing."

Testing Advocates Rejoin

When Arthur Jensen (1969) published his research about intelligence tests, the editors of the journal in which his work was appearing were aware of the discord that his study might create. They indicated that "because of the controversial nature of Dr. Jensen's article," they would devote the subsequent issue to critical rebuttals. As for the gist of the original report, the editors explained that "Jensen argues that the failure of recent compensatory education efforts to produce lasting effects on children's IQ and achievement suggests that the premises on which the efforts have been based should be reexamined" (p. 1). They added that Jensen questioned "a central notion upon which these and other educational programs have recently been based: that IQ differences are almost entirely a result of environmental differences and the cultural bias of IQ tests."

When they simply noted that Jensen's article was controversial, the editors were understating the situation. Critics of the article published furious reactions in newspapers, magazines, and journals. A *Newsweek* reporter ("Born Dumb," 1969) noted that "because of the unusually pessimistic tone of his conclusions, [Jensen's] article has stirred reaction far beyond the [Harvard Educational] Review's 12,000 circulation" (p. 84). This reporter emphasized that "interestingly enough, the board of editors of the *Harvard Educational Review* has no blacks; nor were any black psychologists invited by the Review to comment on Jensen's article." Looking back on the events that followed the publication of his article, Jensen (1974) wrote that "no other single article in the history of psychological publications has been subjected to so many niggling and nit-picking commentaries in so brief a time as my essay" (p. 467). He substantiated this point with a nine-page bibliography of articles, all of which had attempted to dispute his 1969 publication. Jensen's choice of the adjectives "niggling" and "nit-picking" indicated his own impression of these reaction pieces. After referring to the "violent controversy" that this article precipitated, Greenwald (1969) reported that many critics were so upset by Jensen's conclusions that they recommended the suppression of any future research studies that might vindicate those conclusions. Herrnstein and Murray (1994) later recalled that "the reaction to Jensen's article was immediate and violent" and "during the first few years after the...article was published, Jensen could appear in no public forum in the United States without triggering something perilously close to a riot" (p. 9). Ironically, Herrnstein and Murray's remarks, which were made within a controversial book about race and intelligence, revitalized those political liberals who had demanded the suppression of unpopular research ("Issue," 1994).

Because of their anti-intellectual tone, the adjurations to ignore politically unpopular investigations may have actually created sympathy for Jensen's research. For example, Greenwald expressed precisely this type of sympathy when he decried the anti-testing critics for "challenging one of our most strongly held beliefs, i.e., that all knowledge is good" (1969, p. 4). In a two-page introduction to a controversial article (Herrnstein, 1971) about intelligence testing, the editors of the *Atlantic* magazine stipulated that "if differences in mental abilities are inherited, and if success requires those abilities, and if earnings and prestige depend on success, then social standing will be based to some extent on inherited differences among people" (remarks by the editors of *Atlantic Monthly*, in Herrnstein, 1971, p. 43). After asking their readers to agree or disagree with the preceding conclusion, they observed that "it is only lately in America that public discussion requires physical, not to mention intellectual, courage, for the subject is close to taboo." They pointed out some of the similarities between Jensen's 1969 article and the earlier Coleman report, which also had addressed the relationship of race to academic achievement.

> [The Coleman report] was originally authorized by the Civil Rights Act of 1964... [When] Commissioner of Education Harold Howe announced the main findings...the announcement was made the Friday afternoon in July preceding the holiday weekend... No doubt the government was uneasy about the findings. Blacks lagged behind whites in scholastic achievement at every grade level from first to twelfth, and the differences increased with age. Ordinarily, one might blame the general inferiority of segregated black schools for that difference, but the Coleman study sought without success any clear effect of school quality on scholastic achievement for white children. If schools themselves deserve the blame for the poorer performance of blacks, then why shouldn't the whites be similarly affected? (Editors of the *Atlantic*, in remarks that preceded a report by Herrnstein, 1971, p. 44)

The editors concluded that bureaucrats in the Johnson Administration had displayed a mastery of "racial dialectics" in the way they systematically diverted attention from controversial questions about race and education.

Ebel (1975) judged that some of the allegations about culturally biased tests had been crafted to advance peculiarly political objectives. Although he admitted that tests had been "used unwisely, misinterpreted, overinterpreted, or handled as weapons," he still believed "that the argument that educational tests are biased against minorities because the tests reflect middle-class values has a superficial appeal but is probably fallacious."

> Language or experience differences that handicap the minority examinee in his attempt to demonstrate knowledge and skill on the test are likely to handicap him also in his attempt to utilize knowledge and skill in other situations. When this happens, the test cannot be said to be biased against a member of a minority. Rather it reflects quite accurately the usable competence he possesses. (p. 86)

Resorting to overstatement, Ebel warned that proponents of the culturally biased testing hypothesis might someday claim that spelling tests were biased against poor spellers, as evidenced by the fact that the poor spellers did less well on their exams than superior spellers.

Within an earlier article that he had published in an industrial journal, Guion (1966) had made a similar point. He had written candidly that all employment testing, because it was related to employment practices, was "by nature discriminatory." He explained that "an employer cannot be expected to take on all applicants regardless of their qualification; he is expected to be able to distinguish between those who are qualified and those who are not" (p. 25). While pursuing this unavoidable objective, employers had discerned a discrepancy between the test performance of white and African American workers. Although the anti-testing critics could have attributed this differential performance to unequal opportunities in public education, vocational schools, and federal training programs, they had concluded that all employment tests were "the clever subterfuge of confirmed racists" (Guion, 1966, p. 20). Convinced that this divisive conclusion was unfortunate, Guion pointed out ways in which the courts had begun to compensate. For example, they had defined the explicit circumstances under which testing was biased. He counseled employers that these court decisions could serve as a protective bulwark from legal actions. The employers could establish a sound defense by observing four cardinal principles: "tests must be validated as predictors," "validities must be recognized as situation-bound," the "validities of a predictor should be investigated," and "even a valid test should not be the sole basis for decisions" (p. 23).

During the same year that Guion had made the preceding remarks, the Equal Employment Opportunities Commission (EEOC) developed a straightforward but extremely controversial set of principles that were to guide the use of vocational tests. In his history of the civil rights error, Graham (1990) wrote about these 1960s guidelines and the reasons that the federal government had proposed them.

> The EEOC's 1966 guidelines required that any test that rejected blacks at a higher rate than whites must be statistically validated with full documentation by employers, and done so separately for blacks and whites ("differentially validated"). In August of 1970 the EEOC issued a more comprehensive set of guidelines, the professed goal of which was identical rejection rates for minority and non-minority job applicants. Thus the NAACP and the U.S. Solicitor General could argue before the Supreme Court that...a history of inferior segregated schooling had made fair competition impossible between blacks and whites on voting literacy and employment tests alike. (p. 386)

Petersen and Novick (1976) judged that both schools and businesses were trying "to eliminate cultural or racial unfairness arising from the use of tests." Despite their positive dispositions, not all organizations had found the logic of the EEOC helpful or even clear. As such, the task of compliance was complicated by the "many different definitions of what constitutes culture-fair selection," each of which "implicitly, though unfortunately not explicitly, involves a particular set of value judgments with different implications" (p. 3). After analyzing the functionality of the models that had been devised to explain bias, Petersen and Novick concluded that "the concepts of culture-fairness and group parity are neither useful nor tenable, and the models spawned from them should not enjoy institutional endorsement" (p. 28). Writing two years later in the *American Psychologist*, Flaugher (1978), who was associated with the Educational Testing Service, noted that the multiple definitions of test bias exhibited "widely disparate aspects frequently stemming from entirely different universes of discourse" (p. 671). With regard to the research that had been designed to evaluate the impact of test biases, he concluded that "the research results have been insignificant and indicate that [the biases] are not as significant as some supposed" (p. 678). In another *American Psychologist* article, Green (1978) distanced himself from those persons who had attacked tests for their cultural biases. Referring to this criticism in the past tense, he noted that "it was once thought that the tests were culturally biased, with many items requiring knowledge that black urban youths would have had no opportunity to acquire." He added that this attitude had changed because "careful attempts to find such items have had slim success" (p. 668). As to those critics who had maintained that standardized tests lacked objectivity, he curtly retorted that "perhaps the primary value of aptitude testing is objectivity" (p. 664).

In the *Journal of Negro Education*, Coffman (1980), a respected authority on assessment, dutifully paraphrased critical remarks that an opponent of testing had made before a House of Representatives subcommittee. Although Coffman conceded that some children had been assessed inappropriately with standardized tests, he stated firmly that "the critical issues in the testing of children are the same whether they are Black children or White children, boys or girls, poor children or rich children—issues such as whether or not the achievement being measured is what one really wants to measure, whether the questions constitute a fair sample, whether interpretations are legitimate and insightful or distorted and harmful" (pp. 312–313). As far as the current disposition of the public, the cautious Coffman advised that "there is far from unanimous agreement that standardized tests are undesirable" (p. 313).

More and more scholars began to affirm an emerging public view about the appropriateness of standardized testing. They extended their confidence even to those tests that were being completed by minority learners. Like so many analysts, Lennon (1980) acknowledged the unprecedented political pressure that had been placed on standardized tests. He wrote that they had been the "objects of intense scrutiny, often hostile, by educators and lay persons." He specifically reported that tests had been "accused of being unfair to members of minority subgroups..., of fostering lowered expectations..., of fostering inaccurate or irrelevant notions concerning the nature of ability, [and] of providing no useful information about learners" (p. 2). As a simple but effective rejoinder, Lennon reviewed several current tests that exhibited appropriate social adaptations, met educational expectations, contained evidence of effectiveness, and included proof of validity. In the *American Psychologist*, Cole (1981) also made remarks about the intense political dispute over testing. She observed that "the problem of test bias has recently received tremendous scientific and public scrutiny" (p. 1067). She added that this problem had been "a major focus of test critics, the courts, test developers, and scholars of testing." After reviewing the research studies that the controversy had generated, she concluded that "there is not large-scale, consistent bias against minority groups in the technical validity sense in the major, widely used and widely studied tests" (p. 1075). In a review conducted for the U.S. Department of Labor, Hunter (1983) examined "the now massive general literature showing that psychological tests are fair to minorities" (p. v). He stated firmly that "this literature shows that there is no single group validity, there is no differential validity, and tests overpredict rather than underpredict minority job performance."

Kelley (1982) addressed the deliberately biased tests that had been developed by African American scholars. One of these exams, the Black Intelligence Test of Cultural Homogeneity (BITCH), was intended to demonstrate the frustration that African Americans experienced when they took standardized tests. Kelley wrote that the BITCH "is constructed of slang words and phrases that are well known to certain Black residents of New York City" and that "if you do not happen to know this slang, you are going to make a very low score on the test" (p. 126). However, Kelley explained that this patently invalid test had been designed to serve as an example of faulty assessment. He remonstrated that "people who go to the time, effort, and expense of constructing most nationally standardized tests—at least any that have been constructed within the last ten to fifteen years—have had their sensitivities raised to the point that it is quite unlikely that items on their tests will show this kind of gross bias."

Anrig (1985), who was president of the Educational Testing Service, articulated two highly politicized arguments in an attempt to show that standardized testing promoted social egalitarianism. He explained that testing was the corollary to the national assumption that "what a person has…should not be a product of that person's birth, but rather what he or she has earned with labor, diligence, and sweat of the brow" (p. B6). Testing also helped to validate another fundamentally American conviction, namely that "opportunity should be equal, but promotion—whether educational, social, or economic—should be earned."

Anrig's response to the anti-testing critics had been strident, political, and confrontational. However, representatives from the testing corporations sometimes were disarmingly accommodating. In one case, the leaders of Educational Testing Service had not confronted a report (Tittle, McCarthy, & Steckler, 1974) alleging that women, like the members of racial minority groups, had been victimized by standardized tests. The authors of this critical report had not demonstrated that the test scores of female students lagged behind those of males because of sexist biases. Instead, they had paraphrased an earlier report in which one of the authors (Tittle, 1973) had argued that gender biases were significant because "tests, along with textbooks and other instructional materials, play a role in counseling," "any sexist biases in the field of educational testing are likely to have widespread effects," and the results of tainted tests affect "students, parents, and teachers" (p. 118). Not only did executives at the Educational Testing Service refrain from challenging this document, but they actually published it, circulated it within their organization, and encouraged their test developers to heed its advice. The corporation then provided copies of the monograph to scholars and the general public. Because females were scoring competitively on tests, the sexism-in-testing criticism did not generate the wide media attention that the allegations of racism had produced. Nonetheless, the accommodating attitude of the test publishers may have reduced the amount of media sensationalism that this criticism could have received.

During the period from 1980 to 1981, the Educational Testing Service had used a similarly reconciliatory tone while addressing accusations that it had been racially insensitive. The organization had convened conferences at which participants deliberated about biased testing. The papers and transcripts from these meetings were gathered into a compendium (Anderson & Coburn, 1982) in which the authors emphasized the ability of researchers to discourage cultural bias in their tests. The authors also called attention to the ways in which tests could promote equal opportunity. The writer (Wooten, 1982) of the lead article from this volume made this point in a straightforward manner.

> One of the means of identifying group disparities is through group assessment. Obviously, testing becomes a foundation upon which equality is built. Academic freedom, vision, and courage are necessary, if academia is to make its greatest contributions. Educational diversity is protected by the First Amendment of the Constitution of the United States. We must resist vigorously those who advocate control in the name of democratization, pluralism, or other trend-setting terms that sacrifice excellence for all to equality for a few. (p. 15)

Looking back on their efforts to promote fair testing, the managers of the Educational Testing Service (1998) recapitulated some of their reconciliatory actions.

> Since 1980, ETS has required its tests and test materials to be carefully reviewed for sensitivity concerns to ensure that these materials acknowledge the contributions of minority group members and do not include insensitive or offensive material. Since the late 1980s, ETS has also required that its test questions be analyzed for [Differential Item Functioning], not only to assess how individual test questions perform but also to identify patterns of differential performance, which can then be incorporated into the fairness review process by alerting question writers and reviewers about topics that should be avoided. (Educational Testing Service, 1998, pp. 1–2)

Ravitch (2003) identified numerous instances in which publishers had changed the language and content of test items. She demonstrated that voluntary changes had been made over a multi-decade period in response to political pressures from both liberal and conservative factions. She then described the current practices that the publishers were employing.

> Publishers of tests…today routinely engage…panels of bias and sensitivity experts to screen their products. This is a process that effectively removes everything from tests…that might be offensive to any group or individual. It is designed to strip away words and ideas that offend anyone. Bias and sensitivity review has evolved into an elaborate and widely accepted code of censorship that is implemented routinely. (p. 18)

Focusing her attention on the politics of education, Ravitch (2003) had irreverently entitled her book *The Language Police: How Pressure Groups Restrict What Students Learn*. Decades earlier, other scholars had made similar observations. For example, Hechinger (Hechinger, 1977) had written about politics and education in the *New York Times*. He had assumed a brash approach when he attempted to explain why multiple allegations of unfairness had not reduced the schools' commitment to standardized tests. He suggested that each school was "part of a system within a society that loves charts" and that Americans "want to know just exactly how they are doing in everything from sexual performance to their children's third-year reading achievements" (p. 16). Despite the flippant tone of his remarks, Hechinger clearly recognized the pervasive influence of politics on educational assessment. He counseled his readers that the continuing use of tests was connected to "the constant pressure by parents, school administrators, state education authorities, Congress and by colleges—to compare the performance of each child, each school and each district with 'the norm'" (p. 16). He judged that politics had a more significant impact on the fate of testing than the "lip service" that American educators gave "to the idea that the only thing that really matters is the individual child."

Disregarding the stodgy rhetorical routes by which academicians had approached the topic of culturally biased testing, a comic-book artist relied on humor in the February 1980 issue of the *Atlantic* magazine. His cartoon, which is reproduced in Figure 6.1, appeared on the front cover and reflected the changing public attitudes toward the many allegations of culturally biased tests. The cartoon depicted Archie, the popular comic-book hero, taking a standardized high-school exam with two friends. Archie, who displayed great nervousness, was thinking, "Let's see...the opposite of *'abstruse'...'pellucid'...? 'salient'...?* [original emphasis]" A poised and confident Veronica, who is sitting next to Archie was thinking, "This is a cinch! ***Stanford*** here I come!!!" Jughead, who had crumpled his exam and thrown it to the back of the room, was completely indifferent. He cavalierly remarked, "These tests are ***culturally biased***!"

Even while ferocious attacks were being made upon it, the standardized testing movement grew stronger. After examining more than eight decades of research trends, Rudman (1987) detected "a steady development of theory and practices related to the measurement of educational and psychological constructs" (p. 6). Also assuming an historical perspective, Phelps (1998) analyzed 70 polls and surveys that had been conducted during the preceding 25 years. He concluded that "essentially, most adults do not believe that standardized tests are biased against minorities" (p. 9). He added that "the majorities in favor of more testing, more high-stakes testing, or higher stakes in testing have been large, often very large, and fairly consistent over the years" (p. 14).

Financial records comprised the least controversial data with which to confirm the testing industry's resilience to attacks. For example, the Educational Testing

Figure 6.1 Cartoon about Culturally Biased Tests (*"ARCHIE" comic book cover courtesy of Archie Comic Publications, Inc., copyright 1980, 2003. The "ARCHIE" property copyright and trademark of Archie Comic Publications, Inc. All Rights Reserved.*)

Service, which was the largest test publisher during the 1960s and 1970s, was vilified for insensitivity to racial minority groups. However, this criticism did not affect the organization's earnings. Each year, this corporation published a detailed financial statement that indicated its total income. In 1961, that figure exceeded $10,600,000 (Educational Testing Service, 1961). The corporation's income had increased to more than $17,700,000 by 1965 (Educational Testing Service, 1966). By 1969, the amount exceeded $30,500,000 (Educational Testing Service, 1969). A report (Educational Testing Service, 1980) published a decade later indicated that the annual revenue of the corporatio n increased from $58,500,000 to $94,200,000 during the five-year period that had begun in 1975.

Summary

At the beginning of the twentieth century, critics had depicted standardized testing as culturally and linguistically insensitive. Some persons represented it as an explicitly racist procedure. These allegations were restated often, especially during the civil rights era. Although the attacks on testing were widely publicized, the proponents of tests were able to maintain the confidence of business, the community, education, the military, and government. As a result, testing was never truly threatened. In fact, its popularity and financial security increased even during periods of intense assault.

CHAPTER 7

Continuing Criticism

The crucial questions about any test are who decides what's on it, and who sets the standards by which student performance is judged.
—FINN, 1997

Early twentieth-century critics deplored standardized tests because they relied on unnatural tasks, sampling, and statistics. They also worried that these tests provided the basis for racial and ethnic discrimination. Although later critics remained concerned about these issues, they focused a great deal of their attention on the problems that large and powerful testing companies had created. They deprecated these businesses for their excessive earnings, inordinate secrecy, independence, disproportionate influence on society, and inherent conflicts of interests. They especially vilified the Educational Testing Service. Despite these accusations, both the Educational Testing Service and standardized testing flourished.

Allegations of Test Abuse

Persons with positivist dispositions accepted standardized tests as valid measures of students' progress. They were equally optimistic about the ability of tests to promote accountability among teachers, schools, districts, and states. Figure 7.1 is an illustration from a 1950s assessment booklet that was intended for parents (Wrightstone, 1954). Like this picture, the accompanying text represented the scholastic testing program as a cooperative venture in which the thoughtful contributions of parents were solicited and welcomed.

Needless to say, not all persons viewed scholastic testing as an idealistic, cooperative, and beneficial venture. In fact, many individuals considered it to be incompatible with the principles of sound education. Looking back on the early part of the twentieth century, Kandel (1936) indicated that intelligence tests and standardized academic tests had become the two alternatives to traditional examinations. He reported that supporters of the new assessment instruments objected to the traditional examinations "on the ground that the marking is subjective and consequently neither valid nor reliable" (p. 79). The advocates of traditional exams were just as confrontational. They retorted that the new tests were "neither specific nor comprehensive in what they measure" and that the standardized academic tests "set up norms which are not universally applicable" (p. 79).

Kandel explained that the dispute about testing became further complicated after a fourth genre of assessment emerged. Like the other types of testing, this genre had been the object of both praise and criticism.

The construction of the new type test brings together in coöperative [*sic*] effort the teachers of a subject and the experts in measurement. The new type test, may, however, have the

Figure 7.1 Idealized Depiction of Parental Involvement With School Testing

same character of detachment as any other form of external examination. For this reason it is subjected to the criticism that it controls the organization of the content of courses of study, that it leads to special preparation, [and] that it interferes with the flexibility and adaptation of courses of study. (Kandel, 1936, p. 81)

Suspicions about standardized testing were not confined to the early portion of the century. The president of the Educational Testing Service noted that "since World War II, much of the concern about the social effects of testing has been focused on the use and misuse of the scores as predictors of success in college" (Turnbull, 1975, p. vii). He explained that this criticism had intensified as the use of tests had increased. At the college level, admissions officers had begun to rely more on tests because the "demand for college places outran supply of seats in the freshman classes of the high-prestige institutions."

Some critics believed that testing was a sinister force that exacerbated rather than solved academic and social problems. Thompson (1959) depicted testing as a mechanized procedure that could encase "the child in unnatural situations of infinite boredom." She wrote melodramatically that it would create either uncritical robots or "rebels, 'breaking out in all directions' in the demonstrations of juvenile delinquency, with the reactions of savages" (p. 122). Some persons warned that tests had a negative impact on parents as well as children. In the *New York Times Magazine*, Hechinger and Hechinger (1960) wrote of the test "hysteria that is sweeping the country—or at least, the Eastern seaboard" and that was exemplified by "reports of parents in New York City hiring 'tutors' for their infants so that they will pass the tests for admission to 'selective' nursery schools" (p. 14). Although their article purported to highlight the virtues as well as the faults of tests, the authors could not resist the opportunity to underscore the "serious weakness of machine-tested education." They concluded that assessment experts, who had concealed the limitations of tests, could "prevent disaster only if they tell the public what tests *cannot* do" (p. 37). They challenged the advocates of testing to make this confession, even though this act would be unusual "in an age which regards boosting and boasting the essence of 'good public relations.'" Also writing during the early 1960s, Gross (1962) noted that "brain watching" was a "vital twentieth-century sociological phenomenon that has made your mind, inner thoughts, political opinions, frustrations (including the sexual), aspirations—what we commonly call *personality*—the raw material of a humming, seemingly insatiable American industry" (p. 1). He warned readers that brain watchers currently were gathering data on "some 50,000,000 hapless Americans."

A decade later, critics were still underscoring the pervasive weaknesses of standardized tests. Reporting about "the American way of testing" in *Time Magazine*, Wheeler (1979) focused on the academic damage that standardized testing had caused. A byline explained that "many forces have contributed to the decline of American students' writing ability but none has been more effective than the widespread use of multiple-choice tests" (p. 40). An accompanying photo showed adolescents in a crowded room applying themselves to "multiple-choice questions on a College Board test." Switching his focus to preschoolers, McGarvey (1974) endorsed a booklet from a New York City Institute that advised the "parents of low-income children" about the academic liabilities of the Metropolitan Achievement Test in Reading. McGarvey thought that the authors of this booklet had offered "impressive documentation" that the Metropolitan Achievement Test was "ambiguous because there is more than one correct response possible on many items," "deceitful because it takes pains to trick children into choosing a wrong answer," "destructive because it seeks to impose an adult way of thinking on children," and invalid because it "doesn't even do what it claims to do—test reading" (p. 24).

Mixing several metaphors, Murphy (1975) warned that children were "choking in a stranglehold of norms" and that "confinement to a narrow, tight, constrained mental and emotional environment limited by statistically based norms and unrealistically restricted expectations can starve as well as frustrate the child, just as the Berkeley rat cages interfered with optimal development of brain tissue and problem-solving in little rats" (p. 37). Hein (1975) focused on the excessive amount of time that testing consumed. He insisted that in some schools "as many as six weeks of the spring term are essentially lost for instructional purposes while the classes go though the agony of taking the various required tests dictated by the school district, the state and the federal program" (p. 29).

Although Wardrop (1976) optimistically judged that "most objections to standardized testing are directed not at the tests themselves but at thoughtless and inappropriate uses," he still did concede that "there has probably been no other time in history when the arguments—pro and con—have been more heated" (p. vii). In the *New Republic*, Demick (1979b) published an article with the disturbing title, *The Kindergarten Rat Race*. In an equally alarmist *Washington Post* report, Omang (1979) described standardized tests as "the branding irons that have divided a generation of Americans into the sheep and the goats" (p. A10). She alleged that tests contained "racial, sexual and cultural bias that automatically classifies blacks and other minorities as goats."

Downey (1977) advised readers of the *American School Board Journal* that "potent factions within the educational establishment have begun to grow leery of standardized tests" and that "forces are marshaling right now for a struggle with what is being described as 'the multimillion-dollar international testing cartel'" (p. 27). Fiske (1977) reported that testing became a major issue in New York City after a State Supreme Court justice, who had discovered "that some students had been drilled on test questions,...ordered the Board of Education to cancel citywide reading tests" (p. 1). Green (1981) noted that standardized tests had been "severely criticized by several groups...for being secret, biased, and susceptible to coaching" (p. 1).

Lennon (1980) summarized the criticism about standardized educational assessment and speculated about its consequences. He reported that "group intelligence or mental ability tests, never free of some criticism, have in the past thirty years been the objects of intense scrutiny, often hostile, by educators and lay persons." However, he thought this criticism had grown to such proportions that it threatened the future of testing.

> Given the long history of the use of scholastic aptitude tests in American education, their centrality in most established testing programs, it might seem beyond question to anticipate their continued widespread use for the foreseeable future. Indeed this would be true were it not for the fact that these tests have been the type most subject to criticism and attack during the past decade or more. They have been a particular target, for example, of the anti-test advocates in the National Education Association, which has called for a moratorium on their use. The proscription against the use of group intelligence tests in New York City and in California has promoted some other jurisdictions to reconsider the role of these tests in their programs. (p. 8)

Tomlinson and Treacy (1979) paraphrased remarks from John Ryor. Ryor was the president of the National Education Association, which was the largest professional organization of teachers. Ryor had observed that "the whole notion of norm-referenced, standardized tests makes a lie out of the often-stated concern for individual differences." He added philosophically that "the only competition worth the name is competition with oneself" and that "the most tragic aspect of such tests is that they contribute to the training of children to do better than somebody else" (Ryor, 1978, as quoted by Tomlinson & Treacy, 1979, p. 13). Ryor listed additional reasons that he and the members of his organization opposed testing.

> Since 1971, the NEA has sought a moratorium on standardized testing because of beliefs that the tests do not do what they purport to do, that they tend to be culturally biased, that they are norm-referenced, and that they automatically label half the students as losers. Standardized tests seldom correspond significantly to local learning objectives, and they can't be used to measure growth over a short period of time…Further, many school systems tend to misuse the tests in jumping to unwarranted conclusions about curriculum and to justify tracking students into inflexible decisions regarding education and career.…[The NEA maintains a] belief in the importance of evaluation and supported such tools as individual diagnostic tests, teacher-made tests, school letter grades, and criterion-referenced tests—but not standardized tests. (Remarks by Ryor, 1978, as paraphrased by Tomlinson & Treacy, 1979, p. 13)

Even though the National Education Association's political efforts to ban standardized tests were unsuccessful, a later report ("How Other Organizations View," 1982) did not conceal this organization's continued antipathy to large-scale assessment.

> The Association believes that standardized tests should not be administered when they are
> a. Potentially damaging to a student's self-concept
> b. Biased
> c. Used as the only criterion for student placement
> d. Invalid, unreliable, or out-of-date
> e. Used as a basis for the allocation of federal, state, or local funds
> f. Used by testing companies or publishers to promote their own financial interests at the expense of sound educational uses
> g. Used to compare individual schools
> h. Used in an exploitive manner by the media
> i. Used as the sole criterion for graduation or promotion
> j. Inappropriate for the use intended
> k. Used as a criterion for the development of a state system of classification of schools and/or school systems. (p. 17)

Other examples of anti-assessment criticism were easy to locate. Houts (1977) had assembled an anthology of articles about testing, which he entitled *The Myth of Measurability*. In the unlikely event that this title did not convey the authors' attitudes, readers needed only to consult chapter titles such as *The Politics of IQ, The Trouble with IQ Tests, The Bell Shaped Pitfall, The Score against IQ, The Hidden Agenda of IQ, A Case of Cultural Myopia, How the Testing Industry Operates,* and *How to Avoid the Dangers of Testing*. Like Houts, Strenio (1981) wrote a book in which the title of the monograph and the titles of its chapters amply revealed his attitudes toward testing. The book was entitled *The Testing Trap*. Its first five chapters were *You May Be the Next Victim of "Scientific" Testing, The Impact of Test Abuse, An Industry out of Control, False Claims of Objectivity*, and *The Illusion of Precision*.

While describing encounters between the advocates and opponents of tests, Lerner (1980) quoted a passage in which an editor for the *New York Times* compared the disputants to the biblical figures of Goliath and David. Lerner called attention to the one-sided manner in which this writer had depicted the "giant $150 million-a-year testing industry, represented by some fancy Albany lawyers." She contrasted this characterization with the editor's description of the testing opponents as the "representatives of a coalition of student and consumer groups." Lerner speculated that a recent court victory by the anti-testing coalition had convinced it that it was within "sight of its publicly announced goal: the elimination from American life of all objective standardized tests of academic and vocational competence" (1980, p. 119).

In an article entitled *America's Test Mania*, a *New York Times* editor (Fiske, 1988) listed predictable problems with tests. He judged that most educators of the late 1980s agreed with him that these problems were significant and prevalent.

- Tests assume a single correct answer to problems...
- They measure how good students are at recognizing information, not generalizing it...
- Since the tests are timed...they place more value on thinking quickly than on thinking profoundly.
- Most standardized tests focus on basic skills....[and] don't say much about higher-order skills like inferential reasoning or problem-solving [*sic*].
- They emphasize isolated learning, not the integration of facts and ideas. (p. 19)

Also summarizing popular criticism, Swanson and Watson (1989) recapitulated allegations that tests discriminated against learners with disabilities, invaded privacy, and rigidly shaped academic programs. They also believed that the personnel who were administering and interpreting the tests could not discern "individuals of unique cognitive, linguistic, and affective learning styles" (p. 6).

Perrone (1991) reviewed an anti-testing position paper that had been endorsed by the Association for Childhood Education International. He noted that this document complemented a 1976 position paper from that same organization. The earlier paper had called for a moratorium on standardized testing of young students. After conceding that this 1976 paper had failed to restrict the spread of testing, Perrone affirmed the sponsoring organization's enduring confidence in the original recommendations. He wrote that the current membership "believes that no standardized testing should occur through grade 2, and questions the need for testing in the remaining elementary school years" (p. 1).

Public Disclosure Legislation

The anti-testing groups believed that the large testing companies had concealed critical information from the public. This disposition was evident when Zegart (1978) advised an audience that "the tests that ETS administers to millions every year produce reams of data" of which some "is destroyed almost immediately" and "some is kept indefinitely" (p. 5). With regard to those data that were retained, they were protected by the "strictest safeguards." Demick (1979a) displayed an equally antagonistic attitude when he wrote that the "testing agencies, the virtual gatekeepers of the American elite, have become entrusted with the task of preserving the meritocratic [*sic*] system by means of multiple-choice exams" (p. 12). He added that "people who pay to take the tests are powerless to know how the questions were compiled, what the right answers were, or even if their scores have been added up right." Aware of the hostile sentiments toward testing, Smith (1979) wrote that opponents were "fueled by more than just resentment" and that "for ideological reasons, they dislike the near-monopoly of the testing business by the Educational Testing Service" (p. 1110). He continued that "they dislike the secrecy with which this firm and others go about their business" and that "some of them dislike testing per se, viewing it more as a barrier to advancement than as an opportunity for objective evaluation."

Goldstein (1977) identified court challenges that had been brought against standardized testing corporations or the organizations that employed their products. He reported that some of the key issues that had been raised during these challenges included the absence of equal protection for all examinees, the use of an unwarranted amount of secrecy, and the failure of the testing companies to acknowledge the liability that resulted from inappropriate assessment. Also looking for recurring themes in the legal cases that had involved tests, Bersoff (1981) pointed to allegations about cultural bias, invalid test content, and violations of consumer rights. Bersoff thought that some of the censorious court decisions were making psychologists aware "that they will be held responsible for their conduct." He warned that the sheer number of cases contested in court should convince psychologists "that legal scrutiny of psychological testing is both a present and future reality" (p. 1055).

The New York state legislature strengthened the court rulings on standardized assessment with a special "Truth-in-Testing" law. This law was directed at the exams that were being used by colleges and within certain professions. Demick (1979a) reported that the law was designed to ensure that consumers would obtain examination questions, the correct answers to those questions, information about the validity of exams, and information about "how their scores will be computed;

what the tester's contractual obligation to them is; and how test scores have been found to correlate with important background factors such as race" (p. 12). Before the law had taken effect, Smith (1979) surmised that it was intended to regulate "the standardized exams commonly required for admission to college, graduate school, law school, business school, medical school, and in most cases, the professions themselves." He noted that "supporters of the New York law claim it will expose test questions that are culturally biased and reveal errors in scoring." Brownstein and Nairn (1979) reported that bills to enact similar laws had been introduced in 10 other states and the U.S. House of Representatives.

The New York law became effective in January of 1980. Eighteen months later, the *New York Times* published a report with the title *Twenty-two Thousand Scores Revised after Error Is Detected on Law School Exam* (1981). The author of this article noted that the exam scores of law-school applicants were changed "after a test-taker found a flaw in the purported correct answer on a geometry question" (p. A29). The reporter continued that this "was the third time in recent months that errors have been discovered in tests prepared by the Education Testing Service...as a result of students' receiving test questions and answers under new disclosure policies." Making a similar connection, a reporter for *Newsweek* wrote that "what brought the latest error to light was a new policy encouraged by truth-in-testing laws, of disclosing test answers to students" ("Crumbling the Pyramids," 1981). For a front-page story ("Student Outwits PSAT," 1981) in the *Boston Globe*, a reporter selected the simple but telling byline "Exam Flunks." The education editor for the *New York Times* (Fiske, 1981a; 1981b; 1981c; 1981d) portrayed these incidents in a manner that was sure to embarrass the Educational Testing Service.

New York Times reporters depicted the discoveries of errors within the law exam and the Scholastic Aptitude Test as vindications of New York's testing law. A survey from the adversarial Committee for Fair and Open Testing alleged that more than 500,000 students had been victimized by ETS errors during the preceding decade (Jacobson, 1981). Wainer (1983), a senior research scientist in charge of statistics and data analysis at ETS, expressed his indignation about one incident in which a student had successfully challenged a test item that had been prepared by his organization. He was distressed primarily because this incident was "picked up by the national press as few educational testing stories ever were before" (p. 87). Wainer used hermetic statistical techniques to demonstrate that the potential damage from this particular error was not in proportion to the warnings that its discovery had generated. Given the mathematical sophistication of his argument, as well as the scholarly journal in which he published it, it is unlikely that Wainer's report had any impact on the public's attitudes toward the incident in question, standardized testing, or the Educational Testing Service.

Solomon (1981), who was the executive director of the Educational Testing Service, also had wished to discount some of the criticism that had been directed at his organization. However, he cleverly selected rhetorical techniques that made his arguments accessible to the general public. For example, he used multiple-choice questions to highlight the unanticipated consequences of New York's Truth-in-Testing law.

Because tests disclosed under the law can be used only once, some increases in test fees have been necessary to cover the extra cost of developing new tests (as well as to cover inflation). Which is correct?

(a)   The cost of the SAT, which used to be $8.25, is now $11 in New York State.
(b)   The cost of the Graduate Management Admission Test…which used to be $12.50 is now $23.50.
(c)The cost of the Gra   duate Record Exam …, which used to $14, is now $20.
(d)   All of the above. (p. A19)

After revealing the correct answer as item *d*, Solomon pointed to additional unintended consequences of New York's Truth-in-Testing law. For example, some tests were being offered less frequently while others had been eliminated completely from the state. Although one of the medical school exams continued to be offered in New York, Solomon pointed out that this was the case only because a court injunction had shielded that particular exam from the testing law. He challenged his readers to dispute item *d* as the correct answer to the following question, which concerned the effects that the elimination of standardized tests would have on college admissions.

If the opponents of standardized college admissions tests are successful, what factors does history suggest will probably become more important in deciding whom to admit?

(a)   The wealth, influence, and social position of the applicant's parents and friends.
(b)   The reputation of the applicant's high school or prep school.
(c)The whiteness a   nd/or maleness of the applicant.
(d)   All of the above. (p. A19)

Many of the facts that Solomon reported had been forecast before New York's law had even taken effect. Ravitch (1979) predicted that "divulging the answers at the end of each test will require the testing companies to hire more employees, devise more questions, and charge more" (p. 189). Kleiman (1979) advised readers of the *New York Times* that prohibitive costs of complying with the state law had persuaded the Association of Medication Colleges to cease administering its exams to New York residents. Writing in October of 1979 about the likely impact of the newly approved testing law, Fiske (1979) conceded that most of New York's current specialty exams would become unavailable. He explained that "sponsors and publishers of 20 of the 26 tests covered by the law have concluded that it is economically impossible to comply with the requirement to publish questions within 30 days of reporting students' scores" (p. A1). The affected tests included the Entrance Examination for Schools of Practical/Vocational Nursing, the New Medical College Admissions Test, the Minnesota Engineering Analogies Test, the Pharmacy College Admissions Test, and the Veterinary Aptitude Test. Fiske quoted an administrator at the New York Education Department who opined that "some schools will have to simply drop the use of test scores and rely on other kinds of information." This official added ominously that "for students with good grades this [use of other indicators of academic ability] will probably be all right, but for others it could cause serious problems" (remarks by D. R. Bowen, quoted by Fiske, 1979, p. B4).

Less than eight percent of New York's test takers actually paid the fee to receive copies of the questions and answers on the Scholastic Aptitude Test. Owen (1999), who was an opponent of standardized tests, provided his editorialized impression of a reaction from the staff at Educational Testing Service.

> After New York's truth-in-testing law went into effect, ETS gleefully pointed out that virtually all of the people who requested copies of their questions and answers were wealthy, high-scoring whites. This fact, ETS said, discredited the law's supporters by proving that the whole stink had been raised by a small group of rich, white grade-grubbers. (pp. 261–262)

Because requests by New Yorkers created a relatively modest financial strain, the directors of the Educational Testing Service voluntarily decided to extend the same opportunities to students in other states. Critics who questioned the sincerity of the directors were incensed by this action. This ire was discernible when Begley and Carey (1981) interviewed a confrontational spokesperson for the New York Public Interest Research Group. Even though the residents of other states already had access to information from the Educational Testing Service, this spokesperson feared that the company eventually might cease sharing this material. Therefore, this individual recommended that each state pass a truth-in-testing law patterned after that of New York.

Spewing Vitriol at the Educational Testing Service

Because it dominated the assessment field, the Educational Testing Service attracted the attention of the anti-testing factions. Robertson (1980) identified this organization as the primary target at which regulatory testing legislation had been aimed. Alleging that the Educational Testing Service had united with the special interest groups that were resisting New York's truth-in-testing legislation, he identified some of its allies as the "Law School Admissions Council, the Association of American Law Schools, and a large assortment of law school and university admissions personnel." He contrasted these groups with those that were lobbying in support of the regulatory bill. The list of supporters included "the New

York Public Interest Research Group, the Parents and Teachers Association…the National Association for the Advancement of Colored People…the National Education Association…the New York State United Teachers Association, and various educators and student organizations" (p. 181).

In the *Wall Street Journal*, Zonana (1978) had reported that two large nonprofit corporations specialized in college entrance exams. One of these was American College Testing Company, which had reported revenues of $18,000,000 in 1976. The other organization was the Educational Testing Service, which had brought in $70,000,000 that same year. The success of the American College Testing Company was the result of its college entrance exams. Although the Educational Testing Service offered a diversified range of tests, more than 40 percent of its revenue came from college entrance examinations.

Other opponents of testing had not concealed their antagonism to the Educational Testing Service. In *American Psychologist*, McClelland (1973) had depicted the Educational Testing Service as an institution that "employs about 2,000 people…and makes enough money to support a large basic research operation" (p. 1). Even magazine and newspaper reporters began to refer to this corporation in a pejorative fashion. The author of an article ("Pleasures of Nonprofitability," 1976) in *Forbes* wrote that "if Princeton, N.J.'s Education Testing Service were a public company and not a self-contained tax-exempt nonprofit organization, it would probably have long since emerged as one of the darlings of Wall Street" (p. 89). The writer explained that "over the past 30 years, it has easily racked up a record as one of the hottest little growth companies in the U.S. business." This author added that the Educational Testing Service, although it was in theory a nonprofit company, "in fact shapes up as a tough, aggressive and even dynamic growth business." Within the *New Republic*, Masters (1977) warned that "anyone who must deal with [ETS] is completely at the mercy of this private monopoly….[and] must take the tests ETS offers, must supply the information ETS requests, and must pay the fees ETS charges" (p. 13). She concluded that the corporation was "becoming the cradle-to-grave arbiter of social and economic mobility." The president of the Educational Testing Service had no choice but to acknowledge this intense and sustained criticism. However, he cleverly character-ized it as "a corollary of the importance of testing rather than a threat to it" (remarks made by B. Turnbull, quoted in "Ticket of Admission," 1976, p. 94).

The anti-testing critics who had endorsed New York's Truth-in-Testing law were especially confrontational with the Educational Testing Service. In the *New Republic*, Demick (1979a) characterized the Educational Testing Service as "the undisputed lord of the nation's testers." In the *Wall Street Journal*, Zonana (1978) chastised the Corporation for its "posh new $3 million hotel and conference center on the headquarters 'campus'" (p. 21). Building on these remarks, a writer for *Science* noted that "attention is drawn to the firm's headquarters on 400 acres: the eight staff buildings, the president's expensive home, the duck pond, and the $3 million conference-center hotel with tennis courts and swimming pool" (Smith, 1979, p. 1110). A staff member of *Politics & Education* apprized readers that the Educational Testing Service "plows most of its $4 million dollar [*sic*] 'non-profit margin'…into the maintenance of its considerable physical plant, and operation of what is probably the largest educational research facility in the world" (Zegart, 1978, p. 5). Like so many other reporters, this writer could not resist the opportunity to refer to the "400 acre [*sic*] corporate headquarters" and the "$3 million [*sic*] hotel-conference-center."

The most widely discussed assault on the Educational Testing Service may have come from Ralph Nader. Although his 1980 report was identified on its cover page as the "Nader Report," it actually had been written by Allan Nairn (1980), an undergraduate student who had collaborated with Nader. A *New York Times* reporter ("Less than an 'A' for the S.A.T.," 1980) pointed out that "the authors of the 555-page report conclude that multiple-choice examinations, like the Scholastic Aptitude Tests taken by millions each year, do not, in fact, predict much of anything" (p. A22). This reporter added that the authors' conclusions "may be overstated, but should not, in any event, obscure the genuine value of the study." This value was the exposition of "a good deal of research that testmakers heretofore have kept to themselves." This revelation would help "to moderate the inflated importance that many people…now attach to tests."

Haney (1981) described some publicity that Nader arranged for this report.

> The prominence of popular concern over standardized testing was perhaps epitomized by the appearance of Ralph Nader on the Johnny Carson show in January 1980 to publicize the Nader/Nairn report on the Educational Testing Service (ETS). After condemning the "reign of ETS," Nader gave an impassioned plea for wider consideration of traits like perseverance, wisdom, and creativity—traits that cannot be measured with multiple-choice tests. The "Tonight Show" audience broke into spontaneous applause. (p. 1021)

Like many other anti-testing apologists, Nairn (1980) revealed his attitudes in his book's title, *The Reign of ETS: The Corporation That Makes up Minds.* If potential readers still were uncertain about this author's attitudes, they only had to scan the passage about the creation of the Educational Testing Service.

> The Educational Testing Service was a new species of corporate organization, a "soft institution" which combined the techniques and wealth of industry with the privileges and immunities of non-profit education, all beneath the mantle of serving the public good. Insulated from many of the legal and economic obligations which constrain most corporate managers, and shielded politically by a mission under which each act of expansion is by definition an act of benevolence, ETS has become one of the nation's fastest-growing and most profitable corporations. To an extent unmatched by other forms of large-scale government agency…the soft institution operates beyond the reach of economic choice or political will. As an organization endowed by its creators with the right to perform a function central to millions of lives, the ETS test system has been built to absorb shocks from below and outlive the people it serves. (Nairn, 1980, pp. 295–296)

Nairn and Nader had railed against the political insulation of the Educational Testing Service. Nonetheless, they acknowledged that this corporation had been designed to withstand precisely the type of pressure that special interest groups would exert. The Educational Testing Service had been established in 1947 by three influential educational organizations—the Carnegie Foundation for the Advancement of Teaching, the American Council on Education, and the College Entrance Examination Board. The directors of these nonprofit organizations agreed to turn over their testing programs and a portion of their assets, including some of their personnel, to the Educational Testing Service ("Story Behind," 1992).

The oldest testing program transferred to the Educational Testing Service came from the College Entrance Examination Board, which had been established in 1900 to help administrators judge the qualifications of university applicants (Schudson, 1972). Fuess (1950) wrote colorfully that "the College Entrance Examination Board was in its origins an attempt to introduce law and order into an educational anarchy which towards the close of the nineteenth century had become exasperating, indeed almost intolerable, to schoolmasters" (p. 3). Prior to the establishment of the College Board, university officials had relied on high-school transcripts or their own institutional achievement tests when making decisions about the students that they would accept. Because the reliability and validity of these data were questionable, standardized testing seemed to be an ideal solution to the problem. After World War I, the College Board complemented its achievement tests with the Scholastic Aptitude Test (SAT). Wigdor and Garner (1982a; 1982b) observed that students should have been predisposed toward the SAT because, in theory, it helped those who lacked the pre-collegiate experiences that were needed to gain entry to select colleges. Because more students were applying to elite colleges and training programs than could be accommodated, administrators could use SAT scores to identify highly qualified students. The design, management, and administration of the SAT eventually became the responsibilities of the Educational Testing Service.

The architects of the Educational Testing Service had designed this organization to sustain intense political stress. One of the ways that they accomplished this was by ensuring the unit's financial solvency. After describing the fiscal difficulties that the College Board had faced during the years that it had managed the SAT, Fuess (1950) recalled the straightforward manner in which the new managers of the Educational Testing Service dealt with one of their first financial problems.

> The Board was now a purchaser, instead of a producer of tests; and the first report from the ETS of the cost of operations for the Board account indicated that the inflationary trend was affecting even the making of examinations. Accordingly the Board increased its fees by one dollar for each test program or two dollars for the combined series—thus following the practice, not uncommon in industry, of passing increased costs on to the consumer. (p. 192)

How well was the Educational Testing Service able to withstand the political and financial pressures that were placed on it during the late 1970s and early 1980s? The most objective data with which to answer this question may be those from this organization's annual financial reports. Two of these reports (Educational Testing Service, 1981, 1987) itemized the corporation's annual income from 1977 to 1984. During each year of this period, the annual revenue had increased significantly. At the end of 1977, the corporation's total annual income had been $70,300,000. This sum had grown to $106,800,000 by 1980 and then to $148,300,000 after another four years.

Sacks (1999), who was a harsh critic of the Educational Testing Service, recognized that "educators and consumer advocates were expressing some serious concerns about the role of standardized testing in the 1970s and 1980s" (p. 227). As to the impact of this sustained and highly politicized assault, Sacks conceded that "ETS seems to have barely felt it." To substantiate his evaluation, he pointed out the "ETS's sales surged 256 percent from 1980 through 1996" (p. 227).

Vocational Testing

In the 4th edition of their textbook on personnel management, Scott, Clothier, and Spriegel (1949) presented the results of two surveys that they had administered in 1940 and 1947, respectively. The researchers had asked the managers of 325 companies if they relied on vocational tests when hiring workers. The percentage of companies that used tests had decreased from 66 percent in 1940 to 57 percent in 1947. Commenting on this change, the authors simply noted that "the trend shown is by no means a surprising one" (p. v). Because they did not explain why this downturn was predictable, they must have assumed that the reasons were self-evident to their readers. The most significant factor contributing to this change may have been the union movement, which the authors thought was "definitely playing a leading role in personnel relations." Whereas previous versions of their book had addressed this topic only superficially, the authors devoted an entire chapter to it in the 1949 edition.

Immediately after World War II, the rate at which vocational testing was expanding had declined. However, vocational tests never became unpopular. Their use again grew noticeably during the late 1950s and the 1960s. One reporter ("Testing: Can Everyone Be Pigeonholed?" 1959) noted that the Psychological Corporation had "supplied 400,000 clerical job applicant tests in 1958 to firms ranging from banks to laundries" and that "Science Research Associates of Chicago serviced some 10,700 business clients, three times as many as in 1949" (p. 91). The reporter added that the Army "has recently developed some 120 special proficiency tests, and within three or four years expects to have such tests covering every one of its 800 types of jobs for enlisted men" (p. 91).

Wishing to make his readers aware of the increasing use of assessment, a reporter for *Forbes* magazine ("Pleasures of Nonprofitability," 1976) indicated that testing recently had grown to "Orwellian proportions." Using the Educational Testing Service as an example, this writer indicated that more than 250,000 persons annually took this corporation's "50-odd occupational certifying or licensing exams" (p. 89). Three years earlier, McClelland (1973) had provided anecdotal information about the need to score well on vocational tests in order to qualify for jobs that once had been test-free. McClelland's personal feelings were quite apparent in his editorialized remarks about his process.

> Suppose you are a ghetto resident in the Roxbury section of Boston. To qualify for being a policeman you have to take a three-hour-long general intelligence test in which you must know the meaning of words like "quell," "pyromaniac," and "lexicon." If you do not know enough of those words or cannot play analogy games with them, you do not qualify and must be satisfied with some such job as being a janitor for which an "intelligence" test is not required yet by the Massachusetts Civil Service Commission. (p. 4)

In the *Wall Street Journal*, Zonana (1978) assured any reader who had attempted "to become a lawyer, automobile mechanic, podiatrist, or stockbroker" that he or she very likely had taken one of the Educational Testing Service's occupational gate-keeping exams.

Shimberg (1980), who was the associate director of the Education Testing Service unit that developed occupational and professional exams, was aware of the extensive criticism of his company's tests. He acknowledged that "the air is filled with charges and counter-charges about who benefits the most from licensing—the public or the occupational group" (p. 1). Shimberg pointed out that licensing boards had reported originally to occupational groups. Moreover, they had represented the interests of the occupational groups when making decisions. After the federal government documented extensive abuses in the late 1960s and early 1970s, the public lost confidence in this process. Many of the exposed cases had involved unreasonable restrictions on the number of applicants that the boards would approve. The boards had posed these restrictions to create the labor bottlenecks that would raise the salaries of incumbent workers.

Although licensing exams emerged as supposedly objective alternatives to the biased decisions that were being made by employment and certification boards, Shimberg recognized the weaknesses of the licensing exams. Needless to say, the opponents of the exams quickly underscored these limitations. Shimberg addressed the limitations through a series of questions that were to be asked about all vocational tests.

> Are the tests used for licensure clearly related to those aspects of the job that involve protection of the public? Was a systematic job analysis conducted and were the findings documented, or was some other acceptable method used to establish job requirements? Is there a clear linkage between the job analysis and the test specifications? Do the tests meet

professional measurement standards? What assurance is there that the answers labeled correct are not arbitrary? What assurance is provided that tests given at different times are comparable in their coverage and difficulty? Is there a rationale for the way in which passing scores are determined? (Shimberg, 1980, p. 293)

Aware that disgruntled persons had challenged vocational tests in the courts, the editors at Harcourt, Brace, and Jovanovich (Psychological Corporation, 1978) assembled a ten-year summary of those court decisions that had affected employment testing. They had made this compilation as an aid to "those organizations presently using tests for selecting personnel, and to those who are considering using tests as part of their selection process" (p. vii). Booth and Mackay (1980) also reviewed some of the judicial rulings that had restrained the use of vocational tests. However, they detected a recent trend in which judges were showing greater tolerance for tests. Booth and Mackay advised employers that they would prevail in legal suits if they used court-approved procedures to validate their vocational exams. They believed that this strategy, when complemented by the "more reasoned" approach that the judges were displaying, would provide the protection for which employers were searching.

Testing Prevails

Bloom (1970) characterized testing as the "despair" of psychology and education. He thought persons might feel despair because of the perennial criticism that had been directed at testing. However, Bloom simultaneously considered testing to be the "pride" of psychology and education. As to reasons for pride, he explained that testing "is the one area that has shown clearest development and most widespread use in these two fields" and consequently "runs like a powerful minor theme through most of the research and the applied work" (p. 25).

Haney (1979) made a similar point. After examining copies of the *Reader's Guide to Periodical Literature,* he tabulated the number of articles that had been published about intelligence testing or educational testing during the preceding decades. He did this to document the "ebb and flow of public interest in testing as represented in popular periodicals" (p. 1). He was particularly struck by the great number of articles that had been published around 1960, a period when both the criticism of testing and its use had increased. Haney recognized the difficulty of interpreting data that did not indicate whether the original publications had been supportive or opposed to testing. Nonetheless, he concluded that the citations in the *Reader's Guide to Periodical Literature* did contain enough information to reveal the growth of standardized assessment.

Many researchers provided testimonials about the escalation of testing. Some of their remarks were positive, some were negative, and some were accompanied by predictions about the future of testing. In an article about the "history and sociology" of assessment, Tyler (1970) observed that "as the nation has grown and become increasingly complex, it is no longer possible through individual observation or informal procedures to assess our progress and problems." He then anticipated the implications for the decade that was just beginning.

> Increasingly, the public is asking for evidence of educational attainments and school people are recognizing what they term "accountability" for the performance of the schools... Hence, it seems inevitable that educational assessment of various types and for various purposes will be developing widely in the next decade. (p. 473)

During 1975, Paul Houts published numerous anti-testing articles in *National Elementary Principal*, which was the journal he edited. One of these articles (Houts, 1975) contained his conversation with Banesh Hoffman, who had written a 1962 indictment of standardized testing. Hoffman's popular book had included a foreword by Jacques Barzun (1962). Both Hoffman and Barzun had predicted that educational testing was on the verge of decline. Despite his sympathy for these scholars' philosophical views, Houts recognized that their predictions had been inaccurate. He wrote that "Hoffman's book, failed to bring about the immediate reform it should have," which was demonstrated when "the tide did not turn; the revolution never came." He dejectedly but realistically concluded that "standardized testing holds greater sway today than it did in 1962" (Houts, 1975, pp. 30–31).

Many other opponents of testing begrudgingly acknowledged the public's growing respect for educational assessment. They also recognized the inexorable expansion of educational assessment. In the keynote address to the U.S. Education Commissioner's 1978 Conference on Achievement Testing and the Basic Skills, Harold Howe, who had been President Lyndon Johnson's Commissioner of Education, recounted that he and his Democratic colleagues had opposed testing because they believed that "testing in the schools was not the business of the federal government." Because his own attitudes had not changed, he felt he should explain the reason that he and ideologically sympathetic educators were attending a conference about testing. In fact, he felt obliged to clarify why a national conference on testing had been called in the first place. He suggested that "the reason most of us are here is not really our abiding interest in the theory and practice of achievement testing" but because testing had become so important to the "many Americans...deeply concerned about their schools" (Howe, quoted in National School Boards Association, 1978, p. 3). In a précis of Howe's speech, Tomlinson and Treacy (1979) quoted sections in which Howe asserted that "the national mood for improving basic skills performance has hidden within it overtones of racism" (Howe, 1978, quoted by Tomlinson & Treacy, 1979, p. 3). As an alternative to the sponsoring of standardized tests, Howe suggested that the federal government champion initiatives to advance "the soft factors in judging students...those nonquantifiable aspects of human beings that must be considered in decisions about them" (p. 3).

Graham, who was the Director of the National Institute of Education under President Jimmy Carter, did not mask her own resentment of standardized testing. In the foreword to the published proceedings from the assessment conference at which Howe had spoken, she (Graham, 1979) expressed her own skepticism and that of the Carter administration toward standardized testing. She ignored those who were requesting academic accountability, character development, or the connection of the schools to a sound national economy. Instead, she insisted that the appropriate goals for schools were those that liberal Democrats had postulated.

> The primary reason we educate people...is to make persons literate—able to read, write, manipulate symbols, and develop independent means of making judgments and determining actions...[and] we must also continue to work toward improved equity in education—toward reducing obstacles to academic achievement that result simply from a student's being nonwhite, female, or poor. (p. v)

Graham added emphatically that "increasing student achievement is the central issue" for the staff at the National Institute of Education and that "testing is not a central issue" (Graham, 1978, as quoted by Tomlinson & Treacy, 1979, p. 21).

Graham had not concealed her aversion to standardized testing. Her remarks may have been especially irritating to some persons because they were made at a conference on assessment that had been convened because so many citizens were displeased with the attitudes of Graham and like-minded colleagues in the Carter administration. Berry, who was the Assistant Secretary for Education, wrote that a 1978 report about testing from the U.S. Department of Health, Education, and Welfare had been "a central subject of discussion at the recent National Institute of Education Conference" and that it had also "been the subject of extensive media coverage across the country" (Berry, 1978, in National Academy of Education, 1978, initial page of the report). Despite Graham's insistence that the administration did not consider testing to be a central component of a master plan to improve education, she was certainly aware that the authors of a highly publicized federal report had recommended "return to basic skills," "increasing achievement test scores as a governmental goal," "the establishment of 'minimum competency standards,'" "accountability for educational achievement," and acceptance of the fact that "it would be a mistake to regard 'criterion-referenced' tests as necessarily better, more desirable, or more useful than 'norm-referenced' tests" (National Academy of Education, 1978, pp. iii-iv).

One of the critical recommendations from the authors of the National Academy of Education report had been the "return to basic skills." Many of the persons who had supported testing during the 1970s simultaneously had supported the "back to basics" movement. Harnischfeger and Wiley (1976) observed that "after two decades of educational reform and innovation...a strong movement toward restoration" was being "nourished by resource cutbacks" and "alarming news of achievement test score declines" (p. 5). The negative publicity about scholastic failures was not restricted to declining test scores. The author of an article in *U.S. News & World Report* ("Modern Life," 1975) highlighted the results of a federally funded research study about the functional competence of American citizens. This reporter stated that extensive testing had revealed a significant number of persons who could not fill out a check or figure the correct change after making a purchase with a $20 bill.

> About one fifth of the adult population…is found to have difficulty coping with everyday chores like shopping, getting a driver's license or reading an insurance policy. Another 39 million are reported to be just getting by with their skills as workers, consumers, citizens and parents. Less than one half of the adult population…is deemed proficient in dealing with the complexities of modern life. (p. 84)

The researchers who had conducted the study from which the preceding data were taken had drawn several conclusions. As one would expect, they detected a significant literacy problem in the United States. They also noted that the schools did not seem prepared to deal with this problem. After pointing out that the problem might never have been uncovered without standardized testing, they recommended continued, systematic, and expanded testing. The appropriateness of their conclusions and recommendations seemed self-evident to many of the persons who reviewed their exposé.

In an acerbic *Newsweek* editorial, a disillusioned California teacher (Frye, 1979) repeated the chants of those who were sponsoring the back-to-basics movement. He observed that "the quality of public-school education in the United States has been declining for the last decade and a half" and "this almost universal decline has been marked by plummeting Scholastic Aptitude Test scores, functionally illiterate high-school graduates and the general alienation of many students" (p. 13). Relating this situation to the politicized disputes about testing, he derisively referred to the opponents of testing as the "educational Establishment."

> The explosive growth in the educational Establishment has been, and is being, drawn from among the weakest of our college graduates. It is, therefore, entirely consistent that they should attack or drop IQ testing, ability grouping and objective tests for teachers and administrators, while using their energies to develop myriad elective subjects and remedial programs… The ultimate irony is that the fundamental responsibility for this state of affairs lies precisely with those institutions now most vociferously bemoaning the educational product of the schools; that is, with the colleges and universities. (p. 13)

Complementary reports appeared in many other magazines. The byline for an article in the *New York Times Magazine* stated that "last year, $75 billion bought schools filled with new technology, 'innovative' programs—and poorly educated pupils…[and] it's time…to reinstate the old traditions of teaching" (Armbruster,

1977, p. 53). In a *Business Week* editorial, Martland (1978) compared the public school to "a corporation where the workers with the most demanding tasks are at the low end of the pay scale, where the supervisors have no control over personnel, operations, or funds, where the board of directors negotiates directly with the union to set pay scales and working conditions" (p. 9). Although it was hardly necessary in view of the way that he had framed the problem, Martland added his own opinion that "if any corporation tried to operate on the principles widely accepted in American schools, it would soon wind up in bankruptcy."

Jencks (1978) took specific precautions to discourage persons from stereotyping him. For example, he assured his audience that he was not one of those "alarmed traditionalists" who had been "attacking educators for being preoccupied with 'frills' and insisting that schools get 'back to basics.'" Nonetheless, he did recognize that test-verified reports of declining academic abilities had been the driving force behind the back-to-basics movement. He noted that "five years ago the College Entrance Examination Board announced that scores had been falling on its Scholastic Aptitude Test" and that "since then we have had seemingly endless pronouncements about declines on other exams ranging from those of the National Assessment of Educational Progress to the American College Testing Battery" (p. C4). Jencks explained that the traditionalists "blame the declines on school innovations introduced in the 1960s, while those responsible for the innovations...mostly blame the tests themselves." Because these two groups could not be reconciled, Jencks predicted that the public's attitudes would determine which of them would prevail.

A year earlier, a report from the National School Boards Association (1977b) had been directed at the groups who were opposing tests. Although it was not written in a confrontational style, this report did begin with an assertion that "standardized testing in the schools has been an important influence upon educational policy since World War I, and remains pervasive today" (p. 1). To substantiate the point, the authors asked readers to reflect on "the major research studies, evaluation studies, [and] allocation of government moneys, for which standardized test scores have been the chief measure." They also pointed out that "the incessant discussion this year about [the] decline in test scores" demonstrated that educational testing was still a significant matter in the mind of the public.

The authors of an editorial ("Why Tests Are Here to Stay," 1977) from the *American School Board Journal* were not at all worried about starting a dispute with the anti-assessment factions. Their temerity was evident when they recapitulated the "new wisdom" that the anti-assessment critics had proclaimed during 1960s.

> Standardized tests are biased, unreliable and too expensive. The estimated quarter of a billion dollars U.S. schools spend annually on testing is a waste of money, the critics say—an outlay we can ill afford in these hard times. Furthermore, it's said, we may well be testing motor-control in student fingers or the knack of regurgitating white middle-class values. And not only are the tests an invalid gauge of educational quality, according to the

new line, but even such an objective is faulty. The very idea of "quality control" is more appropriate to a factory production line, critics say, than to an institution of learning. (p. 29)

After restating the accusations that had been made by anti-testing critics, the authors concluded that "the public, and perhaps a majority of school board [*sic*] members, don't seem to buy that story." They predicted that tests would "remain solidly with us." They provided several irreverent observations to support this prediction. For example, they observed that the public had "a fundamental distrust—partly of school administrators, but mostly of teachers—that excites a need for an 'objective' indication of what's what in school." Moreover, bureaucrats and administrators wanted "someone else to tell them how one school system stacks up against another." An additional reason that the authors thought tests would persevere was that the "multimillion-dollar testing industry exerts mostly subtle, but sometimes gross, influences in favor of the testing status quo." As a final caveat, they predicted that tests would endure because "news media will accept nothing more than simple-minded indication of whether schools are 'good' or 'bad.'"

Lerner (1980) provided further details of the bickering between the anti-testing and testing factions. She described the 1972 campaign in which "the 1.8-million-member NEA...launched the war on testing by calling for a nationwide moratorium on all standardized testing and by mounting a massive public relations campaign to arouse popular hostility to it" (p. 120). Despite the political intensity of this effort, Lerner concluded that it had been "a total failure." In fact, she pointed out that "the American public responded with the minimum-competence-testing movement—a demand for more, not less, objective test data—that spread across the land with the speed of a prairie fire" (p. 120). She reported that the number of states with minimum-competency-testing programs had increased from one in 1970 to 38 in 1979. To explain how this growth had transpired during a large-scale, highly organized assault on testing, Lerner referred to the public's changing attitudes toward the quality of public education.

Discontent with achievement levels in the public schools was high and rising throughout the [1970s] and has not yet leveled off. Black Americans were and are even more dissatisfied than white ones, and large majorities in both races have repeatedly expressed strong approval for the value of objective, standardized tests, in schools and elsewhere. In its most recent 1979 survey, the Gallup organization once again asked a representative sample of Americans what they thought of standardized tests. Eighty-one percent thought they were "very useful" or "somewhat useful," while only 17 percent rated the tests as "not too useful"—an approval ratio of nearly five-to-one, which rose to six-to-one when the views of non-whites alone were tabulated. (p. 121)

One of the reasons that the attacks on standardized tests were difficult to repel was that they were multifaceted. This complexity was evident when advocates for persons with disabilities joined in the assault. Reschly (1981) reported that a legal dispute had developed as a result of the disproportionate number of children from ethnic minorities who had been assigned to special-education classes. After ruling that this situation was the result of standardized assessment, a judge banned the administration of intelligence tests to California's African American children. Fearing that this "ban on IQ tests and the order to eliminate overrepresentation will not have a significant influence on the overall problem of providing more effective educational services to economically disadvantaged minorities," Reschly (1980) concluded that the judge's ruling represented a case of "right problem—wrong solution." Before the California case had even been argued, Lerner (1978) had anticipated the legal decision that would result. She believed that several earlier testing cases had revealed a tendency by activist judges to "ignore professional-technical experts, deciding essentially scientific questions by judicial fiat" (p. 915).

Hanushek (1986) was another observer who was struck by the complexity of the attacks that were being made on academic testing programs. He noted that some critics thought that tests failed to measure appropriate skills. Others thought they failed to forecast which individuals would be academically successful. Despite the degree to which these accusations had been publicized, the popularity of testing increased. Although Hanushek did not have a straightforward explanation for this paradox, he speculated that tests might have been protected from criticism because they "have an important use in selecting individuals for further schooling." If this were the case, tests might be the best measure of the "'real' outputs" that parents, administrators, and legislators prized. Additionally, high tests scores, because of their social prestige, might be "valued in and of themselves."

Even though he thought that standardized tests were part of "a system that values speed and cleverness over knowledge," Botstein (1985) recognized their secure position within the educational system. He judged that the "quasi-religious" confidence displayed by educators and the public accounted for the increasing use of tests. After acknowledging the expansion of scholastic assessment, Gifford (1989) observed that "the standardized test has become one of the major sources of information for reducing uncertainty in the determination of individual merit and in the allocation of merit-based educational, training, and employment opportunities" (p. ix). To highlight the currently secure status of college entrance exams, he pointed out that "most major institutions of higher education require applicants to supplement their records of academic achievements with scores on standardized tests."

Writing in the same book as Gifford, Jencks (1989) gave a commonsense rationalization for the continued use of college admission tests. He pointed out that those universities that chose to ignore performance on standardized tests had only four alternatives, each of which was problematic. They could rely exclusively on high-school grades, even though these were patently unreliable. They could consult high-school grades, but supplement these with some index to the quality of the applicants' high schools. They could adopt universal admission standards, with the recognition that many unprepared students subsequently would fail. Finally, universities could adopt the community-college model, admitting everyone but providing remedial courses to reduce student failures. Having made these same points decades earlier, Diederich (1963) had concluded that examination-based college admissions were "more sensible, more economical, and more humane than the way offered by most of our state universities" (p. 48).

The universities and the public schools were not the only institutions that preserved their commitment to standardized testing. To demonstrate the enduring prestige of vocational tests, Lee (1988) referred to a survey that the American Society for Personnel Administration had conducted. This study indicated that 84 percent of the responding companies were using vocational tests. Lee reported that 96 percent of the respondents were using tests to select workers, 49 percent to make promotions, and 37 percent to place workers in suitable jobs. He believed that these data demonstrated a reversal of the practices that companies had adopted during an earlier era in which they feared that testing would lead to discrimination lawsuits. He linked the "comeback" of vocational testing to the different demeanors that the Equal Employment Opportunity Commission and other government agencies had exhibited during President Reagan's administration. He also acknowledged that recent court decisions had made it more difficult for plaintiffs to win employment discrimination cases. Lee concluded that these changes had created a "bull market" for vocational tests.

Contrary to the predictions of some critics, standardized testing did not languish. A decline was unlikely as long as the public felt confidence in assessment. Elam, Rose, and Gallup (1993) provided a convincing example of this continued confidence. They conducted a survey in which they asked about the circumstances under which standardized tests should be employed. Ninety-one percent of the respondents supported testing to identify areas in which students needed extra help. Eighty-seven percent endorsed testing to help teachers improve their skills. Seventy-two percent supported it as a way of comparing schools. Seventy percent supported it as a method for determining whether students should be promoted. These same authors analyzed other educational surveys that had been conducted during the preceding 24 years. In response to a proposition about the imposition of national tests to facilitate comparisons among schools, 81 percent of the 1988 respondents had been supportive. This same proposition had recurred on five surveys that had been conducted from 1970 to 1988. This span represented a period during which political activists had publicly denigrated standardized tests. Nonetheless, at least 70 percent of the respondents to each of these surveys had expressed a desire for a national test.

The attitudes of federal bureaucrats and government officials significantly influenced the course of testing. However, their attitudes were far from homogeneous. For example, many conservatives had supported federally mandated and centrally supervised testing in the early 1990s. Despite this support, President George H. W. Bush approached this topic cautiously. In an address about his educational agenda, *America 2000: An Education Strategy* (1991), the president observed that "we spend 33 percent more per pupil in 1991 than we did in 1981—33 percent more in real, constant dollars—and I don't think there's a person anywhere who would say…we've seen a 33 percent improvement in our schools' performance" (p. 3). To correct this problem, he called for a national testing initiative that would "tell parents and educators, politicians and employers, just how well our schools are doing." However, the president reassured the opponents of testing that "we will develop voluntary—let me repeat it—we will develop voluntary national tests for 4th, 8th and 12th graders in the five core subjects" (p. 5).

A year after the president had made these remarks, Gifford and Wing (1992) judged that testing was a "ubiquitous feature of American life" that the public viewed as "a major source of information for reducing uncertainty in the allocation of merit-based educational, training, and employment opportunities" (ix). They added that "test scores are at the center of high-stakes decision making about the future of individuals and of the nation itself." Restating some of the key points from President George H. W. Bush's *America 2000* address, Picus (1996) judged that many features of this plan had been incorporated by President Clinton into his own design for education. Picus encapsulated the current views of "policy makers [who] often point out that despite considerable growth in real pupil expenditures during the past three decades, student performance measures have remained flat or declined" (p. vii). As a result, "these policy makers, along with the business community and the public in general, want to know where this tax money is going and what it is buying." In view of the prevailing sentiments, he predicted "growing pressure for greater accountability in how schools spend the tax funds they receive" (Picus, 1996, p. vii).

Even those liberals who opposed standardized educational testing eventually conceded that it had become a secure component of schooling. Popham (1999) acknowledged the opposition to standardized testing from teachers, especially those who thought that their students' failures were being used to measure their own performance as instructors. Although he believed that standardized tests should not have been used in this fashion, Popham chided discontent educators for failing to recognize their full responsibilities as participants in this conflict.

> Teachers need to show the world that they can instruct children so that those children make striking pre-instruction to post-instruction progress… If educators accept the position that standardized achievement tests scores should not be used to measure the quality of schooling, then they must provide other, credible evidence that can be used to ascertain the quality of schooling [such as] carefully collected, nonpartisan evidence regarding teachers' pre-test-to-post-test promotion of undeniably important skills or knowledge. (p. 15)

Late twentieth-century statements by leaders of the National Education Association indicated their belated recognition of the enduring stature of standardized educational testing. During the 1970s and the early 1980s, National Education Association leaders had attempted to eliminate standardized testing from the schools. Lerner (1980) had described the 1970s campaign in which the National Education Association had tried to organize a nationwide moratorium on all standardized tests. At the end of the 1980s, the retiring president of the National Education Association (Futrell, 1989) was assuring her organization's members that test-based educational reform would be abandoned. Contrary to her prediction, testing became more popular than ever. A subsequent NEA president eventually recognized the futility of these attacks and assumed a distinct political tact. Chase (1999) informed his union's members that "citizens correctly demand high standards and accountability from the public schools" and "like it or not, test scores are popular with the public because they offer a quantifiable measure of school performance" (p. 2). Recognizing that the support for standardized tests was broad and diversified enough to make testing virtually impregnable, Chase made the unqualified declaration that "high-stakes tests are here to stay." He counseled NEA members "to be a constructive, positive force in shaping and implementing these tests." The issue of the NEA-sponsored journal in which Chase had made the preceding remarks contained other articles that complemented the organization's new philosophical stance. Two of these articles contained advice about ways in which teachers could raise their students' scores on high-stakes exams (Gutloff, 1999; "Motivating Students," 1999).

Pellegrino, Chudowsky, and Glaser (2001) thought that some teachers were still "questioning whether current large-scale assessment practices are yielding the most useful kinds of information for informing and improving education" (p. 1). They advised these skeptical teachers to accept the fact that the current assessment practices were part of a decades-long effort to raise academic standards and measure students' progress toward those standards. They pragmatically concluded that educational assessment, despite the unresolved questions about its validity, was "an integral part of the quest for improved education," that it systematically provided "feedback to students, educators, parents, policy makers, and the public," and that it was "playing a greater role in decision making than ever before."

Summary

The opponents of standardized assessment accused test developers of cultural insensitivity, greed, elitism, irresponsible ambition, and political ruthlessness. They especially railed against the Educational Testing Service. In spite of the extensive coverage that the media gave these accusations, the use of testing increased. During the final decades of the twentieth century, its expansion was apparent in public education, higher education, licensing agencies, professional organizations, employment, the government, and the military. The pro-assessment factions acquired power as the nation shifted toward more conservative political values. They gained additional strength after their adversaries reneged on promises to provide practical, cost-effective, bias-free, reliable, and valid alternatives to standardized testing.

CHAPTER 8

Conservatives Reap the Harvest

*Tests are propelled by a lot of fear that the United States will lose
disastrously in international competition.*
—NEILL, 1999

*Even though educational tests were criticized constantly during the second half of the twentieth century, their use and
political prestige rose. The respect for testing was elevated by* **A Nation at Risk***, the 1983 report that portrayed
inadequate educational achievement as a threat to America's economic health and military security. The sponsors of this
report demanded educational changes that would foster essential academic skills. They insisted that these skills be
monitored through ongoing, rigorous, and comprehensive testing. The anti-testing factions were dismayed when powerful
political groups and the general public agreed with this advice.*

Liberal Politicians During the 1960s

Looking back on the 1960s, McLaughlin and Phillips (1991) judged that this was
the period when "modern educational evaluation" had emerged. After noting that
"President Johnson's 'War on Poverty' focused attention on education, and
massive funds were made available," they concluded that "with the money came
the demand for accountability" (p. x). Not all scholars saw a direct link between
the federal initiatives of the 1960s and educational accountability. For example, the
authors of a report from the Center on Education Policy (2003) observed that
"some critics of the original [Elementary and Secondary Education Act of 1965]
say that it failed because it provided money without accountability" (p. vi). This
report's authors contrasted Johnson's educational programs with contemporary
federal initiatives, which they thought required "heavy accountability without much
greater federal financial and technical assistance." Cross (2004a, 2004b), who was
affiliated with the Center on Education Policy, agreed that President Johnson saw
the Elementary and Secondary Education Act of 1965 as a funding stream for
reducing poverty rather than a strategic plan for altering education. Under these
circumstances, the assessing of educational consequences was hardly a high
priority.

If the Johnson administration did require any type of educational accountability, it certainly was not test-based. A reason that the Johnson administration did
not require test-based accountability was the political spirit of the times. Holmen
and Docter (1972) characterized that *zeitgeist* while chronicling the activities of the
Congresses and federal bureaucracies of that era.

> During the summer of 1965, pickets were marching in front of the national headquarters
> of the American Psychological Association in Washington to protest educational testing.
> Less than a mile away, on Capitol Hill, staff members of several Congressmen and Senators

were independently preparing for hearings in which serious charges against certain testing practices would be heard. Distinguished psychologists would add fuel to the fire by applauding some of these charges, while others would testify that isolated examples of poor practice were being overgeneralized. Meanwhile, important concerns about testing were being reviewed in the headquarters of the Equal Employment Opportunity Commission (EEOC). In addition to policy questions, the EEOC was trying to evaluate hundreds of written complaints which involved testing in employment selection and promotion cases. (p. vii)

Writing about the liberals' opposition to standardized testing during the early 1960s, Miller (1963) identified several of their allegations. They had accused exams of promoting unfair comparisons among teachers, unfair comparisons among schools, "deadly uniformity," "undue emphasis on test achievements," and "cramming at the expense of creative work" (p. 44). Because they thought that tests were fundamentally flawed, liberals were not eager to impose them on students, teachers, and the schools. What were the penalties when school systems did not account for the government funds they had received? McLaughlin (1987) concluded that failures to comply with some of the provisions of these lavishly funded programs produced minimal consequences. He gave the example that "most districts did not move beyond *pro forma* response [to the mandated parent involvement provisions of the Elementary and Secondary Education Act of 1965] because teachers and administrators saw little merit in parent participation" (p. 173).

Some critics questioned whether these educational programs could have been successful, irrespective of the casual way in which they were administered. A piece of research (Coleman et al., 1966), which was referred to as the Coleman Report, became critical to this debate. Congress had commissioned this study in 1964 as a component of the Civil Rights Act. The original language in the legislation seemed relatively innocuous when it mandated "a report to the President and the Congress, within two years of the enactment of this title, concerning the lack of availability of equal educational opportunities for individuals by reason of race, color, religion, or national origin in public education institutions at all levels" (statement from Section 402 of the Civil Rights Act of 1964, quoted by Howe, 1966, p. iii). Arthur Jensen (1973), the controversial advocate of intelligence testing, wrote that "when the costly study was proposed there had been some complaints that, like so much educational research, it would only document statistically what had long been common knowledge: that socio-economic status and racial inequalities in scholastic performance were mainly the result of inequalities in school facilities and expenditures" (p. 3). However, Jensen judged that the results of this $1,250,000 study involving over 600,000 students in 4000 schools were "a shocking and disconcerting surprise to nearly everyone." He quoted Coleman's own observation that "within broad geographic regions, for each racial and ethnic group, the physical and economic resources going into a school had very little relationship to the achievements coming out of it" (Coleman, 1966, as quoted by Jensen, 1973, p. 3).

Although partisans argued about the validity of the Coleman study, they all agreed that this report eventually had an immense impact on the schools. An executive at the Educational Testing Service (Barton, 1997) judged that the report instigated "an enduring discussion of whether differences in the expenditure of resources on the schools makes any difference in educational achievement" (p. iii). He added that "research since then has been localized, often without direct measures of student achievement, and with only a gross measure of resources." He applauded the Coleman Report because it had been "based on extensive national tests and surveys." As Jensen (1973) had noted, the report was especially disconcerting to the liberals who had sponsored it but who then refused to accept its conclusions.

Although the Coleman Report (Coleman et al., 1966) was authorized in 1964, it was not published until 1966. This was the same year that Congress authorized the National Assessment of Educational Progress (NAEP). The enactment of this assessment might seem to challenge those critics who chastised the politically liberal Congresses of this era for failing to enforce educational accountability. After all, later NAEP reports (e.g., "Summary of Grades by State," 2001) provided explicit state-by-state comparisons of student achievement in mathematics, reading, writing, and science. The 1999 edition of the annual NAEP Guide contained the following statement about the identity, objectivity, and accountability of the persons who managed this initiative.

> NAEP is a congressionally mandated project of the National Center for Education Statistics, the U.S. Department of Education. The Commissioner of Education Statistics is responsible, by law, for carrying out the NAEP project through competitive awards to qualified organizations. NAEP reports directly to the Commissioner, who is also responsible for providing continuing reviews, including validation studies and solidification of public comment, on NAEP's conduct and usefulness. (Passage on the inside of the front cover of the NAEP Guide, Horkay, 1999)

Despite the high performance standards that eventually were set for this initiative, the original NAEP had quite a different character. Guthrie (1993) noted that comparative, test-based investigations and reporting from the NAEP only began in 1988, when the procedure was reorganized at the prodding of a conservative president. Guthrie judged that the 1966 version of the assessment had been "tightly restricted in format to prevent student achievement and school comparisons among states" (p. 254). Almost a decade before Guthrie had made these comments, Anderson (1985) had noted that "when NAEP was first reporting test results, there was a great reluctance to compare states," which was evident when the Council of Chief State School Officers "flatly refused to have state-by-state comparisons" (p. 23). Messick, Beaton, and Lord (1983) had published an NAEP report in which they suggested the reconfiguration of the assessment initiative so that data could be gathered about "school achievement as it related to *school effectiveness*" (p. 11). They thought this change was critical because of the "erosion of educational credibility" and "growing and pervasive pressures for educational accountability" (p. 5).

Liberal Scholars During the 1960s

Attempting to place standardized testing in a "social perspective," Brim (1963) had warned that "the increasing use of tests in the United Sates constitutes a change in emphasis from traditional bases for the determination of status, such as race, sex, religion, and order of birth, to a greater reliance on this new criterion, performance on a standardized test of ability" (p. 3). He thought this change had transpired as psychologists had attempted to solve an extremely practical problem, which was "how to select the best-qualified individuals for the various educational and occupational positions in society" (p. 3). Although Brim may have been correct, he failed to mention the complex political web in which testing had become entangled. Two years later, Amrine (1965), who was a public information consultant for the American Psychological Association, directly addressed the political ramifications of testing. He reported that standardized tests, which had been "of some concern to the right wing and especially to the extreme right wing of American politics," had recently "become a matter of concern to the other side of the political spectrum." As an indication of the interest that liberals were showing, Amrine pointed to the 1965 "Congressional investigations by Senate and House Committees, accompanied by directives from the Executive side of the Government banning or restricting the use of psychological instruments" (p. 859).

In an article about testing that they subtitled *Politics and Pretense*, Hunter and Rogers (1967) did not attempt to conceal the politicized goals that they and other liberals had set for the schools. These authors explained that they had "no intention...of judging the value of particular programs" of assessment because the more important issue was the fact that "standardized tests are too insensitive to be considered guides to the kind of evaluation that should lead to needed innovation and desirable changes" (p. 5). Because the results of tests were likely to be at odds with the ideological goals that liberals saw as appropriate, Hunter and Rogers dismissed the tests for defeating "one of the primary purposes of testing," which was "to serve as a guide as to how an undesirable educational situation might be remedied" (p. 25).

As he was documenting the politicized attacks that were being made on tests in Congress, Amrine (1965) observed that these assaults were originating not only from persons outside the field of psychology but also from those inside. Anastasi (1967), who was president of the Division of Evaluation and Measurement within the American Psychological Association, was a professional insider who articulated the liberal position on testing. She lectured her colleagues that "the isolation of psychometrics from other relevant areas of psychology is one of the conditions that have led to the prevalent public hostility toward testing" (p. 297). She explained that "the individual does not behave in a vacuum" and that the persons administering tests should qualify the scores on tests by placing them "in a particular environmental context" (p. 304).

Liberals concluded that performance on standardized tests was being accepted without an acknowledgment of the significant influence of environmental learning factors. Consequently, the liberals had little interest in standardized testing. However, they still needed a significant research study that would demonstrate the accuracy of their intuitions to the general public. Because the conservatives had been in a comparable political position, they had looked to Arthur Jensen's 1968 report to validate testing. During the same year, the liberals thought that they had found the forceful research study that would demonstrate the credibility of their own attitudes toward testing. The study, which was published as a popular trade book, was entitled *Pygmalion in the Classroom: Teacher Expectations and Pupils' Intellectual Development*. It was researched and written by Rosenthal and Jacobson (1968).

Within the experiment that they chronicled, Rosenthal and Jacobson had deliberately provided teachers with misinformation about their students. After randomly selecting 20 percent of the students in a single school, they had informed the teachers that these children showed "unusual potential for intellectual growth." Although one might expect that the attitudes of the children would change as a result of the positive labels that were fixed to them, Rosenthal and Jacobson made far more ambitious claims. They alleged that "eight months later these unusual or 'magic' children showed significantly greater gains in IQ than did the remaining children who had not been singled out for the teacher's attention" (pp. vii-viii). The authors of the book stressed that the changes they detected must have been the result of the altered social circumstances because "nothing was done directly for the disadvantaged child" (p. 181). The liberals' fascination with this study was enhanced by the fact that many of the "magic children" came from minority, low-income families.

Looking back on the preceding decade, Gage (1971) estimated that "*Pygmalion in the Classroom* got more attention in the mass media than any other product of the behavioral science in the 1960's [*sic*]" (p. v). Gage, w ho had reviewed the manuscript prior to its publication, had been suspicious of it. He explained that "it seemed implausible…that the IQ, which had proven so refractory, would yield to the admittedly weak treatment administered to the teachers in their experiment." Additionally, he noted flaws in the research design, measurement procedures, and the analysis of data. For all of these reasons, he advised the editors against publication.

Although numerous persons reviewed the Rosenthal and Jacobson study after it was published, Gage questioned whether they were familiar with the technical features of psychological measurement and research. This procedural naiveté may have contributed to the "high praise" that most of them gave the book. The author of a positive review in *Time* magazine had opined that the book's "findings raise some fundamental questions about teacher training [and] they also cast doubt on the wisdom of assigning children to classes according to presumed ability, which may only mire the lowest groups into self-confining ruts" ("Teachers: Blooming by Deception," 1968, p. 62). In the *Saturday Review*, Roberts (1968) applauded Rosenthal and Jacobson for contending that "programs aimed at changing the 'disadvantaged' child directly may be a less effective way of dealing with the failure of the ghetto schools than efforts to change teacher attitudes" (p. 72).

In the *New York Review of Books*, Kohl (1968) predicted that the results of the Rosenthal and Jacobson study would "upset many school people, yet these are hard facts." He saw the research as a refutation of the pervasive practice in which first-grade and second-grade students were grouped according to their alleged ability but where "the determination of ability is made by the teachers or by whatever 'objective' tests of school achievement they administer" (p. 31). In the magazine of the Phi Beta Kappa Society, Doob (1969) characterized the study as a "brilliant experiment" with implications that were "not modestly muted" (p. 6). After reporting that intelligence tests were "banned in the primary grades of the Los Angeles city school system…in an attempt to prevent children from being erroneously labeled as unintelligent," McCurdy (1969) added that "the Board of Education's unanimous action was founded largely on recent findings which show that in many cases the classroom performance of children is based on the expectations of teachers" (p. 1).

Even when they should have known better, reviewers offered fatuous and unwarranted compliments. For example, Aiken (1969), who had reviewed the Rosenthal and Jacobson study for the technically sophisticated audience of *Educational and Psychological Measurement*, had noted that "the control group samples were much larger than the experimental groups, that gain scores are open to question, that many of the significant differences may have been caused by the scores of only a few children, and that the results of the present experiment are in direct contrast to those obtained by [another researcher who had investigated the same question]" (p. 228). After making these observations, Aiken judged that "nevertheless, even as a minimum accomplishment, the results once more call into question the meaning and stability of test scores and other evaluations." Letting logic defer to his political convictions, he concluded that *Pygmalion in the Classroom* was "a provocative experiment" with an "array of significant findings" that made "it difficult [for critics] to destroy."

Thorndike (1968) was a contemporary reviewer who was not enamored with the Rosenthal and Jacobson study. He finished his appraisal by observing that the data were "so untrustworthy" that the researchers' conclusions, if they turned out to be accurate, would be so only as the result of "fortunate coincidence" (p. 711). Three years later, Elashoff and Snow (1971) agreed with Thorndike that the conclusions drawn by Rosenthal and Jacobson had been unjustified. They based their judgment on the many technical weaknesses in the study and the "decades of research suggesting the stability of human intelligence and its resistance to alterations by environmental manipulation" (p. 61). After independent researchers were unable to replicate the results of *Pygmalion in the Classroom*, Elashoff and Snow pointed to this failure as a final demonstration that the study was invalid.

Staunch Support From Conservatives

Ebel (1950) observed that the "literature on testing in education has always been replete with articles intended to direct, stimulate, or retard the construction and use of tests" (p. 88). Referring to these editorialized articles as "hortatory discussions," he lamented that some of them had "been written more on the basis of bias and misinformation than on the basis of experience, insight, and judgment" or that they had been "pitched at a very elementary level" with "over-simplified fundamental problems." Some political liberals undoubtedly had exhibited these faults when they were attacking standardized testing. Many conservatives had behaved in a similar manner when they were attempting to support testing. In fact, Ebel's observations about the late 1940s would have been just as accurate had he made them about the political maneuvering of either liberals or conservatives during any decade from the second half of the century.

Betts (1950) had indicated that teachers should use standardized tests to make decisions about promotions, the suitability of remedial work, and the appropriateness of classroom activities. However, some of his readers might have been surprised when he added that teachers should employ standardized testing because it was a critical component of "the democratic way." Convinced that "an intelligent citizenry" was needed within a democracy, he stipulated that "the intellectual level of our citizenry must continually advance" and that "it dare not mire in mediocrity" (p. 221). He saw standardized testing as a way to stimulate and monitor this advance.

In 1955, Rudolph Flesch (1986) published a best-selling book, *Why Johnny Can't Read—And What You Can Do About It*. The premise of this volume was that the phonics approach was more effective than alternative methods of reading instruction. However, one of the reasons that Flesch's book became so prominent was the alarmist political rhetoric with which it was peppered.

> The word method is gradually destroying democracy in this country; it returns to the upper middle class the privileges that public education was supposed to distribute evenly among the people. The American Dream is, essentially, equal opportunity through free education for all. This dream is beginning to vanish in a country where the public schools are falling

down on the job...Mind you, I am not accusing the reading "experts" of wickedness or malice. I am not one of those people who call them un-American or left-winger or Communist fellow travelers. All I am saying is that their theories are wrong and the application of those theories has done untold harm to our younger generation. (pp. 132–133)

Seven years after Flesch made the preceding remarks, the American Association of School Administrators, the Council of Chief State School Officers, and the National Association of Secondary-School Principals collaborated on a booklet (Joint Committee on Testing, 1962) that was designed to analyze the "tidal wave of public feeling and opinion" that was carrying the testing movement forward. The initial sentence of this report addressed the issue head on. The authors wrote that "since the space race began, the American people have become more and more firmly convinced that the strength and destiny of the nation depend on its educational system" (p. 5). They added that both teachers and lay citizens had developed this conviction because of "national pride and uneasiness about the future." As a result "the general public, powerful individuals in influential positions, and many members of the teaching profession have strongly advocated the increased use of tests as a means of improving the character and quality of the schools" (p. 5).

Trace (1961) had released a book that compared the academic achievement of Russian students with that of their peers in the United States. To ensure that his post-Sputnik audience understood the full political implications of his message, he selected the ominous title *What Ivan Knows That Johnny Doesn't*. Rather than visit Russian schools, Trace drew his conclusions by simply comparing Soviet and American textbooks. He explained the logic behind this method of investigation.

A textbook is in fact a tyrant, because the teacher is fairly well obliged to plan course work around it, particularly in the teaching of the basic subjects...therefore, if a student's textbooks are excellent he may be able to get an excellent education indeed if he has good teachers and if he studies hard; but if his textbooks are poor, his education is bound to be correspondingly poor no matter how excellent his teacher may be or how hard he studies. It matters even less whether his school building has the latest design, whether his classroom is spacious and well-lighted, or whether his gymnasium is fully equipped. (pp. 6–7)

Trace warned potential readers that his exposition would "shock those who have not been in close touch with what has been going on in our schools during the past thirty years" (p. 7). He added that his analyses would prove to them that the "basic subjects are very poorly represented in the curriculum and textbooks of American schools even when compared to the curriculum and textbooks of the schools in a Communist country."

The members of extremist organizations within the conservative movement did not show much tolerance when they made demands about educational practices. This was true of The Committee to Bring Morality to the Mental

Professions. A reporter ("Pickets at APA," 1965) from the *American Psychologist* described a political march that this group had organized.

> Members of the Central Office staff [at the American Psychological Association's Headquarters in Washington, DC] were astonished on June 4 to find that a dozen pickets, half of whom carried signs, were parading up and down in front of our new building. These pickets handed out a statement which indicated they supported something called "The Committee to Bring Morality to the Mental Professions," further described as "a non-profit, non-fund soliciting organization composed of people of all races and creeds who seek to combat immorality practiced under the cover of phony science." (p. 871)

The reporter recorded the messages on some of the signs that the protesters carried. One poster read, "Help stop psychological sex tests—Write your Congressman." Another sign read, "Support Congressional investigations of psychological sex tests in Government, Private Employment, [and] School." Still another placard urged, "Help stop grants from your tax money given to the American Psychological Association—Support Congressional hearings." Figure 8.1 contains two photographs that accompanied this report.

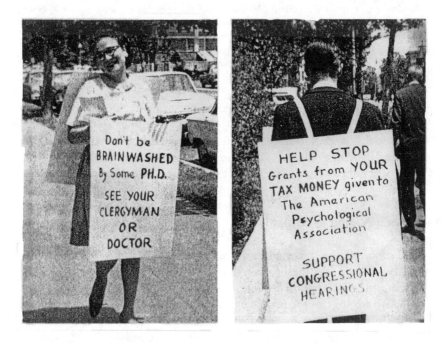

Figure 8.1 1960s Picketers Protest Testing

In an attempt to rally support for their own scholastic programs, some conservative educators had tried to expose the weaknesses in the instructional approaches of their rivals. They claimed that the instruction championed by their adversaries jeopardized the nation's democratic traditions and international security. Other conservatives had underscored the damage caused by undemocratic textbooks or pacifist instructional materials. Choosing a distinct approach, The Committee to Bring Morality to the Mental Professions had tried to direct the public's attention to amoral testing practices. Because these extremist conservative groups represented limited constituencies, they did not have a realistic chance of reforming the schools. Therefore, they had to rely on aggressive media campaigns to attract additional supporters. After reviewing the publicity that they generated, Brandt (1981) judged that their campaigns were extremely effective. He reported that "public education is under attack as never before" and that "popular periodicals feature in-depth analyses of the demoralized, decadent, ineffective state of the public schools" (p. 5). Two years earlier, Lerner (1979) had encapsulated several key aspects of the media hype.

> Unpleasant truths in the educational realm center around the fact that our public schools are doing a seriously inadequate job: children of the poor are not learning the basics; children of the rich are not learning much beyond the basics. We know that because we have current literacy test results showing how widespread illiteracy is among the poor in general and the black poor in particular, and because we have long-term SAT results showing the magnitude of the decline in academic preparedness and competence among the college bound. (p. 4)

Even though they were gaining greater public notice, political conservatives still searched for a rhetorical strategy that would advance their agenda even further. They looked for the opportunity to prevail in the decisive way that they had during World War II and its immediate aftermath. This opportunity presented itself after a 1983 report linked education to America's financial and military security.

Report of a Nation in Jeopardy

The mood of the public toward standardized testing had begun to change before 1983. Two decades earlier, Shellhammer (1963) had chronicled the statewide testing program that California had implemented. He judged that this program had sprung "from a problem that goes back to October 4, 1957, when the Russians announced to the world that they had put a space satellite in orbit" (p. 55). After that event, a committee that had been assembled by the California legislature had recommended "mandatory statewide testing of public schools" (passage from the 1960 report of the Citizens' Advisory Commission, quoted by Shellhammer, 1963, p. 55). Despite the fact that he was a political liberal,

California's Governor Edmund G. "Jerry" Brown made recommendations that infuriated fellow liberals and the teachers who had voted for him. Brown had advised the legislature that "we must now seriously consider a statewide testing program" in order "to give us a measurement of the effectiveness of our schools" (remarks made by Governor Brown in 1961, quoted by Shellhammer, 1963, p. 56). The governor's recommendation became part of a law that went into effect in 1962. Shellhammer observed noncommittally that history would have to judge "whether the venture is destined to be a memorable experience."

Even though many of California's educators were upset by their state's mandatory testing law, Baker (1963) counseled them to recognize that "common sense and obedience to the law leave little choice but to cooperate" (p. 60). He continued that "vitriolic attacks, extreme statements, wails of impending disaster, and similar doom-saying approaches" would simply be "dismissed by critics as petulance." Exhibiting singular political acumen, Baker advised distraught educators that the best way to prevent the enactment of additional restrictions would be to "make an ally of the state testing program."

The editors ("State and National Curriculum," 1963) of the *Journal of Secondary Education* were aware of the pervasive concern about standardized testing. Although they had prepared a report to influence attitudes on this issue, they were upset that this report, which was being ignored, would "insignificantly affect the number and character of state and national testing programs" (p. 26). They explained that the public's disregard of their advice was especially distressing at a time when "deepening concern within states and across the land about the role of education in the national interest and for the development of the individual portends more public scrutiny of what teachers teach, how well they teach, what pupils learn, and how well they learn" (p. 26).

In 1975, the president of the College Board (Marland, 1977) fully recognized the anxiety created by the extensive reporting about scholastic test scores. He reported that "no topic related to the programs of the College Board has received more public attention in recent years than the unexplained decline in scores earned by students on the Scholastic Aptitude Test." In response, he had assembled a "blue-ribbon panel" to investigate "the score decline issue as it relates to candidate population, secondary education, and society" (p. iii). In the report from that panel (Wirtz, Howe, Watson, Tyler, Tucker, Tom, et al., 1977), the members recognized that the public was not so much interested "in the psychometric technicalities of the SAT score decline but in its implications regarding what is widely perceived as serious deterioration of the learning process" (p. 1). Attempting to address this issue conceptually, they pointed to a number of possible causes, such as "a change in the composition of the student group taking the tests." However, the panel's members noted ominously that "more pervasive forces" were contributing to this decline. While they recognized that "the test score statistics do not themselves indicate the nature of these forces," the members made an "informed conjecture about the impact on learning of changes that have taken place in both the schools and the society during a period of turbulence and distraction rarely paralleled in American history" (pp. 1–2).

Because the flood of negative publicity about declining test scores threatened the progressive educational programs that the liberals had sponsored, the liberals felt compelled to retort. Most of them maintained that the low scores were the result of culturally unfair tests. Munday (1979a, 1979b), a vice president in the testing division of Houghton Mifflin Publishers, experimented with a different tactic. Aware of the degree to which falling scores on standardized tests had upset many communities, he argued that the decline was a statistical illusion. The byline for one of his articles (Munday, 1979a) contained reassurances for those teachers and school administrators who had been resisting test-based accountability.

> An authority on testing offers some "uneasy generalizations": 1) Sharp declines beginning in the late 1960s have ended; 2) since 1970 there have been continued achievement gains in the lower grades; 3) since 1970 there has been a leveling off in the middle and upper grades with some small declines; 4) today's achievement levels compare favorably with available history; elementary children may be at a historical high point; and 5) today's high school achievement is about even with that of the early sixties. (Byline accompanying an article by Munday, 1979a, p. 496)

Most critics were not impressed by reassurances of this sort. Howe had been the U.S. Commissioner of Education in President Johnson's administration. Although he did not conceal his anti-testing sentiments, he conceded that testing was more popular than ever. He attributed this situation to the "pervasiveness and the strength of the feeling that American schools suffer shortcomings" (Howe, quoted in National School Boards Association, 1978, p. 3). In fact, he believed that it was precisely this dissatisfaction that had fueled the minimum competency testing movement during the 1970s. Resnick (Resnick, 1981) also detected a cause and effect relationship between the public's dissatisfaction with schools and its insistence upon testing. He observed that "despite the clamor of [the anti-testing] critics, standardized tests enjoy widespread support in U.S. public opinion" (p. 625). Using the responses to a 1979 Gallup survey to substantiate this point, he noted that 81 percent of a national sample of parents had judged standardized tests to be "useful" or "somewhat useful." Two years earlier, Smith and Gallup (1977) discussed the results of a 1976 survey, which had revealed that "the American people, judged from present and past survey data, do not share the skepticism of many educators about the significance of standardized tests." Smith and Gallup added that "by majorities of about 2–1, all segments of the population, in all areas of the nation, believe that the tests are correctly assessing the situation" (p. 27). Lerner (1981b) examined the results of Gallup polls during a several year period to prove that the testing "movement has massive public support." She previously had written that the relatively small group attacking tests had done so because it was threatened by tests that "tell us truths about ourselves and our society; partial truths, to be sure, but truths nonetheless and, in recent years, many of these truths have been unpleasant and unflattering" (Lerner, 1979, p. 4).

In another report, Lerner (1981a) maintained that "public dissatisfaction with the unregulated practice of standardized testing cannot fairly be described as either pervasive or profound." She added that "such dissatisfaction as exists is confined to a small, atypical minority" (p. 274). She pointed to the misunderstandings that had been caused by the inflammatory reporting of the 1960s and 1970s. While acknowledging that "extreme forms of advocacy journalism still exist," she believed that "many responsible investigative reporters and other media people are increasingly unhappy about the role some of their fellows have played, wittingly or unwittingly, as conduits for false claims put forth by new special interest groups" (1981a, p. 275). She added that the public and the press, which were "becoming increasingly leery of self-appointed spokespersons for the public interest," had turned to reputable polls to help them discern the social status of testing. Agreeing that the testing enthusiasts had been able to recruit new constituents, Kearney (1983) reported that "the cast of policy actors has expanded tremendously over the past few years." He noted that the once "loose-knit fraternity" of pro-assessment policymakers had been replaced by an increasingly unified group that included "legislators, legislative staff, executives, executive staff, educators, representatives of interests groups, citizens, parents, students" and all of the "others who make or influence decisions in American education" (p. 9).

Within a book entitled *The Rise and Fall of National Test Scores,* Austin and Garber (1982) explained why recently declining test scores had created so much consternation.

> Every society values education. The institutions it creates for instruction are considered essential to the very survival of the society itself. When evidence emerges suggesting that the outcome of study in the educational institutions is less than it ought to be, public concern is aroused. Test scores are used to measure the health of an educational process. When declining test scores in the nation's schools are reported, public concern is understandably aroused. (p. xv)

In the foreword to Austin and Garber's book, Ebel (1982) adopted a wider historical perspective to explain the escalating concern about test scores. He wrote that the "naturalist 'let's enjoy life' philosophy tends to prevail" when international dangers were not apparent. In contrast, "during periods of threat to the nation, excellence, achievement, and essentialism tend to express the will of the people." Based on contemporary attitudes about the danger of Communism and the critical role of education in national defense, Ebel predicted that the public would rely increasingly on test scores to confirm the health of their schools.

Brandt (1990) calculated that "several dozen national reports and almost three hundred state reports on the condition of education" had been published during the 1980s. A reporter (Walton, 1983) for *Education Week* wrote that "a spate of education reports" had appeared during 1983. Stedman and Smith (1983) commented on four of the national proposals from that year. The Education Commission of the States, the College Entrance Examination Board, and the Twentieth Century Fund had each sponsored publications. The fourth report, which was commissioned by the U.S. Department of Education, was entitled *A Nation at Risk*. Although Stedman and Smith judged that all four reports had engendered interest in educational reform, these authors miscalculated the disproportionate impact of *A Nation at Risk*, which would eclipse all other proposals from that year, that decade, and that quarter of the century.

The National Commission on Excellence in Education had written *A Nation at Risk* in response to a charge from Terrence Bell, the U.S. Secretary of Education. Bell later recounted that 70,000 copies of this report were purchased during the first year that it was available (U.S. Department of Education, 1984). He noted that private groups reprinted 500,000 additional copies during the same period. In a government monograph (U.S. Department of Education, 1984) for which Bell had written the foreword, authors from the Department of Education indicated that "it remains true as the *New York Times* reported in June 1983 that the Commission 'brought the issue [of education] to the forefront of political debate with an urgency not felt since the Soviet satellite shook American confidence in its public schools in 1957'" (p. 11). These authors added that the Department of Education staff had "identified over 700 [newspaper] articles related to *A Nation at Risk* in the 4 months following the report's release" and that "major periodicals, including *Time, Newsweek, The New Republic,* and *Better Homes and Gardens,* have devoted extensive space to commentary on the Commission" (p. 13).

Two decades after the publication of the report, Schouten (2003) wrote a newspaper piece with the title *"At Risk" Report 20 Years Later*. Even though a significant period had passed, Schouten assumed that the general public would recognize this influential document just by the key phrase in its title. In her retrospective, she did not even refer to any of the other reports from the 1980s. The Teaching Commission (2004) used the same rhetorical strategy to call attention to its own proposal for school reform. The members of this unit described themselves as "a diverse group, comprising 19 leaders in government, business, and education." Attempting to associate their current report with that extensively publicized document that had appeared more than two decades earlier, they entitled it *Teaching at Risk: A Call to Action*.

Using low academic test scores as evidence of severe educational problems, the authors of *A Nation at Risk* recommended extensive school reforms. Looking back at the discussions spurred by this report, Koretz (1987) judged that "scores on standardized achievement tests…played a central role in this debate" (ix). He added that the 1983 report increased national attention to current and subsequent test scores because the public became aware "that the test scores of American students declined markedly during the 1960s and 1970s and compared poorly with those of students in other countries." Writing soon after the original report had been released, White (1983) reported that "the latest edition of a national opinion poll...found that the American public largely agrees with the major findings of several recent blue-ribbon panels on education: The quality of the nation's public schools has declined...and broad reforms...are needed" (p. 1).

Timar and Kirp (1988) judged that "since 1983, education has risen to the top of many states' policy agendas" and that "the level of state policy activity is unprecedented in the history of American education" (p. 75). Three years later, Baker and Stites (1991) adopted a similar vantage.

> The 1980s began in the USA with education's retreat from equity issues. This perspective was strengthened by the publication of *A Nation at Risk* in 1983...and raised one more time the alarm that US [*sic*] students were not succeeding at desired levels. What made this cry compelling, however, were two interlocking factors. First, international comparisons revealed that US [*sic*] students were performing significantly poorer than many of our trading partners...and second that the trade balance suggested that US [*sic*] products were not holding their own in the competitive arena. (p. 150)

Gifford (1993) characterized the Department of Education's 1983 report as a document that had "riveted attention on our schools." As a direct result of the report, "the American public came to grips with a crisis in education and its potentially devastating effects on the nation's economic and social life" (p. 3). In the preface to a book that examined the educational reforms of the 1980s, Jacobson (1993) made a similar observation. He concluded that *A Nation at Risk* had made educational change a high political priority. Jacobson summarized the report's central message as a warning that "America's economic preeminence in the global marketplace was being threatened by an erosion in the quality of its public schools" (p. vii).

Many persons and organizations provided testimonials about the impact of *A Nation at Risk*. A report (McLaughlin & Shepard, 1995) from the National Academy of Education examined standards-based educational reforms during the preceding 12 years. In the preface to that report, Kaestle (1995) observed that "most states have begun efforts to improve academic standards or to reform education through innovative assessment" (p. xi). Driscoll (1996) concluded that "most popular accounts agree that *A Nation at Risk*...did impel a slew of reform efforts that continued at breakneck pace throughout the 1980s" (p. 420). In the *Christian Science Monitor*, Kean (2000) underscored the central role of tests within these reforms.

> In the 1980s, many of our governors, educators, and business leaders looked at the poor performance of our students in relation to their peers abroad. Our students' failure to measure up to the rest of the world spurred the development of education standards. To measure these standards, the states created challenging new education assessments. (p. 21)

In agreement with Kean, Hillocks (2002) reckoned that the admonition to commence extensive testing was implemented more widely than any of the other recommendations in *A Nation at Risk*.

Many of the businesspersons who read *A Nation at Risk* reacted in manners that were remarkably similar. The response from the Committee for Economic Development (1985) typified that of other businesspersons. This committee viewed itself as a "nonprofit, nonpartisan, and nonpolitical" research and educational organization. Its 200 members were committed to "steady economic growth at high employment and reasonably stable prices,...greater and more equal [*sic*] opportunity for every citizen, and...[high] quality of life for all" (p. viii). They urged an alliance between educators and businesspersons who were concerned about the "costs of failure." They asked educators to recognize that "employability requires problem-solving skills, command of the English language, self-discipline, and the ability to acquire and apply new knowledge" (p. 3). To ensure that these goals were met, they encouraged states to "set standards, monitor achievement, and intervene if schools fail to perform." Kaestle (1995) recounted that businesspersons came to support "national standards about what students should know and be able to do in each school subject" (p. xi).

A Nation at Risk (National Commission on Excellence in Education, 1983) was subtitled *The Imperative for Educational Reform*. In the introductory passages, the authors made jarring statements.

> Our Nation [*sic*] is at risk. Our once unchallenged preeminence in commerce, industry, science, and technological innovations is being overtaken by competitors throughout the world. This report is concerned with only one of the many causes and dimensions of the problem, but it is the one that undergirds American prosperity, security, and civility....the educational foundations of our society are presently being eroded by a rising tide of mediocrity that threatens our very future as a Nation and a people. What was unimaginable a generation ago has begun to occur—others are matching and surpassing our educational attainments. (p. 5)

Although the U.S. Secretary of Education had explicitly directed this commission to compare "American schools and colleges with those of other advanced nations," its members went further and highlighted reasons that declining academic achievement constituted a threat to military security. They explained that, "if an unfriendly foreign power had attempted to impose on America the mediocre educational performance that exists today, we might well have viewed it as an act of war." The commission's members again emphasized the danger from hostile nations when they chastised the educational community for "committing an act of unthinking, unilateral educational disarmament" (p. 5).

As far as evidence of educational decline, the commissioners made numerous test-based observations. For example, they noted that "average achievement of high school students on most standardized tests is now lower than 26 years ago," "over half the population of gifted students do not match their tested ability with comparable achievement in schools," "the College Board's Scholastic Aptitude Tests (SAT) demonstrate a virtually unbroken decline from 1963 to 1980," "College Board achievement tests…reveal consistent declines in recent years in such subjects as physics and English," "both the number and proportion of students demonstrating superior achievement on the SATs…have…dramatically declined," "there was a steady decline in science achievement scores of U.S. 17-year-olds as measured by assessments of science in 1969, 1973, and 1977," and the "average tested achievement of students graduating from college is also lower" (pp. 8–9).

Becker and Baumol (1996) were struck by the "many studies and proposals for reform of the nation's school system" that the 1983 report had initiated. Although the sheer number of these proposals may have been impressive, the rapidity with which they appeared was also amazing. Just a year after the publication of *A Nation at Risk*, the federal government (U.S. Department of Education, 1984) released a summary of the school changes that were planned in every state. For example, the section on Alabama, which was the first entry in the report's alphabetically organized roster, described that state's new and more stringent testing standards.

> Beginning in 1985, all students must pass a basic skills test to receive a diploma. The test is first offered in 11th grade. *A Plan for Excellence* endorses this requirement and recommends the continuance of the statewide competency and norm-referenced testing programs, adjustments in curricula and parent-teacher conferences. The State Board's resolutions support the report as well as the development of additional instruments to determine students' vocational interests. (p. 22)

As was the case with Alabamians, the citizens of most states accepted the test-based data in *A Nation at Risk* as evidence of a crisis that imperiled the country's economic prosperity and international security. Their worries were exacerbated by other large-scale assessments that followed the 1983 report and that seemed to validate its ominous warnings. For example, Finn and Ravitch (1987) discovered that the 8000 high-school students they had tested knew "shockingly little about history and literature." With regard to history, they pointed out that "one in three of the 17-year-old students do not know when Columbus discovered America," that "two out of five cannot tell in which 50-year period the U.S. Constitution was written," and that "more than half think Jim Crow laws were enacted to *improve* the lot of black people" (p. 31).

Most citizens acknowledged the value of testing because it had revealed fundamental problems in the educational system. Moreover, they believed testing was essential for solving those problems. To demonstrate the impact of these views, Nolen, Haladyna, and Haas (1992) pointed out the changes that had occurred within nine years of the publication of *A Nation at Risk*. They noted that 42 states were requiring standardized tests, the U.S. Department of Education was using test scores as the basis for highly publicized national reports, news media were using test scores to rank school districts, and the public consistently had indicated its overwhelming support for standardized tests.

Continuing to Emphasize Assessment of Teachers

Flanagan (1941) wrote a report in which he referred to the pre–World War II edition of the National Teacher Examinations. Even though he did not question the validity and practicality of these tests, he did wonder whether they actually would help "in predicting the types of things in which school systems are interested." For example, would school administrators agree that persons who scored high on the exams were more effective teachers than those individuals with lower scores? Would they agree on a minimum score below which teachers would not be hired, irrespective of those teachers' other qualifications? Flanagan's questions anticipated some of the political issues that would influence the way that the National Teacher Examinations would be used as well as the extent to which they would be used. These early clashes between advocates and opponents of test-based teacher accountability should have impressed later observers with the politicized positions into which special interest groups already had become entrenched. Like Flanagan, they should have questioned whether these positions were likely to shift noticeably.

In an introductory letter that had accompanied the 1966 Coleman Report, the U.S. Commissioner of Education explained that a group of researchers had been directed by the Congress to assess the opportunities for obtaining a quality education in the United States. The commissioner added parenthetically that some characteristics of quality education were readily discernible. For example, few persons questioned the value of textbooks and libraries. However, quality education had additional features that were less apparent but equally important. These features included "characteristics of the teachers found in the schools—such things as their education, amount of teaching experience, salary level, verbal ability, and indications of attitudes" (Howe, 1966, p. iii). As a member of a liberal Democratic administration that had been endorsed strongly by teacher unions, Howe did not mean to call for greater teacher accountability. In view of the Johnson administration's distrust of standardized tests, Howe certainly did not wish to endorse test-based accountability for teachers. Nonetheless, he had inadvertently called attention to an issue upon which conservatives were waiting to pounce.

Newspapers and magazines provided the ideal venues for conservatives to make their case about the damage that incompetent teachers were causing. In a front-page article in the *Wall Street Journal*, Bulkeley (1978) indicated that "teachers in school systems across the country are being evaluated partly on the basis of what their students learn" (p. 1). He emphasized that this "tough approach to education," which had been implemented in spite of the "strong opposition form teacher organizations," was the result of "national alarm over declining aptitude-test scores and over high-school graduates who can't read newspapers or fill out job applications." One opponent of the educational establishment expressed his frustration about "educators [who] couldn't care less about teaching [because] they get paid no matter what" (Barnes, quoted by Bulkeley, 1978, p. 1). Goldstein (1977) reported about one teacher who believed that the Equal Protection Clause of the 14th Amendment prevented students' test scores from being used as the grounds for her dismissal. He noted curtly that a federal appeals court had disagreed with her.

The authors of a nine-page cover story ("Help," 1980) in *Time* magazine restated some the current educational problems that were being widely publicized.

> Violence keeps making headlines. Test scores keep dropping. Debate rages over whether or not one-fifth or more adult Americans are functionally illiterate. High school [*sic*] graduates go so far as to sue their school systems because they got respectable grades and a diploma but cannot fill in job application forms correctly. Experts confirm that students today get at least 25% more As and Bs than they did 15 years ago, but know less. A Government-funded nationwide survey group, the National Assessment of Educational Progress, reports that in science, writing, social studies and mathematics the achievement of U.S. 17-year-olds has dropped regularly over the past decade. (p. 54)

The authors indicated that different groups had attributed this litany of problems to television, bussing, declining family values, dysfunctional school practices, and the other "usual suspects." However, the authors noted that "parents have begun to blame the shortcomings of the schools on the lone and very visible figure at the front of the classroom." This last observation should not have been a surprise in an article that was entitled *Help! Teacher Can't Teach!* To illustrate the magnitude of instructor incompetence, the authors reproduced a note that had been sent to one student's parents by an Alabama teacher with a master's degree. The note read: "Scott is dropping in his studies he acts as if he don't care. Scott wont pass in his assignment at all, he a had a poem to learn and he fell tu do it" (message from an unidentified teacher, reproduced in "Help!" 1980, p. 59).

Lehmann and Phillips (1987) noted that "report after report, commission after commission, and survey after survey have stated that our schools are in a state of turmoil" (p. 14). Focusing on teachers, they identified studies which had indicated that "our teacher training institution graduates are sorely lacking in basic skills...[that] students enrolled in teacher-training programs score at the lowest decile in verbal and numerical skills...that both full-time, certified teachers, as well as education majors, score lowest on tests of basic skills...that in 1983 16% of Florida's prospective teachers failed the state's proficiency test....that a dispropor-tionate number of minority members fail teacher-competency tests...and that nearly one-fifth of U.S. classroom teachers have not mastered those skills they purportedly are teaching" (p. 14).

Wuhs and Manatt (1983) reported that only six states had required teacher evaluations prior to 1971. That number had jumped to 26 states by 1983. In an article written during the period to which Wuhs and Manatt had referred, reporters recounted that the New Jersey legislature had urged that student performance on standardized tests became "a ground for dismissal of employees, including teachers with tenure" ("Teachers Fail Test," 1978, p. 4). The reporters noted that the New Jersey Education Association had threatened to sue over this proposed policy. They connected this confrontation to a separate incident in which "more than half of the 585 teachers [hired by the Dallas public schools] who took [a commercially prepared standardized intelligence test] failed—even though they only had to answer correctly 31 of the 60 math and language problems" (p. 4). The reporters thought the credibility of the educational establishment diminished even more after "officials in the Dallas public schools fought the *Dallas Times-Herald* and the state's attorney general—unsuccessfully—to prevent publication of scores made by newly hired teachers." The witty reporters characterized the consequences of these incidents in their article's title—*Teachers Fail Test: Tests Fail Teachers*.

An unbridgeable chasm seemed to separate the general public's views on teacher accountability from those of the teachers themselves. The differences were apparent in the 20th anniversary replication of a 1964 study about teachers' attitudes. The researchers (Kottkamp, Provenzo, & Cohn, 1986) asked instructors to identify "the indicator that a good teacher is most likely to use in judging personal effectiveness." As far as the value of reactions from parents, only one percent of the teachers surveyed in 1964 had judged this information to be relevant. Twenty years later, that number had increased by only two percentage points. As for "results of objective examination and various other tests," the percentage of teachers who saw value in these types of data had grown from 13 to 19 in the 20-year period. Attempting to explain the reason that teachers preferred to use personal exams that they had devised rather than standardized tests, Wildemuth (1984) reported that the teachers thought standardized examinations did not "necessarily test what students h ave learned,...what the school has taught,...[and] what the student has achieved" (p. 2).

Berk (1988) reported that 29 states had either implemented or were preparing to implement accountability measures that would affect teachers' salaries. Although these states had not adopted a common procedure for evaluating their teachers, he speculated that the use of student exam scores "seems to be gaining increasing acceptance by legislators and the professionals who are designing the [accountability] programs" (p. 345). Berk protested that these recent teacher assessment programs were unfair because "there are at least 50 factors that can influence a teacher's effectiveness which are beyond his or her control" (p. 348). Some of these uncontrollable elements were the size of the school library, size of the school's building site, age of the school building, quality of the instructional equipment, turnover of staff, and the number of students assigned to each teacher.

In a *New York Times* editorial, Albert Shanker (1988), the president of the American Federation of Teachers, enumerated some of the reasons for teachers' lack of confidence in standardized testing. He indicated that "the tests are very costly...[and] the money spent for the tests could be put to better use for adequate textbooks and materials" (p. 7). The teachers had other reasons for opposing tests. For example, they believed that scores were "misleading if not downright fraudulent," that "students were not being measured against their peers," and that the scores on tests from ten or more years ago were not comparable to those on the current exams with which they were being contrasted. As an additional caveat, Shanker noted that "schools are devoting less time to reading real books, writing essays, and discussing current events and more time teaching kids strategies for filling in blanks and choosing the answers to multiple choice questions" (p. 7).

Although Shanker may have accurately described the dispositions of the members of his labor union, the testing initiatives of the 1980s revealed that the dispositions of teachers were remarkably incongruent with those of the general public. These differences were evident in the remarks that were made by the opponents as well as the supporters of testing. After examining the test-based teacher accountability schemes that had emerged shortly after the publication of *A Nation at Risk*, Freiberg (1984) complained that they were "legislated, top-down plans with little input from the teaching professionals" (p. 20). Freiberg's observations were readily substantiated. Several of the national educational reform groups had displayed their distrust of teachers and school administrators when they called for systematic testing that was "to be administered by an agency external to the local school district" (Madaus, 1985, p. 7). The author of a study that had been prepared for the Congressional Budget Office had indicated the independent manner in which the public was examining the education system. He had written that "test scores have become a common basis of comparisons among schools and districts, and in some communities, newspapers routinely publish test results to facilitate such comparisons" (Koretz, 1986, p. xiv). This author concluded that "test scores have in fact come to be used as a national report card." Looking back on the 1980s, Koretz and Barron (1998) saw this period as one in which the "relatively easy, minimum competency tests" of the previous decade were "supplanted by or supplemented with a program that held educators accountable for scores on standardized, norm-referenced multiple-choice tests" (p. iii).

Despite the public's belief that teachers should share the responsibility for the test scores that their students were earning, most teachers resisted this proposal. Urdan and Paris (1994) reported the results of a survey on which 77 percent of the responding teachers indicated that "tests are bad." In contrast, only three percent agreed with the statement that "tests are good." Although they were aware that most parents had confidence in tests, 68 percent of the teachers judged that the parents were misusing test scores. These teachers had even less confidence in the ability of their own supervisors to accurately comprehend the limitations of tests. Eighty percent of them were dismayed because they thought their administrators believed that standardized tests were valid. Five years later, columnists ("What's Your Opinion," 1999a) for *NEA Today* asked the teachers who read that magazine to indicate whether students' test scores should be used to evaluate teachers. In the subsequent issue, the editors ("What's Your Opinion," 1999b) revealed that 87 percent of the respondents opposed the use of student test scores to evaluate teachers.

Rejecting the advice from the educational establishment, some late twentieth-century critics resolved to use the scores that students were earning on objective tests to judge the effectiveness of teachers. Unlike earlier periods, when a decision about following this type of advice had been left to the discretion of local school districts, the resolutions that followed *A Nation at Risk* were mandated by state and federal legislation. A comparable change characterized the administration of teacher competency tests, which turned out to be another divisive issue for the public and the teachers. As an indication of the views of the public toward teacher competency tests, a 1979 poll (Gallup, 1980) had queried participants as to whether applicants for teaching positions should be "required to pass a state board examination." Eighty-five percent of the respondents indicated that prospective teachers should pass such a test. As for those teachers who had already been hired, 85 percent of the respondents thought that this group "should be tested every few years to see if they are keeping up to date with developments in their fields" (p. 230). Moreover, 85 percent of the respondents wanted applicants for administrative positions and current school administrators to be assessed.

Haney, Madaus, and Kreitzer (1987) observed that "the number of states requiring teachers or would-be teachers to pass some form of entrance or certification examination has grown from only a handful in the mid-1970s to a clear majority by the mid-1980s" (p. 169). Shepard and Kreitzer (1987) reported that "Texas is one of three states with legislated mandates to test the competency of practicing educators [and] 202,000 teachers and school administrators took the TECAT, the Texas Examination of Current Administrators and Teachers, to see if they could keep their jobs" (p. 22). Madaus and Pullin (1987) noted that Arkansas and Georgia had enacted similar requirements for experienced teachers. They also reported that 34 states required prospective teachers to take a national exam from the ETS or some type of locally developed examination.

One reporter ("School Superintendent Fails," 2003) noted that "since 1998, all Massachusetts educators—from teachers to superintendents—have had to pass the Communication and Literacy Skills Test, which measures basic reading and writing skills, including vocabulary, punctuation, grammar, spelling and capitalization" (p. 1). After failing this test, the superintendent of Lawrence, Massachusetts, complained that "I'm trying to understand the congruence of what I do here every day and this stupid test" (Wilfredo Laboy, 2003, as quoted in "School Superintendent Fails," 2003, p. 1). The reporter added that the Massachusetts Education Commissioner "would not say how many chances [the superintendent] would be given to pass or what the consequences of another failure could be." This reporter underscored the irony of this situation when the same superintendent "put 24 teachers on unpaid administrative leave because they failed a basic English test."

Resistance From Post-1960s Liberals

Some of the assaults on tests were primarily, if not exclusively, political. This seemed to be the case when Cohen and Rosenberg (1977) appraised "the role schools have served in the American economic structure." These liberal ideologues judged that previous attempts at educational reform had been "mere cosmetics to keep the contradictory face of capitalism from appearing too ugly" (p. 113). As to the reason that standardized tests had played a central role in these reforms, they concluded that "testing became a pervasive phenomenon because of [the public's beliefs that it would improve scholastic efficiency], but not because the beliefs were true" (p. 129).

During the 1960s and 1970s, the courts had placed restrictions on the scholastic assessment of persons with disabilities (Kirp, 1973; Leary, 1970; Swanson & Watson, 1989; Wildemuth, 1983). Some liberals initiated legal suits in an effort to extend these restrictions to the tests that the general population was taking. In refreshingly forthright remarks, Fincher (1979) admitted that educational testing and politics had become inextricably fused. He wrote that "public policy is the framework in which testing issues must be resolved" and that court decisions, despite their ambiguities, were part of that context. Commenting further on the ambiguities that the courts had created, he wrote insightfully about one historic decision in which "there is more to read between the lines than within the text" (p. 6). In spite of the candor that he had shown while describing the legal process, Fincher was reconciliatory when he explained the motives of those liberals who had been using the courts as a means of assaulting educational assessment.

> The continuing controversies that surround the use of standardized tests, an era of increasingly common litigation, and the emerging directives of public policy imply that traditional test theory and practices may be inadequate...[and] there is an apparent demand for other approaches and procedures that serve the same educational and social purposes... Pluralism and diversity in education have convinced many observers that a different philosophy or theory of testing is needed. (p. 3)

Within another legalistic review, Robertson (1980) made rhetorical points that complemented those of Fincher. He argued that the judges who had used truth-in-testing laws to restrict testing corporations should not be seen as social activists. He preferred that they be viewed as proponents of a social movement that relied on legislation and the courts to define the rights of consumers. The authors of another report ("Legal Issues," 1984) adopted a viewpoint that was extremely similar. They discussed a Florida case in which the judge had considered whether standardized test scores could be imposed as the condition for awarding high-school diplomas. The authors indicated that the plaintiffs, who had cited cases involving persons with disabilities, argued that individuals from racial or linguistic minority groups had experienced educational problems that were comparable to those that had been experienced by persons with disabilities. In this instance, "the Court found that because Florida's black students had not had 12 full years of racially integrated education, they were therefore subject to inferior educational opportunities" (p. 1).

In an article that appeared in the *University of Richmond Law Review*, Commander (1980) reprised court cases in which plaintiffs had alleged that minimum competency testing was discriminatory. Commander pointed out that minimum competency tests actually had two functions—to assess the quality of individual students and to assess the quality of the educational system. With regard to the latter function, he contended that state legislators had crafted testing laws because they were concerned about system-wide declining academic achievement. In many of the cases where student-initiated suits had been rejected, the courts had determined that such laws were significant extenuating factors that justified the use of testing. To demonstrate the degree to which school accountability had been politicized, Commander also cited cases in which the courts had acknowledged the injurious actions of conservative legislators. The conservatives' detrimental influence had been apparent in those cases where students' diplomas had been withheld to advance an exclusively political agenda.

Although heavily politicized arguments from liberals and conservatives appealed to their respective constituencies, they were less persuasive to those persons who had not made up their minds about testing. Rudman (1977) made this observation while he was sorting "fact from fiction, truth from deliberate hyperbole."

> Those who seem to know the least about measurement and who have not used standardized test data in their instructional and curricular decisions are most strongly opposed to testing. But there is a...group, composed primarily of administrators and teachers—a majority, I believe who have had assessment and evaluation responsibilities thrust upon them and are neither for nor against testing. They are seeking help. (p. 179)

Rudman added that many critics of tests were too "poorly qualified to speak with wisdom, knowledge of the facts, and insight." He believed that "what started as an opportunity to stimulate discussion has developed into increasingly nonfactual rhetoric and hysteria" (p. 185).

The logical weaknesses to which Rudman had referred were readily apparent in many of the articles that were published during the 1970s and early 1980s. In these articles, liberals predicted that extensive faults made the future of standardized exams bleak. Attempting to look 25 years into the future, Butler (1975) made precisely this type of forecast.

> Individual and group IQ tests have all but disappeared, and the school psychologist has assumed the same relationship with the child as that of the private physician. The child today is evaluated on a broad range of talents and abilities—not solely on linguistic and culture-specific skills—and the results of those evaluations remain in the possession of the child and his or her family. (p. 75)

Some persons claimed that disaffection with testing already had become a reality. One critical report (Salmon-Cox, 1981) contained a byline indicating that the author would present "a provocative list of reasons why the teachers she studies preferred to rely on their own good judgment" (p. 631). The authors of another article in that same journal warned that the results of tests were so adulterated with extraneous information that "central office administrators do not depend heavily upon test data for decision making" (Sproull & Zubrow, 1981).

The reports made during the 1970s and 1980s about pervasive public hostility to standardized testing were inaccurate. The predictions about an imminent cessation of testing also turned out to be wrong. In the introduction to the annual yearbook of the Politics of Education Association, Malen and Fuhrman (1991) acknowledged these miscalculations. They pointed out that "state governments have assumed a more expansive, aggressive, and prescriptive role in many domains of education policy," and, as a result, had "adopted policies to generate and disseminate more detailed assessment of student performance" (p. 1). Even after they realized that many of their fellow partisans had not been persuaded by forecasts about the doom of standardized assessment, political extremists continued to make these forecasts. In an interview that was published in *NEA Today*, the Executive Director (Neill, 1999) of the Center for Fair and Open Testing opined that the "best way" to measure children's academic performance was "to have student work collected in a portfolio." He railed against standardized tests because "they are not a good measure of a student's ability to think, reason, or problem solve in subject areas," "there are measurement errors in these tests," and "most minority students don't do as well as white students on the tests." In response to a question about the future of tests, he predicted that "we could see fewer when people see testing is not producing large gains and is forcing everything else out of the schools" (p. 6).

Convinced that standardized testing was a liability, Smith (1998) encouraged the trainers of teachers to minimize its negative consequences. An effective way to achieve this goal was to influence the attitudes of those college-level students who would become the next generation of instructors. She discouraged the teacher educators from spreading the "literature of failure," which consisted of "research findings that present repeated comparative test-score profiles of low-achieving minority students and high-achieving White students" (p. 18). Using a grammatically daunting sentence, she explained that "this kind of teacher education program seems not to emphasize that such test profiles are not evidence of inferior levels of potential among minority students but are, in fact, evidence of poor schooling and lack of societal commitment to equal outcomes for minority students."

During the early 1980s, some anti-testing critics gave disingenuous advice about how their opponents could encourage a philosophical rapprochement. Jencks and Crouse (1982) assured the test publishers that students were displaying sloth and frivolity because they did not see the usefulness of the content and the questions on standardized college admission tests. They advised the publishers to make their tests more practical in order to change the attitudes of these students. From a similar perspective, Carpenter (1983) advised the proponents of tests to change teachers' views about the practicality of testing. The proponents could accomplish this objective by "analyzing responses to each test question to identify an individual student's strengths and weakness" (p. 33). One group of educators (Freeman, Kuhs, Porter, Floden, Schmidt, & Schwille, 1983) urged teachers to support only those tests that precisely matched the curricula they were employing in their classrooms. Needless to say, the persons who had made these adjurations realized that their advice would disqualify most large-scale testing programs.

The preceding samples of advice were never intended to close an ideological chasm. To the contrary, they widened the rupture between the opponents and advocates of testing. During the late 1980s, the opponents of testing continued to employ this strategy. McLean and Goldstein (1988) opposed the National Assessment of Educational Progress because it assigned a single score for reading. Even though they must have been fully aware of the impracticality of their suggestion, they recommended that the testers assemble batteries of tests with a separate score for each skill that a reader might employ. McClellan (1988) indicated that he would not support testing programs unless they were locally controlled. Because the conservatives had supported local control of education, McClellan hoped that this criticism would be especially disconcerting to them. Instead of "externally imposed" and "politically motivated" tests, he demanded assessment procedures that would not "challenge the traditional assumptions that educational agendas should be set locally." Using a similar argument, Stiggins (1988) warned about the "whirlpool of publicity, political turmoil, and scholarly debate currently surrounding the development of a national standardized test, of statewide assessments, and of measurement-driven instruction." He urged that all assessments of students defer to the unique perspectives of individual teachers. Meisels (1989) thought this admonition was especially useful when making decisions about young children, who would benefit from low-stakes rather than high-stakes assessment. A year later, the liberal members of the National Commission on

Testing and Public Policy (1990) recommended that "testing programs should be redirected from overreliance on multiple-choice tests toward alternative forms of assessment" (p. x).

The opponents of standardized testing invariably attracted teachers to their ranks. Numerous researchers furnished data or testimonials that verified this allegiance. Boyer (1988) made this point while discussing a largely ignored 1983 report from the Carnegie Foundation for the Advancement of Teaching. Even though he was skeptical about the validity of tests, Boyer recognized that "during the past five years, the nation has been engaged in the most sustained drive for school renewal in its history" (p. 1). Nonetheless, Boyer insisted that most teachers lacked confidence in these reforms. He indicated that he and his staff, after surveying 13,500 instructors, had been "surprised to discover that the vast majority of teachers—nearly 70 percent—said the national push for school reform deserves a 'C' or less [and that] one teacher out of five gave the reform movement a 'D' or 'F'." Boyer and his colleagues judged that school assessment was "marginal at best" because the "testing instruments are crude and often measure that which matters least" (pp. 5–6).

Wolf, LeMahieu, and Eresh (1992) made similar observations. They recognized that the growth in testing was transpiring in spite of the resistance from teachers. However, they also realized that the demands for school accountability were unrelenting. Therefore, they advised teachers to turn away from standardized tests and substitute those forms of assessment to which the teachers were amenable. The byline for this article urged teachers to respond to "the national call…for improved accountability" through "performance tasks and portfolios."

Koretz, Mitchell, Barron, and Keith (1996) also focused attention on the attitudes that teachers maintained toward large-scale standardized assessment. Within a discussion of the Maryland School Performance Assessment Program (MSPAP), they explained that this widely publicized initiative had been "designed to induce fundamental changes in instruction as well as to measure the educational progress of schools, districts, and the state" (p. vii). Because a "sizeable majority of teachers reported that the program has had a moderate amount or great deal of positive impact on instruction," the conclusions of these researchers were not as sensational as those in some of the other studies. Nonetheless, their conclusions did reveal that 35 percent of Maryland's teachers opposed the MSPAP.

Some critics assumed historical or philosophical perspectives when they were explaining their negative attitudes toward standardized testing. Futrell (1989) had served for six years as president of the National Education Association, which had a membership of 2,000,000 teachers. While reminiscing about this service, she predicted that "history will view the 1980s not as the decade of education reform, but as the decade of education posturing" (p. 10). She anticipated that the era of genuine reform, which was just beginning, would be a "grassroots" effort that would replace the initiatives that had "emanated from the statehouse." In this new period of school transformation, test-based educational objectives would be replaced by scholastic goals that were "less parochial, more expansive, and less determined by economic forces" (p. 13). Although Wagner (1989) was not sure that the public was ready to establish new educational priorities, he also tried to articulate the philosophical principles that had guided educational reform during the 1980s. Like Futrell, he thought these principles had been politicized in order to make the schools "less autonomous and more 'accountable.'"

To explain their opposition to standardized assessment, Corbett and Wilson (1991) examined pedagogical rather than historical or philosophical consequences. They criticized the proponents of tests for their naive belief that standardized assessment promoted genuine reform. They suggested that "the paradoxical fallout from statewide testing is that local educators end up rebelling against reform by narrowing their definitions of educational purpose and engaging in 'quick-fix' remedies" (p. 1). Like most educators who opposed standardized assessment, they insisted that "the consequence is that creative visions of what the educational enterprise in a particular locality should be become clouded by the dominating presence of public pressure to improve test performance in the present." From a sympathetic perspective, Smith (1991) presented data to demonstrate that "testing programs substantially reduce the time available for instruction, narrow curricular offerings and modes of instruction, and potentially reduce the capacities of teachers to teach content and to use methods and materials that are incompatible with standardized testing formats" (p. 8). She concluded that "district administrators use test scores as tools to standardize and control what teachers do" and that "it is not the form of these tests that generates these effects on teachers but the political and social uses made of the scores" (p. 11). That same year, Haladyna, Nolen, and Haas (1991) argued that the ways in which teachers prepared their students for tests and the unique circumstance under which they administered exams were sources of "score pollution" that essentially invalidated the tests.

Later twentieth-century critics had predicted that standardized testing would wane. Although this did not transpire, some of their forebodings were accurate. As one example, a reporter (Stecklow, 1997) for the *Wall Street Journal* candidly described the unanticipated consequences of one state's testing program.

> The notion seems simple enough: To improve public education, reward teachers with cash bonuses if their schools' test scores rise. If the scores drop, declare their school is in trouble and provide special assistance. But Kentucky's carrot-and-stick approach...has spawned lawsuits, infighting between teachers and staff, anger among parents, widespread grade inflation—and numerous instances of cheating by teachers to boost student scores. Teachers have allowed students to use textbooks to find test answers, edited essays before they were written in the test booklet and given out questions in advance. (p. A1)

In spite of numerous caustic reports, the proponents of testing claimed that their influence had become stronger than ever during the 1990s. Skeptics might wonder if the conflicting interests of the test supporters prevented them from appraising their political status objectively. Although this could have been the case for the pro-testing factions, conflicting interests could hardly have influenced any of the liberals who eventually provided testimonials about the sustained force of a movement that they resented and opposed. As an instance of this latter type of testimonial, the reporter who had written the styptic essay about Kentucky's standardized testing program still conceded its popularity. He noted that the public had credited the initiative with "helping students to achieve gains in writing and problem solving skills at all grade levels, and improvements in reading, math and science, particularly in elementary schools" (Stecklow, 1997, p. A1). Even though his article was replete with remarks from teachers who claimed that Kentucky's assessment program was oppressive, the reporter noted that those teachers who had earned cash awards for their schools had been permitted to designate how the money would be spent. Given the fact that most of them had stated their opposition to tests stemmed from fear of censure, they could have allayed that fear by purchasing learning materials or equipment. However, in 98 percent of the instances, the teachers had paid themselves bonuses.

Although Koretz (1996) denigrated " accountability-oriented testing," he recognized its popularity, expansion, and success in eliciting progressively greater test performance from students. At the same time, he dismissed rising test scores as "inflation" caused by "degradation of instruction." Convinced that many persons agreed with him, he recommended student portfolios and performance-based measures as alternatives to standardized assessment. Despite his personal enthusiasm for alternative systems of assessment, Koretz was aware that these systems were impractical and expensive. He dejectedly but realistically conceded that "it does not appear…that substituting performance assessment for multiple-choice testing will be sufficient to eliminate many of the fundamental problems of test-based accountability" (p. 174).

Haney (2000) tried to discredit the mandatory testing program that had been implemented in Texas during the 1990s. Despite his personal opposition to it, Haney acknowledged that this program had been praised for "near miraculous progress in reducing dropouts and increasing achievement." A year later, Hoffman, Assaf, and Paris (2001) made similar concessions about the reputed success of the Texas assessment movement. Mixing metaphors, they compared the movement to a "political steamroller" that the public and most teachers had been "seduced" into "accepting if not embracing." In a book with the confrontational title *The Truth About Testing: An Educator's Call to Action*, Popham (2001) warned of the "terrible things" that were happening as a result of testing. However, he acknowledged that the problems he had detected were especially difficult to eliminate precisely because the public trusted and supported testing. A year earlier, he (Popham, 2000) had counseled parents to oppose tests through letter-writing campaigns. He even provided six templates into which they could plug personalized information. The resulting letters were intended to create political pressure when they were sent to those teachers, principals, superintendents, and school board members who were supporting tests.

Although he dreaded the prevailing "test-driven accountability movement," Haney (2002) did acknowledge the skill that its adherents had demonstrated when they attributed rising test scores to exam-based reforms. The testing enthusiasts had cited this progress as a reason for supporting even more drastic educational changes. A year later, Bracey (2003) made a similar observation. Despite a conviction that standardized exams had become the "arsenal" in "the war against America's public schools," he admitted that the scores from these tests had risen to such high levels that "the actual test data from U.S. schools do not give any information to sustain crisis rhetoric or the war on America's public schools" (p. 71). Bracey urged conservatives to desist from a fear-inducing campaign in which data from tests had become the justification for extreme changes to the educational establishment.

Bracey correctly anticipated that supporters and opponents of testing would react differently to the identical information about rising test scores. The accuracy of his prediction had been substantiated on numerous occasions. In one instance, a reporter (Guthrie, 1999) had observed that the San Francisco public schools had "astounded educators nationwide by posting six years of consecutive test score gains." At the same time, the school administrators in this area had been accused of using "smoke and mirrors" to give an illusion of success. Pointing out that "the number of student math scores reported to the public [had] declined by 12 percent and the number of reading scores reported [had] plunged 21 percent" during the preceding decade, some constituents had questioned whether "the big increases in test scores are from class size reduction or certain pupils being removed from the testing base" (p. A1). To validate the significance of the rising test scores, the administrators had investigated other measures of scholastic improvement. They eventually determined that the rising test scores were complemented by increasing numbers of students who had graduated from high school, taken college entrance exams, signed u p for rigorous state tests, and completed advanced college placement exams.

A reporter for *USA Today* (Toppo, 2003) provided another example in which supporters and opponents of assessment had reviewed the same information about rising test scores but reacted differently to it. A pro-assessment faction had concluded that rising test scores on high-school exit exams had vindicated the decision to use the tests. However, an anti-testing faction believed that these rising scores masked the fact that more students were dropping out of school specifically so that they could avoid taking those tests. In a somewhat similar instance, news about changing test scores created political pandemonium in Florida. Vlahos (2003) observed that educational officials had "announced that 41 percent of African-American students scored at or above grade level [on the Florida

Comprehensive Achievement Test] in 2003, compared to 23 percent in 1998," that "51 percent of Hispanic students scored at or above grade level in 2003, compared to 38 percent two years before," and that "73 percent of white students scored at or above grade level, compared to 65 percent in 1998" (p. 1). Although conservatives thought these statistics vindicated test-based reforms, their political opponents viewed them very differently.

> "I call it a testocracy [*sic*]," said Ron Walters, the director of the African-American Leadership Institute at the University of Maryland. He said that the tests used for high school [*sic*] graduation in Florida are culturally biased, as are most tests across the country now being used to measure the performance of schools, teachers and pupils. "The sum total of these tests is that they are a strong reflection of the white Anglo-American-European experience in American culture, and unfair to Hispanic and black test-takers," Walters said. Black Baptist pastor Victor T. Curry, who likens President Bush to a "neo-Nazi" and his brother, Florida Gov. Jeb Bush to "the godfather, the devil," launched a boycott this month of the state's major citrus and tourist industries. (Vlahos, 2003, p. 1)

Summary

During the second half of the twentieth century, critics accused the pro-assessment groups of cultural insensitivity, elitism, unrestrained ambition, conflicts of interest, and greed. They especially remonstrated against the large assessment companies. Testing advocates made defensive maneuvers to counter these allegations. Their tactical agility was evident when they published *A Nation at Risk*. After examining the results of large-scale standardized testing, this federal report called attention to low scores, contrasted the performance of American and foreign students, and declared that the nation was experiencing grave educational problems. The authors went a step further and equated educational decline with military and economic vulnerability. To protect the country from disaster, they demanded that educators emphasize basic academic skills. They also insisted that they monitor learning through systematic testing. To the dismay of the anti-testing critics, the public endorsed both demands.

POSTSCRIPT

Unrelenting Growth of the Testing Industry

[Because] the post "Nation at Risk" years have brought pervasive reforms costing billions of dollars....
is it any wonder that large-scale accountability systems...are a growth industry?
—CATTERALL, 1990

Segel (1944) was an educational consultant who was temporarily detailed to the Secretary of War during World War II. While serving in this position, he witnessed a remarkable increase in testing. On the basis of this experience, he made predictions about the postwar future of assessment. He confidently forecast a "considerable change in the type of testing and in the quantity of testing" (p. 4). He thought that this expansion would include the assessment conducted in high schools, universities, commerce, industry, the government, and the military. Writing a decade later in a book aimed at parents, Wrightstone (1954) also made remarks about the extraordinary expansion of testing. He observed that tests had become the basis for measuring not only intelligence, achievement, and special aptitudes but also personality changes and social adjustment. He estimated that 75,000,000 psychological tests would be administered that year in the United States, with children taking one third of them. A short time later, a *Newsweek* reporter ("Testing: Can Everyone Be Pigeonholed?" 1959) specified that "122 million test booklets and answer sheets were sold to schools last year, 50 percent more than in 1954" (p. 91). The reporter added that "this is enough to give three tests to every U.S. school and college student."

Despite the specificity of the statements that some authors made, they did not know the actual number of tests that had been sold or the number of examinations that had been administered to children in the schools. When they made their estimates, they were constrained by several limitations, one of which was inadequate data. The compilation of accurate data about testing had been complicated by the many ways in which investigators had defined it. Courtis (1938a) had confronted this problem well before the 1950s.

> The determination of trends [about testing] is a matter of judgment and interpretation. Even the tabulation of frequencies of articles rests upon judgment as to the type into which any given article falls. Any value in the discussion of trends...must therefore be sought more in the suggestiveness of its interpretation than in its factual basis. (p. 546)

Throughout the later part of the twentieth century, scholars continued to stress the difficulty of gathering data about testing. McGiverin (1990) pointed to the confusion that scholars had created by interchanging terms such as *testing*, *assessment*, and *evaluation*. This confusion was increased further when researchers categorized tests and information about tests on the basis of specialized applications such as the measurement of learning ability, learning achievement, aptitude, interest, and personality. These sloppy practices made mix-ups inevitable whenever tests were discussed or research papers published. To minimize misunderstanding, some investigators restricted their investigations to budgetary information. As examples, Ebel and Hill (1959) and Boag (1955) had relied on a study that had specified the national annual expense for assessment. The precise expense was 7 cents per student. Ebel and Hill observed parenthetically that this was "far below the recommended minimum of 30 cents to 35 cents" and that even this higher amount would have been "insignificant compared with what a business may spend to determine the effectiveness of its practices." Nonetheless, they judged that testing, even in its current underfunded and underutilized state, would "increase both in quantity…and…scope" (p. 42).

The lack of a common definition was not the only factor that frustrated the researchers who were attempting to survey the extent of testing. Accurate data were hard to acquire because of the multiplicity of agencies and organizations that were involved in assessment. This fact had been underscored by Mayo (1959) when he observed that the "funds available for research on testing and evaluation instruments" were available from "the U.S. Office of Education, National Science Foundation, U.S. Public Health Service, Office of Naval Research, College Entrance Examination Board,…many private foundations" and "too many sources to list all of them" (p. 7). As an example of the degree to which this issue remained troublesome, Haney, Madaus, and Lyons (1993) confronted it again more than 30 years later when they identified the agencies and organizations that currently were producing and distributing tests. The multiple publishers included commercial businesses, nonprofit companies, individual researchers, university centers, the U.S. military, private admissions boards, licensing boards, the civil service, government agencies that sponsored public-sector testing, those private companies that were testing their own employees, governmental licensing boards, therapeutic clinics, and counseling centers. Depending on which types of organizations they recognized, researchers would shrink or inflate their estimates about the extent of testing.

Editorial judgment was still another factor that influenced calculations about the number of standardized tests that were being administered annually. Confining himself just to those tests that had been published by the Educational Testing Service, Yahraes (1951) explained that this organization had been selling two types of exams, custom designed tests and "ready-made tests, sold any time to any school at 10 or 15 cents per test" (p. 22). Yahraes indicated that 7,500 of the ready-made tests had been administered during the preceding year and that "a recent inventory showed that the ETS warehouse contains 2,977,000 copies of 386 different tests" (p. 23).

More than a decade later, Lyman (1963) also wished to underscore the expansion of standardized testing. He conjectured that "one million tests per school day" were administered in American schools. Following the lead of other analysts who had written books about tests, Lyman probably overgeneralized his estimate so that readers would be impressed with the importance of the topic. Within another 1963 book about testing, Chauncey and Dobbin did not specify the number of tests that were being administered. However, they did note that "in a period of sixty years educational testing has developed from a part-time chore of psychologists to a set of techniques that affect every student in school and college" (1963, p. 18). Just five years later, the editors (Stone & Shertzer, 1968) of a general book about testing did make conjecture about the number of tests that were being administered annually in the schools. However, they thought that this number was less than a million.

Many late twentieth-century estimates of the frequency with which tests were administered were based on the political rather than the scholarly viewpoints of the reporters. Even though he had admitted that "information about the extent of testing is sparse," Goslin (1963) still reckoned that "between 150 million and a quarter of a billion standardized ability tests of many different kinds are being administered annually in the United States by schools, colleges, business and industrial firms, and government agencies, including the military services" (p. 13). McGarvey (1974) acknowledged that "the actual number of tests marketed is highly confidential." Nonetheless, he thought he was making a "conservative estimate" when he declared that "ten million children annually use the Metropolitan and Stanford tests alone" (p. 26). A reporter (Rattner, 1977) for the *New York Times* postulated that "each year more than 50 million young Americans take up to three tests" (p. 16). Two years later, a reporter ("Aptitude-Test Scores," 1979) for *U.S. News & World Report* referred to the "400 to 500 million multiple-choice tests...given in schools and workplaces to about one third of the nation's citizens" (p. 76).

During the 1980s and 1990s, analysts continued to make highly variable and unsubstantiated allegations about the extent of testing. *Newsweek* reporters claimed that "more than 100 million standardized achievement and intelligence tests are administered annually in the U.S...[to] youths from nursery to graduate school" (Sewall, Corey, Mors, & Lord, 1980, p. 97). Strenio (1981) reported that 400,000,000 to 500,000,000 tests were administered each year. The National Center for Fair and Open Testing, which was a consumer group concerned about excessive educational assessment, estimated that in the late 1980s more than 100,000,000 tests were given annually to just those students in the elementary schools and high schools (estimate from the National Center for Fair and Open Testing, 1988, reported by Fiske, 1988). In a book with the editorialized title *Standardized Minds: The High Price of America's Testing Culture and What We Can Do to Change It*, Sacks (1999) conjectured that the number of educational tests administered every twelve months ranged between 143,000,000 and 400,000,000.

Because most educators and reporters referred to testing without defining it and then calculated its frequency without revealing the basis for their computations, the accuracy of their remarks could not be confirmed. In contrast, Haney, Madaus, and Lyons (1993) clearly defined their criteria for recognizing tests as well as the sources of their data. Nonetheless, when they attempted to analyze the number of educational tests that were given annually during the late 1980s, they still lacked the data they needed to make precise calculations. Consequently, they concluded that the number of tests administered annually as part of state-mandated testing programs could have ranged from 33,000,000 to 71,500,000. The range was even greater when they estimated the number of annual tests administered through district-imposed assessment programs. They thought this figure could have been as low as 85,621,429 or as high as 271,626,602. They estimated that the number of tests administered annually to select populations, such as children in bilingual or special education programs, was a figure between 11,000,000 and 30,600,000. They judged that the total number of annual college entrance exams was a sum between 13,034,318 and 21,759,548. By adding all of these figures together, they calculated that the average number of educational tests administered annually during the late 1980s was a figure somewhere between 143,175,747 and 395,486,150.

Phelps (1996a) identified three different ways that tests could be counted. Each of these had advantages and disadvantages. He used an illustration to demonstrate the different results that each calculation technique would produce.

> A school district that administers the Metropolitan Achievement Test (MAT), including a multiple-choice achievement battery over five subject areas and an open-ended written composition, could be said to administer one test (the MAT), two tests (multiple-choice and open-ended), or, in the most extreme interpretation, six tests (in six subject areas). (p. 20)

Phelps noted that the amount of testing in the schools also could be estimated by a fourth method, which involved the measurement of the duration of tests. Referring to his example from the Metropolitan Achievement Test, he pointed out that "the duration [of the testing] would always be the same, whether it was counted as the length of time for one test or as the cumulative duration of two to six tests" (p. 20).

Although Haney, Madaus, and Lyons (1993) recognized the degree to which heterogeneous methods of classifying tests had influenced 50 years of reporting, they still were convinced that "standardized testing has been increasing at a rapid rate—by over 10% per annum for the last two or three decades" (p. 125). Attempting to explain this "bull market for testing," they listed four factors: "recurring public dissatisfaction with quality of education," "an array of legislation…promoting or explicitly mandating standardized testing programs," "a broad shift in attention…toward outputs or results produced by our educational institutions," and "the increased bureaucratization of schooling" (p. 125).

Estimates of the numbers of tests published during the final decades of the twentieth century provided more indications of the growth of testing. Within a comprehensive bibliography of the tests used in education, psychology, and industry, Buros (1961) listed 2,126 products. The next edition of this compendium (Buros, 1974) identified 2,467 items. Nine years later, this bibliography contained 2,672 tests (Mitchell, 1983). The two volumes (Murphy, Conoley, & Impara, 1994, Murphy, Impara, & Plake, 1999) that were published during the 1990s respectively catalogued 3,009 and 2,939 tests.

Although the number of tests available was one indication of the size of the testing market, analysts also could consider the number of companies that sold these tests and the revenues that they earned. A reporter from the National School Boards Association (1977b) had employed this approach during the 1970s.

> Standardized testing supports a considerable industry (some would say, a big business). An average test costs $2 including booklet, answer sheet, computerized scoring, and reporting of scores. Over 17 million students are tested each year, which means upwards of $34 million is shared by several publishers including Science Research Associates (SRA); Harcourt, Brace Jovanovich; Educational Testing Service (ETS); and Houghton Mifflin, among others. (p. 3)

Kohn (1975) focused his attention on the prices of tests. He pointed out that these prices, which initially struck many persons as high, had to be balanced against their considerable marketing costs. After conducting some investigative interviews, he reported that Harcourt, Brace, Jovanovich Publishers spent $870,000 to maintain a staff of 29 "test representatives" and then matched this budget with an equal amount to cover the expenses associated with test sales. Houghton Mifflin Publishers supported a force of 180 representatives who marketed that company's textbooks as well as its tests. Although Kohn tried to persuade one of the Harcourt, Brace, Jovanovich test authors to reveal his annual royalties, this author refused. Kohn therefore referred to *The IQ myth*, a CBS television documentary that had alluded to the "best-selling authors [of tests who] may earn royalties amounting to as much as $150,000 a year." Two years later Rattner (1977) pointed out that the prices of tests included development as well as marketing expenses. He explained that "developing a test may take as long as eight years, involve a dozen professionals and cost nearly a million dollars" (p. 16). Providing a specific example, Winter (1985) noted that the actual expenses for the New York Regents exams, if one included no t only the publishing costs but the expenses of development, administration, and scoring, approached $1,000,000.

After examining the profits from testing, Resnick (1982) concluded that "reports of the demise of standardized national testing would seem premature." He added that testing was a business in which both publishers and investors maintained confidence. Two years earlier, he colorfully had described testing as "the arms supplier for a new generation of school reformers"(Resnick, 1980, p. 3).

Some financial analysts focused on the number of companies that were involved in testing as well as the revenue that they were earning. Bencivenga (1985) reported that more than 100 large and small publishers were grossing over $100,000,000 annually through elementary-school and secondary-school tests. However, he did not indicate how this revenue was distributed among these publishers. Haney, Madaus, and Lyons (1993) addressed this issue indirectly. They identified those publishers that had ten or more products indexed in *Tests in Print* during 1961, 1974, 1983, and 1990. A total of 76 publishers had fallen into this category for at least one of these years. A superficial analysis of these data might have led one to conclude that the patterns of test publishing had not shifted substantially during this 30-year period. After all, 41 publishers with ten or more tests were represented in the 1961 edition of *Tests in Print.* That number had only diminished to 36 by 1990. However, these statistics were misleading. Despite the number of publishing houses that were selling tests, six large companies effectively controlled the market (Fremer, 1989).

As an indication of how profitable a single test could be, Hoffman, Assaf, and Paris (2001) alleged that the Texas Assessment of Academic Skills, which was taken by all students in Texas, was "approaching a hundred-million-dollar-a-year industry in direct costs alone" (p. 491). Texas was not the only state to implement a universal testing program. In a discussion of the 1994 law that had reauthorized Title I educational programs, Elmore (1999) noted that "the 1994 law envisioned that by the year 2000 all states would have put in place content and performance standards, aligned with assessments of student performance, and coupled with systems for holding schools accountable for student learning" (p. vii). If states did not comply with these federal requirements, they risked losing their share of the $8,000,000,000 annual Title I budget.

As the markets for tests increased, so did the opportunities for assessment companies to make greater profits. Of the six big companies, the Educational Testing Service was the most successful financially. Fremer (1989) indicated that this corporation's position as the leader in the assessment market had been unchallenged for 14 years. The Educational Testing Service and one other company were concerned chiefly with higher education; the remaining four large companies concentrated on elementary and secondary education. Incidentally, Fremer, who had held professional positions within the Psychological Corporation and the Educational Testing Service, wrote that the financial data demonstrated conclusively that "our field is doing very well." He added proudly that "even though we have critics, we have more supporters than we have had in years" (p. 79).

Although Sacks (1999) agreed that educational assessment had grown enormously, he warned parents that the tests were harming their children. He wrote contemptuously that "the unambiguous beneficiaries of all this testing have been business enterprises themselves, which have invested heavily in the nation's testing obsession" (pp. 221–222). He counseled his readers that, "if one wants to understand the driving forces behind the unmitigated expansion of standardized testing in the United States, then it behooves one to obey the simple adage: Follow the money." Sacks believed that educational testing would not have grown as quickly as it did without the support of businesspersons. However, these businesspersons would not have found such a robust market were it not for the cooperation of powerful politicians.

Politics Redux

Late twentieth-century analysts provided multiple testimonials about the continuing interest of politicians in testing. In an editorial in the *Wall Street Journal*, Finn (1997) argued that "outside opposition" groups, such as the liberals, had fanned educational testing into "one of the hotter issues in Washington." He wrote that the liberals opposed educational testing "on grounds that test scores may harm minorities and more dollars should instead be pumped into school programs" (p. A18). He added that "the public-school establishment is opposed because it wants to continue obfuscating the truth about its dismal performance."

Even though Finn chastised the liberals, many of them actually had softened their opposition after President Clinton endorsed large-scale standardized testing. As one of his educational goals, Clinton had proposed that "students will leave grades four, eight, and twelve having demonstrated competency over challenging subject matter" (statement from Clinton's GOALS 2000, as quoted by Garfield, Garfield, & Willardson, 2003, p. 25). Clinton had used accountability-based educational reform as a tool with which to create a coalition of politically centrist liberals and conservatives. Goodling was one of the moderate Republicans who became fascinated with Clinton's proposal. He reminisced that in 1991 he had believed that "resources would be far better spent on educating our children rather than testing them" (remarks made by Representative William F. Goodling, 1998, Chairman of the House of Representatives Committee on Education and the Workforce, as quoted in "Overview of Testing," 1998, p. 1). Goodling claimed that he changed his mind about testing after he realized the degree to which his attitudes differed from those of the public. He had formed this insight once it had been pointed out that "at least 32 states have developed State [*sic*] standards,…an additional 14 report that standards development is underway…45 States [*sic*] report that they have statewide assessment systems,…23 States [*sic*] report that they have aligned their assessments with their standards…[and] 21 report that they are in the process of doing so."

Finn (1997) had been particularly annoyed at the Clinton administration for recrafting testing initiatives in such an artful manner that they appealed to both liberals and conservatives. A report prepared by Clinton's Department of

Education diplomatically described the Democratic plan as one in which "the President strengthened the nation's commitment to rigorous education standards by proposing a voluntary program of national tests in reading at grade 4 and in mathematics at grade 8 to ensure that individual students across the country are provided equal opportunities to achieve high standards" (Campbell, Voelkl, & Donahue, 1998, p. i). Exhibiting no admiration for the Democratic Department of Education, Finn denigrated it and the President for having "mangled this promising idea to the point that the GOP Congress should either make major repairs or scrap it altogether."

A former assistant secretary of education within a Republican administration, Finn did not conceal his contempt for liberal Democrats. However, he also dismissed those conservatives within his own party who had opposed testing because it was a "new federal intrusion into education." He reserved his single compliment for that faction of conservative congressional Republicans who shared his own belief that "standards-based national tests would provide useful information to students and their parents and put pressure on schools to improve" (Finn, 1997, p. A18).

Although Finn may not have been able to keep his personal political values from coloring his predictions about the fate of testing, he accurately had discerned that the educational testing movement and politics had become inextricably entangled. The Business Roundtable (2001) also recognized the knot into which these two forces were bound. The members of the Business Roundtable described their group as "an association of chief executive officers of leading U.S. corporations with a combined workforce of more than 10 million employees...committed to advocating public policies that foster vigorous economic growth, a dynamic global economy, and a well-trained and productive U.S. workforce essential to future competitiveness." Spokespersons for this organization explained that "policymakers and education reformers who are dismayed by the possibility of a public backlash need not panic...[because] the movement for higher standards and more rigorous testing is on the right course, according to recent public opinion research....among a ll groups: suburban, urban, rural, white, black, Hispanic; wealthy, middle class, poor; Democrat, Republican, independent" (p. ii).

Recognizing that testing and politics were entwined, other conservative organizations attempted to use their political power to influence the course of educational assessment. Like the Business Roundtable, each of these organizations posted reports on the World Wide Web. The titles of these easily accessed reports clearly revealed the partisan attitudes of the sponsoring groups. For example, the Educational Excellence Partnership (n. d.) entitled two of its reports *On the Same Page: Building Local Support for Higher Standards and Better Schools* and *Strengthening Your Child's Academic Future* . The C ommittee for Economi c Development (2001) selected the title *Measuring What Matters: Using Assessment and Accountability to Improve Student Learning*. Public Agenda (2000) published data and press releases under the heading *Survey Finds Little Sign of Backlash against Academic Standards or Standardized Tests*. (Achieve, Inc. , 2000a, 2000b) published reports with the titles *High Standards: Giving All Students a Fair Shot* and *Testing: Setting the Record Straight*.

Both the opponents and the supporters of standardized testing had attempted to advance their initiatives through political alliances. However, liberal analysts were distressed once they realized that these alliances had been more productive for their opponents. Apple (2000) candidly acknowledged that test-based reforms had been successful because of the collaboration between "authoritarian populist," "neo-conservative," and "neo-liberal" educational critics. Elmore (2002), who was another liberal, explicitly blamed Clinton for the aid he had given to the test-based educational reformers. He noted that Clinton, who initially had espoused testing when he was a 1980s governor in Arkansas, had been able to persuade political leaders in other states to endorse performance-based accountability. Elmore wrote cynically that "from the beginning, performance based [*sic*] accountability was an explicitly political idea, designed to bring a broad coalition together behind a single vision of reform" (p. 36). Once they realized that the conservatives were outmaneuvering them, some liberals did try to withdraw their support for testing. Elmore lamented that the tactically acute conservatives immediately responded by "branding" the dissenting liberals as "apologists for a broken system." Jennings (1998) agreed with Elmore's views about Clinton's culpability for the spread of large-scale testing. He argued that "national standards and tests…seemed like an idea whose [*sic*] time had passed" until "at the beginning of 1997, President Clinton raised anew the concept of using national standards and tests" (p. 182). Jennings sputtered in frustration, "Why couldn't things have been left well enough alone [*sic*]?"

Writing about the standardized testing movement during the second half of the twentieth century, the remarks that Linn (2000) made were similar to those of many other liberals. He documented that state and federal policymakers had selected increased testing as a way to respond to changing public moods about education. He added that conservative politicians deliberately had disseminated misinformation about poor student performance during the early stages of test-based reforms. They took advantage of the alarm that this misinformation created to implement remedial educational programs. Only after their programs were in place did they unveil accurate data. They deviously claimed that the new data revealed changed patterns of student performance, which in turn demonstrated the effectiveness of the remedial measures that they had introduced.

Linn identified other political factors that he believed had created support for test-based educational reforms. For example, individuals who lacked confidence in the educational establishment wanted teachers to take tests that were externally mandated and monitored. Some persons saw testing as the basis for rapid and relatively inexpensive changes in the schools. Finally, politicians were attracted to testing because it enabled them to take complex information about the schools and reconstruct it as simple propositions that were accessible to the public. Linn could not suppress his disdain when he wrote that the sponsors of testing found assessment cheap "compared to changes that involve increasing instructional time, reducing class size, attracting more able people to teaching, hiring teacher aides, or implementing programmatic changes that involve substantial professional development for teachers" (Linn, 2000, p. 4). Employing rhetoric similar to that of Linn, Kohn (2000) lambasted those politicians who had used tests "to show they're concerned about school achievement and serious about getting tough with students and teachers" (p. 3). Dismayed by the consensus that liberal and conservatives politicians had reached, Kohn wrote melodramatically that "standardized testing has swelled and mutated, like a creature in one of those old horror movies, to the point that it now threatens to swallow our schools whole" (p. 1).

Following the tact of other liberal analysts, Orfield and Kornhaber (2001) lamented the sustained growth of standardized assessment. They tied this growth to the Reagan administration's famous 1983 report about education.

> The recent widespread adoption of high-stakes testing has roots in a political rhetoric that emphasizes a decline in the quality of public education and its capacity to educate the nation's young people... The 1983 Reagan administration report, *A Nation at Risk*, crystallized this view and created a widespread perception of an educational crisis so severe as to undermine America's economy and future. (pp. 2–3)

Although Orfield and Kornhaber thought that the ideological connection of testing to international threats had been made during the 1980s, they admitted that many persons still respected this warning. They also pointed to an equally popular and enduring corollary, namely that "policies aimed at producing higher test scores will produce a stronger economy" and will limit the "economic dangers of a workforce whose test scores are lower than those of other nations" (p. x).

Throughout the twentieth century, conservatives and liberals recognized that politicians were setting the course for educational assessment. Both groups had encouraged this intervention. However, the liberals eventually recognized the greater damage that their own initiatives were sustaining from political activists. To emphasize this point, Jones, Jones, and Hargrove (2003) highlighted the increasingly deleterious consequences of large-scale standardized testing.

> Testing has recently moved from being an individual student assessment to a system for ranking and comparing students. Students whose scores fail to meet established goals may be denied enrollment in particular courses, retained at a grade level until a specified score is met, or prevented from graduating. These high-stakes tests are also used as a mechanism for public comparisons of teachers, schools, and school systems... Schools whose students score well on tests often receive public celebrations, salary bonuses for teachers, and media recognition. On the other hand, schools that fail to meet the "standards" are provided with mandated assistance teams and receive negative media attention. In some states, low-

performing schools can be taken over by the state, teachers and principals can lose their jobs, and/or teachers may be required to take competency tests. (p. 2)

Even though conservatives and liberals may have deprecated the political pressures that were exerted on educational assessment, they reserved their scorn for those instances in which their opponents had benefitted from these pressures. The conservatives gained a decisive advantage in this debate after they recognized an historical factor that had been critical to their success, namely that their support had grown when their educational programs were seen as deterrents to wartime perils. Resolving to use a comparable form of rhetoric even when the country was not at war, they portrayed incipient international threats as substantive dangers. They then represented conservative educational programs as the best defense against those dangers. In addition to the adoption of their programs, they demanded compliance with national standards and mandatory testing in all schools. Because this line of reasoning struck many persons as reasonable, the political support for testing, which had been unprecedented during two world wars, grew even stronger throughout the second half of the twentieth century.

REFERENCES

Abbott, A. (1923). Tests for English teachers. *English Journal, 12,* 663–671.

Achieve, Inc. (2000a, Fall). *High standards: Giving all students a fair shot* (Policy Brief No. 2). Retrieved July 25, 2003, from http://www.achieve.org/achieve.nsf/publications2?openform

Achieve, Inc. (2000b, Summer). *Testing: Setting the record straight* (Policy Brief No. 1). Retrieved July 25, 2003, from http://www.achieve.org/achieve.nsf/publications2?openform

Achilles, P. S. (1933). Foreword. In G. H. Hildreth, *A bibliography of mental tests and rating scales* (p. v). New York: Psychological Corporation.

Adler, M. (1914). Mental tests used as a basis for the classification of school children. *Journal of Educational Psychology, 5,* 22–28.

Aiken, L. R., Jr. (1969). [Review of the book *Pygmalion in the classroom*]. *Educational and Psychological Measurement, 29,* 226–228.

Alexander, C. (1921). Presenting educational measurements so as to influence the public favorably. *Journal of Educational Research, 3,* 345–358.

Alkin, M. C., & Stecher, B. (1982). A framework for estimating evaluation costs. In M. C. Alkin, *Theoretical issues in the cost of evaluation* (pp. 3–16). Los Angeles: University of California—Center for the Study of Evaluation.

Alkin, M. C., & Stecher, B. (1983). A study of evaluation costs. In M. C. Alkin & L. C. Solmon (Eds.), *The costs of evaluation* (pp. 119–132). Beverly Hills, CA: Sage.

Almack, J. C., Bursch, J. F., & DeVoss, J. C. (1923). Democracy, determinism, and the I.Q. *School and Society, 18,* 292–295.

America 2000: An education strategy sourcebook. (1991). Washington, DC: U.S. Government Printing Office.

Amrine, M. (1965). The 1965 congressional inquiry into testing: A commentary. *American Psychologist, 20,* 859–870.

Anastasi, A. (1967). Psychology, psychologists, and psychological testing. *American Psychologist, 22,* 297–306.

Anderson, B. L. (1985). State testing and the educational measurement community: Friends or foes? *Educational Measurement: Issues and Practice, 4*(2), 22–26.

Anderson, L. D. (1921). Estimating intelligence by means of printed photographs. *Journal of Applied Psychology, 5,* 152–155.

Anderson, S. B., & Coburn, L. V. (Eds.). (1982). *Academic testing and the consumer.* San Francisco: Jossey-Bass.

Anrig, G. (1985, August 23). Standardized tests: Part of US tradition of succeeding by merit. *Christian Science Monitor,* p. B6.

Apple, M. W. (2000). Series editor's introduction. In L. M. McNeil, *Contradictions of school reform: Educational costs of standardized testing* (pp. xv-xix). New York: Routledge.

Aptitude-test scores: Grumbling gets louder. (1979, May 14). *U.S. News & World Report, 86,* 76–80.

Armbruster, F. E. (1977, August 28). The more we spend, the less children learn. *New York Times Magazine,* pp. 9–11, 53–60.

Atwell, C. R., & Wells, F. L. (1933). Army alpha revised—short form. *Personnel Journal, 12,* 160–163.

Austin, G. R., & Garber, H. (Eds.). (1982). *The rise and fall of national test scores.* New York: Academic.

Ayres, L. P. (1909). *Laggards in our schools: A study of retardation and elimination in city school systems.* New York: Russell Sage Foundation.

Ayres, L. P. (1918). History and present status of educational measurements. In G. M. Whipple (Ed.), *The measurement of educational products* (17th yearbook of the National Society for the Study of Education, Part II, pp. 9–15). Bloomington, IL: Public School Publishing.

Bagley, W. C. (1922). Educational determinism; or democracy and the I.Q. *School and Society, 15,* 373–384.

Baker, E. L., & Stites, R. (1991). Trends in testing in the USA. In S. H. Fuhrman & B. Malen (Eds.), *The politics of curriculum and testing: The 1990 yearbook of the Politics of Education Association* (pp. 139–158). London: Falmer.

Baker, W. P. (1963). The compulsory state testing program: Ally or enemy of expertness? *Journal of Secondary Education, 38*(1), 59–64.

Ballard, P. B. (1923). *The new examiner.* London: Hodder & Stoughton.

Baratz, J. C. (1969). Linguistic and cultural factors in teaching reading to ghetto children. *Elementary English, 46,* 199–203.

Barton, P. E. (1997). Preface. In H. Wenglinsky, *When money matters: How educational expenditures improve student performance and how they don't* (p. iii). Princeton, NJ: Educational Testing Service.

Barzun, J. (1962). Foreword. In B. Hoffmann, *The tyranny of testing* (pp. 7–11). New York: Collier.

Bauer, E. A. (1992). NATD survey of testing practices and issues. *Educational Measurement: Issues and Practices, 11*(1), 10–14.

Beard, J. G. (1986). *Minimum competency testing.* Princeton, NJ: ERIC Clearinghouse on Tests, Measurement, and Evaluation, Educational Testing Service. (ERIC Document Reproduction Service No. ED284910)

Becker, W. E., & Baumol, W. J. (Eds.). (1996). *Assessing educational practices: The contribution of economics.* Cambridge, MA: MIT Press.

Begley, S., & Carey, J. (1981, April 6). A sunshine law for SAT's. *Newsweek, 97,* 84.

Bell, J. C. (1912). Recent literature on the Binet tests. *Journal of Educational Psychology, 3,* 101–110.

Bell, J. C., Berry, C. S., Cornell, W. S., Doll, E. A., Wallin, J. E. W., & Whipple, G. M. (1914). Informal conference on the Binet–Simon scale: Some suggestions and recommendations. *Journal of Educational Psychology, 5,* 95–100.

Bencivenga, J. (1985, August 23). Students and teachers face more tests but what do results mean? *Christian Science Monitor,* p. B3.

Berk, R. A. (1988). Fifty reasons why student achievement gain does not mean teacher effectiveness. *Journal of Personnel Evaluation in Education, 1,* 345–363.

Berry, C. S. (1912). A comparison of the Binet tests of 1908 and 1911. *Journal of Educational Psychology, 3,* 444–451.

Bersoff, D. N. (1981). Testing and the law. *American Psychologist, 36,* 1047–1056.

Betts, G. L. (1950). Suggestions for a better interpretation and use of standardized achievement tests. *Education, 71,* 217–221.

Bingham, W. V. (1919). Measuring a workman's skill: The use of trade tests in the army and industrial establishments. In *National Society for Vocational Education, Bulletin No. 30: Proceedings of the St. Louis convention.*

Bingham, W. V. D. (1937). *Aptitudes and aptitude testing.* New York: Harper & Brothers.

Bliss, D. C. (1912, May). The standard test applied. *American School Board Journal, 44,* 12.

Bliss, W. B. (1922). How much mental ability does a teacher need? *Journal of Educational Research, 6,* 33–41.

Block, N. J., & Dworkin, G. (Eds.). (1976). *The IQ controversy: Critical readings.* New York: Pantheon.

Bloom, B. S. (1970). Toward a theory of testing which includes measurement–evaluation–assessment. In M. C. Wittrock & D. E. Wiley (Eds.), *The evaluation of instruction: Issues and problems* (pp. 25–50). New York: Holt, Rinehart, & Winston.

Boag, A. K. (1955, October). Standardized tests: How, when, why. *Instructor, 65,* 24, 115.

Boardman, H. (1917). *Psychological tests: A bibliography.* New York: Bureau of Educational Experiments.

Bond, H. M. (1924a). Intelligence tests and propaganda. *The Crisis, 28*(2), 61–64.

Bond, H. M. (1924b). What the army "intelligence" tests measured. *Opportunity, 2,* 197–202.

Book, W. F. (1924). Voluntary motor ability of the world's champion typists. *Journal of Applied Psychology, 8,* 283–308.

Booth, D., & Mackay, J. L. (1980). Legal constraints on employment testing and evolving trends in the law. *Emory Law Journal, 29,* 121–194.

Boring, E. G. (1923). Intelligence as the tests test it. *New Republic, 35,* 35–37.

Boring, E. G. (1950). *A history of experimental psychology* (2nd ed.). New York: Appleton-Century-Crofts.

Born dumb? (1969, March 31). *Newsweek, 73,* 84.

Botstein, L. (1985, August 23). …or a system that values speed and cleverness over knowledge? *Christian Science Monitor,* p. B7.

Boyce, A. C. (1915). *Methods for measuring teachers' efficiency* (14th yearbook of the National Society for the Study of Education, Part II). Chicago: University of Chicago Press.

Boyer, E. L. (1988). *Report card on school reform: The teachers speak.* Princeton, NJ: Carnegie Foundation.

Bracey, G. W. (2003). *What you should know about the war against America's public schools.* Boston: Allyn & Bacon.

Bradford, M. D. (1917, January). How the superintendent judges the value of a teacher. *American School Board Journal, 54,* 19–20, 69–70.

Brandt, R. M. (1981). *Public education under scrutiny.* Washington, DC: University Press of America.

Brandt, R. M. (1990). *Incentive pay and career ladders for today's teachers: A study of current programs and practices.* Albany: State University of New York Press.

Breed, F. S. (1918). A comparison of two methods of measuring comprehension in reading. *School & Society, 7,* 266–270.

Bregman, E. O. (1926). On converting scores on the Army Alpha examination into percentiles of the total population. *School and Society, 23,* 695–696.

Briggs, T. H. (1923). A dictionary test. *Teachers College Record, 24,* 355–365.

Brigham, C. C. (1923). *A study of American intelligence.* Princeton, NJ: Princeton University Press.

Brim, O. (1963). Foreword. In D. A. Goslin. *The search for ability: Standardized testing in social perspective* (pp. 3–6). New York: Russell Sage Foundation.

Brinkley, S. G. (1924). Values of new type examinations in the high school. *Contributions to Education, No. 161.* New York: Teachers College Press.

Bronner, A. F., Healey, W., Lowe, G. M., & Shimberg, M. E. (1932). *A manual of individual mental tests and testing.* Boston: Little, Brown.

Brooks, S. S. (1921). Measuring the efficiency of teachers by standardized tests. *Journal of Educational Research, 4,* 255–264.

Brooks, S. S., & Buckingham, B. R. (1922). *Improving schools by standardized tests.* Boston: Houghton Mifflin.

Broom, M. E. (1931). Conflicting philosophies concerning educational measurement. *Kadelpian Review, 10,* 175–179.

Brown, H. A. (1916a). *The measurement of ability to read* (2nd ed.). Concord, NH: Rumford.

Brown, H. A. (1916b). The significance of the measurement of ability to read. *Education, 36,* 589–610.

Brownell, W. A. (1937). Some neglected criteria for evaluating classroom tests. *National Elementary Principal, 16,* 485–492.

Brownstein, R., & Nairn, A. (1979). Are truth-in-testing laws a fraud? No! *Phi Delta Kappan, 61,* 189–191.

Brueckner, L. J. (1935). Diagnosis in arithmetic. In G. M. Whipple (Ed.), *Educational diagnosis* (34ᵗʰ yearbook of the National Society for the Study of Education, pp. 269–302). Bloomington, IL: Public School Publishing.

Bruner, F. G. (1914). Racial differences. *Psychological Bulletin, 11,* 384–386.

Buckingham, B. R. (1914). The Courtis tests in the schools of New York City. *Journal of Educational Psychology, 5,* 199–214.

Buckingham, B. R. (1917). Correlation between ability to think and ability to remember, with special reference to United States history. *School & Society, 5,* 443–449.

Buckingham, B. R. (1921). The school as a selective agency. *Journal of Educational Research, 3,* 138–139.

Bulkeley, W. M. (1978, May 30). Some school systems use business methods to make pupils learn. *Wall Street Journal,* pp. 1, 17.

Buros, O. K. (1937). *Educational, psychological and personality tests of 1936: Including a bibliography and book review digest of measurement books and monographs of 1933–36* (Rutgers University Bulletin Vol. 14 No. 2A). New Brunswick, NJ: School of Education, Rutgers University.

Buros, O. K. (Ed.). (1938). *The nineteen thirty eight mental measurements yearbook.* New Brunswick, NJ: Rutgers University Press.

Buros, O. K. (Ed.). (1961). *Tests in print: A comprehensive bibliography of tests for use in education, psychology, and industry.* Highland Park, NJ: Gryphon.

Buros, O. K. (Ed.). (1974). *Tests in print II: An index to tests, test reviews, and the literature on specific tests.* Highland Park, NJ: Gryphon.

Buros, O. K. (1977). Fifty years in testing: Some reminiscences, criticisms, and suggestions. *Educational Researcher, 6*(7), 9–15.

Burtt, H. E. (1926). *Principles of employment psychology.* Boston: Houghton Mifflin.

Business Roundtable. (2001). *Assessing and addressing the "testing backlash."* Washington, DC: Author.

Butler, J. (1975). Looking backward: Intelligence and testing in the year 2000. *National Elementary Principal, 54*(4), 67–75.

Caldwell, O. W. (1935). Foreword. In J. W. Wrightstone, *Appraisal of newer practices in selected public schools* (pp.iii–iv). New York: Teachers College—Columbia University.

Caldwell, O. W., & Courtis, S. A. (1925). *Then and now in education—1845:1923.* New York: World.

Camp, F. S. (1917). Some "marks": An administrative problem. *School Review, 25,* 697–713.

Campbell, J. R., Voelkl, K. E., & Donahue, P. L. (1998). *NAEP 1996 trends in academic progress* (Publication No. 98–531). Washington, DC: National Center for Education Statistics.

Canning, J. B. (1916). The meaning of student marks. *School Review, 24,* 196–202.

Cardozo, F. L. (1924). Test and measurements in public schools. *School and Society, 20,* 797–798.

Carlson, P. A. (1925). A test program in bookkeeping. *The Balance Sheet, 7,* 12–14.

Carpenter, B. (1983). Translate test-score hieroglyphics into clear support for your schools. *American School Board Journal, 170*(2), 33, 44.

Carpenter, D. F. (1913). Mental age tests. *Journal of Educational Psychology, 4,* 538–544.

Cast, G. C. (1919). Selecting text-books. *Elementary School Journal, 19,* 468–472.

Cattell, J. M. (1890). Mental tests and measurements. *Mind, 15,* 373–380.

Cattell, J. M. (1905). Examinations, grades, and credits. *Popular Science Monthly, 66,* 367–378.

Catterall, J. S. (1990). Estimating the costs and benefits of large–scale assessments: Lessons from recent research. *Journal of Education Finance, 16,* 1–20.

Center on Education Policy. (2003). From the Capital to the classroom: State and federal efforts to implement the No Child Left Behind Act. Washington, DC: Author.

Chadwick, E. (1864). Statistics of educational results. *Museum, 3,* 479–484.

Chapman, J. C. (1919). The measurement of physics information. *School Review, 27,* 748–756.

Chapman, J. C. (1921). *Trade tests: The scientific measurement of trade proficiency.* New York: Holt.

Chapman, J. C., & Toops, H. A. (1919). A written trade test: Multiple choice method. *Journal of Applied Psychology, 3,* 358–365.

Chase, B. (1999). Don't get mad, get ready. *NEA Today, 17*(6), 2.

Chassell, C. F., & Chassell, E. B. (1924). A test and teaching device in citizenship for use with junior high school pupils. *Educational Administration and Supervision, 10,* 7–29.

Chauncey, H., & Dobbin, J. E. (1963). *Testing: Its place in education today.* New York: Harper & Row.

Chauncey. H., & Dobbin, J. E. (1966). Testing has a history. In C. I. Chase & H. G. Ludlow (Eds.), *Readings in educational and psychological measurement* (pp. 3–17). Boston: Houghton Mifflin.

Claxton, P. P. (1919). Army psychologists for city public school work. *School and Society, 9,* 203–204.

Cleary, T. A., Humphreys, L. G., Kendrick, S. A., & Wesman, A. (1975). Educational uses of tests with disadvantaged students. *American Psychologist, 30,* 15–41.

Clements, H. M., Duncan, J. A., & Taylor, W. M. (1969). Toward effective evaluation of the culturally deprived. *Personnel and Guidance Journal, 47,* 891–896.

Cobb, M. V. (1922). The limits set to educational achievement by limited intelligence. *Journal of Educational Psychology, 13,* 449–464, 546–555.

Coffman, W. E. (1980). The testing of educational achievement in children. *Journal of Negro Education, 49,* 312–325.

Cohen, D. K., & Rosenberg, B. H. (1977). Functions and fantasies: Understanding schools in capitalist America. *History of Education Quarterly, 17,* 113–137.

Cole, N. S. (1981). Bias in testing. *American Psychologist, 36,* 1067–1077.

Coleman, J. S., Campbell, E. Q., Hobson, C. J., McPartland, J., Mood, A. M., Weinfeld, F. D., et al. (1966). *Equality of educational opportunity.* Washington, DC: U.S. Government Printing Office.

Collings, E. (1926). A conduct scale for the measurement of teaching. *Journal of Educational Method, 6,* 97–103.

Colvin, S. S. (1912). Marks and the marking system as an incentive to study. *Education, 32,* 560–572.

Commander, M. G. (1980). Minimum competency testing: Education or discrimination? *University of Richmond Law Review, 14,* 769–790.

Committee for Economic Development. (1985). *Investing in our children: Business and the public schools.* New York: Author.

Committee for Economic Development. (2001). *Measuring what matters: Using assessment and accountability to improve student learning.* Retrieved July 25, 2003, from http://www.ced.org/docs/report/report_education.pdf

Committee of Southern Educators. (1921). The rating of teachers. *American School Board Journal, 63,* 44–46.

Cook, A., & Meier, D. (n.d.). *Reading tests: Do they help or hurt your child?* Grand Forks: North Dakota Study Group on Evaluation.

Cook, W. A. (1921). Uniform standards for judging teachers in South Dakota. *Educational Administration and Supervision, 7,* 1–11.

Cooprider, J. L. (1925). Information exercises in biology. *School Science & Mathematics, 25,* 807–813.

Corbett, H. D., & Wilson, B. L. (1991). *Testing, reform, and rebellion.* Norwood, NJ: Ablex.

Cottle, T. J. (1975). Going up, going down. *National Elementary Principal, 54* (4), 59–62.

Courtis, S. A. (1911). Standard tests in arithmetic. *Journal of Educational Psychology, 2,* 272–274.

Courtis, S. A. (1915a). Educational diagnosis. *Educational Administration and Supervision, 1,* 89–116.

Courtis, S. A. (1915b). Standards in rates of reading. In S. C. Parker (Ed.), *Minimum essentials in elementary school subjects: Standards and current practices.* (14th yearbook of the National Society for the Study of Education, Part I, pp. 44–58). Chicago: University of Chicago Press.

Courtis, S. A. (1938a). Current criticisms of educational measurement. *Review of Educational Research, 8,* 545–546.

Courtis, S. A. (1938b). Past and present trends in educational measurement. *Review of Educational Research, 8,* 547–550.

Cross, C. T. (2004a). *Political education: National policy comes of age.* New York: Teachers College Press.

Cross, C. T. (2004b, February 9). *The transformation of federal policy in education: Lessons learned-options for the future.* Lecture delivered at the annual meeting of the American Association of Colleges for Teacher Education, Chicago.

Crumbling the pyramids. (1981, March 30). *Time, 117,* 51.

Cubberley, E. P. (1906). *The certification of teachers* (5th yearbook of the National Society for the Scientific Study of Education, part II). Chicago: University of Chicago Press.

Cubberley, E. P. (1917). Editor's introduction. In W. S., Monroe, J.C. DeVoss, & F. J. Kelly, *Educational tests and measurements* (pp. v-ix). Boston: Houghton Mifflin.

Cubberley, E. P. (1918). Editor's introduction. In W. S. Monroe, *Measuring the results of teaching* (pp. v–vii). Boston: Houghton Mifflin.

Cubberley, E. P. (1934). *Public education in the United States: A study and interpretation of American educational history* (rev. ed.). Boston: Houghton Mifflin.

Cubberley, E. P. (1939). Editor's introduction to revised edition. In F. N. Freeman, *Mental tests: Their history, principles and applications* (rev. ed., pp. v–vi). Cambridge, MA: Riverside.

Cutten, G. B. (1922). The reconstruction of democracy. *School and Society, 16,* 477–489.

Davies, D. (1976, March). Harnessing the testing machine. *Citizen Action in Education, 3,* 1, 14.

Davies, G. R. (1912). Mental measurements in school. *Journal of Educational Psychology, 3,* 222–223.

De Avila, E. (1976). Mainstreaming ethnically and linguistically different children: An exercise in paradox or a new approach? In R. L. Jones (Ed.), *Mainstreaming and the minority child* (pp. 93–108). Reston, VA: Council for Exceptional Children.

De Sanctis, S. (1911). Mental development and the measurement of the level of intelligence. *Journal of Educational Psychology, 2,* 498–507.

Deck, I. J. (1932). Does a supervision and testing program pay? *American School Board Journal, 85*(1), 25–26.

Deffenbaugh, W. S. (1925). *Uses of intelligence and achievement tests in 215 cities* [City school leaflet No. 20]. Washington, DC: U.S. Government Printing Office.

Demick, B. (1979a, August 25). Evening the score. *New Republic, 181,* 9, 12–14.

Demick, B. (1979b, September 29). The kindergarten rat race. *New Republic, 181,* 21–25.

Dewey, J. (1922). Education as engineering. *New Republic, 32,* 89–91.

Dickson, V. E. (1920). What first–grade children can do in school as related to what is shown by mental tests. *Journal of Educational Research, 2,* 475–480.

Dickson, V. E. (1923). The test controversy. *Journal of the National Education Association, 12,* 176.

Dickson, V. E. (1924). *Mental tests and the classroom teacher.* New York: World.

Diederich, P. B. (1963). National testing programs: Friend or foe? *Journal of Secondary Education, 38*(1), 48–54.

Dillard, J. L. (1967). The English teacher and the language of the newly integrated student. *Teachers College Record, 69,* 115–120.

Dixon, J. (1929). Are mental tests in the schools democratic? *American School Board Journal, 79*(6), 33–34.

Doll, E. A. (1913). Inexpert Binet examiners and their limitations. *Journal of Educational Psychology, 4,* 607–609.

Doll, E. A. (1914). The need for a measuring scale of pedagogical status. *Journal of Educational Psychology, 5,* 347–349.

Doll, E. A. (1919). The growth of intelligence. *Journal of Educational Psychology, 10,* 524–525.

Doob, L. W. (1969, Spring). [Review of the book *Pygmalion in the classroom*]. *Key Reporter,* p. 6.

Dougherty, M. L. (1913). Report on the Binet–Simon tests given to four hundred and eighty–three children in the public schools of Kansas City, Kansas. *Journal of Educational Psychology, 4,* 338–352.

Downey, G. W. (1977). Is it time we started teaching children how to take tests? *American School Board Journal, 164*(1), 27–30.

Driscoll, M. E. (1996). The name's not the same, but the face is one of my own: Looking at educational policy, past and present. [Review of the book *The politics of curriculum and testing*]. *Journal of Education Finance, 21,* 419–431.

DuBois, W. E. B. (1914). [Review of the book *The mental capacity of the American negro*]. *Journal of Philosophy, 11,* 557–558.

Duckworth, E. (1975). The virtues of not knowing. *National Elementary Principal, 54* (4), 63–66.

Ebel, R. L. (1950). Construction and validation of educational tests. *Review of Educational Research, 20,* 87–97.

Ebel, R. L. (1975). Educational tests: Valid? Biased? Useful? *Phi Delta Kappan, 57,* 83–89.

Ebel, R. L. (1982). Foreword. In G. R. Austin & H. Garber (Eds.), *The rise and fall of national test scores* (pp. xi–xiii). New York: Academic.

Ebel, R. L., & Hill, R. E., Jr. (1959). Development and applications of tests of educational achievement. *Review of Educational Research, 29,* 42–56.

Educational Excellence Partnership. (n.d.). *On the same page: Building local support for higher standards and better schools.* Retrieved July 25, 2003, from http://www.edex.org

Educational Excellence Partnership. (n.d.). *Strengthening your child's academic future.* Retrieved July 25, 2003, from http://www.edex.org

Educational Testing Service. (1961). *Annual report: 1960–1961.* Princeton, NJ: Author.

Educational Testing Service. (1966). *Annual report: 1964–1965.* Princeton, NJ: Author.

Educational Testing Service. (1969). *Twenty–one years later: ETS today.* Princeton, NJ: Author.

Educational Testing Service. (1980). *Annual Report: 1979.* Princeton, NJ: Author.

Educational Testing Service. (1981). *New ways of assessment in a changing time.* Princeton, NJ: Author.

Educational Testing Service. (1987). *Annual report.* Princeton, NJ: Author.

Educational Testing Service. (1998). *Overview: ETS fairness review.* Princeton, NJ: Author.

Elam, S. M., Rose, L. C., & Gallup, A. M. (1993). The 25th annual Phi Delta Kappa/Gallup poll of the public's attitudes toward the public schools. *Phi Delta Kappan, 75,* 137–152.

Elashoff, J. D., & Snow, R. E. (1971). *Pygmalion reconsidered.* Worthington, OH: Jones.

Elmore, R. F. (1999). Preface. In R. F. Elmore & R. Rothman (Eds.), *Testing, teaching, and learning: A guide for states and school districts* (pp. v–vii). Washington, DC: National Academy.

Elmore, R. F. (2002). Testing trap. *Harvard Magazine, 105*(1), 35–37, 97.

Every "examination" passed with honors [Advertisement]. (1931). *American School Board Journal, 83*(2), 92.

Eysenck, H. J. (1947). Student selection by means of psychological tests: A critical survey. *The British Journal of Educational Psychology, 17,* 20–39.

Fernald, G. G. (1912). An achievement capacity test: A preliminary report. *Journal of Educational Psychology, 3,* 331–336.

Fincher, C. (1979). Using tests constructively in an era of controversy. *College Board Review, 113,* 2–7.

Finkelstein, I. E. (1913). *The marking system in theory and practice.* Baltimore: Warwick & York.

Finn, C. E., Jr. (1997, September 9). Throw these tests out of school. *The Wall Street Journal,* p. A18.

Finn, C. E., Jr., & Ravitch, D. (1987). Survey results: U.S. 17–year–olds know shockingly little about history and literature. *American School Board Journal, 174* (10), 31–33.

Fishman, J., Deutsch, M., Kogan, L., North, R., & Whiteman, M. (1963). *Guidelines for testing minority group children.* Ann Arbor, MI: Society for the Psychological Study of Social Issues, American Psychological Association. (ERIC Document Reproduction Service No. ED001649)

Fiske, E. B. (1977, May 1). Controversy over testing flares again. *New York Times,* sec. 12, pp. 1, 14.

Fiske, E. B. (1979, October 8). Colleges may lose 20 entrance exams. *New York Times,* pp. A1, B4.

Fiske, E. B. (1981a, April 14). Pyramids of test question 44 open a Pandora's box. *New York Times,* p. C3.

Fiske, E. B. (1981b, March 24). A second student wins challenge on answer to math exam problem. *New York Times,* p. B2.

Fiske, E. B. (1981c, April 28). Soul-searching in the testing establishment. *New York Times,* pp. C1, C4.

Fiske, E. B. (1981d, March 17). Youth outwits merit exam, raising 240,000 scores. *New York Times,* pp. A1, C4.

Fiske, E. B. (1988, April 10). America's test mania. *New York Times,* pp. EDUC16–EDUC20.

Flanagan, J. C. (1941). A preliminary study of the validity of the 1940 edition of the national teacher examinations. *School and Society, 54,* 59–64.

Flaugher, R. L. (1978). The many definitions of test bias. *American Psychologist, 33,* 671–679.

Flesch, R. (1986). *Why Johnny can't read: And what you can do about it.* New York: Harper & Row.

Flory, C. D. (1930). Personality rating of prospective teachers. *Educational Administration and Supervision, 16,* 135–143.

Freeman, D. J., Kuhs, T. M., Porter, A. C., Floden, R. E., Schmidt, W. H., & Schwille, J. R. (1983). Do textbooks and tests define a national curriculum in elementary school mathematics? *Elementary School Journal, 83,* 501–513.

Freeman, F. N. (1920a). Clinical study as a method in experimental education. *Journal of Applied Psychology, 4,* 126–141.

Freeman, F. N. (1920b). Mental tests. *Psychological Bulletin, 17,* 353–362.

Freeman, F. N. (1923). A referendum of psychologists: A survey of opinion on the mental tests. *Century Magazine, 107,* 237–245.

Freeman, F. N. (1939). *Mental tests: Their history, principles and applications* (rev. ed.). Cambridge, MA: Riverside.

Freiberg, H. J. (1984). Master teacher programs: Lessons from the past. *Educational Leadership, 42*(4), 16–21.

Fremer, J. J. (1989). Testing companies, trends, and policy issues: A current view from the testing industry. In B. R. Gifford (Ed.), *Test policy and the politics of opportunity allocation: The workplace and the law* (pp. 61–80). Boston: Kluwer.

Freyd, M. (1923). The graphic rating scale. *Journal of Educational Psychology, 14,* 83–102.

Frye, C. M. (1979, September 3). Who runs the schools? *Newsweek, 94,* 13.

Fryer, D. (1922). Occupational–intelligence standards. *School and Society, 16,* 273–277.

Fuess, C. M. (1950). *The College Board: Its first fifty years.* New York: Columbia University Press.

Fundamentals in education. (1923). *New Republic, 34,* 57–59.

Futrell, M. H. (1989). Mission not accomplished: Education reform in retrospect. *Phi Delta Kappan, 71,* 8–14.

Gage. N. L. (1971). Foreword. In J. D. Elashoff & R. E. Snow, *Pygmalion reconsidered* (pp. iv–v). Worthington, OH: Jones.

Gallup, G. H. (1980). *The Gallup poll: Public opinion 1979.* Wilmington, DE: Scholarly Resources.

Galton, F. (1890). Remarks. *Mind, 15,* 380–381.

Ganders, H. S. (1932). Is progressive education unscientific? *Educational Research Bulletin, 11,* 379.

Garcia, J. (1972). I.Q.: The conspiracy. *Psychology Today, 6*(4), 40–43, 92–94.

Garcia, J. (1981). The logic and limits of mental aptitude testing. *American Psychologist, 36,* 1172–1180.

Garfield, R. L., Garfield, G. J., & Willardson, J. D. (2003). *Policy and politics in American education.* Atlanta, GA: St. Barthelemy.

Gathany, J. M. (1914). The giving of history examinations. *Education, 34,* 514–521.

Gauss, C. (1927). Should Johnny go to college? *Scribner's Magazine, 82,* 411–416.

Giddings, A. E. (1936). The evolution of tests and examinations. *American School Board Journal, 93*(4), 21–23.

Gifford, B. (Ed.). (1989). *Test policy and test performance: Education, language, and culture.* Boston: Kluwer.

Gifford, B. R. (1992). Introduction. In B. R. Gifford & M. C. O'Connor (Eds.), *Changing assessments: Alternative views of aptitude, achievement, and instruction* (pp. 1–7). Boston: Kluwer.

Gifford, B. R. (Ed.). (1993). *Policy perspectives on educational testing.* Boston: Kluwer.

Gifford, B. R., & Wing, L. C. (Eds.). (1992). *Test policy in defense: Lessons from the military for education, training, and employment.* Boston: Kluwer.

Gilliland, A. R., & Jordan, R. H. (1924). *Educational measurements and the classroom teacher.* New York: Century.

Giordano, G. (2000). *Twentieth-century reading education: Understanding practices of today in terms of patterns of the past.* New York: Elsevier.

Giordano, G. (2003). *Twentieth-century textbook wars: A history of advocacy and opposition.* New York: Lang.

Giordano, G. (2004). *Wartime schools: How World War II changed American education.* New York: Lang.

Goldstein, T. (1977, May 1). Testing for legality. *New York Times,* sec. 12, p. 14.

Goodenough, F. L. (1949). *Mental testing: Its history, principles, and applications.* New York: Rinehart.

Goodman, K. S. (1965). Dialect barriers to reading comprehension. *Elementary English, 42,* 853–860.

Goslin, D. A. (1963). *The search for ability: Standardized testing in social perspective.* New York: Russell Sage Foundation.

Gould, S. J. (1981). *The mismeasure of man.* New York: Norton.

Graham, H. D. (1990). *The civil rights era: Origins and development of national policy 1960–1972.* New York: Oxford University Press.

Graham, P. A. (1979). Foreword. In *Testing, teaching and learning: Report of a conference on research on testing, August 17–26, 1978* (Appendix, p. v). Washington, DC: National Institute of Education, U.S. Department of Health, Education, and Welfare.

Gray, C. T. (1913). A new form of the substitution test. *Journal of Educational Psychology, 4,* 293–297.

Gray, C. T. (1917). *Types of reading ability as exhibited through tests and laboratory experiments: An investigation subsidized by the General Education Board* (Supplementary Educational Monograph, No. 5). Chicago: University of Chicago Press.

Gray, W. S. (1915). Standards in rates of reading. In S. C. Parker (Ed.), *Selected bibliography upon practical tests of reading ability.* (14th yearbook of the National Society for the Study of Education, Part I, pp. 59–60). Chicago: University of Chicago Press.

Gray, W. S. (1916a). Methods of testing reading—I. *Elementary School Journal, 16,* 231–246.

Gray, W. S. (1916b). Methods of testing reading—II. *Elementary School Journal, 16,* 281–298.

Gray, W. S. (1917). *Studies of elementary-school reading through standardized tests* (Supplementary Educational Monograph, No. 1). Chicago: University of Chicago Press.

Gray, W. S. (1918). The use of tests in improving instruction. *Elementary School Journal, 19,* 121–142.

Gray, W. S. (1921). Diagnostic and remedial steps in reading. *Journal of Educational Research, 4,* 1–15.

Gray, W. S. (1946). Preface. In H. M. Robinson, *Why pupils fail in reading: A study of causes and remedial treatment* (pp. v–viii). Chicago: University of Chicago Press.

Green, B. F. (Ed.). (1981). *Issues in testing: Coaching, disclosure, and ethnic bias.* San Francisco: Jossey–Bass.

Green, B. F., Jr. (1978). In defense of measurement. *American Psychologist, 33,* 664–670.

Green, D. R. (1971). *Racial and ethnic bias in test construction* (Project No. 0–I–033). Monterey, CA: McGraw Hill.

Green, R. L. (1975). Tips on educational testing: What teachers and parents should know. *Phi Delta Kappan, 57,* 89–93.

Greene, H. A., & Jorgensen, A. N. (1929). *The use and interpretation of educational tests.* New York: Longmans, Green.

Greenwald, E. (1969, September 21). Letter. *New York Times Magazine,* pp. 4, 12.

Griffith, G. L. (1920). Harlan's American history test in the New Trier Township schools. *School Review, 28,* 697–708.

Gross, M. L. (1962). *The brain watchers.* New York: Random House.

Guion, R. M. (1966). Employment tests and discriminatory hiring. *Industrial Relations, 5*(2), 20–37.

Guthrie, J. (1999, April 12). S.F. test scores questioned: Improvement may be smoke and mirrors. *San Francisco Examiner,* pp. A1, A10.

Guthrie, J. W. (1993). School reform and the "new world order." In S. L. Jacobson & R. Berne (Eds.), *Reforming education: The emerging systemic approach* (pp. 231–255). Thousand Oaks, CA: Corwin.

Gutloff, K. (1999). High-stakes tests: Rethinking curriculum. *NEA Today, 17*(6), 4–5.

Haggerty, M. E. (1916). Scales for reading vocabulary of primary children. *Elementary School Journal, 17,* 106–115.

Haggerty, M. E. (1917). The ability to read: Its measurement and some factors conditioning it. *Indiana University Studies, 4*(34), 39.

Haladyna, T. M., Nolen, S. B., & Haas, N. S. (1991). Raising standardized achievement test scores and the origins of test score pollution. *Educational Researcher, 20*(5), 2–7.

Haller, M. H. (1963). *Eugenics: Hereditarian attitudes in American thought.* New Brunswick, NJ: Rutgers University Press.

Haney, W. (1979). *A review of publications on testing for parents and the public* (National Consortium on Testing Staff Circular No. 5). Cambridge, MA: Huron Institute.

Haney, W. (1981). Validity, vaudeville, and values: A short history of social concerns over standardized testing. *American Psychologist, 36,* 1021–1034.

Haney, W. (2000). The myth of the Texas miracle in education. *Education Policy Analysis Archives, 8*(41).

Haney, W. (2002, July 10). Ensuring failure [Electronic version]. *Education Week,* pp. 56, 58.

Haney, W., Madaus, G. F., & Lyons, R. (1993). *The fractured marketplace for standardized testing.* Boston: Kluwer Academic.

Haney, W., Madaus, G., & Kreitzer, A. (1987). Charms talismanic: Testing teachers for the improvement of American education. In E.Z. Rothkopf (Ed.), *Review of research in education: Vol. 14,* (pp. 169–238). Washington, DC: American Educational Research Association.

Hanushek, E. A. (1986). The economics of schooling: Production and efficiency in public schools. *Journal of Economic Literature, 24,* 1141–1177.

Hard, W. (1918). Captain Smith—77. *New Republic, 15,* 283–285.

Harlan, C. L. (1920). Educational measurement in the field of history. *Journal of Educational Research, 2,* 849–853.

Harnischfeger, A., & Wiley, D. E. (1976). The marrow of achievement test score declines. *Educational Technology, 16*(6), 5–14.

Harris, T. G. (1972). I.Q. abuse. *Psychology Today, 6*(4), 39.

Hartshorne, H., & May, M. A. (1928). *Studies in deceit: Book one—General methods and results*. New York: Macmillan.

Hawkes, D. H. E. (1933). Introduction—The administrator and the testing program. In American Council on Education, *Educational measurement and guidance* (Report of the Second Educational Conference, pp. 136–138). Washington, DC: American Council on Education.

Hawkes, H. E., Lindquist, E. F., & Mann, C. R. (Eds.). (1936). *The construction and use of achievement examinations*. Boston: Houghton Mifflin.

Healy, W. (1914). A pictorial completion test. *Psychological Review, 21*, 189–203.

Hechinger, F. M. (1977, May 1). Why schools use standardized tests. *New York Times*, sec. 12, p. 16.

Hechinger, G., & Hechinger, F. M. (1960, October 2). What the tests do not test. *New York Times Magazine*, pp. 14, 32–37.

Hein, G. E. (1975). Standardized testing: Reform is not enough! In V. Perrone, M. D. Cohen, & L. P. Martin (Eds.), *Testing and evaluation: New views* (pp. 27–31). Washington, DC: Association for Childhood Education International.

Help! Teacher can't teach. (1980, June 16). *Time, 115*, 54–63.

Henmon, V. A. C. (1919). Air service tests of aptitude for flying. *Journal of Applied Psychology, 3*, 103–109.

Herring, J. P. (1919). Derivation of a scale to measure abilities in scientific thinking. *Journal of Educational Psychology, 10*, 417–432.

Herrnstein, R. (1971). I.Q. *Atlantic Monthly, 228*(3), 43–64.

Herrnstein, R. J., & Murray, C. (1994). *The bell curve: Intelligence and class structure in American life*. New York: Free Press.

Hersey, J. (1959). *Intelligence, choice, and consent*. New York: Woodrow Wilson Foundation.

Hildreth, G. H. (1933). *A bibliography of mental tests and rating scales*. New York: Psychological Corporation.

Hildreth, G. H. (1939). *A bibliography of mental tests and rating scales* (2nd ed.). New York: Psychological Corporation.

Hillegas, M. B. (1912). A scale for the measurement of quality in English composition by young people. *Teachers College Record, 13*(4), 1–54.

Hillocks, G., Jr. (2002). *The testing trap: How state writing assessments control learning*. New York: Teachers College, Columbia University.

Hoffman, J. V., Assaf, L. C., & Paris, S. G. (2001). High–stakes testing in reading: Today in Texas—Tomorrow? *The Reading Teacher, 54*, 482–492.

Hollingworth, H. L. (1915). Specialized vocational tests and methods. *School and Society, 1*, 918–922.

Hollingworth, H. L. (1919). *Vocational psychology*. New York: D. Appleton.

Holmen, M. G., & Docter, R. (1972). *Educational and psychological testing: A study of the industry and its practices*. New York: Russell Sage Foundation.

Horkay, N. (Ed.). (1999). *The NAEP guide* (Publication No. 2000-456). Washington, DC: National Center for Educational Statistics.

Horn, E. (1919). Principles of method in teaching spelling, as derived from scientific investigation. In G. M. Whipple (Ed.), *Fourth report of the committee on economy of time in education* (18th yearbook of the National Society for the Study of Education, Part II, pp. 52–77). Bloomington, IL: Public School Publishing.

Horn, E. (1924). General Preface. In G. M. Ruch, *The improvement of the written examination* (pp. iii–v). Chicago: Scott, Foresman.

Houts, P. L. (1975). A conversation with Banesh Hoffmann. *National Elementary Principal, 54*(6), 30–39.

Houts, P. L. (1976). Behind the call for test reform and abolition of the IQ. *Phi Delta Kappan, 57,* 669–673.

Houts, P. L. (Ed.). (1977). *The myth of measurability*. New York: Hart.

How other organizations view testing. (1982). *Educational Measurement: Issues and Practice, 1*(1), 17–19.

Howe, H. (1966). [Introductory Letter]. In J. S. Coleman, E. Q. Campbell, C. J. Hobson, J. McPartland, A. M. Mood, F. D. Weinfeld, et al., *Equality of educational opportunity* (pp. iii–iv). Washington, DC: U.S. Government Printing Office.

Huey, E. B. (1910). The Binet scale for measuring intelligence and retardation. *Journal of Educational Psychology, 1,* 435–444.

Hughes, W. H. (1934). Two educational philosophies: Are they compatible. *The Nation's Schools, 14*(6), 25–28.

Hull, C. L. (1928). *Aptitude testing*. New York: World.

Hunter, H. T. (1919). Intelligence tests at Southern Methodist University. *School and Society, 10,* 437–440.

Hunter, J. E. (1983). *Fairness of the general aptitude test battery: Ability differences and their impact on minority hiring rates* (USES Test Research Report No. 46). Washington, DC: U.S. Government Printing Office.

Hunter, L. B., & Rogers, F. A. (1967). Testing: Politics and pretense. *The Urban Review, 2*(3), 5–6, 8, 25–26.

Hyman, J. D. (1969). Letter. *New Republic, 161*(17), 30–31.

In classroom and on campus: The test dethroned. (1932, July 3). *New York Times,* sec. 9, p. 8.

Issue. (1994, October 31). *New Republic, 211,* 9.

Jacobson, R. L. (1981, March 30). Discovery of second error poses threat to test, College Board chairman says. *Chronicle of Higher Education,* pp. 1, 4.

Jacobson, S. L. (1993). Preface. In S. L. Jacobson & R. Berne (Eds.), *Reforming education: The emerging systemic approach* (pp. vii–xiv). Thousand Oaks, CA: Corwin.

Jencks, C. (1978, February 19). The wrong answer for schools is: Back to basics. *The Washington Post*, pp. C1, C4–C5.

Jencks, C. (1989). If not tests, then what? In B. Gifford (Ed.), *Test policy and test performance: Education, language, and culture* (pp. 115–121). Boston: Kluwer.

Jencks, C., & Crouse, J. (1982). Should we relabel the SAT or replace it? *Phi Delta Kappan, 63,* 659–663.

Jennings, H. M., & Hallock, A. L. (1913). Binet–Simon test at the George Junior Republic. *Journal of Educational Psychology, 4,* 471–475.

Jennings, J. F. (1998). *Why national standards and tests: Politics and the quest for better schools.* Thousand Oaks, CA: Sage.

Jensen, A. R. (1969). How much can we boost IQ and scholastic achievement? *Harvard Educational Review, 39,* 1–23.

Jensen, A. R. (1973). *Educational differences.* London: Methuen.

Jensen, A. R. (1974). The strange case of Dr. Jensen and Mr. Hyde? *American Psychologist, 29,* 467–468.

Johnson, F. W. (1910). A comparative study of the grades of pupils from different elementary schools in the subjects of the first year in high school. *Elementary School Teacher, 11,* 63–78.

Johnson, F. W. (1911). A study of high–school grades. *School Review, 19,* 13–24.

Joint Committee on Testing. (1962). *Testing, testing, testing.* Washington, DC: American Association of School Administrators, Council of Chief State School Officers, and National Association of Secondary-School Principals.

Jones, E. S. (1920). The army tests and Oberlin College freshmen. *School & Society, 11,* 389–390.

Jones, M. G., Jones, B. D., & Hargrove, T. Y. (2003). *The unintended consequences of high-stakes testing.* Lanham, MD: Rowman & Littlefield.

Jordan, A. M. (1920). Some results and correlations of army alpha tests. *School & Society, 11,* 354–358.

Judd, C. H. (1916). *Measuring the work of the public schools.* Cleveland, OH: Survey Committee of the Cleveland Foundation.

Kaestle, C. F. (1995). Preface. In M. W. McLaughlin & L. A.Shepard, *Improving education through standards-based reform* (pp. xi-xii). Stanford, CA: National Academy of Education.

Kamin, L. J. (1975). The politics of IQ. *National Elementary Principal, 54*(4), 15–22.

Kandel, I. L. (1936). *Examinations and their substitutes in the United States.* New York: Carnegie Foundation for the Advancement of Teaching.

Kandel, I. L. (1940). *Professional aptitude tests in medicine, law, and engineering.* New York: Teachers College Press.

Karier, C. J. (1972). Testing for order and control in the corporate liberal state. *Educational Theory, 22,* 154–180.

Karwoski, T. F., & Christensen, E. O. (1926). A test for art appreciation. *Journal of Educational Psychology, 17,* 187–194.

Kean, M. H. (2000, October 4). Educational tests worth keeping. *Christian Science Monitor,* p. 21.

Kearney, C. P. (1983). Uses and abuses of assessment and evaluation data by policymakers. *Educational Measurement: Issues and Practice, 2*(3), 9–12, 17.

Kelley, H. P. (1982). Are culturally biased tests useful? In S. B. Anderson & L. V. Coburn (Eds.), *Academic testing and the consumer* (pp. 125–133). San Francisco: Jossey-Bass.

Kelley, T. L. (1923). Again: Educational determinism. *Journal of Educational Research, 8,* 10–19.

Kelley, T. L., & Krey, A. C. (1934). *Tests and measurements in the social sciences.* New York: Scribner's Sons.

Kellogg, C. E., & Morton, N. W. (1934). Revised beta examination. *Personnel Journal, 13,* 94–100.

Kelly, F. J. (1914). Teachers' marks: Their variability and standardization. *Contributions to Education, No. 66.* New York: Teachers College, Columbia University.

Kemble, W. F. (1917). *Choosing employees by mental and physical tests.* New York: Engineering Magazine.

Kepner, P. T. (1923). A survey of the test movement in history. *Journal of Educational Research, 7,* 309–325.

Keppel, F. (1966). *The necessary revolution in American education.* New York: Harper & Row.

Kevles, D. J. (1968). Testing the Army's intelligence: Psychologists and the military in World War I. *Journal of American History, 55,* 565–581.

Kirkpatrick, E. A. (1911). Tests for class purposes and for research purposes. *Journal of Educational Psychology, 2,* 336–338.

Kirkpatrick, E. A. (1912). The Binet tests and mental ability. *Journal of Educational Psychology, 3,* 337.

Kirp, D. L. (1973). Schools as sorters: The constitutional and policy implications of student classification. *University of Pennsylvania Law Review, 121,* 705–797.

Kleiman, D. (1979, November 9). "Truth in testing law" faces legality test. *New York Times,* p. B3.

Knox, H. A. (1914). A scale, based on the work at Ellis Island, for estimating mental defect. *Journal of the American Medical Association, 62,* 741–747.

Kohl, H. (1968, September 12). Great expectations. [Review of the book *Pygmalion in the classroom*]. *The New York Review of Books, 11,* 30–31.

Kohn, A. (2000). *The case against standardized testing: Raising the scores, ruining the schools.* Portsmouth, NH: Heinemann.

Kohn, S. D. (1975). The numbers game: How the testing industry operates. *National Elementary Principal, 54*(6), 11–23.

Kohs, S. C. (1920). High test scores attained by subaverage minds. *Psychological Bulletin, 17,* 1–5.

Kohs, S. C., & Irle, K. W. (1920). Prophesying army promotion. *Journal of Applied Psychology, 4,* 73–87.

Koretz, D. (1986). *Trends in educational achievement.* Washington, DC: Congressional Budget Office.

Koretz, D. (1987). *Educational achievement: Explanations and implications of recent trends.* Washington, DC: Congressional Budget Office.

Koretz, D. (1996). Using student assessments for educational accountability. In E. A. Hanushek & D. W. Jorgenson (Eds.), *Improving America's schools: The role of incentives* (pp. 171–195). Washington, DC: National Academy Press.

Koretz, D. M., & Barron, S. I. (1998). *The validity of gains in scores on the Kentucky Instructional Results Information System (KIRIS).* Santa Monica, CA: RAND.

Koretz, D., Mitchell, K., Barron, S., & Keith, S. (1996). *Final report: Perceived effects of the Maryland school performance assessment program* (CSE Technical Rep. 409). Los Angeles: National Center for Research on Evaluation, Standards, and Student Testing.

Kornhauser, A. W., & Kingsbury, F. A. (1924). *Psychological tests in business.* Chicago: University of Chicago Press.

Kottkamp, R. B., Provenzo, E. F., Jr., & Cohn, M. M. (1986). Stability and change in a profession: Two decades of teacher attitudes, 1964–1984. *Phi Delta Kappan, 67,* 559–567.

Kuhlmann, F. (1913). The results of grading thirteen hundred feeble–minded children with the Binet–Simon tests. *Journal of Educational Psychology, 4,* 261–268.

Landsittel, F. C. (1917). Evaluation of merit in high-school teachers. *School and Society, 6,* 774–780.

Lathrop, H. O. (1927). Testing in commercial geography. *Journal of Geography, 26,* 356–362.

Laycock, S. R. (1925). The Laycock test of biblical information. *Journal of Educational Psychology, 16,* 329–334.

Lazarus, M. (1975). On the misuse of test data: A second look at Jencks's "Inequality." *National Elementary Principal, 54* (4), 76–78.

Leary, M. E. (1970). Children who are tested in an alien language: Mentally retarded? *The New Republic, 162*(22), 17–18.

Lee, C. (1988). Testing makes a comeback. *Training, 25*(12), 49–59.

Legal issues in minimum competency testing. (1984). Princeton, NJ: ERIC Clearinghouse on Tests, Measurement, and Evaluation, Educational Testing Service. (ERIC Document Reproduction Service No. ED286942)

Lehmann, I. J., & Phillips, S. E. (1987). A survey of state teacher-competency examination programs. *Educational Measurement: Issues and Practice, 6* (1), 14–18.

Lennon, R. T. (1980). The anatomy of a scholastic aptitude test. *NCME Measurement in Education, 11*(2), 1–8.

Lerner, B. (1978). The Supreme Court and the APA, AERA, NCME, test standards. *American Psychologist, 33,* 915–919.

Lerner, B. (1979). *The war on testing: Detroit Edison in perspective.* Princeton, NJ: Educational Testing Service. (ERIC Document Reproduction Service No. ED182348)

Lerner, B. (1980). The war on testing: David, Goliath, and Gallup. *Public Interest, 60,* 119–147.

Lerner, B. (1981a). Representative democracy, "men of zeal," and testing legislation. *American Psychologist, 36,* 270–275.

Lerner, B. (1981b). The minimum competence testing movement. *American Psychologist, 36,* 1057–1066.

Less than an "A" for the S.A.T. (1980, January 21). *New York Times,* p. A22.

Lind, J. E. (1914). Diagnostic pitfalls in the mental examination of negroes. *New York Medical Journal, 99,* 1286–1287.

Lingenfelter, E. (1930). The visiting teacher. *Journal of Education, 112,* 56.

Link, H. C. (1920). *Employment psychology.* New York: Macmillan.

Link, H. C. (1923). What is intelligence? *Atlantic Monthly, 132,* 374–385.

Linn, R. L. (2000). Assessments and accountability. *Educational Researcher, 29*(2), 4–16.

Lippmann, W. (1922a). A future for the tests. *New Republic, 33,* 9–11.

Lippmann, W. (1922b). Tests of hereditary intelligence. *New Republic, 32,* 328–330.

Lippmann, W. (1922c). The abuse of the tests. *New Republic, 32,* 297–298.

Lippmann, W. (1922d). The mental age of Americans. *New Republic, 32,* 213–215.

Lippmann, W. (1922e). The mystery of the "A" men. *New Republic, 32,* 246–248.

Lippmann, W. (1922f). The reliability of intelligence tests. *New Republic, 32,* 275–277.

Lippmann, W. (1923a). A defense of education. *Century Magazine, 106,* 95–103

Lippmann. W. (1923b). A judgment of the tests. *New Republic, 34,* 322–323.

Lippmann. W. (1923c). Mr. Burt and the intelligence tests. *New Republic, 34,* 263–264.

Lippmann. W. (1923d). Rich and poor, girls and boys. *New Republic, 34,* 295–296.

Lippmann. W. (1923e). The great confusion. *New Republic, 33,* 145–146.

Long, H. H. (1923). Race and mental tests. *Opportunity, 1,* 22–28.

Loree, D. H. (1925). The predictive value of the IQ. *American School Board Journal, 71*(3), 53–54, 142.

Loretan, J. O. (1965). The decline and fall of group intelligence testing. *Teacher's College Record, 67,* 10–17.

Lowell, F. (1919). A group intelligence scale for primary grades. *Journal of Applied Psychology, 3,* 215–247.

Lyman, H. B. (1963). *Test scores and what they mean.* Englewood, NJ: Prentice-Hall.

Madaus, G. F. (1985). Public policy and the testing profession: You've never had it so good? *Educational Measurement: Issues & Practice, 4*(4), 5–16.

Madaus, G. F., & Pullin, D. (1987). Teacher certification tests: Do they really measure what we need to know? *Phi Delta Kappan, 69*, 31–38.

Madsen, I. N. (1920a). High school students' intelligence ratings according to the army alpha test. *School & Society, 11*, 298–300.

Madsen, I. N. (1920b). The army intelligence test as a means of prognosis in high school. *School & Society, 11*, 625–627.

Madsen, I. N., & Sylvester, R. H. (1919). High school students' intelligence rating according to the army alpha test. *School & Society, 10*, 407–410.

Malen, B., & Fuhrman, S. H. (1991). The politics of curriculum and testing: Introduction and overview. In S. H. Fuhrman & B. Malen (Eds.), *The politics of curriculum and testing: The 1990 yearbook of the Politics of Education Association* (pp. 1–9). London: Falmer.

Malin, J. E. (1930a). History of the measurement movement. *Educational Outlook, 4*, 72–80.

Malin, J. E. (1930b). History of the measurement movement (continued). *Educational Outlook, 4*, 149–155.

Marland, S. P. (1977). Prefatory note. In W. Wirtz, H. Howe, B. C. Watson, R. W. Tyler, L. R. Tucker, V. H. T. Tom, et al., *On further examination: Report of the advisory panel on the Scholastic Aptitude Test score decline* (pp. iii–iv). New York: College Entrance Examination Board.

Martin, E. M. (1923). An aptitude test for policemen. *Journal of the American Institute of Criminal Law and Criminology, 14*, 376–404.

Martland, T. H. (1978, January 30). Costly schools that do not educate. *Business Week, 2519*, 9.

Masters, K. (1977, February 5). Why your daughter didn't get into law school: ETS's star chamber. *New Republic, 176*, 13–14.

May, M. A., & Hartshorne, H. (1928). *Studies in deceit: Book two—Statistical methods and results.* New York: Macmillan.

Mayo, M. J. (1913). The mental capacity of the American negro. In R. S. Woodworth (Ed.), *Archives of Psychology: No. 28*. New York: Science.

Mayo, S. T. (1959). Testing and the use of test results. *Review of Educational Research, 29*, 5–14.

McAndrew, W. (1920). Ratings of teachers [Letter]. *Journal of Education, 91*, 243.

McCall, W. A. (1920). A new kind of school examination. *Journal of Educational Research, 1*, 33–46.

McCall, W. A. (1923). *How to measure in education.* New York: Macmillan.

McClellan, M. C. (1988). Testing and reform. *Phi Delta Kappan, 69*, 768–771.

McClelland, D. C. (1973). Testing for competence rather than for "intelligence". *American Psychologist, 28*, 1–14.

McConn, M. (1931). The co–operative test service. *Journal of Higher Education, 2*, 225–232.

McConn, M. (1935). Academic standards vs. individual differences: The dilemma of democratic education. *American School Board Journal, 91*(6), 44–46, 73.

McConn, M. (1936). The use and abuse of examinations. In H. E. Hawkes, E. F. Lindquist, & C. R. Mann (Eds.), *The construction and use of achievement examinations* (pp. 443–478). Boston: Houghton Mifflin.

McCurdy, J. (1969, January 31). Testing of IQs in L.A. primary grades banned. *Los Angeles Times*, part II, p. 1.

McGarvey, J. (1974, May/June). Standardized tests: Five steps to change. *Learning, 2,* 24–26.

McGiverin, R. H. (1990). *Educational and psychological tests in the academic library*. New York: Haworth.

McLaughlin, M. W. (1987). Learning from experience: Lessons from policy implementation. *Educational Evaluation and Policy Analysis, 9,* 171–178.

McLaughlin, M. W., & Phillips, D. C. (Eds.). (1991). *Evaluation and education: At quarter century* (90th yearbook of the National Society for the Study of Education, Part II). Chicago: National Society for the Study of Education.

McLaughlin, M. W., & Shepard, L. A. (1995). *Improving education through standards-based reform*. Stanford, CA: National Academy of Education.

McLean, L. D., & Goldstein, H. (1988). The U.S. national assessments in reading: Reading too much into the findings. *Phi Delta Kappan, 69,* 369–372.

McLeod, L. S. (1918). The influence of increasing difficulty of reading material upon rate, errors, and comprehension in oral reading. *Elementary School Journal, 18,* 523–532.

Mead, C. D. (1915). Silent versus oral reading with one hundred sixth–grade children. *Journal of Educational Psychology, 6,* 345–348.

Measurement and utilization of brain power in the army. (1919). *Science, 49,* 221–226, 251–259.

Meier, D. (1973). *Reading failure and the tests*. New York: Workshop Center for Open Education.

Meisels, S. J. (1989). High-stakes testing in kindergarten. *Educational Leadership, 46* (7), 16–22.

Mental test: Selection of teachers through our agency [Advertisement]. (1930). *American School Board Journal, 81*(3), 158.

Mercer, J. R. (1972, September). I.Q.: The lethal label. *Psychology Today, 6*(4), 44–47, 95–97.

Messick, S., Beaton, A., & Lord, F. (1983). *National assessment of educational progress reconsidered: A new design for a new era* (NAEP Rep. No. 83–1). Princeton, NJ: National Assessment of Educational Progress.

Miller, D. G. (1963). State and national curriculums and testing programs—Friend or foe of expertness in the classroom? *Journal of Secondary Education, 38,* 41–47.

Miller, H. W. (1927a). Segregation on the basis of ability. *School and Society, 26,* 84–88.

Miller, H. W. (1927b). Segregation on the basis of ability, II. *School and Society, 26,* 114–120.

Mills, L. S. (1925). A superintendent's observations on intelligence tests. *American School Board Journal, 71*(4), 50, 141–142.

Mitchell, J. V., Jr. (Ed.). (1983). *Tests in print III: An index to tests, test reviews, and the literature on specific tests.* Lincoln: Buros Institute of Mental Measurements, University of Nebraska–Lincoln.

Mitchill, T. C. (1913). Loss of efficiency in the recitation. *Educational Review, 45,* 8–28.

Modern life is too much for 23 million Americans. (1975, November 10). *U.S. News & World Report, 79,* 84.

Monk, D. H. (1995). The costs of pupil performance assessment: A summary report. *Journal of Education Finance, 20,* 363–371.

Monk, D. H. (1996). The importance of balance in the study of educational costs. *Journal of Education Finance, 21,* 590–591.

Monk, D. H., & King, J. A. (1993). Cost analysis as a tool for education reform. In S. L. Jacobson & R. Berne (Eds.), *Reforming education: The emerging systemic approach* (pp. 131–150). Thousand Oaks, CA: Corwin.

Monroe, W. S. (1918a). Existing tests and standards. In G. M. Whipple (Ed.), *The measurement of educational products* (17th yearbook of the National Society for the Study of Education, Part II, pp. 71–104). Bloomington, IL: Public School Publishing.

Monroe, W. S. (1918b). Monroe's standardized silent reading tests. *Journal of Educational Psychology, 9,* 303–312.

Monroe, W. S. (1919). Principles of method in teaching arithmetic, as derived from scientific investigation. In G. M. Whipple (Ed.), *Fourth report of the committee on economy of time in education* (18th yearbook of the National Society for the Study of Education, Part II, pp. 78–95). Bloomington, IL: Public School Publishing.

Monroe, W. S., DeVoss, J. C., & Kelly, F. J. (1917). *Educational tests and measurements.* Boston: Houghton Mifflin.

Morrison, P. (1975). The bell shaped pitfall. *National Elementary Principal, 54*(4), 34–37.

Morse, J. (1914). A comparison of white and colored children measured by the Binet scale of intelligence. *Popular Science Monthly, 84,* 75–79

Mort, P. R., & Gates, A. I. (1932). *The acceptable uses of achievement tests: A manual for tests users.* New York: Teachers College Press.

Motivating students. (1999). *NEA Today, 17*(6), 4–5.

Munday, L. A. (1979a). Changing test scores, especially since 1970. *Phi Delta Kappan, 60,* 496–499.

Munday, L. A. (1979b). Changing test scores: Basic skills development in 1977 compared with 1970. *Phi Delta Kappan, 60,* 670–671.

Münsterberg, H. (1913). *Psychology and industrial efficiency.* Boston: Houghton Mifflin.

Murphy, L. B. (1975). The stranglehold of norms on the individual child. In V. Perrone, M. D. Cohen, & L. P. Martin (Eds.), *Testing and evaluation: New views* (pp. 37–42). Washington, DC: Association for Childhood Education International.

Murphy, L. L., Conoley, J. C., & Impara, J. C. (Eds.). (1994). *Tests in print IV: An index to tests, test reviews, and the literature on specific tests.* Lincoln: Buros Institute of Mental Measurements, University of Nebraska–Lincoln.

Murphy, L. L., Impara, J. C., & Plake, B. S. (Eds.). (1999). *Tests in print V: An index to tests, test reviews, and the literature on specific tests.* Lincoln: Buros Institute of Mental Measurements, University of Nebraska–Lincoln.

Myers, C. E., & Myers, G. C. (1919). A group intelligence test. *School and Society, 10,* 355–360.

Myers, G. C. (1922). Teachers vs. mental tests as prophets of school progress. *School and Society, 16,* 300–303.

Myers, G. C. (1926). Teaching versus testing. *American School Board Journal, 72*(2), 47, 137.

Nairn, A. (1980). *The reign of ETS: The corporation that makes up minds* (Ralph Nader Report on the Educational Testing Service). Washington, DC: Ralph Nader.

National Academy of Education. (1978). *Improving educational achievement: Report of the National Academy of Education—Committee on Testing and Basic Skills.* Washington, DC: Author.

National Commission on Excellence in Education. (1983). *A nation at risk: The imperative for educational reform.* Washington, DC: Author.

National Commission on Testing and Public Policy. (1990). *From gatekeeper to gateway: Transforming testing in America.* Chestnut Hill, MA: Boston College.

National School Boards Association. (1977a). School board attitudes toward standardized testing. *NSBA Research Report, 1,* 25–29.

National School Boards Association. (1977b). *Standardized achievement testing* (Research Rep. 1977–1). Washington, DC: Author.

National School Boards Association. (1978). *Minimum competency* (Research Rep. 1978–3). Washington, DC: Author.

Negro efficiency. (1916). *Eugenical News, 1*(11), 79.

Neill, M. (1999). Is high-stakes testing fair? *NEA Today, 17*(6), 6.

New! Diagnostic tests and practice exercises in arithmetic [Advertisement]. (1929). *American School Board Journal, 79*(6), 136.

Newark system of rating teachers. (1930). *Elementary School Journal, 30,* 409–412.

Newkirk, L. V., & Greene, H. A. (1935). *Tests and measurements in industrial education.* New York: Wiley.

Noble, E. L., & Arps, G. F. (1920). University students' intelligence ratings according to the Army Alpha test. *School and Society, 11,* 233–237.

Nolen, S. B., Haladyna, T. M., & Haas, N. S. (1992). Uses and abuses of achievement test scores. *Educational Measurement: Issues and Practice, 11*(2), 9–15.

Now have a taste of what cultural bias means. (1977). *American School Board Journal, 164*(1), 31.

Olson, P. A. (1975). Power and the National Assessment of Educational Progress. *National Elementary Principal, 54*(6), 46–53.

Omang, J. (1979, December 26). Making the grade: Standardized tests are under attack. *Washington Post,* pp. A10–A11.

Orfield, G., & Kornhaber, M. L. (Eds.). (2001). *Raising standards or raising barriers: Inequality and high–stakes testing in public education.* New York: Century Foundation.

Orleans, J. S., & Sealy, G. A. (1928). *Objective tests.* New York: World Book.

Orr, E. F. (1925). A principal's observations on intelligence testing. *American School Board Journal, 70*(5), 50, 136, 139.

Overview of testing/standards and assessments in the states: Hearing before the Committee on Education and the Workforce, House of Representatives, 105th Cong., 1 (1998).

Owen, D. (1983, May). 1983: The last days of ETS. *Harper's, 266,* 21–37.

Owen, D. (1999). *None of the above: The truth behind the SATs, revised and updated.* Lanham, MD: Rowman & Littlefield.

Parsons, R. P., & Segar, L. H. (1918). Barany chair tests and flying ability. *Journal of the American Medical Association, 70,* 1064–1065.

Partch, C. E. (1938). Foreword. In O. K. Buros, *The nineteen thirty eight mental measurements yearbook* (pp. xi–xii). New Brunswick, NJ: Rutgers University Press.

Passes every test in school service [Advertisement]. (1937). *American School Board Journal, 94*(2), 64.

Paterson, D. G. (1940). Applied psychology comes of age. *Journal of Consulting Psychology, 4,* 1–9.

Patterson, J. L., Czajkowski, T. J., Hubbard, E., Johnson, G., Slater, C., & Kaufman, D. (1975). How to avoid the dangers of testing. *National Elementary Principal, 54*(6), 93–94.

Pellegrino, J. W., Chudowsky, N., & Glaser, R. (Eds.). (2001). *Knowing what students know: The science and design of educational assessment.* Washington, DC: National Academy Press.

Perrone, V. (1991). *On standardized testing* (Report No. EDO–PS–91–8). Washington, DC: Office of Educational Research and Improvement. (ERIC Document Reproduction Service No. ED338445)

Petersen, N. S., & Novick, M. R. (1976). An evaluation of some models for culture–fair selection. *Journal of Educational Measurement, 13,* 3–29.

Peterson, J. (1925). *Early conceptions and tests of intelligence.* New York: World.

Phelps, R. P. (1996a). Are U.S. students the most heavily tested on Earth? *Educational Measurement: Issues and Practice, 15*(3), 19–27.

Phelps, R. P. (1996b). Mis-conceptualizing the cost of large-scale assessment. *Journal of Education Finance, 21,* 581–589.

Phelps, R. P. (1998). The demand for standardized student testing. *Educational Measurement: Issues and Practice, 17*(3), 5–23.

Phelps, R. P. (2000). Estimating the cost of standardized student testing in the United States. *Journal of Education Finance, 24,* 343–380.

Phillips, B. A. (1912). Retardation in the elementary schools of Philadelphia. *Psychological Clinic, 6,* 79–90, 107–121.

Phillips, B. A. (1914). The Binet tests applied to colored children. *The Psychological Clinic, 8,* 190–196.

Pickets at APA headquarters protest psychological tests. (1965, November). *American Psychologist, 20,* 871–872.

Picus, L. O. (1996). Preface. In L. O. Picus & J. L. Wattenbarger (Eds.), *Where does the money go?—Resource allocation in elementary and secondary schools* (pp. vii-x). Thousand Oaks, CA: Corwin.

Pintner, R. (1919). A non-language group intelligence test. *Journal of Applied Psychology, 3,* 199–214.

Pintner, R. (1923). *Intelligence testing: methods and results.* New York: Holt.

Pintner, R., & Paterson, D. G. (1917). *A scale of performance tests.* New York: Appleton.

Pleasures of nonprofitability. (1976, November 15). *Forbes, 118,* 89–94.

Popham, W. J. (1999). Why standardized tests don't measure educational quality. *Educational Leadership, 56*(6), 8–15.

Popham, W. J. (2000). *Testing! Testing! What every parent should know about school tests.* Boston: Allyn and Bacon.

Popham, W. J. (2001). *The truth about testing: An educator's call to action.* Alexandria, VA: Association for Supervision and Curriculum Development.

Pressey, S. L., & Pressey, L. C. (1922). *Introduction to the use of standard tests.* New York: World.

Pressey, S. L., & Teter, G. F. (1919). A comparison of colored and white by means of a group scale of intelligence. *Journal of Applied Psychology, 3,* 277-282.

Pritchett, H. S. (1923). Are our universities overpopulated? *Scribner's Magazine, 73,* 556–560.

Psychological Corporation. (1978). *Summaries of court decisions on employment testing: 1968–1977.* New York: Author.

Public Agenda. (2000). *Survey finds little sign of backlash against academic standards or standardized tests.* Retrieved July 25, 2003, from http://publicagenda.org/aboutpa/pdf/standards-backlash.pdf

Purvin, G. (1975). The hidden agendas of IQ. *National Elementary Principal, 54*(4), 44–48.

Pyle, W. H. (1912). A suggestion for the improvement and extension of mental tests. *Journal of Educational Psychology, 3,* 95–96.

Pyle, W. H. (1913). Standards of mental efficiency. *Journal of Educational Psychology, 4,* 61–70.

Pyle, W. H. (1915). The mind of the Negro child. *School and Society, 1,* 357–360.

Rating scale. (1918). *Psychological Bulletin, 15,* 203–206.

Rattner, S. (1977, May 1). In business terms, testing is a success. *New York Times,* sec. 12, p. 16.

Ravitch, D. (1979). Are truth-in-testing laws a fraud? Yes! *Phi Delta Kappan, 61,* 189–190.

Ravitch, D. (2003). *The language police: How pressure groups restrict what students learn.* New York: Knopf.

Reigner, C. G. (1924). The measurement movement—And the man in the street. *Education, 44,* 571–575.

Reschly, D. J. (1980). Psychological evidence in the Larry P. opinion: A case of right problem–wrong solution? *School Psychology Review, 9,* 123–135.

Reschly, D. J. (1981). Psychological testing in educational classification and placement. *American Psychologist, 36,* 1094–1102.

Resnick, D. (1982). History of educational testing. In A. K. Wigdor & W. R. Garner (Eds.), *Ability testing: Uses, consequences, and controversies,* Part I (pp. 173–194). Washington, DC: National Academy Press.

Resnick, D. P. (1980). Minimum competency testing historically considered. *Review of Research in Education, 8,* 3–29.

Resnick, D. P. (1981). Testing in America: A supportive environment. *Phi Delta Kappan, 62,* 625–628.

Rhoads, L. C. (1926). Some practical uses of the intelligence tests. *American School Board Journal, 72*(2), 67–68.

Rice, J. M. (1896). Obstacles to rational educational reform. *The Forum, 22,* 385-395.

Rice, J. M. (1897a). The futility of the spelling grind. *The Forum, 23,* 163–172.

Rice, J. M. (1897b). The futility of the spelling grind–II. *The Forum, 23,* 409–419.

Rivers, L. W., Mitchell, H., & Williams, W. S. (1975). I.Q. labels and liability: Effects on the black child. *Journal of Afro–American Issues, 3*(1), 63–76.

Roberts, G. L., & Brandenburg, G. C. (1919). The army intelligence tests at Purdue University. *School & Society, 10,* 776–778.

Roberts, W. (1968, October 19). Voices in the classroom. *Saturday Review, 51,* 72.

Robertson, D. F. (1980). Examining the examiners: The trend toward truth in testing. *Journal of Law and Education, 9,* 167–199.

Robinson, E. S. (1919). The analysis of trade ability. *Journal of Applied Psychology, 3,* 352–357.

Rogers, D. L., Roach, B. W., & Short, L. O. (1986). *Mental ability testing in the selection of Air Force officers: A brief historical overview* (Report No. AFHRL–TP–86–23). Washington, DC: U.S. Government Printing Office.

Rosenthal, R., & Jacobson, L. (1968). *Pygmalion in the classroom: Teacher expectations and pupils' intellectual development.* New York: Holt, Rinehart, & Winston.

Ross, C. C. (1941). *Measurement in today's schools.* New York: Prentice-Hall.

Rowan, C. T. (1970). How racists use "science" to degrade black people. *Ebony, 25* (7), 31–40.

Ruch, G. M. (1924). *The improvement of the written examination.* Chicago: Scott, Foresman.

Ruch, G. M. (1929). *The objective or new-type examination: An introduction to educational measurement.* Chicago: Scott, Foresman.

Ruch, G. M., & Rice, G. A. (1930). *Specimen objective examinations: A collection of examinations awarded prizes in a national contest in the construction of objective or new-type examinations, 1927–1928.* Chicago: Scott, Foresman.

Ruch, G. M., & Stoddard, G. D. (1927). *Tests and measurements in high school instruction.* New York: World.

Rudman, H. C. (1977). The standardized test flap. *Phi Delta Kappan, 59,* 179–185.

Rudman, H. C. (1987). The future of testing is now. *Educational Measurement: Issues and Practice, 6*(3), 5–11.

Rugg, E. U. (1919). Character and value of standardized tests in history. *School Review, 27,* 757–771.

Rugg, H. O. (1915). Teachers' marks and the marking system. *Educational Administration & Supervision, 1,* 117–142.

Rugg, H. O. (1920). Self–improvement of teachers through self-rating: A new scale for rating teachers' efficiency. *Elementary School Journal, 20,* 670–684.

Rugg, H., & Shumaker, A. (1928). *The child–centered school.* New York: World Book.

Ruml, B. (1919). The extension of selective tests to industry. *Annals of the American Academy of Political & Social Science, 81,* 38–46.

Russell, C. (1926). *Classroom tests: A handbook on the construction and uses of non–standard tests for the classroom teacher.* Boston: Ginn.

Russell, R. D. (1925). The use of educational and intelligence tests in the county schools of California. *American School Board Journal, 70*(6), 68.

Sacks, P. (1999). *Standardized minds: The high price of America's testing culture and what we can do to change it.* Cambridge, MA: Perseus.

Salmon-Cox, L. (1981). Teachers and standardized achievement tests: What's really happening? *Phi Delta Kappan, 62,* 631–634.

Sangren, P. V. (1932). *Improvement of reading through the use of tests.* Kalamazoo, MI: Western State Teachers College.

Scates, D. E. (1937). The costs of standardized testing. *American School Board Journal, 94*(4), 56.

Scates, D. E. (1938). The improvement of classroom testing. *Review of Educational Research, 8,* 523–536.

Scates, D. E. (1947). Fifty years of objective measurement and research in education. *Journal of Educational Research, 41,* 241–264.

School superintendent fails must–pass English test. (2003, August 3). *CNN Student News.* Retrieved August 4, 2003, from http://www.cnn.com/2003/EDUCATION/08/03/

Schouten, F. (2003, April 20). "At Risk" report 20 years later. *Salt Lake Tribune*, A13.

Schudson, M. S. (1972). Organizing the 'meritocracy': A history of the College Entrance Examination Board. *Harvard Educational Review, 42*, 34–69.

Schwegler, R. A., & Winn, E. (1920). A comparative study of the intelligence of white and colored children. *Journal of Educational Research, 2*, 838–848.

Score against IQ: A look at some test items. (1975). *National Elementary Principal, 54*(4), 42–43.

Scott, C. A. (1913). General intelligence or "school brightness." *Journal of Educational Psychology, 4*, 509–524.

Scott, W. D. (1915). The scientific selection of salesmen. *Advertising and Selling, 25* (5), 5–6, 94–96.

Scott, W. D. (1916, May). Selection of employees by means of quantitative determinations. *Annals of the American Academy of Political and Social Science, 65*, 182–193.

Scott, W. D. (1922). Intelligence tests for prospective freshmen. *School and Society, 15*, 384–388.

Scott, W. D., & Clothier, R. C. (1949). Preface to the first edition. In W. D. Scott, R. C. Clothier, & W. R. Spriegel, *Personnel management: Principles, practices, and point of view* (4th ed., pp. v–x). New York: McGraw Hill. (Original work published 1923)

Scott, W. D., Clothier, R. C., & Spriegel, W. R. (1949). *Personnel management: Principles, practices, and point of view* (4th ed.). New York: McGraw Hill.

Segel, D. (1944, April 20). An appraisal of the influences of World War II on testing practices. *Education for Victory*, pp. 3–4.

Sewall, G., Carey, J., Simons, P. E., & Lord, M. (1980, February 18). Tests: How good? How fair? *Newsweek, 95*, 97–104.

Shanker, A. (1988, April 24). Exams fail the test. *New York Times*, sec. 4, p. 7.

Sheldon, W. H. (1924). The intelligence of Mexican children. *School and Society, 19*, 139–142.

Shellhammer, T. A. (1963). Teaching and statewide testing. *Journal of Secondary Education, 38*(1), 55–58.

Shepard, L. A., & Kreitzer, A. E. (1987). The Texas teacher test. *Educational Researcher, 16*(6), 22–31.

Shimberg, B. (1980). *Occupational licensing.* Princeton, NJ: Educational Testing Service.

Shumaker, A. (1931). Editorial. *Progressive Education, 8*, 98–100.

Shuy, R. W. (Ed.). (1964). *Social dialects and language learning: Proceedings of the Bloomington, Indiana Conference.* Champaign, IL: National Council of Teachers of English.

Simpkins, G., Gunnings, T., & Kearney, A. (1973, October). The black six-hour retarded child. *Journal of Non-White Concerns, 2*, 29–34.

Slater, J. (1973, October). Sterilization: Newest threat to the poor. *Ebony, 28,* 150–156.

Smith, G. P. (1998). *Common sense about uncommon knowledge: The knowledge bases for diversity.* Washington, DC: AACTE.

Smith, L. W. (1933). A quantitative study of an activity program. *Elementary School Journal, 33,* 669–677.

Smith, M. L. (1991). Put to the test: The effects of external testing on teachers. *Educational Researcher, 20*(5), 8–11.

Smith, R. J. (1979). "Truth–in–testing" attracts diverse support. *Science, 205,* 1110–1114.

Smith, V., & Gallup, G. H. (1977). *What the people think about their schools: Gallup's findings.* Bloomington, IN: Phi Delta Kappa.

Snow, A. J. (1926). Tests for chauffeurs. *Industrial Psychology, 1,* 30–45.

Sokal, M. M. (1981). The origins of the psychological corporation. *Journal of the History of the Behavioral Sciences, 17,* 54–67.

Solomon, R. J. (1981, March 10). "Truth-in-testing" is: (A) (B) (C). *New York Times,* p. A19.

Speaking of tests [Advertisement]. (1936). *American School Board Journal, 93*(3), 84.

Sproull, L., & Zubrow, D. (1981). Standardized testing from the administrative perspective. *Phi Delta Kappan, 62,* 628–631.

Squire, C. R. (1912a). Graded mental tests, Part I. *Journal of Educational Psychology, 3,* 363–380.

Squire, C. R. (1912b). Graded mental tests, Part II. *Journal of Educational Psychology, 3,* 430–443.

Squire, C. R. (1912c). Graded mental tests, Part III. *Journal of Educational Psychology, 3,* 493–506.

Starch, D. (1915). The measurement of efficiency in reading. *Journal of Educational Psychology, 6,* 1–24.

Starch, D. (1917). *Educational measurements.* New York: Macmillan.

Starch, D. (1918). The reliability of reading tests. *School & Society, 8,* 86–90.

Starch, D., & Elliott, E. C. (1912). Reliability of the grading of high–school work in English. *School Review, 20,* 442–457.

Starch, D., & Elliott, E. C. (1913a). Reliability of grading work in history. *School Review, 21,* 676–681.

Starch, D., & Elliott, E. C. (1913b). Reliability of grading work in mathematics. *School Review, 21,* 254–259.

Stark, W. E. (1925). When the scientific mind meets popular prejudice. *Journal of Educational Research, 11,* 79–84.

State and national curriculum and testing programs: Ally or enemy of expertness? (1963). *Journal of Secondary Education, 38*(1), 26–27.

Stecklow, S. (1997, September 2). Kentucky's teachers get bonuses, but some are caught cheating. *The Wall Street Journal,* pp. A1, A6.

Stedman, L. C., & Smith, M. S. (1983). Recent reform proposals for American education. *Contemporary Education Review, 2,* 85–104.

Stenquist, J. L. (1921). The case for the low I.Q. *Journal of Educational Research, 4,* 241–254.

Stenquist, J. L. (1929a). Getting research into practice in a large school system. *American School Board Journal, 79*(5), 41–42.

Stenquist, J. L. (1929b). Getting research into practice in a large school system (continued). *American School Board Journal, 79*(6), 41–42, 131–132.

Stenquist, J. L. (1933). Recent developments in the uses of tests. In B. D. Wood, W. J. Osburn, G. M. Ruch, M. R. Trabue, G. A. Kramer, J. L. Stenquist, et al. (Eds.), Educational tests and their uses. *Review of Educational Research, 3*(1), 49–61.

Stenquist, J. L. (1935). Vocational interests, ability, and aptitude. In G. M. Whipple (Ed.), *Vocational interests, ability, and aptitude.* (34th yearbook of the National Society for the Study of Education, pp. 435–445). Bloomington, IL: Public School Publishing.

Stetson, G. R. (1897). Some memory tests of whites and blacks. *Psychological Review, 4,* 285–289.

Stiggins, R. J. (1988). Revitalizing classroom assessment: The highest instructional priority. *Phi Delta Kappan, 69,* 363–368.

Stoddard, L. (1923). *The revolt against civilization: The menace of the under man.* New York: Scribner's Sons.

Stone, C. W. (1908). *Arithmetical abilities and some factors determining them.* New York: Teachers College Press.

Stone, S. C., & Shertzer, B. (1968). Editors' Introduction. In N. M. Downie, *Types of test scores* (p. ix). Boston: Houghton Mifflin.

Story behind the 1947 merger of testing programs that established Educational Testing Service. (1992). *ETS Development, 37*(2), 4–9.

Strayer, G. D. (1911). Measuring results in education. *Journal of Educational Psychology, 2,* 3–10.

Strayer, G. D. (1913). Is scientific accuracy possible in the measurement of the efficiency of instruction? *Education, 34,* 249–258.

Strayer, G. D. (1924). Editor's Introduction. In M. R. Trabue, *Measuring results in education* (pp. 5–6). New York: American.

Strenio, A. J., Jr. (1981). *The testing trap.* New York: Rawson, Wade.

Strong, A. C. (1913). Three hundred fifty white and colored children measured by the Binet–Simon measuring scale of intelligence: A comparative study. *Pedagogical Seminary, 20,* 485–515.

Student outwits PSAT, raising 240,000 scores. (1981, March 18). *Boston Globe,* pp. 1, 4.

Summary of grades by state [Electronic version]. (2001, January 11). *Education Week.*

Sundberg, N. D. (1954). A note concerning the history of testing. *American Psychologist, 9,* 150–151.

Swanson, H. L., & Watson, B. L. (1989). *Educational and psychological assessment of exceptional children* (2nd ed.). Columbus, OH: Merrill.

Symonds, P. M. (1928). *Measurement in secondary education.* New York: Macmillan.

Taylor, E. F., & Schwartz, J. L. (1975). A due process procedure for testing. *National Elementary Principal, 54*(6), 95.

Taylor, F. W. (1998). *The principles of scientific management.* Norcross, GA: Engineering & Management Press. (Original work published 1911)

Taylor, H. C., & Russell, J. T. (1939). The relationship of validity coefficients to the practical effectiveness of tests in selection: Discussion and tables. *Journal of Applied Psychology, 23,* 565–578.

Taylor, J. S. (1912). Measurement of educational efficiency. *Educational Review, 44,* 348–367.

Teachers fail test: Tests fail teachers. (1978). *Phi Delta Kappan, 60,* 4.

Teachers: Blooming by deception. (1968, September 20). *Time, 92,* 62.

Teaching Commission. (2004). *Teaching at risk: A call to action.* New York: Cuny Graduate Center.

Terman, L. M. (1918). The use of intelligence tests in the army. *Psychology Bulletin, 15,* 177–187.

Terman, L. M. (1919). *The intelligence of school children.* Boston: Houghton Mifflin.

Terman, L. M. (1922a). The great conspiracy. *New Republic, 33,* 116–120.

Terman, L. M. (1922b). Were we born that way? *World's Work, 44,* 655–660.

Terman, L. M. (1924). In V. E. Dickson, *Mental tests and the classroom teacher* (pp. xiii-xvi). New York: World.

Terman, L. M. (1928). Editor's introduction. In C. L. Hull, *Aptitude testing.* New York: World.

Testing: Can everyone be pigeonholed? (1959, July 20). *Newsweek, 54,* 91–93.

This window will pass your examination [Advertisement]. (1931). *American School Board Journal, 82,* 87.

Thompson, D. (1959, August). Are we developing a robot education? *Ladies Home Journal, 76,* 11–12, 122.

Thompson, R. B. (1943). Total war challenges educational measurements. *Education, 63,* 565–568.

Thorndike, E. L. (1908). *The elimination of pupils from school* (Education Bureau Bulletin No. 4). Washington, DC: Government Printing Office.

Thorndike, E. L. (1913). *An introduction to the theory of mental and social measurements.* New York: Teachers College, Columbia University.

Thorndike, E. L. (1914). The measurement of ability in reading: Preliminary scales and tests. *Teachers College Record, 15*(4), 1–71.

Thorndike, E. L. (1916a). An improved scale for measuring ability in reading (concluded). *Teachers College Record, 17,* 40–67.

Thorndike, E. L. (1916b). The measurement of achievement in reading: Word knowledge. *Teachers College Record, 17,* 430–454.

Thorndike, E. L. (1917). Reading as reasoning: A study of mistakes in paragraph reading. *Journal of Educational Psychology, 8,* 323–332.

Thorndike, E. L. (1918). The nature, purposes, and general methods of measurements of educational products. In G. M. Whipple (Ed.), *The measurement of educational products* (17th yearbook of the National Society for the Study of Education, Part II, pp. 16–24). Bloomington, IL: Public School Publishing.

Thorndike, E. L. (1920a). Intelligence and its uses. *Harper's Monthly Magazine, 140,* 227–235.

Thorndike, E. L. (1920b). Introduction. In H. C. Link, *Employment psychology* (pp. ix-x). New York: Macmillan.

Thorndike, E. L. (1923). *Education: A first book.* New York: Macmillan.

Thorndike, E. L. (1948). The future of measurements of abilities. *The British Journal of Educational Psychology, 18,* 21–25.

Thorndike, E. L., & Gates, A. I. (1931). *Elementary principles of education.* New York: Macmillan.

Thorndike, R. L. (1968). [Review of the book *Pygmalion in the classroom*]. *American Educational Research Journal, 5,* 708–711.

Thurstone, L. L. (1919a). A standardized test for office clerks. *Journal of Applied Psychology, 3,* 248–251.

Thurstone, L. L. (1919b). Mental tests for prospective telegraphers, a study of the diagnostic value of mental tests for predicting ability to learn telegraphy. *Journal of Applied Psychology, 3,* 110–117.

Ticket of admission. (1976, November 15). *Forbes, 118,* 94.

Tiegs, E. W. (1928). *An evaluation of some techniques of teacher selection.* Bloomington, IL: Public School Publishing.

Tiegs, E. W. (1931a). *Tests and measurements for teachers.* Boston: Houghton Mifflin.

Tiegs, E. W. (1931b). The faith of our fathers: What school–board members should know about intelligence testing. *American School Board Journal, 83*(1), 45–46.

Timar, T. B., & Kirp, D. L. (1988). State efforts to reform schools: Treading between a regulatory swamp and an English garden. *Educational Evaluation and Policy Analysis, 10,* 75–88.

Tinker, M. A. (1932). Diagnostic and remedial reading, I. *Elementary School Journal, 33,* 293–306.

Tinker, M. A. (1933). Diagnostic and remedial reading, II. *Elementary School Journal, 33,* 346–357.

Tittle, C. K. (1973). Women and educational testing. *Phi Delta Kappan, 55,* 118–119.

Tittle, C. K., McCarthy, K., & Steckler, J. F. (1974). *Women and educational testing: A selective review of the research literature and testing practices.* Princeton, NJ: Educational Testing Service.

Todd, E. J., & Powell, W. B. (1899). *How to teach reading: A treatise showing the relation of reading to the work of education.* Boston: Silver, Burdett.

Tomlinson, T. M., & Treacy, M. E. (1979). Appendix: The National conference on achievement testing and basic skills. In *Testing, teaching and learning: Report of a conference on research on testing, August 17–26, 1978* (pp. 1–33). Washington, DC: National Institute of Education, U.S. Department of Health, Education, and Welfare.

Toops, H. A. (1925). A general science test. *School Science & Mathematics, 25,* 817–822.

Toppo, G. (2003, June 18). Are exit exams boosting dropout rates? *USA Today,* p. 6D.

Trabue, M. R. (1924). *Measuring results in education.* New York: American Book.

Trace, A. S. (1961). *What Ivan knows that Johnny doesn't.* New York: Random.

Turnbull, W. W. (1975). Foreword. In R. J. Samuda (Ed.), *Psychological testing of American minorities: Issues and consequences* (pp. vii-xi). New York: Dodd, Mead.

Twenty-two thousand scores revised after error is detected on law school exam. (1981, May 7). *New York Times,* p. A29

Twiss, G. R. (1919). A plan for rating the teachers in a school system. *School and Society, 9,* 748–756.

Tyler, R. W. (1970). National assessment: A history and sociology. *School and Society, 98,* 471–477.

Tyler, R. W., & White, S. H. (1979). Chairmen's preface. In *Testing, teaching and learning: Report of a conference on research on testing, August 17–26, 1978* (pp. v-vi). Washington, DC: National Institute of Education, U.S. Department of Health, Education, and Welfare.

U.S. Department of Education. (1984). *The nation responds: Recent efforts to improve education.* Washington, DC: U.S. Government Printing Office.

Uhl, W. L. (1916). The use of the results of reading tests as bases for planning remedial work. *Elementary School Journal, 17,* 266–275.

Urdan, T. C., & Paris, S. G. (1994). Teachers' perceptions of standardized achievement tests. *Educational Policy, 8,* 137–156.

Van Wagenen, M. J. (1919). Historical information and judgment in pupils of elementary schools. *Contributions to Education, No. 101.* New York: Teachers College Press.

Van Wagenen, M. J. (1920). Some results and inferences derived from the use of the army tests at the University of Minnesota. *Journal of Applied Psychology, 4,* 59–72.

Viteles, M. S. (1925). Research in selection of motormen. *Journal of Personnel Research, 4,* 100–115, 173–199.

Vlahos, K. B. (2003, May 30). Florida boycotters say standardized tests unfair to minorities. Retrieved from http://www.foxnews.com/story/0,2933,88107,00.html

Vold, D. J. (1985). The roots of teacher testing in America. *Educational Measurement: Issues and Practice, 4*(3), 5–7.

Wagner, R. B. (1989). *Accountability in education: A philosophical inquiry.* New York: Routledge.

Wainer, H. (1983). Pyramid power: Searching for an error in test scoring with 830,000 helpers. *American Statistician, 37,* 87–91.

Walden, J. C. (1975). Law and the school principal: The courts look at standardized testing. *National Elementary Principal, 54*(4), 80–81.

Wallin, J. E. W. (1914). *The mental health of the school child.* New Haven, CT: Yale University Press.

Walton, S. (1983, December 7). States' reform efforts increase as focus of issues shifts [Electronic version]. *Education Week,* p. 5.

Wardrop, J. L. (1976). *Standardized testing in the schools: Uses and roles.* Monterey, CA: Brooks/Cole.

Washburne, C. (1932). *Adjusting the school to the child: Practical first steps.* New York: World.

Webb, L. W., & Shotwell, A. M. (1932). *Standard tests in the elementary school: Nursery school to sixth grade.* New York: Farrar & Rinehart.

Webb, L. W., & Shotwell, A. M. (1939). *Testing in the elementary school.* New York: Farrar & Rinehart.

Weintrob, J., & Weintrob, R. (1912). The influence of environment on mental ability as shown by Binet–Simon tests. *Journal of Educational Psychology, 3,* 577–583.

Weiss, A. P. (1911). On methods of mental measurement, especially in school and college. *Journal of Educational Psychology, 2,* 555–563.

Weitzman, E., & McNamara, W. J. (1949). *Constructing classroom examinations: A guide for teachers.* Chicago: Science Research Associates.

Weld, L. D. (1917). A standard of interpretation of numerical grades. *School Review, 25,* 412–421.

Wells, F. L. (1932). Army alpha—Revised. *Personnel Journal, 10,* 411–417.

Wells, G. F. (1916). Some significant facts in the history of reading as a school subject. *Education, 36,* 585–588.

Wesman, A. G. (1968). Intelligent testing. *American Psychologist, 23,* 267–274.

What's your opinion? (1999a). *NEA Today, 17*(6), 43.

What's your opinion? (1999b). *NEA Today, 17*(7), 43.

Wheeler, T. C. (1979, September 2). The American way of testing. *New York Times Magazine,* p. 40.

Whipple, G. M. (1913). Editor's Preface. In I. E. Finkelstein, *The marking system in theory and practice* (pp. 1–2). Baltimore: Warwick & York.

Whipple, G. M. (1921). The national intelligence tests. *Journal of Educational Research, 4,* 16–31.

Whipple, G. M. (1923). The intelligence testing program and its objectors–conscientious and otherwise, I & II. *School & Society, 17,* 561–569, 596–604.

Whipple, G. M. (1935). Editor's preface. In G. M. Whipple (Ed.), *Educational diagnosis* (34th yearbook of the National Society for the Study of Education, pp. viii–x). Bloomington, IL: Public School Publishing.

White, E. (1983, August 31). Poll finds public endorsement of school reforms [Electronic version]. *Education Week,* pp. 1–10.

White, J. S. (1888). *Recent examination papers.* Boston: Ginn & Company.

Whitley, M. T. (1911). *An empirical study of certain tests for individual differences.* New York: Science Press.

Who should go to college [Editorial]. (1922). *New Republic, 32,* 137–138.

Why tests are here to stay. (1977). *American School Board Journal, 164*(1), 29.

Wigdor, A. K., & Garner, W. R. (Eds.). (1982a). *Ability testing: Uses, consequences, and controversies,* Part I. Washington, DC: National Academy Press.

Wigdor, A. K., & Garner, W. R. (Eds.). (1982b). *Ability testing: Uses, consequences, and controversies,* Part II. Washington, DC: National Academy Press.

Wiggam, A. E. (1922). The new Decalogue of science. *Century Magazine, 103,* 643–650.

Wildemuth, B. M. (1983). *Minimum competency testing and the handicapped.* Princeton, NJ: ERIC Clearinghouse on Tests, Measurement, and Evaluation, Educational Testing Service. (ERIC Document Reproduction Service No. ED289886)

Wildemuth, B. M. (1984). *Alternatives to standardized tests.* Princeton, NJ: ERIC Clearinghouse on Tests, Measurement, and Evaluation, Educational Testing Service. (ERIC Document Reproduction Service No. ED286938)

Williams, R. L. (1974, May). The silent mugging of the black community. *Psychology Today, 7,* 32–41, 101.

Williams, R. L. (1975). The politics of I.Q., racism, and power. *Journal of Afro-American Issues, 3*(1), 1–3.

Winter, M. (1985, August 23). New York Regents' exams: Emulated and criticized for toughness. *Christian Science Monitor,* p. B5.

Wirtz, W., Howe, H., Watson, B. C., Tyler, R. W., Tucker, L. R., Tom, V. H. T., et al. (1977). *On further examination: Report of the advisory panel on the Scholastic Aptitude Test score decline.* New York: College Entrance Examination Board.

Witham, E. C. (1914). School and teacher measurement. *Journal of Educational Psychology, 5,* 267–278.

Wolf, D. P., LeMahieu, P. G., & Eresh, J. (1992). Good measure: Assessment as a tool for educational reform. *Educational Leadership, 49*(8), 8–13.

Wolff, R. P. (1971). Letter. *Atlantic Monthly, 228*(6), 106.

Woody, C. (1917). Tests and measures in the schoolroom and their value to the teachers. *School and Society, 6,* 61–66.

Woody, C., & Sangren, P. V. (1933). *Administration of the testing program.* New York: World.

Woolley, P. V. (1921). The use of a scale for judging manual arts teachers. *Manual Training Magazine, 23,* 5–8.

Wooten, K. L. (1982). Tests: The foundation for equality. In S. B. Anderson & L. V. Coburn (Eds.), *Academic testing and the consumer* (pp. 11–16). San Francisco: Jossey-Bass.

Wrightstone, J. W. (1933, May). Analyzing and measuring democracy in the classroom. *The Nation's Schools, 11*(5), 31–35.

Wrightstone, J. W. (1934a). A social background data sheet. *Journal of Educational Sociology, 7,* 525–527.

Wrightstone, J. W. (1934b). An instrument for measuring group discussion and planning. *Journal of Educational Research, 27,* 641–650.

Wrightstone, J. W. (1934c). Measuring teacher conduct of class discussion. *Elementary School Journal, 34,* 454–460.

Wrightstone, J. W. (1935). *Appraisal of newer practices in selected public schools.* New York: Teachers College—Columbia University.

Wrightstone, J. W. (1938). *Appraisal of newer elementary school practices.* New York: Teachers College Press.

Wrightstone, J. W. (1954). *What tests can tell us about children.* Chicago: Science Research Associates.

Wrinkle, W. L. (1927). The diagnosis and guidance of teaching. *Journal of Educational Method, 6,* 425–433.

Wuhs, S. K., & Manatt, R. P. (1983). The pace of mandated teacher evaluation picks up. *American School Board Journal, 170*(5), 28.

Yahraes, H. (1951, May 19). They know all the answers. *Collier's, 127,* 22–23, 53–54.

Yerkes, R. M. (1918). Psychology in relation to the war. *Psychological Review, 25,* 85–115.

Yerkes, R. M. (1920). Introduction. In C. S. Yoakum & R. M. Yerkes (Eds.), *Army mental tests* (pp. vii–xiii). New York: Holt.

Yerkes, R. M. (Ed.). (1921). *Psychological examining in the United States Army* (Memoirs of the National Academy of Sciences, Vol. 15). Washington, DC: National Academy of Sciences.

Yerkes, R. M. (1923a). Foreword. In C. C. Brigham, *A study of American intelligence* (v–viii). Princeton, NJ: Princeton University Press.

Yerkes, R. M. (1923b). Testing the human mind. *Atlantic Monthly, 131,* 358–370.

Yoakum, C. S., & Yerkes, R. M. (Eds.). (1920). *Army mental tests.* New York: Holt.

Young, K. (1923). The history of mental testing. *Pedagogical Seminary, 31,* 1–48.

Zegart, D. (1978, Summer). Educational testing service: Who tests the testers? *Politics and Education, 1*(3), 5–7.

Zirbes, L. (1925). Attacking the causes of reading deficiency. *Teachers' College Record, 26*, 856–866.

Zonana, V. F. (1978, February 28). Who gets ahead? *Wall Street Journal*, pp. 1, 21.

AUTHOR INDEX

SUBJECT INDEX